"This book by my friend Robin Hadaway is [...] ...ogical and historical perspective. It is also practical and relevant to the twenty-first-century context. It will serve well as a college or seminary textbook for years to come."

—*Daniel L. Akin, president, Southeastern Baptist Theological Seminary*

"Dr. Robin Hadaway has spent decades on the mission field, and teaching missions and missionaries in training. Thus, he has the unique combination of theory and experience . . . as well as a track record of missionary commitment and accomplishment. That combination is what makes Dr. Hadaway such a gift to the church, and this book such a treasure for it."

—*Jason K. Allen, president, Midwestern Baptist Theological Seminary*

"No matter should concern the Christian more than accomplishing the very mission for which Christ called his church into existence. Thus, understanding that mission is crucial. Drawing from a lifetime of Great Commission passion, missionary experience, and scholarship, Robin Hadaway has produced what I predict will become the standard textbook for introducing the study of missions . . . [He] covers all the bases in providing an accessible and succinct overview of missions history, philosophy, and strategy."

—*Paul Chitwood, president, International Mission Board*

"I have long admired Robin Hadaway's infectious zeal for missions and his thoughtful insights as a missiologist. In *A Survey of World Missions*, both of these exemplary attributes will be obvious to readers as Hadaway superbly introduces the concept, work, and scope of missions from a linguistic, biblical, theological, and historical perspective. . . . It is a joy to enthusiastically recommend this excellent resource."

—*David S. Dockery, distinguished professor of theology and theologian-in-residence, Southwestern Baptist Theological Seminary*

"In *A Survey of World Missions*, Robin Hadaway provides a thorough presentation of the field of missiology, while also providing helpful explanations and illustrations of complex issues . . . Hadaway brings his expertise in World Religions, Worldview, and missions methodology to bear on the current conversations and scholarship in the field . . . Yet, what makes this volume most valuable is its clarity. Hadaway's writing style successfully educates the reader and makes a helpful case for why complicated concepts and debates matter."

—*Jason G. Duesing, provost and associate professor of historical theology, Midwestern Baptist Theological Seminary*

"Robin Hadaway's *A Survey of World Missions* is a fine introduction to Christian missions. This work by an experienced and wise scholar-practitioner offers a comprehensive and accessible overview of missions thought and practice, past and present. It engages with multiple dimensions of missions, including theology, history, anthropology, philosophy, and methodology. This book is a pleasure to read, and will be greatly appreciated, not only by students of missiology, but also by pastors and laypeople."

—*Mark Durie, vicar, Oaktree Anglican Church, Melbourne, Australia, and research fellow, Melbourne School of Theology*

"Hadaway's *A Survey of World Missions* should find a prominent place in the reading and library of every serious proponent of missions. This book is fresh, well researched, and encompassing in its scope. Unlike most texts on this critical subject, Hadaway's writing enables you to become well acquainted with the author himself as a man, a missionary, and as a respected missiologist. The reader senses that he or she is being 'conversed with,' rather than 'talked at.' This is a refreshing achievement for any textbook."

—*Tom Elliff, former president, International Mission Board*

"While our mission and the message of the gospel never change, the mission field is always shifting—today at a faster pace than ever before. . . . Robin Dale Hadaway has compiled an outstanding overview for pastors, missionaries, and anyone who wants to gain a greater understanding of these foundational issues. I would call it an essential book to add to your collection."

—*Kevin Ezell, president, North American Mission Board*

"This is one of the rare books that spiritual leaders and growing Christians need to have in their library. *A Survey of World Missions* is . . . not the words from a novice, but words from a proven missionary leader and gifted scholar. As [Hadaway] tells the story of God's work across the world, you will be inspired to give yourself to the completion of the Great Commission. If you want to learn more about advancing the gospel to the world, get a copy of this book, read it, and share it with a friend."

—*Ronnie Floyd, president and CEO, Executive Committee of the Southern Baptist Convention*

"Robin Hadaway draws on a wealth of personal experience, wide-ranging research, and sound biblical theology in his *Survey of World Missions*. With a plethora of field examples peppering every chapter, he treats controversial issues judiciously.... In short, he covers all one might hope to see in an introductory volume."

—*Ant Greenham, associate professor of missions and Islamic studies, Southeastern Baptist Theological Seminary*

"Robin Hadaway has provided the students of mission and missiology with a readable and wider-ranging overview. He frequently roots his discussion in the Scriptures, not just with the citation of verses but with discussion of exegetical questions and implications for praxis. I know Robin personally within the context of deep discussion of areas where we differ profoundly, and have found him to be warmhearted, compassionate, and fair-minded even when engaged with people holding distinctly divergent views from his own.... I am grateful to be able to commend Robin in this regard!"

—*Kevin Higgins, president, William Carey International University, and general director, Frontier Ventures*

"Robin Hadaway ... has produced a resource that will be helpful for professors and students alike. This introductory text covers topics related to theology, history, world religion, and mission strategy. *A Survey of World Missions* is ... well researched, well written, and relevant for today's students. Robin's passion for the Lord and his mission is contagious; this book will inform the mind and warm the heart."

—*D. Scott Hildreth, George Liele director, Center for Great Commission Studies, and assistant professor of global studies, Southeastern Baptist Theological Seminary*

"I have known Robin Hadaway as a church planter in Africa, a director of missionaries in South America, a professor of missions in Kansas City, and a senior pastor in California and Arizona. He draws on these experiences to produce a mission text equally valuable for the North American and international contexts. *A Survey of World Missions* ... [is] sufficiently academic for the scholar, easily usable for the practitioner, and clearly phrased for the layman. I highly recommend this important book for every student, pastor, missionary, and church member."

—*Johnny Hunt, senior vice president, Evangelism and Leadership, North American Mission Board*

"It is delightful and helpful to find a book about missions written by a person who is both a missionary and a missiologist. Some books are long on theory, short on practice. Others reverse the polarities. This excellent survey speaks authoritatively from both perspectives.... This remarkable book will inform and inspire a new generation to join the mission of God to the nations."

—*Jeff Iorg, president, Gateway Seminary*

"Robin Hadaway has accomplished something that is as rare as it is masterful. He has written a book of missiology that is at the same time comprehensive in scope and laser-precise in detail, exhaustive in research and exhilarating through personal touch, intellectually stimulating and inspirationally challenging. How is all that possible in one volume? ... This is a must-read for everyone from the curious student to the seasoned veteran who has spent a lifetime in Christian ministry."

—*Richard A. Jackson, pastor emeritus, North Phoenix Baptist Church, Phoenix, AZ*

"Robin Hadaway's *A Survey of World Missions* is born out of many years of the author's field missions experience and lengthy time as a missions administrator.... The work does not shy away from controversial issues related to missions strategy or contentious theological issues that shape missions practice. He is irenic in tone and expansive in his survey of various views on missions."

—*John Massey, dean, Roy Fish School of Evangelism and Missions, associate professor of Missions, Southwestern Baptist Theological Seminary*

"Are you looking for an up-to-date overview of world missions? If so, *A Survey of World Missions* by Robin Dale Hadaway is the book to ... read! It is both comprehensive and readable; a major accomplishment. It explains the biblical/theological foundations, the major theories, and the possible future of missions. Missiologists will find this book a must have for their libraries, classes, and students."

—*Gary L. McIntosh, professor of Christian ministry and leadership, Talbot School of Theology, Biola University*

"How will the church reach the nations with the gospel of Jesus Christ? What is the shape of Christian missions today? Robin Hadaway is a capable guide and this book is a helpful survey of Great Commission ministry around the world today."

—*R. Albert Mohler Jr., president, The Southern Baptist Theological Seminary*

"Robin writes about missions as he leads and mentors missionaries—clear, practical, helpful, deep, and solid. The book flows well and covers simply yet thoroughly the foundations and task of missions. Robin has done, taught, and preached everything he talks about. A book that could only be produced by an accomplished practitioner and scholar!"

—*Eddie Pate, professor of evangelism, Gateway Seminary*

"As a professor of missions after forty years of active missionary service, I have discovered it is difficult to find a relevant mission text that is not outdated. After many years of teaching and missionary leadership, Dr. Robin Hadaway has provided a classroom resource that not only presents refreshing insights into the biblical and historical background of missions."

—*Jerry Rankin, former president, International Mission Board*

"As a mother of a missionary myself, I found this book to be educational, inspirational, and practical. I have been greatly blessed! My late husband, Dr. Adrian Rogers, knew Dr. Hadaway for many years and I know that he would have been excited to endorse this wonderful book."

—*Mrs. Joyce (Adrian) Rogers, former pastor's wife, Bellevue Baptist Church, Cordova, TN*

"In Robin Hadaway, you have a missionary, pastor, and professor all in one. Writing as both a scholar and practitioner, Robin provides a sound biblical, historical, and missiological survey of world missions that will be a valuable resource for the twenty-first-century mission student—whether they be in the pulpit, classroom, or pew."

—*Ed Stetzer, Billy Graham Distinguished Chair for Church, Mission, and Evangelism, and executive director, Billy Graham Center for Evangelism, Wheaton College*

"Robin Hadaway has produced a well-written, accessible introduction to missions which demonstrates the breadth of the church's biblical, theological, historical, and anthropological reflections on the missionary enterprise, without losing sight of the unifying core which has driven the church throughout the ages to bring the gospel to the ends of the earth."

—*Timothy C. Tennent, president & professor of world Christianity, Asbury Theological Seminary*

"This book will serve well as a textbook for introductory college and seminary courses on missions. Robin Hadaway brings to the book a lifetime of service as a field missionary, missions administrator, and professor of missions. Indeed, he shares personal experiences throughout the book, and these illustrate the points he makes. His explanation of contextualization will clarify this complex topic for beginning students. Further, his comments on the use of money and missions will prove helpful to novice and veteran missionaries alike. I can recommend this book with enthusiasm."

—*J. Mark Terry, professor emeritus of missions, Mid-America Baptist Theological Seminary*

"Robin Hadaway has turned in an opus on the history of missions backed by a lifetime of experience and generations of perspective. He reviews where the church has been to help us discern what leaders can do next. The perspective found in this book will help any church leader understand the true health of the local church is measured by its sending capacity, not its seating capacity!"

—*Rick Warren, founding and lead pastor, Saddleback Church*

A SURVEY
of
WORLD
MISSIONS

A SURVEY
of
WORLD
MISSIONS

ROBIN DALE HADAWAY

B&H
ACADEMIC
NASHVILLE, TENNESSEE

Contents

Preface

N o one feels 100 percent qualified to write a comprehensive book about missions, especially me. Missions texts with multiple authors are beneficial because they offer a great pool of knowledge and experience. These books sometimes suffer, however, from repetitiveness and writing styles that vary in style and quality. Single-author books have the advantage of a sole focus, but no person knows the subject matter of missions with such breadth that he or she can cover every concept comprehensively. I served as a career missionary church planter and regional director (eastern South America) overseas for eighteen years. My family lived in Tanzania, Kenya, Brazil, and a closed, North African Muslim nation. I have also been a senior pastor in California and Arizona in the Los Angeles and Phoenix areas, respectively. For the past sixteen years I have taught missions at Midwestern Baptist Theological Seminary in Kansas City, Missouri. Despite this experience as a missionary, pastor, and professor, there are parts of the world and areas of missions about which I am still learning. The purpose of this book is to share what I know about missions and to explore the subject for the benefit of students, laypeople, church workers, and the Christian community. It is my aim and hope that this book will serve as a textbook to assist pastors, students, missionaries, and theologians in understanding and practicing international and home missions.

Acknowledgments

I would like to acknowledge those who have contributed to my life and work. My wife, Kathy, and our children, Bethany, Seth, and Joy, partnered with me in missions to the ends of the earth on this great adventure. It was with their encouragement and support that I was able to write this book.

Missiologically, I am indebted to the late David Hesselgrave, Keith Eitel, and the late Paul Hiebert, for the mission lessons learned from each over the years. Additionally, I appreciate the support of president Jason Allen and provost Jason Duesing, of Midwestern Baptist Theological Seminary, for granting me liberty from teaching duties and a year's sabbatical to write this book. Both are dear friends who have continually supported me during the writing process.

1

Introduction

WHAT IS MISSIONS?

In the mid-1970s I served as the weapons and administrative officer of the Tactical Warfare Training Squadron (TEWTS) at Nellis Air Force Base, Nevada. Now part of the Nevada Test and Training Range, their mission "provides the warfighter a flexible, realistic and multidimensional battle-space to conduct testing tactics development, and advanced training in support of U.S. national interests."[1] On a mission trip to Myanmar, I visited the U.S. embassy in Burma. The seal at the entrance proclaims the building as "The American Mission to Burma." A management textbook defines "mission" as that "which defines the fundamental purpose the organization attempts to serve and identifies its services, products, and customers."[2] Of course, Christian organizations have mission statements too. How is Christian missions different from these?

The term *mission* springs from the Latin word *missio* and denotes a "sending off" or "to send."[3] Although David Bosch calls missions undefinable, he

---

[1] "Mission," Nevada Test and Training Range, Units, Nellis Air Force Base website, accessed August 30, 2018, https://www.nellis.af.mil/Units/NTTR/.

[2] Donald C. Mosely, Leon C. Megginson, and Paul H. Pietri, *Supervisory Management: The Art of Inspiring, Empowering, and Developing People* (Mason, OH: Thomson-Southwestern, 2005), 43.

[3] *Random House Webster's College Dictionary* (New York: Random House, 1992), s.v. "mission."

distinguishes between the singular *missio Dei*, God's mission, and the plural *missions*, the activities of Christians and the church.[4] The term's present meaning emerged in the sixteenth century when the Jesuit order spread the Roman Catholic faith abroad.[5] Usually the singular, "Mission," is capitalized while the plural "missions" is not. Christopher Wright says, "So the phrase [*missio Dei*] originally meant 'the sending of God'—in the sense of the Father's sending of the Son and their sending of the Holy Spirit."[6] George Peters defines "missions" as

> the sending forth of authorized persons beyond the borders of the New Testament church and her immediate gospel influence to proclaim the gospel of Jesus Christ in gospel-destitute areas, to win converts from other faiths or non-faiths to Jesus Christ, and to establish functioning, multiplying local congregations who will bear the fruit of Christianity in that community and to that country.[7]

From *missions* comes *missiology*, a subdivision of the field of Christian theology. The term came into English from the French *missiologie*, a compound from the Latin *missio* and the Greek *logos* (Λόγος).[8] According to Justice Anderson, "The word missiology, therefore, connotes what happens when the mission of God comes into holy collision with the nature of man. It describes the dynamic result of a fusion of God's mission with man's nature. It is what occurs when redeemed mankind becomes the agent of God's mission. . . . missiology,

---

[4] David J. Bosch, *Transforming Mission: Paradigm Shifts in Theology of Mission* (Maryknoll, NY: Orbis Books, 1991), 9–10.

[5] David Bosch says, "Until the sixteenth century the term was used exclusively with reference to the doctrine of the Trinity, that is, of the sending of the Son by the Father and of the Holy Spirit by the Father and the Son." Bosch, 1. The sending of the Son is called the *filioque*. During this controversy, the Byzantine Church rejected the *filioque*, holding the Spirit only proceeded from the Father. The Western church's insistence on including the *filioque* doctrine (the procession of the Spirit from both the Father and the Son) was a major cause in the Great Schism of 1054. See Angel F. Sanchez Escobar, *A Brief History of the Byzantine Church* (Winston-Salem, NC: St. Stephen Harding College, 2009), 98, 102.

[6] Christopher J. H. Wright, *The Mission of God: Unlocking the Bible's Grand Narrative* (Downers Grove, IL: IVP Academic, 2006), 63.

[7] George W. Peters, *A Biblical Theology of Missions* (Chicago: Moody, 1972), 11.

[8] Justice Anderson, "An Overview of Missiology," in *Missiology: An Introduction to the Foundations, History, and Strategies of World Missions,* ed. John Mark Terry, 2nd ed. (Nashville: B&H, 2015), 3–4.

etymologically speaking, is the study of this redemptive relationship."[9] This book explores the subject.

Recently, the related term *missional* has gained popularity. A *missional* person or church focuses on mission work. Michael Goheen says the word *mission* connotes a geographical expansion, whereas *missional* describes "not a specific *activity* of the church but the very *essence and identity* of the church."[10] Ed Stetzer and Daniel Im say, "*Missional* means adopting the *posture of a missionary*, joining Jesus on mission, and learning and adapting to the culture around you while remaining biblically sound."[11] Therefore, *missions* is the activity of the church, while *missional* focuses on what the church does.

VIEWS ON MISSIONS

This begs the question: What is God's mission? Bosch says the Christian faith sees "all generations of the earth as objects of God's salvific will and plan of salvation."[12] There are numerous ways missiologists, theologians, and churchmen observe missions.

The Soteriological View

This represents the traditional rationale for missions: the people of the world need saving from their sin, therefore, evangelism and missions communicates the good news of God's reconciliation to humanity. Proponents point to Luke 19:10 and the words of Jesus: "For the Son of Man came to seek and to save the lost." Dwight L. Moody pronounced, "I look upon this world as a wrecked vessel. God has given me a lifeboat and said, 'Save all you can.'"[13] Most conservative missiologists and practitioners until recently have held this view. Preston Nix says:

---

[9] Anderson, 4.

[10] Michael W. Goheen, *A Light to the Nations: The Missional Church and the Biblical Story* (Grand Rapids: Baker Academic, 2011), 4.

[11] Ed Stetzer and Daniel Im, *Planting Missional Churches: Your Guide to Starting Churches That Multiply*, 2nd ed. (Nashville: B&H, 2016), 21.

[12] Bosch, *Transforming Mission*, 9.

[13] Augustus Warner Williams, *The Life and Work of Dwight L. Moody: The Great Evangelist of the XIX Century* (Philadelphia: P. W. Ziegler, 1900), 149.

The method, or strategy, God has chosen to employ in order for the Great Commission to be accomplished is the evangelistic witness of his followers in his church. According to the Great Commission passages . . . [t]he object of proclamation is the gospel revealing that mankind through repentance of sin and faith in Jesus can receive forgiveness and enter a right relationship with the Father (Acts 20:21).[14]

The Eschatological View

This perspective holds that missions can usher in the end times. Jesus states in Matt 24:14, "This good news of the kingdom will be proclaimed in all the world as a testimony to all nations [*ethnos*, ἔθνος], and then the end will come." Advocates juxtapose this verse with Rev 5:9,[15] concluding Christ cannot return until representatives from "every tribe and language and people and nation"[16] have heard the gospel.[17] Furthermore, proponents interpret 2 Pet 3:12[18] to mean the activities of God's people can hasten the return of the Lord. This dispensational view was popularized by writers such as Charles F. Baker, J. Dwight Pentecost, and C. I. Scofield.[19] This perspective has birthed an increased urgency for winning the world for Christ in this generation. Some criticize this view because God's actions are linked to the works of men.

The Doxological View

This perspective sees missions as a vehicle for glorifying God. Those holding this view proclaim the gospel and insist souls are saved only by believing in

---

[14] Preston Nix, "Commentary on Article 10: The Great Commission," in *Anyone Can Be Saved: A Defense of 'Traditional' Southern Baptist Soteriology*, ed. David L. Allen, Eric Hankins, and Adam Harwood (Eugene, OR: Wipf and Stock, 2016), 151.

[15] "And they sang a new song: You are worthy to take the scroll and to open its seals, because you were slaughtered, and you purchased people for God by your blood from every tribe and language and people and nation."

[16] *ethnos*, ἔθνος

[17] Lynne Bryan, *Understanding Bible Prophecy* (Bloomington, IN: WestBow, 2012), 29.

[18] "as you wait for the day of God and hasten its coming" (or "and speed its coming," NIV).

[19] Charles F. Baker, *A Dispensational Theology*, 2nd ed. (Grand Rapids: Grace Bible College Publications, 1972), 331. See also J. Dwight Pentecost, *Things to Come: A Study in Biblical Eschatology* (Grand Rapids: Zondervan, 1958), 472.

Christ. They claim, however, missions is the by-product of the activity and not the chief aim of it. Representing this perspective, John Piper says:

> Missions is not the ultimate goal of the church. Worship is. Missions exists because worship doesn't. Worship is ultimate, not missions, because God is ultimate, not man. . . . The goal of missions is the gladness of the people in the greatness of God. . . . But worship is also the fuel of missions. Passion for God in worship precedes the offer of God in preaching. . . . Missions begins and ends in worship.[20]

According to this view, missions exists, not primarily to save the lost, but to increase the praise offered to God. As missionaries proclaim the gospel and the lost are saved, God is glorified. This, in their view, is the primary purpose of missions. As more Reformed pastors have emphasized missions, this view has gained more traction. Due to the immense influence of John Piper, a former pastor and fervent supporter of missions, this perspective of missions is widely held.

The Kingdom View

This outlook holds missions is an expansion of the kingdom of God. Popularized by George Eldon Ladd, the Kingdom View sees the aim of missions as furthering God's kingdom on earth. Ladd says the gospel must be preached to all nations (Mark 13:10) and equates this with the proclamation of the good news about the kingdom of God. He says, "[I]t will be the mission of the church to witness to the gospel of the Kingdom in the world."[21] Proponents see Matt 4:17 as an example: "From that time Jesus began to preach and say, 'Repent, for the kingdom of heaven is at hand'" (NASB). The Kingdom View says the Lord desires obedience under his rule, not simply converts who may or may not alter their lifestyles and profess Christianity in name only.

---

[20] John Piper, *Let the Nations be Glad: The Supremacy of God in Missions* (Grand Rapids: Baker, 1993), 11–12.

[21] George Eldon Ladd, *A Theology of the New Testament* (Grand Rapids: Eerdmans, 1974), 114–15.

The Holistic View

This vantage point of missions sees the gospel from a humanitarian perspective. Its adherents see the mission of Jesus as renewing mankind in body, soul, and spirit. They view the church's primary mission as healing the sick, feeding the poor, sheltering the homeless, educating the ignorant, liberating the oppressed, and fostering world peace. Holistic missions, also known as the social gospel, often stresses political concerns, social justice issues, environmental causes, gender equality, and class consciousness over theological issues. They cite Jesus's words in the Beatitudes, Matt 5:3–12.[22]

Proponents note the apostle James's admonition in Jas 1:27, "Pure and undefiled religion before God the Father is this: to look after orphans and widows in their distress and to keep oneself unstained from the world." Many Roman Catholics, mainline Protestant denominations, and Eastern Orthodox communions subscribe to this view. The World Council of Church's mission statement advocates a solidarity with the poor and considers this stance as part and parcel with the gospel.[23]

Gustavo Gutierrez, considered one of the founders of *liberation theology*, took the social gospel to the extreme. Liberation theology sees Christ as more of a liberator of the oppressed than a savior. To their credit, many evangelical

---

[22] "Blessed are the poor in spirit, for the kingdom of heaven is theirs. Blessed are those who mourn, for they will be comforted. Blessed are the humble, for they will inherit the earth. Blessed are those who hunger and thirst for righteousness, for they will be filled. Blessed are the merciful, for they will be shown mercy. Blessed are the pure in heart, for they will see God. Blessed are the peacemakers, for they will be called sons of God. Blessed are those who are persecuted because of righteousness, for the kingdom of heaven is theirs. You are blessed when they insult you and persecute you and falsely say every kind of evil against you because of me. Be glad and rejoice, because your reward is great in heaven. For that is how they persecuted the prophets who were before you."

[23] "The mission of the Church ensues from the nature of the Church as the body of Christ, sharing in the ministry of Christ as Mediator between God and his creation. At the heart of the Church's vocation in the world is the proclamation of the kingdom of God inaugurated in Jesus our Lord, crucified and risen. Through its internal life of eucharistic worship, thanksgiving, intercessory prayer, through planning for mission and evangelism, through a daily life-style of solidarity with the poor, through advocacy even to confrontation with the powers that oppress human beings, the churches are trying to fulfill this evangelistic vocation." *The Church: Towards a Common Vision, Faith and Order Paper No. 214*, World Council of Churches (Geneva: WCC Publications, 2013), 6.

churches attempt to engage in social action and gospel proclamation at the same time. Some churches have excellent programs for meeting human needs.

THEORIES OF MISSIONS

In addition to these views of missions, missiologists conceptualize missions in very different ways. The following theories remain prominent in missions.

The Geographic Theory

The original theory of missions was that missionaries were sent to specific countries and evangelized everyone in that nation. This could also be called "presence missions," whereby missions agencies seek to place missionaries in as many fields as possible without regard to either their receptiveness or what percentage of the population was unreached. For example, the practice of planting an Assembly of God congregation or Baptist church in every county seat town in North American stems from this view. Although tribes and ethnicities were known by the missionaries of previous generations, people-group consciousness had not yet been conceptualized. When I was appointed as a missionary to Tanzania in 1983, my assignment focused on a country, not specifically the Sukuma tribe who were the majority people group in the northwestern part of the nation. Proponents of geographical missions point to the apostle Paul's intention of journeying to the region of Spain in Rom 15:24 and to Rome in Acts 19:21.

Urban missions represents another kind of geographic strategy. Deployed to large population centers, urban strategists evangelize those living in the city, not limiting their vision to a particular people group within the metropolitan area. The rationale is that since most of the people of the world live in cities,[24] the greatest need exists where most people live. Advocates assert the apostle Paul employed a city strategy, evangelizing the population centers of the world, including Jerusalem, Athens, Corinth, and Ephesus. After Paul visited

---

[24] Whereas a little over half of the world's population lives in cities now, the UN predicts this will soar to two-thirds of the world's population by the year 2030. See Edith M. Lederer, "UN Report: By Year 2030 Two-Thirds of the World Will Live in Cities," Associated Press, May 18, 2016, https://www.apnews.com/40b530ac84ab4931874e1f7efb4f1a22.

Ephesus, Acts 19:21 records, "After these events, Paul resolved by the Spirit to pass through Macedonia and Achaia and go to Jerusalem. 'After I've been there,' he said, 'It is necessary for me to see Rome as well!'" This is an example of an urban strategy in the geographic sense.

The Church Growth Theory

Donald McGavran advocates concentrating mission activity in the most receptive places. McGavran believes that Christians can most effectively evangelize within their own family, caste, or tribal group.[25] These clusters he identifies as *homogeneous units*. Known as *people groups* today, homogeneous units represent populations possessing something major in common. Also known as harvest missions or receptivity missions, the church growth view believes the responsive should hear the gospel first and have priority over the unreached and less receptive. Winston Crawley says, "From the beginning, McGavran was concerned primarily for the rapid evangelization of potentially responsive people groups around the world. To encourage that, he emphasized research and strategic planning, the primacy of evangelism in mission work, [and] focus on those people groups that are most responsive and cultural adaptation."[26] Church growth advocates point to Jesus's words in Matt 9:37–38: "Then he said to his disciples, 'The harvest is abundant, but the workers are few. Therefore, pray to the Lord of the harvest to send out workers into his harvest.'" McGavran asserts:

> That receptivity should determine effective evangelistic methods is obvious. . . . Unless Christian leaders in all six continents are on the lookout for changes in receptivity of homogeneous units within the general population, and are prepared to seek and bring persons and groups belonging to these units into the fold, they will not even discern what needs to be done. . . . An essential task is to discern receptivity and—when this is seen—to adjust methods, institutions, and

---

[25] "The major insight that Donald felt God had shown him was that the normal way in which people confessed their faith in Christ was through a family, caste or tribal group." Gary L. McIntosh, *Donald A. McGavran: A Biography of the Twentieth Century's Premier Missiologist* (Boca Raton, FL: Church Leader Insights, 2015), 107.

[26] Winston Crawley, *World Christianity, 1970–2000: Toward a New Millennium* (Pasadena: William Carey Library, 2001), 72.

personnel until the receptive are becoming Christians and reaching out to win their fellows to eternal life. Effective evangelism is demanded. It finds the lost, folds those found, feeds them on the word of God, and incorporates them into multitudes of new and old congregations.[27]

People Group Theory

Ralph Winter, a colleague and contemporary of Donald McGavran at Fuller Theological Seminary, adopted his *Homogeneous Unit Principle* but renamed the concept *unreached peoples*. Winter advocates sending missionaries, not to the most responsive ethnic groups, but to peoples who have not yet heard the gospel. Many of this persuasion repeat the maxim, "Why should anyone hear the Gospel twice before everyone has heard it once?"[28] They say God desires representatives among all people groups in heaven, citing Rev 5:9.[29] Commenting on this, Ralph D. Winter and Bruce A. Koch urge:

> Jesus says that before the end comes, there will be "a witness to all the nations." The "nations" Jesus was referring to are not countries or nation-states. The wording He chose (the Greek word *ethne*) points to the ethnicities, the languages and the extended families which constitute the people of the earth. . . . In order to work together strategically, mission leaders have been redefining the concept of "people groups" as a rough measure of our progress toward completing the entire task. There are four useful ways of looking at the idea of people groups: blocs of peoples, ethnolinguistic peoples, sociopeoples, and unimax peoples.[30]

Winston Crawley notes that the unreached peoples theory emerged out of the church growth school, the former supplanting the latter. Crawley says:

---

[27] Donald A. McGavran, *Understanding Church Growth*, 3rd rev. ed., ed. C. Peter Wagner (Grand Rapids: Eerdmans, 1990), 192.

[28] This famous quotation is attributed to Oswald J. Smith in Lois Neely, *Fire in His Bones: The Official Biography of Oswald J. Smith* (Wheaton, IL: Tyndale House, 1982), 13.

[29] "And they sang a new song: You are worthy to take the scroll and to open its seals, because you were slaughtered, and you purchased people for God by your blood from every tribe and language and people and nation."

[30] Ralph D. Winter and Bruce A. Koch, "Finishing the Task: The Unreached Peoples Challenge," in *Perspectives on the World Christian Movement: A Reader*, 4th ed., ed. Ralph D. Winter and Steven C. Hawthorne (Pasadena: William Carey Library, 2009), 533–34.

Winter effectively shifted the main theme of today's missiology from church growth to unreached peoples, thereby becoming the most influential missiologist of the 1980s and '90s. It is interesting that McGavran first directed Christian attention to people groups, as a lead-in to his concern for growth; he and Winter were colleagues at Fuller, but their strategy thrusts move in different directions. McGavran wanted major effort to concentrate on responsive peoples, where the harvest is ripe, but Winter urges concentration on places where the gospel seed has yet to be sown.[31]

The people group theory has become the dominant view in missions today, by far superseding all other theories.

Supernatural Theory

Often of the charismatic and Pentecostal persuasion, proponents of the supernatural theory argue that missions and evangelism must be approached spiritually. They say it is useless to talk about strategies, methods, people groups, and receptivity before the spiritual ground has been researched and discerned. Such preparation identifies territorial spirits[32] and spiritually maps them.[33] A spiritual warfare strategy often includes strategic intercession to "bind the strong man," power encounters to combat the forces of darkness, and signs and wonders to prove the authenticity of the gospel. Advocates cite Jesus's words in Matt 12:25–29 as evidence.[34] Writers such as John Wimber and Peter Wagner juxtapose this verse with Eph 6:12[35] and say intercessors must identify the principalities and powers in the heavenly places, confront them through power

---

[31] Crawley, *World Christianity*, 74–75.

[32] C. Peter Wagner, *Territorial Spirits: Practical Strategies for How to Crush the Enemy through Spiritual Warfare* (Shippensburg, PA: Destiny Image, 2012), 67, 72.

[33] George Otis Jr., *Informed Intercession: Transforming Your Community through Spiritual Mapping and Strategic Prayer* (Ventura, CA: Renew Books, 1999), 81.

[34] "Every kingdom divided against itself is headed for destruction, and no city or house divided against itself will stand. If Satan drives out Satan, he is divided against himself. How then will his kingdom stand? And if I drive out demons by Beelzebul, by whom do your sons drive them out? For this reason they will be your judges. If I drive out demons by the Spirit of God, then the kingdom of God has come upon you. How can someone enter a strong man's house and steal his possessions unless he first ties up the strong man? Then he can plunder his house."

[35] "For our struggle is not against flesh and blood, but against the rulers, against the authorities, against the cosmic powers of this darkness, against evil, spiritual forces in the heavens." Referring to this verse, John Wimber says, "As Christ's instruments, we wage war against these

encounters,[36] and spiritually bind them before evangelism can take place.[37] This, in their view, represents the starting point and essence of missions. Peter Wagner writes:

> An area of power encounter which is just beginning to be taken seriously is the confrontation of demons associated with specific locations or geo-political units. The whole concept of the gods of the nations in the Old Testament and the references in Daniel to the Prince of Persia (Dan. 10:13, 20) provide us with a biblical insight into this, and Jesus' statement about binding the strong man (Matt. 12:29) may also apply. I have come to believe that Satan does indeed assign a demon or a corps of demons to every geo-political unit in the world and that they are among the principalities and powers against whom we wrestle.[38]

Although odd to evangelical ears, supernatural missions reigns supreme in Charismatic Christian circles. Many evangelicals would be surprised to learn that the strategy of prayer walking comes from this theory of missions.

The Spontaneous Theory

This outlook holds that believers should evangelize where they go, and as "targets of opportunity" arise, they should engage in their own personal missions. Proponents observe Paul and Barnabas participating in this kind of missions as they departed Antioch in Acts 13:4–12. This view of missions distrusts goal setting and strategic planning, and advocates "moving according to the Spirit." Henry Blackaby writes:

> When you get to the place where you trust Jesus to guide you one step at a time you experience a new freedom. If you don't trust Jesus to guide you this way, what happens if you don't know the way

---

strongholds, replacing their dominion with the Kingdom of God." John Wimber, *Power Evangelism* (Bloomington, MN: Chosen Books, 2009), 32.

[36] John Wimber claims "a power encounter is a visible, practical demonstration that Jesus Christ is more powerful than the false gods or spirits worshiped or feared by a group of people." Wimber, *Power Evangelism*, 49.

[37] Harold Caballeros, "Defeating the Enemy with the Help of Spiritual Mapping," in *Breaking Strongholds: How to Use Spiritual Mapping to Make Your Prayers More Strategic, Effective and Targeted*, ed. C. Peter Wagner (Shippensburg, PA: Destiny Image, 2015), 131.

[38] Wagner, *Territorial Spirits*, 76.

you are to go? You worry every time you must take a turn. You often freeze up and cannot make a decision.... I told our students, "If someone starts asking you spiritual questions, whatever else you have planned, don't do it. Cancel what you are doing. Go with that individual and look to see what God is doing there." That week our students went out to see where God was working and joined Him.... Why do we not realize that it is always best to do things God's way? We cause some of the wreck and ruin in our churches because we have a plan.... The key to knowing God's voice is not a formula. It is not a method you can follow. Knowing God's voice comes from an intimate love relationship with God.[39]

The concept of being "On Mission with God," asserts that God has a mission and each believer must join God where he is already working. Avery Willis describes the concept: "On the way you discover that you may not get to the destination you first had in mind, but you will get to His destination for your life—a far better arrival point than you had planned. That's what it means to be on mission with God."[40] According to this view, missionaries should follow God's direction and not overstrategize. Of course, this view has its critics. Such a "no plan" plan waits for intuition and circumstances to lead the missionary in their daily endeavors; although this is laudable in theory, goals and action plans help keep ministers on task and accountable for their work.

PHILOSOPHIES OF MISSIONS

In addition to these views and theories of missions, philosophies of missions differ widely from one another. Justice Anderson says one's theology of missions plus a study of the history of missions yields a philosophy of missions.[41] A philosophy of missions deals with how to organize the mission enterprise.

---

[39] Henry T. Blackaby and Claude V. King, *Experiencing God: Knowing and Doing the Will of God* (Nashville: LifeWay Press, 1990), 11, 26, 29, 37.

[40] Avery T. Willis Jr. and Henry T. Blackaby, *On Mission with God: Living God's Purpose for His Glory* (Nashville: LifeWay Press, 2001), 11.

[41] Justice Anderson, "Overview of Missiology," 10.

Individualism (Unilateralism)

Somewhat associated with spontaneous missions, individualism asserts that each person and each local church should be involved in missions. This view holds that mission boards should not be involved in missions; rather, missions should be the purview of either the local church or the individual. Some assert that this was the view of the Reformers, including Martin Luther. John W. Montgomery says, "For Luther, the proclamation of the gospel is the Christian's highest privilege and he should begin by exercising it in the normal situations of life. . . . It was Luther's conviction that missionary work ideally proceeds from the home base."[42]

Colonialism

In this view of missions a government authority channels funds through a state church for distribution. For instance, the Danish-Halle Mission to South India was funded by the Danish Crown in the eighteenth century. Today many Lutheran state churches in Scandinavia serve as the conduits for their governments' relief and development resources.[43] In the city square of most of the major cities in the former British Empire stands a majestic Anglican church. The state Church of England benefited from its relationship with the colonial power.

Cooperative Missions

As the name suggests, this view believes churches, denominations, parachurch groups, missions, and individuals should cooperate to evangelize the world. There are different types of cooperative missions.

Denominationalism. Local churches within a particular faith tradition unite to support their own denominational mission program. The International Mission Board of the Southern Baptist Convention and the Assemblies of God World Missions Board are examples of this type of missions. A synonym

---

[42] John Warwick Montgomery, "Luther and Missions," *Evangelical Missions Quarterly* 3, no. 4 (1967): 193–202.

[43] Norwegian Church Aid, "Our History," accessed December 12, 2017, https://www.kirkensnodhjelp.no/en/about-nca/our-history/.

of this view, *ecclesiasticism*, describes a liturgical body of churches uniting to send missionaries. The Society of Jesus (Jesuits) and the White Fathers orders of the Roman Catholic Church exemplify this kind of denominationalism.

Societal Missions. Missions societies operate independently of governments and denominations. Most mission entities follow this organizational model. African Inland Mission (AIM), Sudan Interior Mission (SIM), Baptist Bible Fellowship, Frontiers, Pioneers, Avant, Youth with a Mission (YWAM), and Operation Mobilization (OM) represent this kind of missions. Each of these missions have a board that sets the vision, determines the doctrinal parameters, prescribes missionary qualifications, and directs the work. Any church or individual can join the society and support its work.

MISSIONARY ACTIVITIES

In addition to the views, purposes, and philosophies of missions, missionary-sending bodies often specialize in certain kinds of missionary activities.

Ancillary Missions

This kind of missions facilitates the work of other mission groups, churches, and individuals. Missionary Aviation Fellowship (MAF), Wycliffe Bible Translators, and Gospel Recordings Network are examples of mission support agencies. Support missions undergird the activities of other mission entities by providing either resources or services. Ancillary missions do not usually major in evangelism themselves but assist other agencies in fulfilling this task.

Institutionalism

These mission societies exist primarily to operate or fund a particular orphanage, school, hospitals, or media outlet. They may also deploy teachers, medical personnel, and humanitarian workers to work in these institutions. Founded in 1896, the German Evangelical Mission Hospital in Aswan, Egypt, operates a clinic, hospital, and bookstore along the Nile to minister to the spiritual and physical needs of Egyptians.[44] Although limited to one kind of ministry, institutional missions perform good work in needy and neglected parts of the world among the marginalized of society.

Marketplace Missions (associated with individualism)

Also known as Business as Missions (BAM), marketplace-ministry sending agencies facilitate missionaries in establishing business overseas or working as tentmakers for existing companies. These missionaries are either self-employed or work for an overseas business, institution, or government. As more and more Americans engage in international business and travel, this kind of missions has increased exponentially. Many new missionaries are going overseas as self-employed tentmakers rather than serving with a mission-sending agency.

Direct Missions

This kind of missions focuses on evangelism, church planting, and discipleship. This is the principle type of mission work normally associated with the overseas missionary enterprise. Institutional missions and BAM efforts assist agencies in gaining entry to both closed and open countries. Ancillary mission organizations offer support for all categories of mission groups. Direct missions, however, remains the focus of the missionary effort.

Eclectic Missions

Many mission agencies, especially denominational mission groups, purport to "do it all," but most concentrate on one or two of the above categories. Speaking of the Southern Baptist mission board, Winston Crawley states, "Our foreign missions philosophy and strategy have always been eclectic. That is, we have adopted insights, concepts, or approaches derived from many different sources, if we feel they can be useful and are harmonious with our basic understanding of our mission and with the main thrust of our work."[45] An eclectic mission

---

[44] Samir Boulos, *European Evangelicals in Egypt (1900–1956): Cultural Entanglements and Missionary Spaces* (Leiden, Netherlands: Koinklijke Brill, 2016), 177.

[45] Winston Crawley, *Global Mission: A Story to Tell: An Interpretation of Southern Baptist Foreign Missions* (Nashville: Broadman, 1985), 275.

attempts to incorporate all missionary functions, even ancillary missions, into its operations. Inevitably, however, an eclectic mission group does some kinds of ministries better than others.

CONCLUSION

Missions seems simple at first glance, but its complexity becomes apparent during an analysis of the different views, perspectives, and theories of missions. Espousing a particular view of missions is usually not intentional. One's view evolves, often unconsciously, due to experience and their Christian background. A person may even hold to two or more of the mission perspectives simultaneously. These categories are presented, not to limit one's thinking, but to help the missiologist and practitioner process where they fit along the mission spectrum.

All evangelical Christians understand the world desperately needs Christ and the task of proclaiming his gospel is great. Believers, however, differ markedly on ascertaining the task and prioritizing the delivery of the message. Succeeding chapters of this book will explore the issues involved in formulating sound mission theology and practice.

READING FOR FURTHER STUDY

Bosch, David J. *Transforming Mission: Paradigm Shifts in Theology of Mission*. Maryknoll, NY: Orbis Books, 1991.
Crawley, Winston. *World Christianity, 1970–2000: Toward A New Millennium*. Pasadena: William Carey Library, 2001.
Piper, John. *Let the Nations be Glad: The Supremacy of God in Missions*. Grand Rapids: Baker, 1993.
Stetzer, Ed, and Daniel Im. *Planting Missional Churches: Your Guide to Starting Churches That Multiply*, 2nd ed. Nashville: B&H Academic, 2016.
Wright, Christopher J. H. *The Mission of God: Unlocking the Bible's Grand Narrative*. Downers Grove, IL: IVP Academic, 2006.

2

The Biblical Basis of Missions

Two national Christian workers in an Islamic fundamentalist country told me the following story. A woman came to Christ in a Muslim village in their North African nation. The leaders of the church gave her a Bible after her baptism. Her husband was incensed when he learned of her newfound faith. He seized his wife's Bible and set it on the ground outside their mud home. Then he poured gasoline over the Bible and lit a match. The woman told Jonadab[1] the Bible would not burn. Over and over, the woman's husband attempted to ignite the Scriptures, but to no avail. This story illustrates the primacy of the Word of God and its indestructibility. The Bible is the foundation and basis of missions.

Moses and John, the authors of the first and last books of the Bible, received unparalleled insights into the timeless past and eternal future. The revelations include Moses's accounts of creation and early human history,[2] John's prophecy about the end times, and the final disposition of the universe. Chapters 1 and 2 of Genesis declare God's creation as perfect. Genesis 2:1–3 says, "So the heavens and the earth and everything in them were completed. On the

---

[1] "Jonadab" is a pseudonym for a Muslim-background believer in North Africa who partnered with me in planting churches.
[2] H. C. Leupold says the Bible treats this as pure history. He suggests that Moses could have received this by direct revelation from God, or Adam and Eve received this by direct revelation and passed the stories down by tradition. H. C. Leupold, *Exposition of Genesis*, vol. 1 (Grand Rapids: Baker, 1942), 36.

seventh day God had completed his work that he had done, and he rested on the seventh day from all his work that he had done. God blessed the seventh day and declared it holy, for on it he rested from all his work of creation." Chapters 21 and 22 of the Apocalypse describe God's "re-creation" of the heavens and the earth. The apostle John proclaims in Rev 21:1, "Then I saw a new heaven and a new earth; for the first heaven and the first earth had passed away, and the sea was no more." As Köstenberger and O'Brien say, "The notion of mission is ultimately bound up with his saving plan which moves from creation to recreation, and has to do with his salvation reaching the ends of the earth."[3]

In Genesis 3, Adam and Eve both cause and experience the first death. The first death constitutes the judgment for their disobedience. Pronouncing a curse, God told the first couple they would return to the dust from which they were formed. Additionally, women would "bear children with painful effort"[4] and men would toil upon an afflicted ground. In Revelation 21–22, the curse departs.[5] The second death now exists only for the unbeliever. Indeed, the tree of life in the garden of Eden[6] reappears in the New Jerusalem near the river of living water close to the throne of God and the Lamb.

Between the first two chapters of Genesis and the last two chapters of the Revelation, the human experience unfolds. This includes sin, redemption, reconciliation, and salvation. Missions consists of the activities of God and his representatives to bring Adam's race back into fellowship with him through his Son, Jesus Christ.

MISSIONS AND THE OLD TESTAMENT

After Adam and Eve's sin in chapter 3, Genesis 4 and 5 depict mankind's downward spiral into iniquity, rebellion, and debauchery. These transgressions include murder (4:8), polygamy (4:19), and manslaughter (4:23). As a result of humanity's iniquity, God's judgment severely limits the lengthy life spans recorded in the first five chapters of Genesis. God says in Gen 6:3, "My Spirit

---

[3] Andreas J. Köstenberger and Peter T. O'Brien, *Salvation to the Ends of the Earth: A Biblical Theology of Missions* (Downers Grove, IL: InterVarsity Press, 2001), 25.

[4] Gen 3:16.

[5] Rev 22:12.

[6] Gen 3:24.

will not remain with mankind forever, because they are corrupt. Their days will be 120 years." Despite this judgment, wickedness spreads over the earth, so much that God regrets he made the human race and therefore decides to destroy it (6:5–8).

One person, however, found favor with God. In fact, when Noah was born, his father, Lamech said, "This one will bring us relief from the agonizing labor of our hands, caused by the ground the LORD has cursed" (5:29). God reached out to Noah and saved him and his family from the destruction of the flood, preserving a remnant on the earth. Noah's actions resulted in the physical salvation of his family[7] while his obedience brought some relief from Adam's curse. After Noah offered animal sacrifices to the Lord, God declared in Gen 8:21, "I will never again curse the ground because of human beings, even though the inclination of the human heart is evil from youth onward." The full reversal of the curse, however, would occur much later in Rev 22:3.[8] Unfortunately, not long after leaving the ark, Noah's inebriation (Gen 9:21) demonstrated that man's propensity toward sin continued unabated.

Genesis 11 records how mankind devolved into various nations and peoples. According to these Scriptures, everyone in the world spoke the same language and used the same words. Earlier, God commanded Noah and his sons (9:7), "But you, be fruitful and multiply; spread out over the earth and multiply on it." Those who built the tower of Babel were determined to stay together. The descendants of Noah said in Gen 11:4, "Come, let us build ourselves a city and a tower with its top in the sky. Let us make a name for ourselves; otherwise, we will be scattered throughout the earth." God desired mankind to multiply and fill the earth, whereas mankind rebelled against his decree. The Lord, therefore, intervened by confusing the language of the people of Babel, dividing and scattering them over the globe. The table of nations in the previous chapter records the result.

---

[7] Hebrews 11:7 says, "By faith Noah, after he was warned about what was not yet seen and motivated by godly fear, built an ark to deliver his family."

[8] Revelation 22:3 reads, "[A]nd there will no longer be any curse. The throne of God and of the Lamb will be in the city, and his servants will worship him."

In the Old Testament, the most common word for "nations" or "peoples" is the Hebrew term *goy* [גּוֹי], and its plural, *goyim* [גּוֹיִם].[9] The Septuagint[10] translates *goyim* [גּוֹיִם] "Gentiles" and the Greek word *ethnos* [ἔθνος][11] as "nations." Of some 160 occurrences of *ethnos* in the New Testament, about 40 instances are quotes from the Old Testament, words for nation or Gentile.[12] The *ethnos* (nations, ἔθνος) constitute the object of God's love, mercy, and mission in the New Testament. These nations or people groups began at Babel and are important in missions.

Paul, in his address to the Athenians, describes the reason God confused Babel's languages and divided the world into different ethnicities. In Acts 17:26–27 he writes, "From one man he has made every nationality to live over the whole earth and has determined their appointed times and the boundaries of where they live. He did this so that they might seek God, and perhaps they might reach out [*psailaphao*, ψηλαφήσειαν][13] and find him, though he is not far from each one of us." As one entity, mankind was determined to rebel against God. A divided humanity, however, would be more willing to seek the Lord.

---

[9] *The Theological Wordbook of the Old Testament* states, "One must conclude that the basic idea is that of a defined body or group of people, or some specific large segment of a given body. . . . The synonym *'am* is used largely for a group of people or for people in general. However, sometimes, especially in poetic parallel with *goyim*, it [*goyam*] may refer to a nation, whether a foreign nation or Israel. *Goyim* on the other hand more usually refers to nations, especially the surrounding pagan nations. . . . The term *goy* is used especially, to refer to specifically defined political, ethnic or territorial groups of people without intending to ascribe a specific religious or moral connotation. Thus, in Gen. 10:5 the writer speaks of defined groups of people according to their territories. . . . In this general ethnic sense the term may even be used of Abraham's seed. Thus, God said to Abraham, 'I will make you a great nation,' i.e., a political, territorial, identified people." *Theological Wordbook of the Old Testament*, vol. 1, ed. R. Laird Harris, Gleason J. Archer Jr., and Bruce K. Waltke (Chicago: Moody, 1980), 326–27.

[10] The Septuagint received its name because seventy Hebrew scholars translated the Hebrew Old Testament into Greek since more Jews in the Diaspora read Greek more easily than Hebrew. The word Septuagint stands for "seventy."

[11] Karl Ludwig Schmidt writes, "The word ἔθνος (*ethnos*), which is common in Greek from the very first, probably comes from ἔθος (*ethos*) and means "mass" or "host" or "multitude" bound by the same manners, customs or other distinctive features. . . . In most cases ἔθνος [*ethnos*] is used of men in the sense of a 'people.'" Karl Ludwig Schmidt, "ἔθνος (*ethnos*)," in *TDNT*, vol. 2.

[12] Schmidt, "ἔθνος (*ethnos*)."

[13] The New American Standard Bible translates this verb "grope." Moulton and Milligan define the term to mean "touch" or "feel." However, they say "*psailaphao* [ψηλαφήσειαν] comes in late Greek to denote 'examine closely.'" James Hope Moulton and George Milligan, *The Vocabulary of the Greek Testament: Illustrated from the Papyri and other Non-Literary Sources* (London: Hodder and Stoughton, 1914–1929; Grand Rapids: Eerdmans, 1976), 697.

Although Noah's three sons fathered all the peoples of the world, the latter part of Genesis 11 narrows the focus of the Old Testament to the descendants of Shem—particularly one descendant, Abram (later to become Abraham). Whereas previously God dealt with the entire human race as one, from Genesis 12 until the coming of the Messiah, the Lord deals principally with one people: the Jewish people, the nation of Israel.

Abram was not a missionary in the sense of the word today. His call in Gen 12:1 was to relocate to a faraway land, not reach another people with God's message. As a result of this obedience, God changed Abram's name to Abraham[14] and the peoples of the earth were blessed (12:3). Indirectly, the missionary intention of God passes down through the patriarchs. God's intention was to bless the nations through his chosen people. This is not the same as asserting that Israel had a missionary mission. Andreas Köstenberger and Peter O'Brien caution, "To contend that Israel had a missionary task and should have engaged in mission as we understand it today goes beyond the evidence. There is no suggestion in the Old Testament that Israel should have engaged in 'cross cultural' or foreign mission."[15]

More missions content exists in the Mosaic era than usually meets the eye. In Exod 19:5–6, God told Moses to say to Israel, "Now if you will carefully listen to me and keep my covenant, you will be my own possession out of all the peoples, although the whole earth is mine, and you will be my kingdom of priests and my holy nation." God implores Israel to serve as priests to the other nations. Since a priest represents God to others, so Israel would embody the Almighty to the peoples of the world. This constitutes Old Testament missions.

Missions in the two testaments flows in different directions. George Peters says:

> In regard to methodology, the Scriptures prescribe a twofold way— the *centrifugal* and the *centripetal*. It must be recognized that the Old Testament is wholly built around the latter method, whereas the New Testament enjoins the former method.
>
> The Old Testament upholds the centripetal method which may be thought of as a sacred magnetism that draws to itself.... Also

---

14 The father of a multitude.
15 Köstenberger and O'Brien, *Ends of the Earth*, 35.

> because of Old Testament methodology, the disciples found it very
> difficult to understand their Master in His commission to go into
> all the world. According to the Old Testament, the world of nations
> is to come to Jerusalem. . . . But why must they go *from* Jerusalem?
> It constituted a turnabout in methodology but not in principle and
> purpose.[16]

These principles are in view today. Some ministries are content to construct large buildings and say, "Come and see." Although edifices are neutral in
merit, the New Testament thrust is for the church to "go and tell." Of course,
both emphases are possible to practice simultaneously, but it is difficult to sus-
tain equal and opposite thrusts.

Scriptures in the Davidic era repeatedly expose God's missions heart.
Psalm 96:3 exhorts, "Declare his glory among the nations, his wondrous works
among all peoples [*goyim*, גוֹיִם]." In other words, Israel was supposed to speak
to the Gentiles about the Lord of the earth. The true purpose for Israel is revealed in Solomon's prayer at the dedication of the first temple. In one of the
longest chapters of the Bible, David's son and successor states that the aim of
the temple would be so that "all peoples of earth will know your name, to fear
you as your people Israel do and to know that this temple I have built bears
your name" (1 Kgs 8:43). Solomon summarizes his prayer in 1 Kgs 8:60, saying
the rationale for the temple is so that "all the peoples of the earth know that
the LORD is God. There is no other!" No verses in the Old Testament so clearly
define Israel's reason for their existence as a chosen people as these.

Of course, many of the prophetic books display distinct mission thrusts.
The book of Isaiah seems to possess the clearest view of God's heart. Almost
immediately, the prophet presents a missionary theme, as he writes in Isa 2:2–3,
"In the last days the mountain of the LORD's house will be established at the
top of the mountains and will be raised above the hills. All the nations will
stream to it, and many peoples will come and say, 'Come, let us go up to the
mountain of the LORD.'" Furthermore, the prophet quotes God in Isa 49:6,
writing, "He says, 'It is not enough for you to be my servant raising up the
tribes of Jacob and restoring the protected ones of Israel. I will also make you a
light for the nations, to be my salvation to the ends of the earth.'" In Isa 52:10,

---

[16] Peters, *Biblical Theology of Missions*, 21 (see chap. 1, n. 7).

the Lord's servant writes, "The LORD has displayed his holy arm in the sight of all the nations; all the ends of the earth will see the salvation of our God." All these verses demonstrate the true purpose of Israel—they were to be a light to the nations.

There are many other Old Testament passages that point to missions. Except for the negative example of Jonah, who was called to preach a message of repentance to another nation, but first refused, there is not a model of actual missions in the New Testament sense. George Peters calls the Old Testament a missionary book[17] and states, "The Old Testament does not contain missions but is itself 'missions' in the world."[18] By the time the New Testament begins, Israel had become self-absorbed and legalistic. God's message of salvation to the nations would not change, but the coming of the Messiah would alter Israel and how God dealt with other nations.

MISSIONS AND THE NEW TESTAMENT

This book argues that the New Testament possesses a missionary perspective. The New Testament explains the person of Jesus Christ, records the activities of those proclaiming his message, and teaches doctrine and proper behavior to missionary churches. As Peters says:

> We need only remind ourselves of the fact that the book of Acts is the authentic record of the apostles and the early church and all the epistles were written to churches established through missionary endeavors. Were Christianity not a missionary religion and had the apostles not been missionaries, we would have no book of Acts and no epistles. With the exception of Matthew, even the Gospels were written to missionary churches. The New Testament is a missionary book in address, content, spirit and design.[19]

---

17 Peters, 130.
18 Peters, 129.
19 Peters, 131.

The Gospels

It is evident in the Gospels that the mission of Jesus was directed toward the nation of Israel. In Matt 15:24 Jesus says, "I was sent only to the lost sheep of the house of Israel." It is clear, however, that from the beginning all the peoples of the earth were in view. Guided by the Holy Spirit, Simeon took the Christ child in his arms and said, "Now, Master, you can dismiss your servant in peace, as you promised. For my eyes have seen your salvation. You have prepared it in the presence of all people [*laou*, λαῶν][20]—a light for revelation to the Gentiles [*ethnos*, ἔθνος] and glory to your people [*laou*, λαῶν] Israel."[21] Jesus concentrated primarily on a mission to the Jews until just after his triumphal entry into Jerusalem on Palm Sunday in John 12:20–24.[22] After healing the sick in Matt 8:4, Mark 1:43, Mark 7:36, and Luke 5:14, Jesus instructed the recipients of God's grace to not tell anyone about his miracles. Once some of the Greeks, however, expressed interest, Jesus launched his larger mission to redeem all the people of the world. Many see this as a pivotal point in the New Testament—the turning to the Gentiles by Jesus.

On May 12, 1971, I received a "small commission." On that date, the president of the United States of America, Richard Nixon, commissioned me as an officer in the United States Air Force. As a lieutenant and later a captain, I obeyed the chief executive officer of the USA and commanded several military units in order to fulfill the mission objectives of the United States.

In the same manner and in a much larger sense, Jesus Christ commissioned the apostles and their successors to fulfill his primary task: reaching the world with the message of salvation. There are four generally recognized commissions in the four Gospels (and another in Acts), the first considered to be the Great Commission. Each commission commands Jesus's disciples to represent him

---

[20] See n. 32 in this chapter for an explanation of the Greek word *laou* (λαῶν). This word forms the root of the English term "laity."

[21] Luke 2:29–32.

[22] "Now some Greeks were among those who went up to worship at the festival. So they came to Philip, who was from Bethsaida in Galilee, and requested of him, 'Sir, we want to see Jesus.' Philip went and told Andrew; then Andrew and Philip went and told Jesus. Jesus replied to them, 'The hour has come for the Son of Man to be glorified. Truly I tell you, unless a grain of wheat falls to the ground and dies, it remains by itself. But if it dies, it produces much fruit.'"

in the cause of world evangelization. Each commission, however, possesses a different emphasis.

Jesus said in the Great Commission of Matt 28:18–20:

> All authority has been given to me in heaven and on earth. Go, therefore, and make disciples of all nations, baptizing them in the name of the Father and of the Son and of the Holy Spirit, teaching them to observe everything I have commanded you. And remember, I am with you always, to the end of the age.

In the days when Rome ruled the world, this was a startling claim. Although Israel and Rome rejected the humble Jewish rabbi, the resurrected Messiah claimed worldwide dominion. The clear emphasis of Matthew 28 involves making disciples. Speaking of these verses, McNeile writes, "The Lord is no longer 'sent to the lost sheep of the house of Israel'; His authority being now limitless, all nations are to become His disciples. On *mathaitusate* [μαθητεύσατε—discipling], it is not 'instruct,' but describes a comprehensive term of which the *Baptizontes* [βαπτίζοντες—baptizing], and *didaskontes* [διδάσκοντες—teaching], each form a part."[23] In other words, the mission of the infant church would focus on not just retelling the gospel story, but evangelizing the lost, baptizing converts, and then discipling them intensely. In a reference in the secular *papyri*, James Hope Moulton and George Milligan describe a μαθητεῖ (*mathaitai*, disciple), who "is regular in his attendance at his studies, . . . eager in acquiring knowledge."[24] In other words, a disciple should not be just an adherent, but an active and participative learner.

A remarkable feature in Matt 28:18 concerns the object of the missionary mandate. Whereas the Old Testament primarily focuses on Israel with a secondary emphasis on the Gentiles, in the New Testament the nations (*ethnos*, ἔθνος) are front and center in God's plan and purpose. Cornell Goerner says, "Jesus found God's purpose for all nations in the books of Moses, in the

---

[23] Alan Hugh McNeile, *The Gospel According to St. Matthew: The Greek Text with Introduction, Notes, and Indices* (Grand Rapids: Baker, 1980; London: Macmillan, 1915), 435.

[24] Moulton and Milligan, *Vocabulary of the Greek Testament*, 385.

writing of the Prophets, and in the Psalms."[25] In Matt 28:19, he proclaims that the evangelization of the nations is God's primary task.

Mark's commission is shorter and has a different emphasis. He writes in Mark 16:15–16, "Then he said to them, 'Go into all the world and preach the gospel to all creation. Whoever believes and is baptized will be saved, but whoever does not believe will be condemned.'" The objects of the Matthew and Mark commissions are roughly equivalent. Matthew presses for an outreach to "all nations," while Mark looks to reaching "all creation." The makeup of the creation (*ktisei*, κτίσει) is defined by the term "world" (*kosmon*, κόσμον) later in the sentence. The most important part of Mark's commission is the phrase "preach [*karuxate*, κηρύξατε] the Gospel [*euaggelion*, ευαγγέλιον]." The former term speaks of a public announcement by an official, sometimes in connection to the public games or official financial documents.[26] According to Moulton and Milligan, in secular Greek the word *gospel* meant "good tidings."[27] Of course, this term was adopted by the New Testament writers to mean "good news." In other words, the preaching of the good news of God consists of a solemn and official process by which those who believe could and would be saved. The apostle Paul later defines the content of the word *gospel* in 1 Cor 15:3–8.[28]

According to the New Testament writers, this message has the power to save anyone who "believes" (*pisteusas*, πιστεύσας). The term meant much more than the simple intellectual assent "believe" often signifies in English. The derivation of the word points to "trusting" or "entrusting."[29] As many have contended, baptism is not a condition for salvation, because only unbelief, not failure to be baptized, condemns.

---

[25] H. Cornell Goerner, *All Nations in God's Purpose: What the Bible Teaches about Missions* (Nashville: Broadman, 1979), 21.

[26] Moulton and Milligan, *Vocabulary of the Greek Testament*, 343.

[27] Moulton and Milligan, 259.

[28] "For I passed on to you as most important what I also received: that Christ died for our sins according to the Scriptures, that he was buried, that he was raised on the third day according to the Scriptures, and that he appeared to Cephas, then to the Twelve. Then he appeared to over five hundred brothers and sisters at one time; most of them are still alive, but some have fallen asleep. Then he appeared to James, then to all the apostles. Last of all, as to one born at the wrong time, he also appeared to me."

[29] Moulton and Milligan, 515. One instance in the papyri speaks of the word in the sense of "one entrusted with the management of a ship."

Luke's commission is longer and more substantive than either of the two previous commissions. Luke, writing to Theophilus, a Greek man, adds a more Jewish flavor to the commission narratives. This is evident in Luke 24:44–49.[30] Luke presents Jesus as the Jewish Messiah and speaks of the testimony of the Old Testament. Neither Matthew nor Mark's commissions refer to Jesus's Jewish background. In order to understand Jesus and the gospel message, especially in places unfamiliar with Judaism, some aspects of Jesus's national heritage have to be addressed by today's missionaries. Additionally, it is clear the Lord Jesus must still unlock men's minds if they are to understand the gospel, as Jesus did with his disciples. Every missionary should understand that without the Lord opening the minds of those in the culture, no one could be saved out of Islam, Hinduism, Buddhism, or atheism. Like the apostle Paul in 1 Corinthians 15, Luke grounds his commission in the resurrection of Christ. The most unique contribution of Luke's commission consists of his inclusion of repentance (*metanoia*, μετάνοια) in his Gospel. The origin of the term lies in the idea of changing one's mind or breaking a contract.[31] Moulton and Milligan say, "Its meaning deepens with Christianity, and in the NT it is more than 'repent,' and indicates a complete change of attitude, spiritual and moral, towards God."[32] Luke mentions that the object of the missionary effort should be the nations (*ethnos*, ἔθνος), but designates the point of departure as Jerusalem. In other words, the Jews would not be forgotten. Paul wrote in Rom 1:16, "For I am not ashamed of the gospel, because it is the power of God for salvation to everyone who believes, first to the Jew, and also to the Greek." Indeed, Paul's missionary band would go first to a synagogue or a place of prayer to preach the gospel. Jesus then tells his disciples (Luke 24:48), "You are witnesses [*marturais*, from the singular μάρτυς or "martyr"] of these things." This term possesses tremendous gravity, as the papyri uses the word in the sense of "solemnly

---

[30] "He told them, 'These are my words that I spoke to you while I was still with you—that everything written about me in the Law of Moses, the Prophets and the Psalms must be fulfilled.' Then he opened their minds to understand the Scriptures. He also said to them, 'This is what is written: The Messiah would suffer and rise from the dead the third day, and repentance for the forgiveness of sins would be proclaimed in his name to all the nations, beginning at Jerusalem. You are witnesses of these things. And look, I am sending you what my Father promised. As for you, stay in the city until you are empowered from on high.'"

[31] Moulton and Milligan, *Vocabulary of the Greek Testament*, 403.

[32] Moulton and Milligan, 404.

charge" and "bearing witness to the facts."[33] Indeed, Jesus was depending on these eleven men to represent him in the courts of humanity throughout the world. They would not be up to the task without the power of the Holy Spirit promised in Luke 24:49.

The commission in John's Gospel is very short. John 20:21 says, "Jesus said to them again, 'Peace be with you. As the Father has sent [*apostello*, ἀποστέλλω] me, I also send [*pempo*, πέμπω] you.'" Moulton and Milligan say the latter constitutes the common word for "send."[34] Westcott claims:

> The contrast between the verbs (*apostello, pempo*) in the two clauses is obviously significant. Both verbs are used of the mission of the Son, and of the mission of believers, but with distinct meanings. The former (*apostello*) corresponds with our own words "dispatch" and "envoy," and conveys the accessory notions of a special commission, and so far of a delegated authority in the person sent. The simple verb *pempo* marks nothing more than the immediate relation of the sender to the sent.[35]

Although originally spoken to the eleven apostles, missionaries today can rest in the knowledge that as God the Father sent God the Son to earth on his mission of salvation, today he now sends us into the world as his representatives. All Christians should stand in awe that God has not only entrusted the message of salvation to every believer, but also that Christ identifies so closely with those who represent him. This is only possible because the Holy Spirit indwells every Christian.

The Book of Acts

Written about the initial spread of Christianity, the Acts of the Apostles is the most missionary book in the Scriptures. Reading like a fifth Great Commission, Acts 1:8 says, "But you will receive power when the Holy Spirit has come on you, and you will be my witnesses, in Jerusalem, in all Judea and Samaria,

---

[33] Moulton and Milligan, 390.

[34] Moulton and Milligan give the example from the papyri, "had it not been for the fact that I was ill, I would have sent them to you long ago." Moulton and Milligan, *Vocabulary of the Greek Testament*, 502.

[35] Brooke Foss Westcott, *The Gospel According to St. John: The Authorized Version with Introduction and Notes* (1882; repr., Grand Rapids: Eerdmans, 1975), 298.

and to the ends of the earth." The Greek construction of this verse deserves attention. When the conjunction *kai* (καί), is followed by the particle *te* (τῆ), as is the case in this passage, the verse can read as follows (as it does in the Phillips translation): "You will be witnesses to me, not only in Jerusalem, not only throughout Judea, not only in Samaria, but to the very ends of the earth!" In other words, missions should occur simultaneously, not only sequentially.[36] The temptation always exists to feel there is so much mission work needed in one's home country, resources are too scarce to fund endeavors in other places. Additionally, there is the opposite inclination to starve mission work in historic fields and concentrate only on countries at the ends of the earth. This Scripture seems to indicate that mission work should be accomplished simultaneously throughout the world.

The power Luke speaks about in 24:49 and Acts 1:8 arrives in force in Acts 2. The coming of the Holy Spirit at Pentecost seems to reverse the language difficulty created in Gen 11:7–9[37] when the disciples began to speak with other languages in Acts 2:7–11.[38] Here, at Pentecost, the focus of evangelism returns

---

[36] Here's how the NASB and KJV translate Acts 1:8: "[B]ut you will receive power when the Holy Spirit has come upon you; and you shall be My witnesses both in Jerusalem, and in all Judea and Samaria, and even to the remotest part of the earth" (NASB); "But ye shall receive power, after that the Holy Ghost is come upon you: and ye shall be witnesses unto me both in Jerusalem, and in all Judaea, and in Samaria, and unto the uttermost part of the earth" (KJV). The translation of the term "both" represents a rather strange construction here to the English ear. In English when one says "both" he usually refers to the linking together of two ideas. However, here there are four places mentioned. The translation of the passage turns on the meaning of the enclitic particle *te* (τῆ). The Greek word *te* (τῆ) is usually rendered by the English word "and" when the particle stands alone. The NIV, CSB, and most other translations translated the term in this manner. However, when the *te* (τῆ) is followed by a *kai* (καί), the words can have the meaning of "not only, but also." See Eugene Van Ness, *The Language of the New Testament* (New York: Charles Scribner's Sons, 1977), 320. The Phillips translation renders the *te* (τῆ) so that the passage implies that one does not start at home base (Jerusalem) and when one finishes there, go to Judea, and when one finishes there, go to Samaria and when one finishes there, go to the ends of the earth. Robin Dale Hadaway, "Balancing the Biblical Perspective: A Missiological Analysis," *Journal of Evangelism and Missions* 2 (Spring 2003): 103–14.

[37] "'Come, let's go down there and confuse their language so that they will not understand one another's speech.' So from there the LORD scattered them throughout the earth, and they stopped building the city. Therefore it is called Babylon, for there the LORD confused the language of the whole earth, and from there the LORD scattered them throughout the earth."

[38] "They were astounded and amazed, saying, 'Look, aren't all these who are speaking Galileans? How is it that each of us can hear in our own native language? Parthians, Medes, Elamites; those who live in Mesopotamia, in Judea and Cappadocia, Pontus and Asia, Phrygia

to the nations. Although these were primarily Jews living within these nations, these Jews considered the languages of their homelands their own native tongues. Additionally, there were also proselytes (Gentiles who became Jews) from these nations. These proselytes would become the seedbed for the nascent missions movement.

After the church scattered among the nations following the death of Stephen (Acts 8:1) and Paul's dramatic conversion (Acts 9), the missionary-minded Antiochian church commissions and sends out the first missionaries. Mission endeavors can be traced to Acts 13:1–4.[39]

The passage speaks to the reciprocal importance of the local church to missions and missions to the local church. Of the church's leadership, fully 40 percent were sent out as missionaries. Speaking of how man and God partner in ministry, the first missionaries were dispatched in equal measure by the church (13:3) and the Holy Spirit (13:4). Much more can be said concerning the apostle Paul's three missionary journeys, aspects of which will be covered later. This book, however, will return often to the Acts of the Apostles in the coming theological, cultural, contextualization, and strategy chapters for further exploration.

The book of Acts closes with Paul pronouncing the direction Christianity would shift from Israel to the nations when the leaders of the Jewish community in Rome rejected his message. Paul said in Acts 28:28, "Therefore, let it be known to you that this salvation of God has been sent to the Gentiles [ethnos, ἔθνος]; they will listen." Christianity began as a mission to the Jews and Gentiles but by the end of Acts the emphasis had been reversed.

---

and Pamphylia, Egypt and the parts of Libya near Cyrene; visitors from Rome (both Jews and converts), Cretans and Arabs—we hear them declaring the magnificent acts of God in our own tongues.'"

[39] "Now in the church at Antioch there were prophets and teachers: Barnabas, Simeon who was called Niger, Lucius of Cyrene, Manaen, a close friend of Herod the tetrarch and Saul. As they were worshiping the Lord and fasting, the Holy Spirit said, 'Set apart for me Barnabas and Saul for the work to which I have called them.' Then after they had fasted, prayed, and laid hands on them, they sent them off. So being sent out by the Holy Spirit, they went down to Seleucia, and from there they sailed to Cyprus."

The Epistles

Most of the Epistles were written either to missionary churches or to other missionaries, pastors, or individuals associated with the missionary churches. Romans, 1 and 2 Corinthians, Galatians, Ephesians, Philippians, Colossians, 1 and 2 Thessalonians, and 1 and 2 Peter fit the first category; while 1 and 2 Timothy, Titus, Philemon, 2 and 3 John form the second. The books of Hebrews and James appear to be written primarily for Jewish believers throughout the Diaspora,[40] while 1 John and Jude are general letters that do not match any particular classification.

Paul's epistles are filled with both missionary stories and references to them. His account of his missionary trials in 2 Cor 11:23–28 are both sobering and inspiring.[41] Paul also writes of his passion for reaching the world for his Master. He writes in Rom 15:19–20, "I have fully proclaimed the gospel of Christ from Jerusalem all the way around to Illyricum. My aim is to preach the gospel where Christ has not been named, so that I will not build on someone else's foundation." Paul, more than any other disciple, obeyed Christ's commission, evangelizing Jerusalem, Judea, and Samaria throughout and to the ends of the earth. Paul's epistles resonate with passion to evangelize and disciple unbelievers. The apostle presents his message and mandate in Rom 10:8–15.[42]

These verses reveal, not only the content and process of God's saving work through Christ, but also the urgency of the gospel's proclamation. Furthermore,

---

[40] The Diaspora refers to the scattering of the Jewish people among the nations.

[41] "…with far more labors, many more imprisonments, far worse beatings, many times near death. Five times I received the forty lashes minus one from the Jews. Three times I was beaten with rods. Once I received a stoning. Three times I was shipwrecked. I have spent a night and a day in the open sea. On frequent journeys, I faced dangers from rivers, dangers from robbers, dangers from my own people, dangers from the Gentiles, dangers in the city, dangers in the wilderness, dangers at sea, and dangers among false brothers; toil and hardship, many sleepless nights, hunger and thirst, often without food, cold, and without clothing. Not to mention other things, there is the daily pressure on me: my concern for all the churches."

[42] "This is the message of faith that we proclaim: If you confess with your mouth 'Jesus is Lord,' and believe in your heart that God raised him from the dead, you will be saved. One believes with the heart, resulting in righteousness, and one confesses with the mouth, resulting in salvation. For the Scripture says, **Everyone who believes on him will not be put to shame,** since there is no distinction between Jew and Greek, because the same Lord of all richly blesses all who call on him. For **everyone who calls on the name of the Lord will be saved**. How, then, can they call on him they have not believed in? And how can they believe without hearing about him? And how can they hear without a preacher? And how can they preach unless they are sent? As it is written: **How beautiful are the feet of those who bring good news.**"

the apostle Paul presents four questions, all answered in the negative. The first query is the evangelism question: "How, then, can they call on him they have not believed in?" (v. 14). The answer is, they cannot. Here Paul presents, as has already been mentioned, the act of believing as the entry point to salvation. This is accomplished by confessing Jesus verbally and believing with one's heart.

The second question represents the missions question. Romans 10:14 asks, "And how can they believe without hearing about him?" The answer is the same—they cannot. In other words, if the lost are to believe, someone has to tell them. The lost do not become believers apart from a verbal witness to them. This is the reason for missions—so the unsaved will hear about Jesus Christ.

The third question resembles the second one. Romans 10:14 reads, "And how can they hear without a preacher [*kairusontos*, κηρύσσοντος]?" Again, the answer must be, they cannot. The term translated "preacher" also means "proclaimer." This is the missionary question. In order for the gospel to spread over the earth, proclaimers must verbally present the good news.

The final question remains as important as the preceding ones, "And how can they preach unless they are sent?" (v. 15). The answer for the fourth time is, they cannot. This is why churches and mission agencies have sent out missionaries ever since Paul and Barnabas departed Antioch. This is the deputation question. The task is too dangerous, the work too complex, and the logistics too expensive for individuals to send themselves—they must be sent.

Paul closes his fourfold questionnaire by quoting Isa 52:7, "How beautiful are the feet of those who bring good news." Although John MacArthur says it is the gospel that is beautiful and not the evangelist's feet,[43] I believe that truly anyone who shares the gospel possesses beautiful feet, at least spiritually.

The Apocalypse

The Revelation of John presents an interesting case regarding missions. The Apocalypse, the only prophetic book in the New Testament, features neither a historical sketch of missions like Acts nor doctrinal instruction as in the Epistles. Instead, the Revelation peers far into the future, observing individuals

---

[43] John MacArthur, *Romans 9–16*, MacArthur New Testament Commentary Series (Chicago: Moody, 1994), 83–84.

from every people group on earth entering the New Jerusalem. Revelation 5:9–10 says, "And they sang a new song: You are worthy to take the scroll and to open its seals, because you were slaughtered, and you purchased people for God by your blood from every tribe and language and people [*laiou*, λαῶν][44] and nation [*ethnos*, ἔθνος]. You made them a kingdom and priests to our God, and they will reign on earth."

In the Old Testament, Israel was to be a priestly nation and the peoples of the earth were to journey to the old temple from all over the world to learn of God's ways. As observed earlier, missions in the old covenant was centripetal, "come and see," so to speak. In the New Testament from Matthew until the Revelation, the mission of the church presents as a centrifugal endeavor, as in "go and tell,"[45] as the Gospels and Epistles proclaim the missionary-sending mandate of the church. However, with the Revelation, the New Testament ends with all redeemed humanity, whether Jew or Gentile, serving as a kingdom of priests to God. By the end of the last book of the Bible, representatives of all the nations dwell within the walls of the New Jerusalem. Speaking of the Holy City, Rev 21:24–26 says, "The nations [*ethnos*, ἔθνος] will walk by its light, and the kings of the earth will bring their glory into it. Its gates will never close by day because it will never be night there. They will bring the glory and honor of the nations [*ethnos*, ἔθνος] into it." Now as a result of missions past and present in the world and due to the saving power of Jesus Christ, until the events prophesied in the Apocalypse transpire, the emphasis will remain centrifugal. When the curtain falls on earth's history and all saved humanity streams into the New Jerusalem to live forever, the days of evangelism and missions will end. Around the throne in the New Jerusalem, the emphasis will not be centrifugal (go and tell) or centripetal (come and see), but rather in the moment, as in "be."

---

[44] Moulton and Milligan say, "In the Papyri *laioi* [from λαῶν] is the regular term for 'natives,' '*fellaheen*' [common people]. . . . [T]he editor remarks, 'an ancient and poetical form for people both in the LXX and in the Papyri.'" Moulton and Milligan, *Vocabulary of the Greek Testament*, 370. Whereas "nations" refers often to ethnicity, "people" here refers to all classes of humanity.

[45] Peters, *Biblical Theology of Missions*, 21. See the quote from George Peters on pages 21–22 for a longer definition of centrifugal and centripetal missions.

CONCLUSION

The books of the Bible from Genesis to Revelation present the story of missions. This includes the creation of the world, the sin of Adam and Eve, and God's redemption story encompassing the Old and New Testaments. Although not always overtly missional in theme, each book of the Bible displays God's grace toward Israel and the nations of the world. Missiology rests on the firm foundation of God's Word, the Bible, and the Living Word, Jesus Christ our Lord.

READING FOR FURTHER STUDY

Goerner, H. Cornell. *All Nations in God's Purpose: What the Bible Teaches about Missions.* Nashville: Broadman Press, 1979.

Köstenberger, Andreas J., and Peter T. O'Brien. *Salvation to the Ends of the Earth: A Biblical Theology of Missions.* Downers Grove, IL: InterVarsity Press, 2001.

Peters, George W. *A Biblical Theology of Missions.* Chicago: Moody, 1972.

3

The Theological Foundation of Missions

On January 12, 2007, the *Washington Post* asked classical violin phenomenon Joshua Bell to perform inside the *L'Enfant* subway station in Washington, DC, to see if anyone recognized him. The violinist played six pieces on his 1713, handcrafted, $3.5 million Stradivarius violin. He laid his violin case on the subway floor for tips. During the performance, 1,097 people walked by; seven stopped and twenty-seven donated money. The total receipts for the forty-three minutes were $32.17. Bell's concerts routinely sell out at $125 a ticket. There was never a crowd. Only three of the people who stopped truly appreciated the quality of the music. Only one person recognized him. Stacy Furukawa, a demographer at the Commerce Department, had attended a Bell concert three weeks earlier. She said, "It was the most astonishing thing I've ever seen in Washington. Joshua Bell was standing there playing at rush hour and people were not stopping, and not even looking."[1] In a similar way, Jesus, the Son of God, arrived on the earth. Few thought him special. Even fewer recognized his deity.

When the apostle Paul completed his gospel presentation to the Athenians in Acts 17, most scoffed when they heard about Jesus's resurrection. Of

---

[1] Gene Weingarten, "Joshua Bell," *Washington Post*, reprinted in *Kansas City Star*, April 22, 2007.

the few who believed, Luke mentions only two by name: a man, Dionysius the Areopagite, and a woman, Damaris. Concerning Jesus, John 1:11–12 says, "He came to his own, and his own people[2] did not receive him. But to all who did receive him, he gave them the right to be children of God." Despite Christ's miracles and teaching, most Jews and Gentiles failed to recognize God's incarnation as man.

From his lifetime down to the present day, most either reject Christ or remain indifferent to him. In Acts 17:30–31 Paul says, "Therefore, having overlooked the times of ignorance, God now commands all people everywhere to repent, because he has set a day when he is going to judge the world in righteousness by the man he has appointed. He has provided proof of this to everyone by raising him from the dead." The fallen nature of man, the judgment of God, the need for repentance, and faith in the Savior constitute some of the theological issues that impact missions. As George Peters says:

> Christian missions makes sense only in the light of an existing abnormality or emergency and in the conviction that an answer to and remedy for such a malady is available. . . . The emergency is the fact of sin in the world which has overpowered and infected the human race and which threatens the very existence of mankind. There would be no need for Christian missions if sin were not a serious reality. . . . Sin made salvation necessary and sin makes Christian missions necessary.[3]

MANKIND'S CONDITION AND NEED

Mark Twain remarks, "Whoever has lived long enough to find out what life is, knows how deep a debt of gratitude we owe to Adam, the first great benefactor of our race. He brought death into the world."[4] The previous chapter asserts the

---

[2] The apostle John does not use either *ethnos* (ἔθνος) or *laios* (λαῶν) here, but rather another Greek term, *idioi* (ἴδιοι). Moulton and Milligan say that in the New Testament "the word is rendered 'one's own,' 'private,' 'personal,' without any mention of a weaker meaning." Furthermore, they say the word when used as an adjective implies, "sequestrated from the common stock." Moulton and Milligan, *Vocabulary of the Greek Testament*, 298 (see chap. 2, n. 13).

[3] Peters, *Biblical Theology of Missions*, 15 (see chap. 1, n. 7).

[4] Mark Twain, "Youth, Aging," in *The Wit and Wisdom of Mark Twain: A Book of Quotations*, Dover Thrift Editions, ed. Paul Negri (Mineola, NY: Dover, 1999), 31.

sin of Adam and Eve initiated iniquity, triggering physical and spiritual death, which spread to all mankind. In Rom 5:16–19,[5] Paul addresses how the first couple's sin affects their descendants today. All mankind inherits sin unknowingly but later each chooses to transgress individually. The term "lost" describes mankind's pre-salvific condition. After the tax collector Zacchaeus repented, Luke 19:9–10 says, "'Today salvation has come to this house,' Jesus told him, 'because he too is a son of Abraham. For the Son of Man has come to seek and to save the lost [*apoloulos, ἀπολωλός*].'"[6] Jesus portrays salvation as the remedy for Zacchaeus's lost, sinful condition.

Paul asserts in Rom 3:9–12 that iniquity resides within all humanity. He writes, "For we have already charged that both Jews and Gentiles are all under sin, as it is written: There is no one righteous, not even one. There is no one who understands; there is no one who seeks God. All have turned away; all alike have become worthless. There is no one who does what is good, not even one." The pervasiveness of mankind's wickedness and his lost state requires a resolution in the form of salvation. Martin Luther said, "If sin proved itself so powerful that a single transgression has perverted many, or rather all, then divine grace is much more powerful; for the act of grace can save many, indeed, all men, of many sins, if they only would desire it."[7]

Paul depicts the manner of Christ's salvation in Rom 10:8–10, writing, "This is the message of faith that we proclaim: If you confess with your mouth, 'Jesus is Lord,' and believe in your heart that God has raised him from the dead, you will be saved. One believes with the heart, resulting in righteousness, and one confesses with the mouth, resulting in salvation." Furthermore, Paul

---

[5] "And the gift is not like the one man's sin, because from one sin came the judgment, resulting in condemnation, but from many trespasses came the gift, resulting in justification. Since by the one man's trespass, death reigned through that one man, how much more will those who receive the overflow of grace and the gift of righteousness reign in life through the one man, Jesus Christ. So then, as through one trespass there is condemnation for everyone, so also through one righteous act there is justification leading to life for everyone. For just as through one man's disobedience the many were made sinners, so also through the one man's obedience the many will be made righteous."

[6] This is the simple Greek word for "lose," "loss," or "lost." The following example appears in the papyri; "I am quite upset over Helenos' loss of the money." Moulton and Milligan, *Vocabulary of the Greek Testament*, 66.

[7] Martin Luther, *Commentary on Romans*, trans. Theodore Mueller (Grand Rapids: Kregel, 1954), 98.

negates the role of works in salvation, writing in Eph 2:8–9, "For you are saved by grace through faith, and this is not from yourselves; it is God's gift—not from works, so that no one can boast."

Peter's experience in the house of Cornelius the Roman centurion in Acts 10–11 indicates God welcomes all tribes and peoples. The apostle told the assembled Gentiles in Acts 10:42–43, "He commanded us to preach to the people and to testify that he is the one appointed by God to be the judge of the living and the dead. All the prophets testify about him that through his name everyone who believes in him receives forgiveness of sins." After they believed, Peter returned to Jerusalem, where certain Jewish Christians criticized him for fraternizing with Gentiles. Peter described his experiences and how the centurion and his household had come to faith. Upon hearing this, the Jewish believers exclaimed, "So then, God has given repentance resulting in life even to the Gentiles."[8] Finally, Israel began to see the fulfillment of Isaiah's prophecies concerning the nations coming to God.

THE PROCESS OF SALVATION

Theological terms describing the complexity of the salvation process include "atonement," "redemption," "reconciliation," "propitiation," "adoption," "ransom," "justification," and "sacrifice." Although each of these words reflects a different facet of Christ's salvific work, Rom 3:23–26 summarizes the legal transaction constituting it.[9] The term "redemption" (*apolutroseos*, ἀπολυτρώσεως) describes the payment to an abductor to purchase a person's liberty. Appearing ten times in the New Testament, the popular usage of the word describes "the purchase-money for manumitting slaves."[10] Henry P. Lidden says of verse 24, "But the *lutron* [redemption, λυτρῶν] was not paid to Satan, whose power was

---

[8] Acts 11:18.

[9] "For all have sinned and fall short of the glory of God. They are *justified* freely by his grace through the *redemption* that is in Christ Jesus. God presented him as an *atoning sacrifice* in his blood, received through faith, to demonstrate his *righteousness*, because in his restraint God passed over the sins previously committed. God presented him to demonstrate his *righteousness* at the present time, so that he would be *righteous* and *declare righteous* the one who has faith in Jesus" (italics added).

[10] Moulton and Milligan, *Vocabulary of the Greek Testament*, 382.

a usurpation, but to God, whose eternal and necessary morality also required a satisfaction for sin."[11] The redemption price in this case consists of a propitiatory payment of the highest value—the very blood of the Son of God. The term "propitiation" (*ilastairion*, ἱλαστήριον) in verse 25 refers to the place of expiation on the mercy seat in the holy of holies in the Jewish temple, which, "according to Exodus 25:22 and Leviticus 16:2 . . . is the central seat of God's saving presence on earth and of His gracious revelations to man."[12] Luther writes concerning Rom 3:25:

> This is a perplexing and difficult text that must be explained and understood as follows: God from eternity has ordained and set forth Christ as the propitiation for our sins, but that only for those who believe in Him. Christ wanted to become a propitiation for us only through His blood, that is, He first had to make amends for us through the shedding of His blood. And all this God did "*to declare his righteousness*," that is, to make it known that all men are sinners and in need of His righteousness. The very fact that Christ suffered for us, and through His suffering became a propitiation for us, proves that we are (*by nature*) unrighteous, and that we for whom He became a propitiation, must obtain our righteousness solely from God, now that forgiveness for our sins has been secured by Christ's atonement.[13]

The words translated "justified," "righteous," and "declare righteous" all come from the same Greek word, *dikaios* (δικαιος). The adjectival term portrays a "just measurement," but as a noun signifies "duty," "rights," "legal claim," or "justice."[14] This passage describes how Jesus's sacrifice of himself on the cross expiates man's sin, justifying those who trust him by faith.

Colossians 2:13–14 provides further clarity concerning the legal nature of Christ's redemption of mankind. Paul writes, "And when you were dead in the trespasses and in the uncircumcision of your flesh, he made you alive with him and forgave us all our trespasses. He erased the certificate of debt, with its obligations, that was against us and opposed to us, and has taken it away by

---

[11] Henry P. Liddon, *Explanatory Analysis of St. Paul's Epistle to the Romans* (1899; repr., Minneapolis: James and Klock, 1977), 74.

[12] Liddon, 75.

[13] Luther, *Commentary on Romans*, 78.

[14] Moulton and Milligan, *Vocabulary of the Greek Testament*, 162.

nailing it to the cross." The term "certificate of debt" describes a handwritten promissory note. Generally, at crucifixion, an inscription describing the perpetrator's crimes rested above their heads. The image depicts the expunging of their transgressions and debts to society. Upon Jesus's death in John 19:30, he cried out, "It is finished [*tetelestai*, Τετέλεσται]!" The term also signifies "complete," "accomplish," "paying," or "fulfill."[15] It also means "to execute a deed," as in the closing of escrow. This declaration marks the moment of the reversal and payment for the sin of Adam and the entire human race.

Second Corinthians 5:18–21 effectively summarizes the core theological aspects of the crucifixion and its implication for missions.[16] After reconciling mankind to himself by sacrificing his Son, God commissions Christians as ambassadors to proclaim this message. Mired in iniquity, active in rebellion, and lost without direction, individuals must repent and trust Christ by faith in order to appropriate this reconciliation. This constitutes the theological basis for missions.

Many years ago, I flew between London and North Africa, changing planes in Amsterdam. KLM Royal Dutch Airlines carefully checks all passports and visas due to the nature of the Muslim fundamentalist government and restrictions placed on Westerners at the destination. Just ahead of me, the gate agent questioned a boarding passenger, "Do you have a passport?" The man replied no. The airline employee continued, "Do you possess a visa?" He countered, "No, I do not." Somewhat exasperated, the agent asked, "Then what do you have?" The British traveler produced a gilded-edged letter, replete with a thick, waxed, stamped seal, and announced, "I am a personal representative of the Queen." Without delay, the envoy was welcomed on the aircraft. Similarly, believers have received the Great Commission, providing authority to proclaim the message of salvation as Christ's ambassadors. Furthermore, he has entrusted to each this matchless message of reconciliation.

---

[15] Moulton and Milligan, *Vocabulary of the Greek New Testament*, 630.

[16] "Everything is from God, who has reconciled us to himself through Christ and has given us the ministry of reconciliation. That is, in Christ, God was reconciling the world to himself, not counting their trespasses against them, and he has committed the message of reconciliation to us. Therefore, we are ambassadors for Christ, since God is making his appeal through us. We plead on Christ's behalf: 'Be reconciled to God.' He made the one who did not know sin to be sin for us, so that in him we might become the righteousness of God."

PATHS TO SALVATION

There are various views regarding different religions and their claims concerning truth, revelation, salvation, and eternity. Alan Race explores the theology of religions using three typological headings: Pluralism, Inclusivism, and Exclusivism; his work is useful to assist in examining the various beliefs and approaches.[17]

Pluralism

Pluralists hold that all religions possess equal truth and value. Many of the major world religions, such as Hinduism, Buddhism, and most traditional religions, subscribe to this position. Ebbie Smith observes, "For pluralists, Christianity is neither the one true religion, nor even the highest expression of religion, nor even the fulfillment of other religions. All religions are true; none may claim supremacy; Christianity should surrender its claims to exclusivity."[18] Pluralists see God as one, mankind as one, and view all religions as equal in man's quest for truth. Alan Race says, "The Pluralist approach in the theology of religions sets out an hypothesis which affirms the other major religions as valid and equally salvific paths in relation both to ultimate transcendent reality and to the journey toward mutual critical acceptance of one another."[19] The pluralist may favor one faith over another, but does not believe that one religion is weightier than any other.

Inclusivism

The inclusivist, however, deems Christ unique but declares Jesus's redeeming sacrifice makes salvation accessible to all mankind. Inclusivists fall into four major categories.

Classic Universalism. This perspective holds that all will ultimately be saved because Christ died for all and God is good. Unitarian and Universalist

---

[17] Alan Race, *Thinking about Religious Pluralism: Shaping Theology of Religions for Our Times* (Minneapolis: Fortress, 2015), 19.

[18] Ebbie Smith, "Contemporary Theology of Religions" in *Missiology: An Introduction to the Foundations, History, and Strategies of World Missions*, ed. John Mark Terry, Ebbie Smith, and Justice Anderson, 1st ed. (Nashville: Broadman and Holman, 1998), 416.

[19] Race, *Thinking about Religious Pluralism*, 39.

churches, and some Trinitarian churches, hold this view. This interpretation mirrors the Pluralism view but with the caveat that Christ's sacrifice is what saves the individual, not their non-Christian belief system.

New Universalism. This view declares that Christ died for sinners but the world remains largely ignorant of this fact. In this perspective, Christ saves everyone, with or without their knowledge or even their consent. They interpret Rom 5:18 to mean Christ has saved everyone without their recognition, belief, or repentance.[20] Karl Barth held that God's forgiving power eventually saves everyone.[21] General Charles "Chinese" Gordon,[22] a prominent Victorian-age Christian, subscribed to this view. His message of evangelism constituted proclaiming the "secret" that all were already saved.[23]

Wider Hope. Clark Pinnock's Wider Hope view holds that not all will be saved but God remains merciful. Somewhat similar to New Universalism, Wider Hope proponents believe sincere seekers and those who follow other religions will be saved because of God's impartiality. As individuals came to God before Christ's incarnation in the Old Testament, so they can enter his fold today due to the mercy of God.[24] Pinnock adopted this view later in his life and was criticized by evangelicals.

New Wider Hope. In this view, the sincere receive the opportunity at death or after death to change their minds and become believers. Only those who reject the gospel absolutely will be eternally lost. In *The Great Divorce*, C. S. Lewis expresses the view that everyone receives a chance to repent from a kind of purgatory and go to heaven. In this view, the choice for heaven and hell can be made both before and after death. In this interesting novel, most

---

[20] "So then, as through one trespass there is condemnation for everyone, so also through one righteous act there is justification leading to life for everyone."

[21] Sven Ensminger wrote, "For Barth ... every human being is elected in Christ and being rejected by God is not a possibility. Whether they realize it or not, everyone is elected in Christ—and not just for the promise of election. Even O'Neil has to conclude that 'Barth asserts an objective universal reconciliation in the incarnation and atonement, with the result that none are rejected.'" Sevn Ensminger, *Karl Barth's Theology as a Resource for a Christian Theology of Religions* (London: Bloomsbury T&T Clark, 2014), 131.

[22] Charles Gordon discovered Gordon's Calvary and the Garden Tomb in Israel. After this he traveled to Khartoum, Sudan, to become the governor general. He died at the hands of a Sudanese Mahdi. Anthony Grant, *Israel*, 7th ed. (New York: Frommer Media LLC, 2017), 139–40.

[23] Lord Elton, *General Gordon* (London: Collins Press, 1954), 123.

[24] Smith, "Contemporary Theology of Religions," 424.

of those in hell decide to remain even after visiting paradise on a day trip aboard a London bus.[25] Lewis's novel seems to present a "second chance" view of salvation.

Exclusivism

The exclusivist takes seriously Christ's words in John 14:6, "Jesus told him [Thomas], 'I am the way, the truth, and the life. No one comes to the Father except through me." Ebbie Smith identifies three kinds of exclusivists.

Hopeful Exclusivism. With some relationship to Inclusivism, the hopeful exclusivist embraces the view that God may accept the unevangelized person who dies without hearing or receiving the gospel. They leave open the possibility of the annihilation of the wicked or a postmortem encounter with God or Christ. Ebbie Smith says, "Hopeful exclusivists recognize and acknowledge the lack of biblical teaching of salvation outside of Christ. They hope, however, God may have some other way for the unevangelized."[26] Tom Johnston remarks concerning Billy Graham's view on inclusivism and exclusivism:

> While Graham maintained that Christ was the only way of salvation, by 1978 he had moved from the universal affirmation that the preaching of the gospel was the only way, to the sub-contrary negative that God could use any way he chose to save men. His presumed openness to salvation outside of the preaching of the gospel *as the only means of salvation* marked a clear change in the theology of Graham. Earlier in his ministry, Graham was a vocal exclusivist.[27]

---

[25] C. S. Lewis, *The Great Divorce: A Fantastic Bus Ride from Hell to Heaven—A Round Trip for Some but Not for Others* (New York: Macmillan, 1946), 124.

[26] Smith, "Contemporary Theology of Religions," 429.

[27] Thomas Paul Johnston, *Examining Billy Graham's Theology of Evangelism* (Eugene, OR: Wipf and Stock, 2003), 294–95. Johnston also references in these pages a *Christianity Today* article that reads, "Explaining the reference to 'other ways of recognizing the existence of God,' Graham pointed out that the Bible 'says all men have some light given by God, both in creation and in human conscience. Whoever sees the footsteps of the Creator in nature can ask for help, and I believe God—in ways we may not fully understand—will give that person further light and bring him to a knowledge of the truth that is in Jesus Christ so that he will be saved. He may use our preaching or he may use any other way he chooses, but ultimately it is God . . . who saves men.'" "Graham's Beliefs: Still Intact," *Christianity Today*, January 13, 1978, 49. In the same year, Johnston notes, Graham told *McCall's* (January 1978, 156), "I used to play God, . . . but I can't do that anymore. I used to believe that pagans in far-off countries were lost—were

Some hopeful exclusivists, like John Stott, believe in annihilation.[28] In addition, annihilation is the view of Seventh-day Adventism.[29] Although annihilation may seem more merciful than eternal punishment in hell, the doctrine does not offer hope for the afterlife other than oblivion without suffering.

Realistic Exclusivism. Seeing some value in other religions, realistic exclusivists hold that only faith in Christ achieved in this life before death results in salvation. Proponents point to John 3:35–36, which says, "The Father loves the Son and has given all things into his hands. The one who believes in the Son has eternal life, but the one who rejects the Son will not see life; instead, the wrath of God remains on him." They see no hope for anyone who does not accept Christ. Realistic exclusivists may hold hope for the salvation of the mentally handicapped and those dying as young children, but they do not believe that those who have never heard the gospel can somehow enter heaven without consciously believing in Christ before death. These exclusivists may see some moral value in other religions but not for salvation.

Rigid Exclusivism. This category does not differ from Realistic Exclusivism so much in content as in attitude. According to Ebbie Smith, rigid exclusivists "see neither value nor hope in the religions. These religions are, in the sight of these writers, evil and perhaps demonic."[30] Proponents in the previous category might see some value in the concepts and insights within other non-Christian religions. This classification would not.

Ecclesiastical Exclusivism. I add this grouping because of its prominence in church history. Some churches believe only the members of their own church will be saved. This is the historic position of the Catholic Church before Vatican II. Other minor groups sometimes contend only their church's members are truly saved.

---

going to hell—if they did not have the Gospel of Jesus Christ preached to them. I no longer believe that.'"

[28] Robert A. Peterson, "Undying Worm, Unquenchable Fire: What Is Hell—Eternal Torment or Annihilation? A Look at the Evangelical Alliance's *The Nature of Hell*," *Christianity Today,* October 23, 2000, https://www.christianitytoday.com/ct/2000/october23/undying-worm -unquenchable-fire.html.

[29] Walter R. Martin, *The Kingdom of the Cults: An Analysis of the Major Cult Systems in the Present Christian Era* (Minneapolis: Bethany Fellowship, 1965), 372–73.

[30] Smith, "Contemporary Theology of Religions," 430.

Eligibility for Salvation

One of the most perplexing and controversial issues in the theology of missions concerns the question of who can be saved. David Hesselgrave summarizes the dilemma:

> When we inquire into the relationship between God's sovereignty and human free will, we are inquiring into foundational questions having to do with everything from the very nature and attributes of God himself to the meaning and method of Christian missions. What part do sinners play in their salvation? Do sinners "elect" God, or has he already elected them? Do they exercise saving faith, or is faith as well as salvation a gift of God? Does God determine not only the course of human history but also personal histories—yours and mine? Or are humans free to write their own ticket and reap the results, whether good or bad?[31]

Entire books of systematic theology seek to answer these kinds of questions. Such issues cannot be sufficiently addressed, much less settled, in a volume this size. Explaining the scaffolding upon which each view rests, however, holds value for the missiologist for developing a theology of evangelism and missions. One's perspective on these questions affects their assessment of the missionary task. Building upon the categories of C. Gordon Olson, David Hesselgrave presents five views for understanding mankind's eligibility to receive salvation.[32]

1. Augustinian deterministic Calvinism—God alone determines all events independently of man's will, including those having to do with salvation and lostness.

---

[31] David J. Hesselgrave, *Paradigms in Conflict: 15 Key Questions in Christian Missions Today*, 2nd ed., ed. Keith E. Eitel (Grand Rapids: Kregel, 2018), 23–24.

[32] Steve Lemke lists five categories using different names: 1. Hard Determinism/Causal Determinism. 2. Soft Determinism/Compatibilism. 3. Molinism/Middle Knowledge. 4. Decisionism/Congruentism/Soft-Libertarian Freedom. 5. Strong-Libertarian Freedom/Self-Determination. Steve W. Lemke, "Five Theological Models Relating Determinism, Divine Sovereignty, and Human Freedom," in Allen, Hankins, and Harwood, eds., *Anyone Can Be Saved*, 169–76 (see chap. 1, n. 14).

2. Moderate Calvinism—Man's free will is limited, and God's sovereignty and foreknowledge operate in such a way that saving grace is restricted to the elect.

3. A mediate theological view—God's sovereignty and man's free will are somehow synergistic, working together in ways that accomplish his plan and purpose, including those matters having to do with salvation and lostness.

4. Moderate Arminianism—God has limited his sovereignty and shown his love in such a way that his grace is extended to all on the condition of repentance and faith in the gospel of Christ, with the expectation that all are free to accept or reject it.

5. Open Theism or extreme Arminianism—God's sovereignty is subject to the limits of his foreknowledge and the largeness of his love so that man's freedom is unimpeded in any way or to any degree.[33]

Category one certainly presents as the tidiest and most logical theological system because little is left to speculation. In this view, God elects certain men and women unconditionally for salvation based solely on God's favor without any exercise of will by mankind.[34] Furthermore, God foreordains all events, including the choices people make for or against Christ. Louis Berkhof, writing about spiritual rebirth and the effectual call, rejects synergistic regeneration:

> The only adequate view is that of the Church of all ages, that the Holy Spirit is the efficient cause of regeneration. This means that the Holy Spirit works directly on the heart of man and changes its spiritual condition. There is no co-operation of the sinner in this work whatsoever. It is the work of the Holy Spirit directly and exclusively, Ezek. 11:19; John 1:13; Acts 16:14; Rom. 9:16; Phil. 2:13. Regeneration, then, is to be conceived monergistically. God alone works, and the sinner has no part in it whatsoever.[35]

---

[33] Hesselgrave, *Paradigms in Conflict*, 23–24.

[34] James White, "Unconditional Election," in *Debating Calvinism*, by Dave Hunt and James White (Sisters, OR: Multnomah, 2004), 91–92.

[35] Louis Berkhof, *Systematic Theology: With a Complete Textual Index*, 4th rev. ed. (Grand Rapids: Eerdmans, 1949), 473.

Despite this declaration, Hesselgrave notes that Roger Greenway trumpets the zeal and effectiveness of missionaries of the Reformed persuasion. Greenway says a belief in God's sovereignty and Christ's lordship constitutes an impetus for missionary zeal, rather than an impediment against it.[36] Missionaries of this persuasion follow the command of Christ to preach the gospel in order to be obedient. This view presents some theological problems for the missionary. If this perspective is true, then many, if not most, of those the missionary meets on the mission field lack the capability to believe even if they possessed the desire to do so.

Presenting a moderating perspective on Calvinism, D. A. Carson, Wayne Grudem, and others posit the notion of *compatibilism*. Robert Peterson and Michael Williams say:

> Where incompatibilism holds that divine sovereignty and responsi-
> ble human freedom are logically inconsistent, and that the affirma-
> tion of one necessarily entails either the rejection or attenuation of
> the other, compatibilism holds that the Bible affirms both the abso-
> lute, unlimited sovereignty of God and the responsibility of human
> beings for their choices and actions. Further, while Scripture teaches
> both the sovereignty of God and the moral responsibility of human
> beings, the two are not equally ultimate. God's sovereign lordship
> over his creation includes the moral responsibility and freedom of
> human beings.[37]

Often called the Reformed position, compatibilism holds that God causes good, but not evil. In a mysterious way, according to this view, God remains sovereign while mankind exercises some free will.[38] Steve Lemke, however, questions whether soft determinism (compatibilism) successfully combines limited human freedom with Calvinism. Lemke asserts, "Compatibilist free-dom is not really freedom at all—it is voluntary but not free. Just being willing to do something does not mean that a person is free. . . . [C]ompatibilism re-ally does not qualify as a variety of freedom, since freedom requires the ability to choose between alternatives. In compatibilism, we act willingly according

---

[36] Hesselgrave, *Paradigms in Conflict*, 26.

[37] Robert A. Peterson and Michael D. Williams, *Why I Am Not an Arminian* (Downers Grove, IL: InterVarsity Press, 2004), 144.

[38] Hesselgrave, *Paradigms in Conflict*, 28.

to our greatest desire, but we do not choose freely."[39] Reformed theologians counter they are content to allow the sovereignty of God and freedom of man to remain in tension. They believe the Bible teaches these "doctrines of grace" and feel compelled to proclaim these truths on the mission field.

Named for Luis de Molina, a sixteenth-century theologian, *Molinism* seeks to strike even more of a balance between God's sovereignty and human free will. According to the mediate theological view of C. Gordon Olson, God limits his sovereignty by delegating authority to his created beings.[40] Drawing on a concept called "middle knowledge," Lemke summarizes:

> God knows not only all the myriad possibilities of what could happen (his "general knowledge") but he also conceives (by his own omniscience, not by his perception of future human choices) what persons would actually do in every possible situation (his "middle knowledge"). Based upon his natural knowledge and middle knowledge of all the "possible worlds" (i.e., each different future series of events in which there is at least one choice that is different from all the other series of events), God actualizes the possible world of free human choices that he desires (his "free knowledge"). Molinism thus allows for both genuinely free human choices and God determining which possible world he desires.[41]

William Lane Craig, a proponent of the middle knowledge view, gives the example of the apostle Peter denying Christ in one possible world while affirming him in another. Peter exercises his free will in both scenarios, but God chooses the correct cosmos according to his foreknowledge, sovereignty, and divine will.[42] Craig says, "Once one grasps the concept of middle knowledge, one will find it astonishing in its subtlety and power. Indeed, I would venture to say that it is the single most fruitful theological concept I have ever encountered. I have applied it to the issues of Christian particularism, perseverance of the saints and biblical inspiration."[43] C. Gordon Olson illustrates Molinism in terms of a chess match. He says, "A chess player with no real prescience is working with

---

[39] Lemke, "Five Theological Models," 172–73.
[40] Hesselgrave, *Paradigms in Conflict*, 34.
[41] Lemke, "Five Theological Models," 173–74.
[42] William Lane Craig, "The Middle Knowledge View," in *Divine Foreknowledge: Four Views*, ed. James K. Beilby and Paul R. Eddy (Downers Grove, IL: InterVarsity Press, 2001), 121.
[43] Craig, 125.

probabilities. God, however, has real prescience of both events that eventuate and counterfactuals. This helps understand how God can manipulate history to what extent He desires without coercion of the players involved. By virtue of middle knowledge, God works out His plan of redemption of humanity without being a puppeteer pulling the strings."[44]

As might be expected, Molinism does not satisfy everyone either. In this scenario, God seems to "tip the scale" in this cosmic chess game in favor of his desired outcome, rendering mankind's "free choice" illusory at best. Hesselgrave remarks that Olson "reaches a view that is actually more Amyraldian (i.e., basically Calvinist but more Arminian with respect to the doctrine of grace)."[45] Amyraldians hold to an unlimited atonement position, often called "four-point Calvinism," rather than the limited atonement view of the Reformed positions. Recently, a number of evangelicals, including Kenneth Keathley and John Mark Terry, have turned to the middle knowledge view.[46]

Although Hesselgrave calls category number four "Moderate Arminianism,"[47] Steve Lemke prefers the terms "Decisionism, Congruentism, and Soft-Libertarian Freedom"[48] to describe his view, which he calls the "Traditional view of Southern Baptists."[49] Lemke says, "In soft libertarianism, limited choices are available in almost every aspect. While our decisions are not determined by prior causes and events, our decisions are definitely impacted by forces outside ourselves. We do not make decisions in a vacuum; we often face profound pressures which weigh heavily on our choices. However, at the end of the day, we are still able to decide freely."[50] This view holds that all have the capacity to be saved and can repent and believe if they so desire. When they do, they become the "elect." As with most of the positions, proponents see an element of mystery. In the same book, Eric Hankins speaks of concurrence in election: "Concurrence in election means that God's sovereignty in election

---

[44] C. Gordon Olson, *Beyond Calvinism and Arminianism: An Inductive Mediate Theology of Salvation*, 3rd ed. (Lynchburg, VA: Global Gospel, 2012), 427–28.

[45] Hesselgrave, *Paradigms in Conflict*, 33.

[46] John Mark Terry, "Update Reflection on *Sovereignty and Free Will: An Impossible Mix or a Perfect Match*," in Hesselgrave, *Paradigms in Conflict*, 45.

[47] Hesselgrave, *Paradigms in Conflict*, 24.

[48] Lemke, "Five Theological Models," 174.

[49] Lemke, 176.

[50] Lemke, 175.

extends ultimately to the individual behavior in such a way that, without God's electing, initiating, and superintending, no individual has the hope of salvation. It, however, also means that the free response of humans to God's electing activity is real and essential to salvation."[51] This view postulates a strong synergy between man and God in the salvation process.

This category has its detractors. In this view, the sinner (whom God foreknew) chooses God, triggering God's "election" of the new believer. Calvinists see this as "works salvation," as the sinner participates in the salvation process. Furthermore, some facets of life are predetermined—such as gender, race, and the time and place of one's birth. The decisionist must decide what part of life is decreed by God and what portion mankind determines.

The final category, Open Theism, Extreme Arminianism, or Strong Libertarian Freedom, stands on the opposite end of the scale from the Reformed positions. This perspective declares that God has limited his sovereignty so some future events are not yet known, even to him. Supporting this perspective, Gregory Boyd says:

> The view I shall defend agrees unequivocally with the classical view that God is omniscient, but it embraces a different understanding of creation. It holds that the reality that God perfectly knows not only excludes some possibilities as what might have been, but also includes other possibilities as what might be. Reality, in other words, is composed of both settled and open aspects. Since God knows all of reality perfectly, this view holds that he knows the possible aspects as possible and knows the settled aspects as settled. In this view, the sovereign Creator settles whatever he wants to settle about the future, and hence he perfectly foreknows the future as settled *to this extent*.[52]

Advocates of this view emphasize differing aspects of mankind's freedom. This perspective holds that in regard to salvation, man is totally free to choose or reject Christ. Critics such as Bruce Ware say Open Theism rejects historic

---

[51] Eric Hankins, "Commentary on Article 6: Election to Salvation," in Allen, Hankins, and Harwood, eds., *Anyone Can Be Saved*, 97.

[52] Gregory A. Boyd, "The Open-Theism View," in *Divine Foreknowledge: Four Views*, ed. James K. Beilby and Paul R. Eddy (Downers Grove, IL: InterVarsity Press, 2001), 14.

Christianity's belief in the omniscience and omnipotence of God.[53] Furthermore, in this view missions and evangelism become totally man's responsibility, with little or no synergy with God. Most evangelicals reject Open Theism.

This chapter devotes space to the discussion of the five major views of the sovereignty of God and the free will of mankind because of its relevancy to missions and evangelism. If God predetermines all history, then why expend time, energy, and resources preaching to those who will believe anyway? Conversely, if God sets the cosmos in motion with chance and human freedom reigning, then all responsibility for missions and evangelism rests with humans. Between these opposites, more moderate views advocate some synergy within God's sovereignty and man's responsibility.

I directed more than 400 missionaries during an eighteen-year career as a missionary and supervisor of missionaries. I oversaw missionaries with beliefs on this issue spanning the theological spectrum (excepting Open Theism).[54] As long as missionaries possess a knowledge of the gospel (defined in chapter 2), a compassion for the lost, and a zeal for sharing Christ's message, they can be effective. Those of the Decisionist, Soft-Libertarian perspective witness to everyone because they believe God elects to salvation those who freely choose the gospel. Reformed missionaries share the good news with passion so God can be glorified. This is because Calvinists do not know the identity of the elect but are commanded to obey the Great Commission.

I recall a story D. James Kennedy related at the Billy Graham School of Evangelism in Las Vegas, Nevada, on November 21, 1980. Kennedy, a Reformed pastor, authored the Evangelism Explosion (EE) method of church evangelism. The EE system consists of visiting prospects who attend a church's services. Kennedy related that when he knocked on the door of one home, a large, unshaven man appeared, holding a can of beer. The man glared at him and gruffly said with belligerence, "What do ya want?" Kennedy thought to himself, *Surely he is of the non-elect.* After a moment that seemed like an eternity, Kennedy recalled the man uttering the words that terrify every evangelistic

---

[53] Boyd states Bruce Ware's criticism of the Open Theism view in Boyd, "Open-Theism View."

[54] The International Mission Board of the Southern Baptist Convention, my former sending organization, requires missionaries to affirm the Baptist Faith and Message (BF&M) 2000, which endorses the eternal security of the believer that Open Theism denies.

visitor: "Come in." Kennedy shared that within the hour this supposedly non-elect man had come to faith in Christ.

Despite the missionary zeal of many Calvinists, most of the more prominent mission pioneers have held the Decisionist position. These include Philipp Spener, August Francke, and Ludwig von Zinzendorf. According to David Hesselgrave, although originally Reformed, William Carey "moved to this position [Decisionism] after his rejection by some members of his own presbytery and it became the theological position of his Baptist missions board."[55] Missionaries should know what they believe about this issue because of its effect on evangelism and missions. Any Calvinist, Molinist, or Decisionist may serve well as a missionary. Each, however, will have different motivations for their preaching and differing expectations.

My theology professor at Southwestern Baptist Theological Seminary, William Hendricks, carved out a sixth perspective. Although unnamed specifically, I will call it the "existential view." Hendricks told me, "God knows in a different way than man. In our way of knowing, man's free will and God's sovereignty cannot both be true. In God's way of knowing, however, since he is above time and outside our knowledge, free choice and foreordination can be true simultaneously." This theory attempts to reconcile the irreconcilable and no doubt also fails in this regard.

Mission boards and denominations contain missionaries and members representing all these beliefs. Since Paul speaks of the danger of fighting about words in 2 Tim 2:14,[56] each missionary practitioner should choose their own view carefully but hold it with humility because in this life Christians see as in a "glass, darkly."[57]

---

[55] Hesselgrave, *Paradigms in Conflict*, 27.

[56] "Remind them of these things, and charge them before God not to fight about words. This is useless and leads to the ruin of those who listen."

[57] "For now we see through a glass, darkly; but then face to face: now I know in part; but then shall I know even as also I am known" (1 Cor 13:12 KJV).

THOSE WHO PROCLAIM SALVATION

The Church

The term "church" (*ekklesia*, ἐκκλησία),[58] a compound Greek word, combines the ideas of "to call" (*kaleo*, καλέω) and "out from" (*ek*, ἐκκ) and describes an assembly, "the called-out ones." When Christ says in Matt 16:18, "And I also say to you that you are Peter, and on this rock I will build my church, and the gates of Hades will not overpower it," most commentators see the universal church composed of all Christians. According to George Peters, of the 115 times the term appears in the New Testament, 85 occurrences refer to a local congregation or congregations of believers.[59] Christopher Wright says, "Finally the biblical narrative introduces us to ourselves as the church with a mission."[60]

Although disparaged by many as antiquated, irrelevant, and flawed, the Christian church represents God's chosen vessel to constitute his presence on earth. Without the church, Christianity is reduced to a moral philosophy, like Buddhism, or a series of traditions, like Hinduism. Churches are where the lost hear the gospel, receive Christian baptism, and are discipled. Churches retain the results of evangelism and pass the faith on to the next generation.

Henry C. Thiessen says the mission of the church is "to glorify God, to edify itself, to purify itself, to educate its constituency, to evangelize the world, to act as a restraining and enlightening force in the world, to promote all that is good."[61] Many authors have described the purposes of the church. Focusing on fulfilling the Great Commandment and the Great Commission, Rick Warren summarizes everything the church does through the lens of the five New Testament purposes: worship, fellowship, discipleship, ministry, and missions.[62] The missions portion of the church's task is the focus of this book. The church accomplishes this duty through the church offices and ministries.

---

[58] The term originally meant in Greek literature "any public assembly of citizens summoned by a herald" and appears in an inscription on an image of the Greek god Artemis given to the assembly at the theatre in Ephesus. Moulton and Milligan, *Vocabulary of the Greek Testament*, 195.

[59] Peters, *Biblical Theology of Missions*, 200–201.

[60] Wright, *Mission of God*, 66 (see chap. 1, n. 6).

[61] Henry C. Thiessen quoted in Peters, *Biblical Theology of Missions*, 209.

[62] Rick Warren, *The Purpose Driven Church: Growth without Compromising Your Message and Mission* (Grand Rapids: Zondervan, 1995), 103–6.

Charles Spurgeon said, "The mission of the church is to go into all the world . . . and tell out the gospel to every creature."[63] Missions is central to the church. Every church should be focused on missions. George Miley insists, "God designed churches to be agents of missions. . . . Each member of the church can participate in missions."[64] Craig Van Gelder and Dwight Zscheile ask an interesting question: "How is it that ordinary Christians can authentically imagine and enter into participation in God's mission in their workplaces, their homes, neighborhoods, and the world?"[65] They urge local churches to fully engage in missions at all these levels. Jesus gave the Great Commission to Christians and these believers are in local churches. The church carries the gospel into the world today.

The Apostles

The previous chapter demonstrates how the twelve apostles received the Great Commission. Some argue that the original apostles fulfilled the Great Commission in the first century. William Carey, however, presents three reasons why the Great Commission retains validity and binds believers in each generation to fulfill the task. He writes:

> FIRST, If the command of Christ to teach all nations be restricted to the apostles, or those under the immediate inspiration of the Holy Ghost, then that of baptizing should be too; and every denomination of Christians, except the Quakers, do wrong in baptizing with water at all. SECONDLY, If the command of Christ to teach all nations be confined to the apostles, then all such ordinary ministers who have endeavored to carry the Gospel to the heathens, have acted without a warrant, and run before they were sent. . . . THIRDLY, If the command of Christ to teach all nations extends only to the apostles, then, doubtless, the promise of the divine presence in this work must be so limited; but this is worded in such a manner

---

[63] Charles Spurgeon, quoted in John Sypert, "What Is the Mission of the Church?," blog of the Spurgeon Center for Biblical Preaching at Midwestern Seminary, February 20, 2018, https://www.spurgeon.org/resource-library/blog-entries/what-is-the-mission-of-the-church.

[64] George Miley, *Loving the Church, Blessing the Nations: Pursuing the Role of Local Churches in Global Mission* (Waynesboro, GA: Authentic Media, 2003), 68, 70.

[65] Craig Van Gelder and Dwight J. Zscheile, *The Missional Church in Perspective: Mapping Trends and Shaping the Conversation* (Grand Rapids: Baker Academic, 2011), 153.

as expressly precludes such an idea. Lo, I am with you always, to the end of the world.[66]

The apostle Paul delineates the officers of the church in Eph 4:11–12, writing, "And he himself gave some to be apostles, some prophets, some evangelists, some pastors and teachers, equipping the saints for the work of ministry, to build up the body of Christ." These offices are given in order for the church to prosper and expand. George Peters groups these into two categories: (1) apostles and evangelist (2) prophets and pastor-teacher.[67] Concerning the origin of the word "apostle," Karl Rengstorf says:

> In the older period ἀπόστολος [apóstolos] was one of the special terms bound up with sea-faring and more particularly with military expeditions.... In the first instances this simply denotes the dispatch of a fleet (or army) on a military expedition.... [I]t comes to be applied on the one side to a group of men sent out for a particular purpose, e.g., not merely to an army but to a band of colonists and their settlement (Dion. Hal. Ant. Rom., IX, 59), and on the other to the commander, e.g., the admiral.[68]

The question arises, Are today's missionaries apostles? Some see apostleship as an ongoing office in the church.[69] According to George Peters, the successors of the apostles were not apostles, nor was there a generational transfer of apostleship. He writes:

> There is a theory which would like to raise the modern missionary movement into a certain type of "apostolate," a successor to the apostolic band, and make its ministry independent of church associations, direction and control. This may be a noble aspiration, at times much desirable, and under certain circumstances it may even become necessary. It must be stated emphatically, however, that such theory is extra-biblical.[70]

---

[66] William Carey, "An Enquiry into the Obligation of Christians to Use Means for the Conversion of the Heathens," in Winter and Hawthorne, *Perspectives on the World Christian Movement*, 313–14 (see chap. 1, n. 30).

[67] Peters, *Biblical Theology of Missions*, 246.

[68] Karl Heinrich Rengstorf, "ἀπόστολος [apostolos]," *TDNT*, vol. 1.

[69] Don Dent, *The Ongoing Role of Apostles in Mission: The Forgotten Foundation* (Bloomington IL: Crossbooks, 2011).

[70] Peters, *Biblical Theology of Missions*, 255–56.

The term "apostle" carries with it an authority and power not present today. On the other hand, just as nonevangelists are exhorted to perform evangelism,[71] nonapostles can engage in apostolic work. It is obvious that certain ministers are gifted in church founding and directing such work. This, however, does not render them apostles. Then who are today's missionaries?

B. F. Westcott, W. E. Vine, and Gerhart Kittel see the New Testament evangelist as the successor of the apostles.[72] Appearing three times in the New Testament, the term literally means, "gospeler," or "one who proclaims the gospel." The modern missionary's role seems more related to the role of the evangelist than that of the apostle. Eusebius writes:

> Then starting out upon long journeys they performed the office of evangelists, being filled with the desire to preach Christ to those who have not yet heard the word of faith and to deliver to them the divine Gospels. And when they had only laid the foundation of the faith in foreign places, they appointed others as pastors, and entrusted them with the nurture of those who had been recently brought in, while they themselves went on again to other countries and nations.[73]

Although the modern concept of evangelist denotes an itinerant preacher, the usage in the New Testament and the early church resembles more of a missionary. The second grouping, prophets and pastor-teacher, presents an interesting case. The Old Testament office of the foretelling prophet resurfaces with the advent of John the Baptist and occurs sporadically in the New Testament (with Agabus in Acts 21:10 and perhaps with Philip's prophesying daughters in Acts 21:9). At the close of the first century, the revelatory function of the prophet disappears and the teaching function remains, effectively subsumed by the New Testament office of pastor-teacher.

The pastor-teacher role remains important in the conduct of missions. The pastor-teacher shepherds, instructs, and leads a congregation started initially by the evangelist. In the North American context, a church planter serves as

---

[71] "But as for you, exercise self-control in everything, endure hardship, do the work of an evangelist, fulfill your ministry" (2 Tim 4:5).

[72] Peters, *Biblical Theology of Missions*, 259–60.

[73] Eusebius, *Eccles III* (New York: Mason and Lane, 1839), 123.

a missionary evangelist performing the apostolic work of church founding. The church planter may transition into a pastor-teacher role, similar to the apostle Paul's two-year pastoral stint in Ephesus. Critical to the conduct of missions, the office of pastor-teacher conserves the results of the evangelist-missionary and fulfills the never-ending "teaching all things" portion of the Great Commission.

CONCLUSION

This chapter analyzes the major underlying theological issues related to the theory and practice of missions. Many more theological issues intersect with missions than appear in this chapter. Some topics, such as the missionary call and baptism, will be addressed later. A full treatment of every theological topic in missions exceeds the scope of this book. This theological underpinning, however, assists in going forward to the next subject, the historical foundation of missions.

READING FOR FURTHER STUDY

Allen, David L., Eric Hankins, and Adam Harwood, eds. *Anyone Can Be Saved: A Defense of "Traditional" Southern Baptist Soteriology*. Eugene, OR: Wipf and Stock, 2016.

Berkhof, Louis. *Systematic Theology: With a Complete Textual Index*, 4th rev. ed. Grand Rapids: Eerdmans, 1949.

Grudem, Wayne. *Systematic Theology: An Introduction to Biblical Doctrine*. Grand Rapids: Zondervan, 1994.

Johnston, Thomas Paul. *Examining Billy Graham's Theology of Evangelism*. Eugene, OR: Wipf and Stock, 2003.

Olson, C. Gordon. *Beyond Calvinism and Arminianism: An Inductive Mediate Theology of Salvation*, 3rd ed. Lynchburg, VA: Global Gospel, 2012.

Race, Alan. *Thinking about Religious Pluralism*. Minneapolis: Fortress, 2015.

4

The Historical Foundation of Missions

Writing late in the second century to the Roman governor of his North African province about the spread of Christianity, church father Tertullian said:

> We are but of yesterday, and we have filled every place among you—cities, islands, fortresses, towns, market-places, the very camp, tribes, companies, palace, senate, forum,—we have left nothing to you but the temples of your gods.... For now it is the immense number of Christians which makes your enemies so few,—almost all of the inhabitants of your various cities being followers of Christ. Yet you choose to call us enemies of the human race, rather than of human error.[1]

INTRODUCTION

How could a small Jewish sect become a dominant force in the Roman Empire? The answer emerges in the study of history. Earle Cairns defines history as the "interpreted record of the socially significant human past, based upon

---

[1] *ANF* 3 37:45. Philip Schaff, *Latin Christianity: Its Founder, Tertullian*, https://www.ccel.org/ccel/schaff/anf03/Page_45.html.

organized data collected by the scientific method from archaeological, literary or living history."[2] Church history, a subset of the discipline, can be further subdivided into a number of specialties. Philip Schaff splits church history into six parts, listing first the history of missions.[3] This includes home and international missions and, to some extent, evangelism. This chapter, devoted to mission history, also contains elements of church history. Emphasizing the importance of history, Cairns says, "The present is usually the product of the past and the seed of the future."[4]

THE APOSTOLIC AGE (AD 1–100)

Preparation for the Gospel

Galatians 4:4–5 proclaims, "When the time came to completion, God sent his Son, born of a woman, born under the law, to redeem those under the law, so that we might receive adoption as sons." According to Scripture, Jesus arrived at the perfect time in human history. Jews were dispersed around the Roman empire and with their piety, monotheism, and understanding of a personal relationship with God, provided a seedbed for the gospel. The practical Romans built roads, bridges, and aqueducts uniting the empire and fostering a *pax Romana*.[5] In the middle to late first century the apostles preached the gospel across the empire due to this technology. Roman law and justice with emphasis on individual rights allowed non-Romans to obtain citizenship, providing cohesion to the empire beyond the walls of the mother city-state.[6] Although the Romans conquered the Greeks in 146 BC, the culture of the latter vanquished the conquerors. The Greek language and philosophical categories facilitated

---

[2] Earle E. Cairns, *Christianity through the Centuries: A History of the Christian Church*, rev. ed. (Grand Rapids, Zondervan, 1954), 13.

[3] Philip Schaff, *History of the Christian Church*, vol. 1, *Apostolic Christianity, A.D. 1–100* (Grand Rapids: Eerdmans, 1971), 6.

[4] Cairns, *Christianity through the Centuries*, 19.

[5] Roman peace.

[6] Cairns, *Christianity through the Centuries*, 38.

the transmission and understanding of the truth of the gospel message.[7] Concurrently, the gods of the Romans and Greeks, and local deities seemed inadequate. These gods appeared not to care about the economic dislocations, regime changes, and barbarian conquests that plagued the Roman Empire until its fall centuries later. Into this milieu the Son of God arrived.

The Mission of Jesus

Secular sources document that Jesus lived as a historical person. The Roman writer Lucian penned a satire about Christ around AD 170, describing the new cult as "worshipping that crucified sophist."[8] Writing about the arrest of the apostle James and some others, the Jewish author Josephus said of Jesus, "He was the Christ."[9] Teaching as no man ever taught, Christ centered his instruction on the inner man rather than on the outward legalistic observances favored by the Pharisees. He proclaimed the inauguration of the kingdom of God, but limited his message initially to his own people, the Jews. Furthermore, authenticating his authority, Jesus healed the sick, raised the dead, cast out demons, turned water into wine, multiplied bread and fish, walked on water, and calmed a raging sea. This was only the beginning. Christ's real mission involved dying on a Roman cross to purchase by his blood the salvation of those who would believe in him. This did not complete his work, however, for on the third day he rose from the dead, proving his divinity. Christ's resurrection, the most pivotal event in human history, became the focus of the gospel message. The five previously mentioned Great Commissions charge the apostles with heralding this gospel to the ends of the earth.

The Mission of the Apostles

The remarkable accomplishments of the twelve apostles and their first-century contemporaries stand the test of time. Without mechanized transportation or modern communication devices, they crisscrossed the Roman Empire and

---

[7] John Mark Terry and Robert L. Gallagher, *Encountering the History of Missions: From the Early Church to Today* (Grand Rapids: Baker Academic, 2017), 3.

[8] Cairns, *Christianity through the Centuries*, 50.

[9] Flavius Josephus, *The Antiquities of the Jews*, chap. 3, in *Josephus Complete Works*, trans. William Whiston (Grand Rapids: Kregel, 1960), 426.

beyond with the gospel. The book of Acts provides something of a beginning history to the expansion of the church, with Philip evangelizing the Samaritans and the Ethiopian eunuch and the three missionary journeys of Paul. Acts demonstrates that the gospel is not just for the Jews but for Gentiles as well. After Acts closes with Paul under house arrest in Rome, only a scattering of writings remains about what the apostles accomplished afterward. Tradition associates Peter's name with the founding of the church in Britain and ministry in Corinth, Antioch, Babylon, and Rome, where he died.[10] Other traditions record Andrew's stoning and consequent crucifixion in Scythia.[11] John started churches in Asia Minor, escaped miraculously from a cauldron of boiling oil, and was later exiled to Patmos, where he wrote the book of Revelation. Long connected with the church at Ephesus, John alone among the apostles died a natural death.[12] According to church tradition, Thomas established the church in India,[13] dying a martyr's death by a lance. In addition, after evangelizing much of the Roman Empire, James the Less, Phillip, Matthew, Mark, Matthias, Jude, Bartholomew, and Luke died as witnesses for their faith.[14] Indeed, as Tertullian would later say, "The blood of the martyrs is the seed of the church."[15]

Missions during the Remainder of the First Century

According to the early church fathers, Jesus's disciples divided the world into twelve parts, evangelized the nations, and started churches in every city.[16] Although the apostles and their successors took the lead, the task of further evangelization fell to itinerant prophets and ordinary Christians.[17] Due to a lack

---

[10] William Steuart McBirnie, *The Search for the Twelve Apostles* (Wheaton, IL: Tyndale House, 1973), 53–56.

[11] McBirnie, 80.

[12] *Foxe's Book of Martyrs*, ed. Marie Gentert King (Old Tappan, NJ: Fleming H. Revell, 1968), 13.

[13] Kenneth Scott Latourette, *A History of Christianity*, vol. 1, *Beginnings to 1500*, rev. ed. (New York: Harper and Row, 1975), 80, 324.

[14] *Foxe's Book of Martyrs*, 13.

[15] Michael A. Smith, *From Christ to Constantine* (Downers Grove, IL: InterVarsity Press, 1971), 107.

[16] Alan Kreider, *The Patient Ferment of the Early Church: The Improbable Rise of Christianity in the Roman Empire* (Grand Rapids: Baker Academic, 2016), 74.

[17] Kreider, 75–76.

of written records, the size and strength of the church at the end of the first century remains a mystery. John Mark Terry says, "At the end of the apostolic age ... one can say that the church was limited in size, perhaps no more than one hundred congregations, mainly urban, and primarily Greek speaking."[18]

ANTE-NICENE MISSIONS (AD 100–325)

Kenneth Scott Latourette asserts less is known about the spread of Christianity in the second century than the first. By AD 200, however, Christians inhabited every province of the empire, penetrating as far as Mesopotamia.[19] Although uneven growth persisted, by the end of the third century, estimates of the number of Christians in the Roman Empire reached 3 or 4 million.[20] Only two missionaries during this period are known by name: Pantaenus journeyed from Alexandria to India[21] and Gregory, a disciple of Origen, who returned in the middle of the third century to evangelize Pontus in Asia Minor.[22] The church grew as missionary bishops, itinerant prophets, and evangelists carried the gospel message from town to town. According to Alan Kreider, however, "migration missions" figures prominently in the church growth of the Ante-Nicene period.[23] Christians traveling to new areas because of persecution or to improve their economic situations brought the gospel as they relocated. Others shared the good news while living their daily lives. Church growth in this period follows a pattern of gradual fermentation more than sudden explosion.[24] Several reasons explain why the early church grew, when accepting the gospel often brought death and persecution instead of prestige.

Perhaps almost counterintuitively, persecution time and again brings solidarity and purpose. In my work in North Africa, I saw persecuted nationals tortured and ostracized for their faith who developed a remarkable resilience

---

[18] John Mark Terry, "The History of Missions in the Early Church," in Terry, *Missiology*, 142 (see chap. 1, n. 18).

[19] Latourette, *History of Christianity*, 76.

[20] Terry and Gallagher, *Encountering the History of Missions*, 6.

[21] Kreider, *Patient Ferment*, 10.

[22] *Eusebius' Ecclesiastical History*, trans. C. F. Cruse (Peabody, MA: Hendrickson, 2013), 218.

[23] Kreider, *Patient Ferment*, 75.

[24] Kreider, 12.

and esprit de corps in the face of injury or death. Remarkable among the martyrs of the third century were two young women of Carthage named Perpetua and Felicitas. Rather than deny their Lord, they perished in the arena before many witnesses, attacked first by a wild animal and then dispatched with a sword.[25] Since Christians refused to participate in the worship of the Roman, Greek, and local gods, the believers were deemed atheists who practiced all sorts of immoralities during secret assemblies.[26] The ten major persecutions of the first three centuries of Christianity purified and solidified the church.

The spiritual content of the meetings and the changed lives of the Christians are other reasons the church grew. Alan Kreider writes:

> Greco-Roman culture valued banquets, which customarily had two parts: an evening meal (Greek *deipnon*, δεῖπνον; Latin *cena*) was followed by a time of entertainment (*symposium*, συμπόσιο), at which people gave speeches, conversed, and drank. This two-part meal took place in domestic settings, lasted several hours, and enabled face-to-face encounters. The earliest description we have of Christian worship is the meal described in 1 Corinthians 11 in which all shared an evening meal. The meal was followed by the symposium in chapter 14, to which "each one" could contribute (1 Cor 14:26).

The Pauline model—an evening meal providing real sustenance and also remembering Jesus; a multivoiced symposium in which all could pray and contribute; face-to-face relationships in a domestic setting—was still present 150 years later in Tertullian's community in Carthage.[27]

The early church grew, not as the result of a mission board or an outreach program, but rather because the members simply loved one another and desired their unsaved friends to find Christ. This commitment against all odds proved contagious. Although some parts of the worship service were open to the public, the *agape* (ἀγάπην, love) feast was not. The early church attracted adherents because of the witness of the lives of the members. Thomas Lindsay says, "The brotherly love of these early Christians was a real and practical

---

[25] Philip Schaff, *History of the Christian Church*, vol. 2, *Ante-Nicene Christianity, AD 100–325* (Grand Rapids: Eerdmans, 1971), 58.

[26] Latourette, *History of Christianity*, 81–82.

[27] Kreider, *Patient Ferment*, 186–87.

thing which no experience of imposition seems to have damped."[28] This indirect evangelism and outreach was culturally appropriate in a society where suspicion, betrayal, and persecution abounded. The early church membership multiplied as a watching world admired their love of one another, charity toward the marginalized of society, and their grace under persecution.

POST-NICENE MISSIONS (AD 325–1073)

The status of the church changed abruptly with the proclamations of the Edict of Toleration (311) by Galerius and the Edict of Milan (313) by Constantine. The former provided relief from persecution for Christians, while the latter gave religious freedom to all creeds within the Roman Empire.[29] Only ten years had passed since Diocletian (303) ordered churches destroyed, meetings suspended, Scriptures burned, and believers imprisoned or executed.[30] These edicts meant Christian churches and missionaries could worship and witness unimpeded. Not long after assuming power, Constantine called the First Church Council, also known as the Council of Nicaea.[31] The young emperor Constantine encouraged missions within his empire to such an extent that the number of Christians quadrupled over the following 100 years.[32]

Missionary work began among the Goths when Ulfilas (311–383) translated the Bible into the vernacular language.[33] Martin of Tours (316–397), the patron saint of France, preached to the Burgundians in southern Gaul, bringing that part of the Roman Empire under the banner of the cross.[34] Captured by pirates while working in England as a shepherd, Patrick (389–461) spent years as slave in Ireland. Subsequent to his release, Patrick's burden for the Irish compelled him to return to Ireland as a missionary. There he baptized

---

[28] Thomas M. Lindsay, *The Church and Ministry in the Early Centuries* (Minneapolis: James Family Publishing, 1977), 173.

[29] Schaff, *History of the Christian Church*, 2:71–73.

[30] Cairns, *Christianity through the Centuries*, 101

[31] Church history in the first millennium is often divided into the Pre-Nicene years and the Post-Nicene era.

[32] Terry, "Missions in the Early Church," 150.

[33] Philip Schaff, *History of the Christian Church*, vol. 3: *Nicene and Post-Nicene Christianity, AD 311–600* (Grand Rapids: Eerdmans, 1971), 641.

[34] Cairns, *Christianity through the Centuries*, 138.

thousands and ordained many clergy.[35] Due to Patrick's efforts, the island became a center for Celtic Christianity and missions.[36]

While Patrick served as the apostle of Ireland, Columba (521–597) became the leader of the Celtic mission to Scotland. Preaching both to the nobility and common people, Columba and his missionaries succeeded in winning
most of the Scottish population to Christianity.[37]

In the first half of the fourth century, in the highlands of East Africa,
Christianity found a foothold when two young travelers, Frumentius and Ae-
dessius, became captives in Abyssinia. After preaching the gospel, the former
sought out Athanasius, the bishop of Alexandria, who appointed him as the
bishop of Axum. This resulted in the founding of the Ethiopian Orthodox
Church, which continues to this day.[38]

By AD 500 Christianity had reached into Arabia, Mesopotamia, Persia,
India, Germany, and Georgia. The expansion was so great that by this time a
majority in the empire called themselves Christians.[39] What kind of Christians, however, were these? Philip Schaff observes:

> But the elevation of Christianity as the religion of the state pres-
> ents also an opposite aspect to our contemplation. It involved great
> risk of degeneracy to the church. The Roman state, with its laws,
> institutions, and usages, was still deeply rooted in heathenism, and
> could not be transformed by a magical stroke. The Christianizing of
> the state amounted therefore in great measure to a paganizing and
> secularizing of the church. The world overcame the church, as much
> as the church overcame the world, and the temporal gain of Christi-
> anity was in many respects cancelled by spiritual loss.[40]

During this period, another major missionary movement emerged—the
Nestorians. Nestorius, a monk and presbyter from Antioch, became the patri-
arch of Constantinople in AD 428. Although an able opponent of Arianism

---

[35] Latourette, *History of Christianity*, 101–2.
[36] Cairns, *Christianity through the Centuries*, 139.
[37] John Finney, *Recovering the Past: Celtic and Roman Missions* (London: Darton, Longman & Todd, 1996), 29.
[38] Latourette, *History of Christianity*, 104.
[39] Terry, "Missions in the Early Church," 154–55.
[40] Schaff, *History of the Christian Church*, 3:93.

and staunch defender of the full divinity of Jesus, Nestorius argued against the hypostatic union. In other words, the Nestorians believed that Christ not only had two natures but possessed two persons. On the contrary, the orthodox view holds that Christ possesses two natures, human and divine, but exists as one person—the God-Man. Nestorians viewed Christ's humanity as God-bearing, but not divine.[41]

Despite their nonorthodox views concerning the person of Christ, the Nestorians engaged in significant missionary activities. Nestorians planted churches in Nubia (northern Sudan), Kurdistan, Persia, India, and China.[42] A Chinese imperial edict in 845 against Buddhists and Christians caused such a sharp reduction in the Nestorian churches that no trace of them could be found by a survey team sent in 980.[43]

The Eastern Orthodox Church produced outstanding missionaries during this period. Whereas the Western church insisted on worship being conducted only in Latin, the Eastern church advocated translating it into the language of the people.[44] This "Incarnational approach" fostered missionary activities represented by Cyril and Methodius. Originally from Thessalonica, these brothers planted a church among the Tartar tribe in what is today Russia. Next, they evangelized the Moravians and Bulgarians, earning them the title "Apostles of the Slavs."[45] Furthermore, Cyril translated parts of the Bible into the Slavic vernacular, creating in the process the Slavic alphabet that bears his name.[46] Unfortunately, in this age of Muslim expansion, the Eastern church's missionary zeal was tempered by efforts to stem the tide of Islam.[47]

---

[41] Schaff, 715–19.

[42] William Chauncey Emhardt and George M. Lamsa, *The Oldest Christian People: A Brief Account of the History and Traditions of the Assyrian People and the Fateful History of the Nestorian Church* (Eugene: Wipf and Stock, 2012), 66.

[43] Latourette, *History of Christianity*, 325.

[44] Terry and Gallagher, *Encountering the History of Missions*, 64.

[45] Philip Schaff, *History of the Christian Church*, vol. 4, *Mediaeval Christianity, A.D. 590–1073* (Grand Rapids: Eerdmans, 1971), 128–29.

[46] Latourette, *History of Christianity*, 307. This translation engendered some controversy. Latourette says the German clergy, jealous of Byzantine influence, "maintained that only the languages permissible in the Eucharist were the three which were alleged to have been in Pilate's placard on the cross of Christ—Hebrew, Greek, and Latin." Latourette, 308.

[47] Terry and Gallagher, *Encountering the History of Missions*, 87.

The most significant event of the Middle Ages involves the rise of a new religion from the sands of Arabia—Islam. When an orphaned caravan operator received God's call to become a prophet, he would change not only medieval history, but would affect modern times as well.[48] By the time of Muhammad's death in 612, all Arabia had capitulated. The Prophet's successors, Caliphs Omar and Othman, began absorbing Christian kingdoms in both the East and the West. Jerusalem fell in 636, Alexandria in 641,[49] and by the end of the seventh century, Islam had spread across North Africa and into Spain. Without Charles "the Hammer" Martel halting the Arab forces at the Battle of Poitiers (732) near Tours, France, all of Europe might have succumbed to the Muslim advance. In the East, Leo the Isaurian halted the progress of the Saracens at the walls of Constantinople (718). This, despite the fact Islam had spread past modern-day Turkey into Persia and Afghanistan.[50]

This period of church history ends with the Great Schism between the Roman Church and the Eastern Orthodox churches in 1054.[51] Up to this time, Christianity was more or less unified. From here on, however, the two streams of Christianity would proceed separately. Although the Eastern and Western churches agreed with the decisions of the seven church councils and about most other doctrines and practices, disagreements persisted that could not be bridged. The Eastern Orthodox churches objected to the authority of the pope, the celibacy of lower clergy, the withdrawal of the cup from the laity, and the insertion of the *filioque*, the double procession of the Holy Spirit from both the Father and the Son.[52]

---

[48] W. Montgomery Watt, *Muhammad: Prophet and Statesman* (London: Oxford University Press, 1961), 7, 10–12.

[49] Shibli Numani, *'Umar: An Abridged Edition of Shibli Numani's 'Umar al-Faruq* (London: I. B. Tauris, 2004), 59.

[50] Michael Auckland Smith, *The Church under Siege* (Downers Grove, IL: InterVarsity Press, 1976), 212.

[51] At ecumenical councils at Ferrara (1438) and Florence (1438), Pope Eugenius IV was able to get the Church of the East to accede to Rome's demands. After Constantinople fell to the Muslims, a synod in that city (1472) with the backing of the new Sultan repudiated the reunion and the Great Schism became permanent and remains in effect until today. Latourette, *History of Christianity*, 621–22.

[52] Schaff, *History of the Christian Church*, 4:307–8. Schaff says a further difference emerged in 1854 when the Western Church proclaimed Mary's immaculate conception official dogma. The Eastern Church does not accept this in theory but does in practice. Schaff, 308.

MISSIONS IN THE MIDDLE AGES (AD 1054–1517)

"Christianity survived despite medieval Christians, not because of them,"[53] observes William Manchester.[54] Speaking of the mass conversions during this period, noted historian Kenneth Scott Latourette asks and then answers an important question:

> How far in these conversions in the West was the Gospel understood and really accepted? Could the professedly Christian communities be knit together into an inclusive fellowship exemplifying the basic Christian tie of love? Much of the alleged Christianity was obviously very superficial and quite without comprehension. That meant that they were in principle fully committed to the Christian faith and to carrying out thoroughly its precepts in their own lives.[55]

Philip Schaff devotes three volumes of his *History of the Christian Church* to medieval Christianity. Latourette calls the ninth and tenth centuries "years of deep darkness."[56] Indeed, the latter half of the first millennium (the first half of the Middle Ages) is often called the Dark Ages, not because they were worse than the second half of the Middle Ages, but because history knows so little of the content of this period.[57] Latourette speaks for most Christians when he observes this time period "may seem disheartening for any who would share the dream of Jesus for the coming of the kingdom of God. What had happened to that vision, with its confident assertion that the reign of God was at hand?"[58]

Indeed, the prospects seemed bleak. In November 1095, Pope Urban II proposed a crusade against the Muslims with the objective of retaking the Holy Land for Christianity. Although many joined the Pope's call seeking adventure or the lure of the spoils of war, many were sincere in their desire to assist the Eastern Orthodox Church in regaining Christianity's lost real

---

[53] William Manchester, *A World Lit Only by Fire: The Medieval Mind and the Renaissance: Portrait of an Age* (New York: Little, Brown, 1991), xvii.

[54] After falling ill, William Manchester, best known as the most skilled of Winston Churchill's biographers, took a break from writing the third volume about the former prime minister to research the Middle Ages. Manchester died before completing his last Churchill biography, so *A World Lit Only by Fire* became his last published work.

[55] Latourette, *History of Christianity*, 352.

[56] Latourette, 365.

[57] Manchester, *Lit Only by Fire*, 3.

[58] Latourette, *History of Christianity*, 374.

estate in Palestine. More than a million people joined the First Crusade, which recovered Nicaea, Antioch, and Jerusalem. As a result, the "Christians" held Jerusalem for almost a hundred years. Six more crusades were less successful before this period ended in 1291.[59]

The effects of the Crusades linger until today. Millions of people traveling from Europe to the Holy Land introduced soldiers to a civilization and culture more advanced than their own.[60] This progress in knowledge paved the way for the Renaissance. When the Crusades began, the institution of feudalism was in full bloom. When the period ended, feudalism had largely disappeared, as sovereigns extended their authority.[61] The recruiting of Crusaders from nations across Europe gave birth to the concept of nation states, contributing to the rise of monarchies and the loss of papal influence.[62] Many Muslims, however, recall the Crusades as a time when Christianity picked up the sword to conquer Islam. Schaff says:

> The Crusades failed in three respects. The Holy Land was not won. The advance of Islam was not permanently checked. The schism between the East and the West was not healed. These were the primary objects of the Crusades. They were the cause of great evils. As a school of practical religion and morals, they were no doubt disastrous for most of the Crusaders. . . . The vices of the Crusading camps were a source of deep shame in Europe. . . . The schism between the East and the West was widened by the insolent action of the popes in establishing Latin patriarchies in the East. . . . Another evil was the deepening of the contempt and hatred in the minds of the Mohammedans. . . . Again, the Crusades gave occasion for the rapid development of the system of papal indulgences which became a dogma of the medieval theologians.[63]

These indulgences and the veneration of more than 1,000 shrines (which charged admission to visit them) paved the way for the Protestant Reformation. William Manchester says citizens of the modern world struggle in their efforts to fathom the fears of the medieval mind.

---

[59] Cairns, *Christianity through the Centuries*, 241.

[60] Justice Anderson, "Medieval and Renaissance Missions (500–1792)," in *Missiology*, 162.

[61] Schaff, *History of the Christian Church*, vol. 5, *The Middle Ages, A.D. 1049–1294* (Grand Rapids: Eerdmans, 1971), 292.

[62] Cairns, *Christianity through the Centuries*, 235.

[63] Schaff, *History of the Christian Church*, 5:290–91.

Everyone also knew—and every child was taught—that the air all around them was infested with invisible, soulless spirits, some benign but most of them evil, dangerous, long-lived, and hard to kill; that among them were the souls of unbaptized infants, ghouls who snuffled out cadavers in graveyards and chewed their bones, water nymphs skilled at luring knights to death by drowning, dracs who carried little children off to their caves beneath the earth, wolfmen—the undead turned into ravenous beasts—and vampires who rose from their tombs at dusk to suck the blood of men, women, or children who had strayed from home. At any moment, under any circumstances, a person could be removed from the world of the senses to a realm of magic creatures and occult powers. Every natural object possessed supernatural qualities.[64]

Into this dark and superstitious world, a few lights of missions flickered to brighten the Middle Ages. In 1272 Marco Polo reported encountering Nestorians ministering in Asia Minor among the Muslims in Mosul.[65] In 1215 Dominic Guzman founded the Order of Preachers, also known as the Dominicans. With a concern for the marginalized, the Dominicans later championed the spiritual and physical rights of the indigenous people of Latin America, pointing out the injustices of the Spanish conquistadores.[66] Giovanni di Pietro di Bernardone (Francesco) founded the Franciscans in 1210. Francis of Assisi spread the Catholic gospel from Italy to Tunis. His followers preached in England (1224), Syria (1217), Germany (1219), India, and China (1254).[67]

Of the Franciscans, missionary Ramon Llull's contributions continue to inspire. Llull made three missionary trips to North Africa to reach Muslims before being stoned to death in 1316 in Tunis. As he devised a system of presenting the gospel, Llull's "chief concern was to see all men won to the Christian faith."[68] Novel at the time, Llull advocated winning converts through understanding, reasoning, and love, by learning the language and culture of the Arabs.[69]

---

[64] Manchester, *Lit Only by Fire*, 62.

[65] Lawrence Bergreen, *Marco Polo: From Venice to Exandu* (New York: Random House, 2007), 45.

[66] Terry and Gallagher, *Encountering the History of Missions*, 90–93.

[67] Terry and Gallagher, 99–102.

[68] Latourette, *History of Christianity*, 404.

[69] Terry and Gallagher, *Encountering the History of Missions*, 104–5.

Peter Waldo (1140–1218) and the Waldensians

Peter Waldo founded the Waldensians, a restoration movement that began in France. Although they were not missionaries in the international-mission sense, Waldo dispatched lay followers two by two to preach the gospel. The Waldensians interpreted the Bible literally, translating it into the vernacular. When excommunicated for these practices and their beliefs, "they replied that 'they ought to obey God, rather than men'."[70] Many were imprisoned and some executed. This group emphasized the priesthood of the believer and claimed any layman could preach and preside over the Lord's Supper. They anticipated the Protestant Reformation, with its belief in a return to the apostolic faith.[71] According to Philip Schaff, "They were the strictly biblical sect of the Middle Ages."[72]

John Wycliffe (1328–1384) and the Lollards

John Wycliffe taught at Oxford University for most of his life, until he was removed from his professorship for denouncing the abuses of the Catholic clergy and questioning the primacy and authority of the pope.[73] Furthermore, Wycliffe taught the Bible as the sole authority for faith, church structure, and practice. He translated the first full manuscript of the Bible into English to put copies of the Scriptures in the hands of the people.[74] Although not a missionary himself, Wycliffe founded a group of lay itinerant preachers called the Lollards, who preached all over England.[75] They would be considered home missionaries today. Wycliffe anticipated the more radical beliefs of the Protestant Reformation by opposing the Catholic doctrine of transubstantiation.[76] The Catholic Church hated him to the extent that forty-four years after his

---

[70] Schaff, *History of the Christian Church*, 5:493–94.

[71] Cairns, *Christianity through the Centuries*, 248–49.

[72] Schaff, *History of the Christian Church*, 5:493.

[73] Manchester, *Lit Only by Fire*, 104.

[74] Cairns, *Christianity through the Centuries*, 276.

[75] Schaff, *History of the Christian Church*, vol. 6, *The Middle Ages, A.D. 1294–1517* (Grand Rapids: Eerdmans, 1971), 319.

[76] John Wycliffe posted his views on this and other subjects in twelve theses (as opposed to Luther's ninety-five theses), declaring the church's doctrine unscriptural and misleading. Schaff, *History of the Christian Church*, 6:320.

death, the pope ordered Wycliffe's bones exhumed, burned, and thrown into a stream.[77] Philip Schaff calls him "the Morning Star of the Reformation."[78]

John Huss (1373–1415) and the Hussites

John Huss[79] of Bohemia,[80] after reading the views of Wycliffe, determined to reform his nation's church along the lines of the Lollard model.[81] Although not an international missionary, Huss also participated in home missions, preaching Wycliffe's evangelical ideas to throngs of listeners all over the nation in the open air.[82] He simultaneously preached in a local church and served as dean of the faculty of philosophy and rector of the University of Prague. Despite the support of the masses and many aristocrats, John Huss, a national hero, was burned at the stake on July 6, 1415, for refusing to recant his Wycliffian views. His last words were, "Lord, into thy hands I commend my spirit."[83]

MISSIONS DURING THE REFORMATION AND POST-REFORMATION ERA (1517–1792)

Martin Luther (1483–1546)

Martin Luther, the son of a miner, set off the Protestant Revolution by nailing ninety-five theses to the door of the church at Wittenberg.[84] Luther's ninety-five theses mainly involved the sale of indulgences and papal power.[85]

---

[77] Latourette, *History of Christianity*, 666.

[78] Schaff, *History of the Christian Church*, 6:315.

[79] John Huss's surname means "goose" in the Czech language. Huss often referred to himself by this term, claiming that his followers "loved the Goose." Schaff, 6:360.

[80] Now known as the Czech Republic.

[81] Cairns, *Christianity through the Centuries*, 277.

[82] Schaff, *History of the Christian Church*, 6:362.

[83] Latourette, *History of the Christian Church*, 668–69.

[84] Manchester, *Lit Only by Fire*, 140. Manchester says, "In Wittenberg, as in many university towns of the time, the church door was customarily used as a bulletin board; an academician with a new religious theory would post it there, thus signifying his readiness to defend it against all challengers."

[85] A translation of Luther's lengthy ninety-five theses appears in Philip Schaff, *History of the Christian Church*, vol. 7, *Modern Christianity, the German Reformation* (Grand Rapids: Eerdmans, 1971), 160–66.

Later he would advocate salvation by faith alone, the priesthood of the believer, and the authority of the Scriptures—translating the Bible into German, standardizing the Teutonic literary language.[86] Luther, indeed most of the Reformers, did not pursue international missions. Gordon Olson calls this lack of missionary zeal of the Reformers[87] the "Great Omission."[88] Although many in that day believed the Great Commission had been fulfilled by the twelve apostles in the first century, John Mark Terry believes the reason for the Reformers' lack of missionary activity lies in another direction. None of the Reformers could conceive of a missionary force apart from one of the Roman Catholic missionary orders. Without such a force, the churches of the Reformation were slow to engage in international missions.[89]

John Calvin (1509–1564)

There were exceptions, however. John Calvin trained oppressed Protestants from his center in Geneva, returning them to their native countries to preach the gospel.[90] Specifically, he instructed many Huguenots, sending the French Protestants to their home country to start churches.[91] In this sense, Calvin engaged in regional missions to countries in other parts of Europe. Additionally, he sent a theologian and a number of pastors to minister with French Calvinists in Guanabara Bay, Brazil,[92] to assist in the colonization efforts of Nicolas Durand de Villegaignon in 1555.[93] Additionally, Verceslaus Budovetz, a Hungarian, became the first post-Reformation missionary to Muslims, working in Istanbul from 1577 to 1581.

---

[86] Kenneth Scott Latourette, *A History of Christianity*, vol. 2, *Reformation to the Present*, rev. ed. (n.p.: Prince Press, 1997), 719.

[87] Martin Luther, Ulrich Zwingli, John Calvin, and John Knox.

[88] Justice Anderson, "Medieval and Renaissance Missions," 167–68.

[89] Terry and Gallagher, *Encountering the History of Missions*, 139.

[90] Latourette, *History of Christianity*, 2:758.

[91] Terry and Gallagher, *Encountering the History of Missions*, 137.

[92] Now Rio de Janeiro, Brazil.

[93] Jean de Léry, *History of a Voyage to the Land of Brazil, Otherwise Called America*, trans. Janet Whatley (Berkeley: University of California Press, 1992), 4–6.

The Anabaptists

Among the Reformers, the Anabaptists should not be ignored, not because they were missionaries, but because their doctrines hold sway among many mission boards today. Some of Ulrich Zwingli's followers in Zurich became known as Anabaptists because they taught all converts should be rebaptized. Conrad Grebel (1498–1526), considered the father of Swiss Anabaptists, held meetings for Bible study while advocating separation of church and state, the authority of the Bible and adult believer's baptism.[94] Balthasar Hubmaier (1481–1528) became the principal leader and theologian of the German Anabaptists. Called the "Doctor of Anabaptism," he famously advocated for religious liberty.[95] Hubmaier argued religious beliefs should be matters of individual conscience, not issues for the government. When he refused to recant, the authorities burned Hubmaier at the stake and drowned his wife, the latter a common mode of execution for Baptists.[96] The Anabaptist preachers were not international missionaries, but they functioned as home missionaries by preaching the gospel at great risk.

For Roman Catholics, the term "evangelical" describes those who adhere to the importance of the four Gospels. During the Reformation, however, the word referred to a political party that opposed the papacy. Anabaptists, Pietists, Quakers, Moravians, and Methodists became what Ralph Winter calls a "third force," redefining the term "evangelical." Winter writes:

> It began to refer to individuals who had a personal "evangelical experience," by which they meant that something real had happened in a person's heart and life, not just purely mental assent to some sort of intellectual creed.... The concept of a "born again" experience was almost entirely unknown at the time of the Reformation. But in 1738 John Wesley, a university-trained Anglican, in a little Moravian chapel on a street called Aldersgate, sensed the warming of his heart as he listened to a verse being read out loud from the Book of

---

[94] Cairns, *Christianity through the Centuries*, 329, 331.
[95] Jason G. Duesing, *Seven Summits in Church History* (Nashville: Rainer, 2016), 78.
[96] Schaff, *History of the Christian Church*, 7:609.

Romans in a commentary by Luther. The verse spoke of being "saved by faith."[97]

Evangelicals today generally believe that some kind of personal experience normally accompanies the conversion event. Evangelicals would be the ones to take up the cause of world missions in the future.

Philipp Spener (1635–1705)

A little more than a hundred years after the Reformation, lethargy had crept into the Protestant church. The Pietist movement rose to fill the spiritual void within Lutheranism. Philipp Spener, the father of Pietism, emphasized evangelism, missions, prayer, Bible study, and personal piety. Spener founded the University of Halle, which August Francke (1663–1727) developed into a large ministerial training center.[98] When Frederick IV of Denmark embraced Pietism, he desired to send missionaries to the Danish colony in India. As a result, Danish-Halle missionaries Heinrich Plütschau and Bartholomew Ziegenbalg traveled to Tranquebar, India, staying five and fifteen years, respectively.[99] While on a furlough from India at Halle, Ziegenbalg's mission stories influenced a young nobleman who would change missions forever.

Nicolas Ludwig von Zinzendorf (1700–1760)

If Christianity considers John Wycliffe the "Morning Star of the Reformation," then Count Nicolaus Ludwig von Zinzendorf qualifies as the "Morning Star of Missions." Although the Moravians began under John Huss in the late fifteenth century, persecution from the Counter-Reformation caused a remnant to seek refuge in one of Zinzendorf's estates in 1722.[100] A committed Pietist, the nobleman was ordained a bishop of the Moravian Church in 1737,

---

[97] Ralph D. Winter, "The Future of Evangelicals in Mission," in *MissionShift: Global Mission Issues in the Third Millennium*, ed. David J. Hesselgrave and Ed Stetzer (Nashville: B&H Academic, 2010), 165.

[98] J. Herbert Kane, *A Global View of Christian Missions: From Pentecost to the Present*, rev. ed. (Grand Rapids: Baker, 1975), 77.

[99] Joseph Muthuraj, *We Began at Tranquebar*, vol. 1, *SPCK, the Danish-Halle Mission and Anglican Episcopacy in India (1706–1843)* (Delhi: ISPCK-Indian Society for Promoting Christian Knowledge, 2010), 30.

[100] Kane, *Global View of Christian Missions*, 78–79.

leading them to establish missions in St. Thomas (1732), Greenland (1733), St. Croix (1734), Surinam (1735), the Gold Coast, South Africa (1737), North America, (1740), Jamaica (1754), and Antigua (1756). Herbert Kane ranks Zinzendorf and Francke as the greatest missionary leaders of the eighteenth century. He writes:

> The missionary impulse came about in a strange way. Zinzendorf, on a visit to Copenhagen in 1730, met a Negro from the West Indies and two Eskimos from Greenland, each of whom pleaded for missionaries. He was deeply moved by the appeal and decided to do something about it. On his return to *Herrnhut* he placed the challenge before the group. The response was immediate and enthusiastic.[101]

John Wesley (1703–1791) and Jonathan Edwards (1703–1758)

John Wesley of England and Jonathan Edwards of New England were born the same year. Although the former was an Arminian and the latter a Calvinist, both were powerful preachers and participated in spiritual awakenings in their respective countries during what became known as the First Great Awakening. These revivals raised the spiritual temperature of both nations, ushering in the Great Century of Missions.

David Brainerd (1718–1747)

One of those who responded to the preachers of the First Great Awakening was David Brainerd (1718–1747). Expelled from Yale due to his evangelistic exuberance, Brainerd became an itinerant preacher and then missionary to the Native Americans. He died of tuberculosis in the home of Jonathan Edwards, who published Brainerd's diary to the Christian world. Brainerd's mission passion became a model and inspiration for William Carey and Henry Martyn.[102]

---

[101] Kane, 79.
[102] Terry and Gallagher, *Encountering the History of Missions*, 246.

George Liele (1750–1820)

A former slave, George Liele, was converted as an adult on a plantation in Georgia at the time of the American Revolution. A British Loyalist, Liele left with others opposed to colonial independence and settled in Canada. Shortly thereafter, Liele; his wife, Hannah; and their four children migrated to Jamaica. After two years working as an indentured servant, Liele received his freedom and began preaching to the slaves there. Liele preached at a racecourse, won a number of converts, and started the first of many churches.[103] George Liele influenced David George, a fellow slave in Georgia, to establish a mission to Sierra Leone, where the latter planted the first Baptist church in West Africa.[104] Although not formally sent out by a mission agency, Liele represents the first of many who launched their mission work from a secular occupation.

THE GREAT CENTURY OF MISSIONS (1792–1910)

William Carey (1761–1834)

William Carey, the "Father of Modern Missions," created the first missions sending agency[105] in 1792. Not finding anyone who would go, Carey volunteered himself and arrived in Bengal the following year.[106] Since the British East India Company opposed missionaries, Carey and two others settled in Serampore, a Danish colony near Calcutta, India. Despite his wife's mental illness and the death of a child, Carey and the "Serampore Three" preached the gospel, translated the Bible into several languages, and started a training school for national believers.[107] Carey opposed the prevailing notion that the apostles had already fulfilled the Great Commission. In his treatise "An Enquiry into the Obligation of Christians to Use Means for the Conversion of

---

[103] Winston A. Lawson, "Pioneer George Liele in Jamaica, the British Colony," in *George Liele's Life and Legacy: An Unsung Hero*, ed. David T. Shannon Sr. (Macon, GA: Mercer University Press, 2012), 115–18.

[104] Jeneen Blease Roscoe, "David George: George Liele's Legacy in Sierra Leone," in Shannon, 140–41.

[105] Baptist Missionary Society.

[106] Duesing, *Seven Summits*, 100–103.

[107] Latourette, *History of Christianity*, 2:1033.

the Heathens," Carey argued, "If the command of Christ to teach all nations be restricted to the apostles, or those under the immediate inspiration of the Holy Ghost, then that of baptizing should be, too."[108] William Carey almost single-handedly brought about the modern mission movement.

Henry Martyn (1781–1812)

Henry Martyn was born the son of a poor miner on the southwest coast of England. After becoming a fellow at Cambridge, Martyn was turned down in marriage by a woman who considered herself his social superior. Therefore, he surrendered for missionary service, arriving in India in 1806 to serve as a chaplain for the East India Company.[109] Martyn said upon his arrival, "Now let me burn out for God."[110] Indeed, Martyn poured out his life, translating the New Testament into the predominantly Muslim languages of Arabic, Urdu, and Farsi in just six years before his untimely death at the age of thirty-one. His translation work enabled Henry Martyn to preach to thousands in India, Singapore, and Persia.[111]

Robert Morrison (1782–1834)

Robert Morrison of the London Missionary Society served as the first Protestant missionary to China. Prevented by the East India Company from accessing China, Morrison traveled to Canton[112] on an American ship, with an introduction from James Madison. Herbert Kane writes, "The owner of the ship considered Morrison's venture a little rash. Said he one day with a cynical smile: 'And so, Mr. Morrison, you really expect to make an impression on the idolatry of the great Chinese Empire?' Morrison famously replied; 'No, sir, but I expect God will.'"[113] Morrison was opposed by the British, the Chinese, and the Catholic Church in Portuguese Macao, where he worked as a translator.

---

[108] William Carey, "Conversion of the Heathens," in Winter and Hawthorne, *Perspectives on the World Christian Movement*, 314 (see chap. 1, n. 30).

[109] Sarah J. Rhae, *Life of Henry Martyn: Missionary to India and Persia, 1781–1912* (Create Space Publishing Platform, 2016), 7, 9.

[110] Latourette, *History of Christianity*, 2:1034.

[111] Rhae, *Life of Henry Martyn*, 20.

[112] Now Guangzhou, China

[113] Kane, *Global View of Missions*, 212.

Although Morrison won only twelve converts during his lifetime, the Chinese Bible he completed in 1823 after sixteen years of work remains as the first and most respected of the Chinese-English translations.[114] Morrison's mammoth Chinese-English dictionary and his Chinese Bible caused him to remark, "By the Chinese Bible, when dead, I shall still speak."[115]

Adoniram Judson (1788–1850)

Adoniram Judson represents for American Baptists what William Carey symbolizes for British Baptists—their pioneering missionary hero. The wayward, unbelieving son of a Congregationalist minister, Judson found the Lord at age twenty while attending Andover Seminary as a special student because he was not yet a Christian. After his conversion, Judson joined a missionary student group that became known as the Haystack Prayer Meeting because the members sought refuge under a haystack during a rainstorm. This led to the formation of the American Board of Commissioners for Foreign Missions and a number of Haystack members, including Judson, surrendered for missions.[116] Two weeks after their marriage, Adoniram and Ann Judson departed for India. During the voyage, a study of the Greek New Testament convinced the Judsons that baptism by immersion represented the biblical mode of the ordinance.

William Ward, an associate of William Carey, baptized the Judsons, and after a short stay in South Asia, the couple departed for Burma[117] as Baptist missionaries. Since they forfeited the support of the Congregationalist mission board, the Judsons urged Baptists in America to form a missionary society.[118] This mission board birthed the Baptist denomination in the United States, the precursor of both American Baptists and Southern Baptists. Judson translated the Bible into the Burmese language, buried two wives and a number of

---

[114] One of my students, a house-church leader in China, says Morrison's translation is still used and revered.

[115] Terry and Gallagher, *Encountering the History of Missions*, 253.

[116] Jason G. Duesing, "Ambition Overthrown," in *Adoniram Judson: A Bicentennial Appreciation of the Pioneer American Missionary*, ed. Jason G. Duesing (Nashville: B&H, 2012), 69–70.

[117] Known today as Myanmar.

[118] Courtney Anderson, *To the Golden Shore: The Life of Adoniram Judson* (Valley Forge, PA: Judson Press, 1987), 146.

children, while tirelessly preaching the gospel. As the first American mission-ary, Judson modeled a brand of self-sacrifice, while enduring persecution and imprisonment, that still inspires succeeding generations of missionaries.

Robert Moffat (1795–1883)

Robert Moffat pioneered missionary work in South Africa for the London Missionary Society, serving for fifty years as Bible translator, church planter, and publisher. He also founded a medical clinic and an experimental farm.[119] Moffat wrote to his parents, "Oh, that I had a thousand lives and a thousand bodies! All of them should be devoted to no other employment but to preach Christ to those degraded, despised, yet beloved mortals."[120] Moffat's daugh-ter married the controversial David Livingstone (1813–1873). Livingstone also served with the London Mission Society but simultaneously represented the Royal Geographical Society as an explorer searching for the source of the Nile.[121] This caused many to conclude Livingstone preferred scientific inquiry to mission work.

J. Hudson Taylor (1832–1905)

J. Hudson Taylor founded the China Inland Mission (CIM) after serving for four years with the Chinese Evangelization Society.[122] Most missions to China preferred life along the country's coastline, but Taylor favored the more difficult interior areas. CIM did not stress education for their missionaries, advocated national dress, and permitted single women to serve as mission-aries.[123] Taylor's mission group spread across the globe and survives today as the Overseas Missions Fellowship. Unlike other mission groups, China Inland Mission's headquarters remained on the mission field rather than in its host country. Although other mission groups raised funds, this society refused to

---

[119] Terry and Gallagher, *Encountering the History of Missions*, 254.
[120] Robert Moffat, quoted in Ethel Daniels Hubbard, *The Moffats* (New York: Friendship Press, 1944), 21.
[121] Kane, *Global View of Christian Missions*, 404.
[122] Warren W. Wiersbe, *50 People Every Christian Should Know: Learning from Spiritual Gi-ants of the Faith* (Grand Rapids: Baker, 2009), 136–37.
[123] Terry and Gallagher, *Encountering the History of Missions*, 264–65.

advertise their needs, depending on the Lord to reveal those needs to donors.[124] CIM inspired the creation of mission groups such as the Sudan Interior Mission (1893) and the Africa Inland Mission (1895).

Charlotte (Lottie) Moon (1840–1912)

Following the example of the China Inland Mission, Charlotte "Lottie" Moon and her sister Edmondia became the first women to serve as unmarried Southern Baptist missionaries. Besides her women's work in China, Lottie Moon became a force in the Shantou revival, participating in evangelism and church starting.[125] During a time of severe famine in northern China, she became malnourished herself and died on the voyage home. Lottie Moon and Annie Armstrong were instrumental in founding the Woman's Missionary Union and conceived of a special offering for mission causes due to the paucity of funds available at the time for missionaries.[126] The Lottie Moon Christmas Offering for International Missions bears testimony to her influence in missions.[127] The Annie Armstrong Easter Offering for North American Missions subsequently was named for the leader of Baltimore, Maryland, women, Annie Armstrong.

William "Buck" Bagby (1855–1939) and Anne Luther Bagby (1859–1942)

Named after Anne Judson, Anne Luther received her call to missions before her future husband. Will Bagby desired to enter the pastorate but after much prayer surrendered to the call of missions. When urged by officials at the Foreign Mission Board in Richmond, Virginia, to travel to the Orient as a missionary, William "Buck" Bagby declared that he would not travel to the Chinese Empire but would by all means go to Brazil.[128] Bagby and his wife, Anne, were among the first career Protestant missionaries in South America.

---

[124] Wiersbe, *50 People*, 139.

[125] Charlotte (Lottie) Moon, February 29, 1888, letter to *Foreign Mission Journal*, in *Send the Light: Lottie Moon Letters and Other Writings*, ed. Keith Harper (Macon, GA: Mercer University Press, 2002), 226–28.

[126] Regina D. Sullivan, *Lottie Moon: A Southern Baptist Missionary to China in History and Legend* (Baton Rouge: Louisiana State University Press, 2012), 100, 105.

[127] Terry and Gallagher, *Encountering the History of Missions*, 255.

[128] Daniel B. Lancaster, *The Bagbys of Brazil: The Life and Work of William Buck Bagby and Anne Luther Bagby, Southern Baptist Missionaries* (Austin, TX: Eakin Press, 1999).

After a year of Portuguese language school near São Paulo, the Bagbys started their ministry in Salvador, Brazil. After a year in northern Brazil with another missionary couple and establishing the first Baptist church, they moved to Rio de Janeiro. The Bagbys reported to the Foreign Mission Board that although experiencing much persecution, their church of three couples was thriving and storming the gates of hell. These three couples became the foundation for the Brazilian Baptist Convention, now more than one million strong. Buck and Anne Bagby served in Brazil as missionaries for fifty-six years.[129]

Erik Alfred Nelson (1862–1939)

Erik Nelson, the "Apostle of the Amazon," traveled down the Amazon River in a nonmotorized boat, planting churches along the way. Born in Sweden, but growing up in Kansas, Erik Nelson described himself as a cowboy. Inspired by a letter from Brazil pioneer missionary Buck Bagby, Nelson sailed for Brazil, serving as a self-supported Swedish Baptist missionary. After Bagby spent one year in Brazil by himself, Ida Lundberg traveled from Kansas to Brazil to marry him.[130] After Erik and Ida labored for six years as independent missionaries, they were appointed by the Foreign Mission Board of the Southern Baptist Convention and served in Brazil for forty-eight years.[131] Erik Nelson traveled by steamboat up the Amazon and planted churches in the major cities. He visited the smaller towns by paddling a canoe.[132] For many, Nelson embodies pioneer missionary exploration and evangelizing to the ends of the earth.

Amy Carmichael (1867–1951)

Amy Carmichael established a mission to children at risk in India. Under her leadership, the Dohnavur Fellowship in Tinnevelly grew to a ministry of more than 900 boys and girls.[133] Carmichael sought to indigenize her society, beginning a non-Catholic lay order called "Sisters of the Common Life." Open to

---

129 William R. Estep, *Whole Gospel Whole World: The Foreign Mission Board of the Southern Baptist Convention, 1845–1995* (Nashville: B&H, 1994), 127–28.

130 L. M. Bratcher, *The Apostle of the Amazon* (Nashville: Broadman Press, 1951), 21.

131 Howard Gallimore, *Erik (Eurico) Alfred Nelson Papers: 1891–1975, AR 363* (Nashville: Southern Baptist Historical Library and Archives, 2012), 2–3.

132 Bratcher, *Apostle of the Amazon*, 68–69.

133 Terry and Gallagher, *Encountering the History of Missions*, 295.

Indian and European single women, this order opposed both Hinduism and sex trafficking.[134] Amy Carmichael's self-sacrifice and commitment brought her unsought fame as a servant of God during her lifetime. Carmichael's dedication was such that she spent sixty years on the field, never coming home to report to her board. Like her ministry model, the China Inland Mission, she did not solicit funds but depended on the Lord to meet her needs.[135]

Samuel Zwemer (1867–1952)

The thirteenth of fifteen children, Samuel Zwemer was born to Dutch emigrants who settled in Michigan. He founded the Arabian Mission in 1889, by convincing the board of Foreign Missions and the General Synod of the Reformed Church to support his work.[136] Zwemer established stations in Iraq, Bahrain, Egypt, Persia, and Yemen. Along with Temple Gardner, Zwemer developed the "Irenic approach" of reaching Muslims. They believed evangelism with Muslims should be courteous, not polemic. Zwemer thought only by encountering the person of Christ and understanding the value of the cross could a Muslim come to Christ and be saved.[137] Samuel Zwemer became known as the "Apostle to Islam" due to his pioneering efforts to reach Muslims from North Africa to China.[138]

Roland Bingham (1872–1942)

Although born into a "Dissenter" family in England, Roland Bingham heard the gospel through the Salvation Army and joined the movement.[139] Bingham was among three single men who arrived in Nigeria as missionaries in 1894. His two companions died shortly after their arrival, and Bingham returned

[134] Elisabeth Elliot, *A Chance to Die: The Life and Legacy of Amy Carmichael* (Grand Rapids: Revell, 1987), 240, 243–44.

[135] Wiersbe, *50 People*, 299, 303.

[136] J. Christy Wilson Sr., *Apostle to Islam: A Biography of Samuel M. Zwemer* (Baker, 1952; repr., Pioneer Library, 2017), 27–28.

[137] Peter Pikkert, *Protestant Missionaries to the Middle East: Ambassadors of Christ or Culture?* (Hamilton, ON: WEC Canada, 2008), 82, 101.

[138] Kenneth Scott Latourette, introduction to *Apostle to Islam* by Wilson, vii.

[139] James Hogg Hunter, *A Flame of Fire: The Life and Work of Rowland V. Bingham* (Toronto: Sudan Interior Mission, 1961), 44.

to England very ill. Bingham subsequently moved to Newburg, New York, where he accepted the pastorate of a church. With missions still on his mind, he and his new wife founded the interdenominational Sudan[140] Interior Mission (SIM)[141] in 1898.[142] The vision of SIM was to reach the interior of Africa where the Muslim north meets the traditional religion of the south. SIM established work in Ethiopia, Sudan, Somalia, Eritrea, Niger, Ghana, Nigeria, Benin, Upper Volta (Burkina Faso), and Liberia. Under Bingham's thirty-five-year leadership, SIM grew to become the largest interdenominational mission agency in the world.

MISSIONS FROM 1910 TO 2020

Missions from the time of the first worldwide mission conference[143] until the present day defies easy description. Pre–World War I Christianity exuded optimism about the dawn of a new Christian century. Unfortunately, World War I, the "war to end all wars," dashed these hopes. Supposedly Christian nations fought each other in destructive battles heretofore unimaginable. World War II exceeded World War I in both scope and intensity, with institutionalized genocide carried out on civilian populations. The Korean War, the Vietnam War, and the First Gulf War followed in rapid succession. The twentieth century could be called the "war century" without fear of exaggeration. The twenty-first century seems little better in terms of the prospects for peace. The year 2001 began with a war against Afghanistan that still continues. The Second Gulf War (Iraq War) commenced in 2003.

The two world wars disrupted missionary activities. The advent of communism in Russia (1917) and China (1949), and its spread in Southeast Asia, forced missionaries to exit these countries until the Berlin Wall fell in 1989. Amazingly, missionary societies have multiplied and expanded during the

---

[140] The greater Sudan encompasses an area of Africa that spreads across the continent from Mauretania to Somalia.

[141] Although "Sudan Interior Mission" was Bingham's first name for the mission, in its early days it was also known as the "African Industrial Mission" and "African Evangelical Mission." Hunter, *Flame of Fire*, 82–83.

[142] Hunter, 66, 71.

[143] The Edinburgh Conference of 1910

period after World War II (1946) until the present day. Ralph Winter calls the years between 1945 and 1970 the "Twenty-Five Unbelievable Years" of missionary expansion.[144] Southern Baptists expanded from working in thirteen countries to seventy-seven countries and more than doubled their number of missionaries.[145] From 1970 until 2020, the number of missionaries and agencies has continued to swell. The North American Mission Handbook lists no fewer than 907 agencies in the United States and Canada that are working overseas.[146]

William Cameron Townsend (1896–1982)

Although unknown to many, William Cameron Townsend influences missions as much in the twenty-first century as during his ministry in the twentieth century. A native of Los Angeles, after completing high school, Townsend went to Occidental College, leaving after three years to go to the mission field. As a new missionary in Guatemala, Townsend observed that the Cakchiquel Native Americans in his region could not understand, much less read or write, the Spanish language. Townsend learned Cakchiquel, developed a written alphabet for it, and then translated the Bible into it.[147] Opposed by his mission board, the Central American Mission, in his quest to translate the Bible into other Native American languages, Townsend resigned in 1934 to begin Camp Wycliffe to train missionaries and linguists in Bible translation. At Camp Wycliffe, the Summer Institute for Linguistics (SIL) was born, as well as a new mission—the Wycliffe Bible Translators (1942). Today Wycliffe/SIL works in more than fifty countries, translating the Bible and training indigenous linguists and missionaries to do the same.[148] Cameron Townsend's vision was to translate the Bible into the languages of tribes who had no Scripture in their

---

[144] Ralph D. Winter, *The Twenty-Five Unbelievable Years* (Pasadena: William Carey Press, 1971).

[145] Estep, *Whole Gospel Whole World*, 284, 310.

[146] Peggy E. Newell, ed., *North American Mission Handbook: US and Canadian Protestant Ministries Overseas, 2017–2019*, 22nd ed. (Pasadena: William Carey Library, 2017), 97–412.

[147] James Hefley and Marti Hefley, *Uncle Cam: The Story of William Cameron Townsend, Founder of the Wycliffe Bible Translators and the Summer Institute of Linguistics* (Huntington Beach, CA: Wycliffe Bible Translators, 1995), 25, 62.

[148] Terry and Gallagher, *Encountering the History of Missions*, 316.

native tongues. By 1971 Wycliffe had engaged their five hundredth language with a goal to complete two thousand more.[149]

Eric Liddell (1902–1945)

Eric Liddell was born to Scottish missionary parents in China. According to the practice of the times, the Liddell children were sent away to boarding school during their elementary school years, growing up in Britain. While in college in Edinburgh, Eric became a popular youth preacher and an Olympic athlete. The story of his stand for Christ and winning a gold medal in the 1924 Olympic games was made into a film, *Chariots of Fire*, which won an Academy of Motion Pictures Oscar for Best Picture in 1981.[150] After completing college, Liddell was appointed a missionary by his parents' mission, the London Mission Society. Eric Liddell served as a teacher, pastor, and church starter in China from 1925 until 1945. Eric and his wife, Florence, lived in China during turbulent times. They experienced the revolution and civil war between the communist and nationalist factions. After sending his wife and three children away to safety in Canada, Liddell was interred in a Japanese prisoner of war camp during World War II, where he died in 1945.[151]

Bill Wallace (1908–1951)

On September 6, 1935, Bill Wallace sailed from San Francisco Bay toward China. Although his father was a medical doctor, Wallace originally wanted to become an automobile mechanic. God, however, called him into medical missions at age seventeen. After completing medical school and working as a physician in Tennessee, Wallace responded to a request for a surgeon at the Stout Memorial Hospital in Wuchow, China.[152] Wallace learned Chinese and served there as a surgeon for fifteen years. After surviving the Japanese occupation of

---

[149] Hefley and Hefley, *Uncle Cam*, 121, 269.

[150] Sally Magnusson, *The Flying Scotsman: A Biography* (New York: Quartet Books, 1981), 182.

[151] Ellen Caughey, *Eric Liddell: Olympian and Missionary* (Ulrichville, OH: Barbour, 2000), 172, 199.

[152] Philip A. Pinckard, "Bill Wallace: Missionary Martyr and Model," in *The Message* (Louisiana Baptist state paper), April 1, 2015, https://baptistmessage.com/category/premium/page/129/.

China during World War II, Wallace was arrested by Chinese Communists in 1950 and accused of spying. Despite his protestations of innocence, the Communists beat and tortured him mercilessly.[153] As he did during his medical career in China, Wallace continued witnessing for Christ while in prison, dying a martyr's death on February 10, 1951.

Winfred "Wimpy" Harper (1920–1958)

Wimpy Harper served as an evangelist, church planter, teacher, and administrator in Nigeria and Tanganyika (Tanzania). Beginning their career as "bush" missionaries in a primitive area of Nigeria, Wimpy and his wife, Juanita, evangelized, baptized converts, and taught in a boys' school.[154] Despite suffering periodically with severe bouts of malaria, Harper so excelled in relating to African people that he was chosen to lead the language and orientation center for Nigerian missionaries. After two terms there, Wimpy and Juanita Harper, along with two other couples,[155] founded the Baptist Mission of East Africa in 1956.[156] Harper led the fledging work in Tanganyika and Kenya before his untimely death by drowning in Dar es Salaam in 1958. On furlough just a few months before his death, Wimpy Harper decried the racial prejudice that existed at that time in the US. Speaking at the Texas Baptist Convention, he said:

> The prejudice of your churches [is] affecting the lives of your young people who may someday be called to serve on a foreign mission field. I have decided in light of my own youngster's experience on the mission field that all children are color blind until we teach them otherwise. . . . How do you think we feel when we have to tell African young people that they would not be welcomed in the churches that send missionaries to them?[157]

Although his service in East Africa was cut short, upon hearing of his death, many new missionaries volunteered to take his place.

---

[153] Jesse C. Fletcher, *Bill Wallace of China*, ed. Timothy George and Denise George (Nashville: B&H, 1996), 204–7.

[154] Jesse C. Fletcher, *Wimpy Harper of Africa* (Nashville: Broadman Press, 1967), 43.

[155] The other couples were Davis and Mary Saunders and Jack and Sally Walker.

[156] Laura Lee Stewart, *Through Christ Who Strengthens: A History of the Baptist Mission of East Africa, 1956–1976* (Nairobi: Baptist Publications, 1976), 13, 23.

[157] Winfred Harper, quoted in Fletcher, *Wimpy Harper of Africa*, 124.

Wana Ann G. Fort (1924–2015) and Giles Fort (1923–2013)

Wana Ann and Giles Fort Jr., both missionary medical doctors, served in Southern Rhodesia (Zimbabwe) from 1952 until their retirement in 1986. The Forts represent the thousands of ordinary people who labor as extraordinary servants of God in relative obscurity in difficult places. Working in a "bush" station in the remote Sanyati Reserve, the Forts battled the elements and the traditional religious beliefs of the inhabitants.[158] The two doctors built a hospital where they treated and performed surgery on patients. Although providing for the physical needs of the African people, their primary ministry was spiritual. The Forts shared their faith one-on-one and in worship services, leading many to faith in Christ. These converts often followed the Lord in baptism and were incorporated into local churches. Once in 1953 after Giles Fort preached, forty people accepted Christ and asked for baptism. Since there was no baptistery or other water in the vicinity, a termite hill was hollowed out, cemented, and filled with water for the occasion.[159] In addition to their medical work, the Forts raised five boys on the mission field. While ministering, they still found time to homeschool their children and felt the hardship of sending each away to boarding school as they matured. Their youngest, Grady, was born with Down syndrome. Three of the boys returned to Africa, serving with their wives[160] as missionaries with the International Mission Board (IMB) of the Southern Baptist Convention.

Jim Elliot (1927–1956) and Elisabeth Elliot (1926–2015)

These two Wheaton College graduates were married in a simple civil ceremony in Ecuador. Jim Elliot was raised in the Pacific Northwest but attended college in the Chicago area. Although a promising youth speaker, Elliot felt a call to missions. He attended Camp Wycliffe to learn how to translate the Bible into the Quechua language. Elliot arrived in Ecuador in 1952 and a year and a half later married Elisabeth Howard, a single missionary already on the field.

---

[158] Wana Ann G. Fort with Kim P. Davis, *A Thousand Times Yes: Two Doctors Who Answered God's Call* (Birmingham: New Hope, 2013), 75, 78.

[159] Sammie Johnston, *Dream Builders: The Story of the Forts of Africa* (Birmingham: New Hope, 1989), 29.

[160] David and Laurel Fort, Gordon and Leigh Ann Fort, and Greg and Donna Fort.

Howard was born in Belgium to missionary parents but grew up in the United States. Her dream was to translate the Bible into Quechua, a vision that also gripped her future husband. Soon after their marriage, the Elliots decided God was leading them to attempt to reach a far more dangerous tribe. The Huaorani people of Ecuador were called by the pejorative name "Auca," derived from Quechua *áukka*, meaning "enemy" or "rebel."[161] On a trip with three other missionaries to contact the Huaorani, Jim Elliot, Nate Saint, Ed McCully, Peter Fleming, and Roger Youderian were speared to death.[162] Despite her heartbreak, Elisabeth and her daughter, Valerie, returned to live, work, and witness among the very people who had killed their husband and father. Elisabeth Elliot returned to the US in 1963 and became a noted author and speaker. She married twice more, dying in 2015 at age eighty-eight, almost sixty years after her first husband's death.

CONCLUSION

Kenneth Scott Latourette's concern about the Christian church straying from its moorings continues to puzzle.[163] A study of church history helps solve the problem. Except in a few places, such as China, Eritrea, Sudan, Iran, Afghanistan, Pakistan, and North Korea, the persecuted environment of the early church cannot be reproduced. Indeed, although it may be an excellent catalyst for church growth, those experiencing persecution do not really enjoy or recommend it. Furthermore, oppression in each of these countries differs in intensity and focus. Even within each of these nations, maltreatment varies widely according to locale. It is nothing short of remarkable that Christianity flourishes in many of these places. Perhaps the below-the-surface "slow ferment" of the early church simmers in China today. Conceivably, by the middle of the twenty-first century, Chinese Christians, like their Roman early church

---

[161] *Merriam-Webster*, s.v. "auca," accessed July 27, 2019, https://www.merriam-webster.com/dictionary/auca.

[162] Elisabeth Elliot, *Through Gates of Splendor* (Carol Stream, IL: Tyndale House, 2005), 194–96.

[163] Latourette, *History of Christianity*, 1:374.

counterparts, might become the majority in the very land that attempted to eliminate them.[164]

Perhaps another cause of the lowering of the spiritual temperature of the modern church occurred during the second and third centuries. Due to the imperial suspicion of immorality at the evening banquets of Roman societies, Christians began meeting on Sunday mornings instead of Sunday evenings. Instead of a full repast, the Eucharist was "tokenized" to a piece of bread and a single cup.[165] This changed the character of the *agape* love feast (ἀγάπην) from a time of fellowship and spiritual interaction[166] to a more formalized worship service.[167] When persecution of the early church halted in the early fourth century, coupled with the tokenizing of the Lord's Supper, Christianity slowly lost its distinctive vitality. The liturgy of the medieval church replaced the evangelistic fervor of the early church. Of course, the opposite tendency of idolizing the early church beyond its merit exists as well. Even Origen said about AD 240 that there were "bad Christians" within the Christian communities, with some joining to gain "a little prestige."[168]

What is the way forward for the twenty-first-century church? Persecution certainly purifies the church and is a positive factor in church growth. The Christians I know in limited-access countries, however, pray persecution will stop in their nation, although they acknowledge it eliminates most insincere believers. The church in the nonpersecuted world should focus on meaningful small groups, including, but not exclusively, house and cell churches, to recapture something of the esprit de corps and vitality of the early church. Although a weekly dinner might be a stretch in the modern world, pastors and church leaders should attempt to imitate the intimate fellowship of the early church that such practices encourage.

---

[164] Kreider, *Patient Ferment*, 12.

[165] Kreider, 189–90.

[166] Ralph Neighbour, a proponent of home cell churches, says the *Koinonia* (κοινωνία) that happens at home meetings around the table is essential for Christian growth and is one of the distinctives of biblical Christianity.

[167] Kreider, 190.

[168] Kreider, 128–29.

READING FOR FURTHER STUDY

Latourette, Kenneth Scott. *A History of the Expansion of Christianity*. Vol. 7, *Advance through Storm: A.D. 1914 and After*. New York: Harper & Bros., 1945.

Kreider, Alan. *The Patient Ferment of the Early Church: The Improbable Rise of Christianity in the Roman Empire*. Grand Rapids: Baker Academic, 2016.

Manchester, William. *A World Lit Only by Fire: The Medieval Mind and the Renaissance: Portrait of an Age*. New York: Little, Brown, 1991.

Shenk, Wilbert R., ed. *North American Foreign Missions 1810–1914: Theology, Theory & Policy*. Grand Rapids: Eerdmans, 2004.

Walls, Andrew F. *The Missionary Movement in Christian History: Studies in the Transmission of Faith*. Maryknoll, NY: Orbis, 1996.

Winter, Ralph D. *The Twenty-Five Unbelievable Years*. Pasadena: William Carey Press, 1971.

5

World Religions

The following article appeared in the *New York Times*:

> José Argüelles, the father of the Harmonic Convergence, the mammoth New Age event that in 1987 drew thousands of humming adherents to sites around the globe, died in the Australian bush on March 23, ... from peritonitis. ... He was 72. ...
>
> His philosophy was an eclectic amalgam of Mayan and Aztec cosmology, the I Ching, the Book of Revelation, ancient-astronaut narratives and more.
>
> ... The Convergence drew followers to Mount Shasta in California, Central Park in New York, Ayers Rock in Australia and many other spots in August 1987. ... The ultimate objective, simply put, was to stave off the end of the world. That, Mr. Argüelles said, ... would take place in 2012, at the winter solstice.[1]

INTRODUCTION

Religions often defy definition. There was a day when everyone belonged to one of the major world religions. Now people such as Argüelles mix and match elements of multiple faiths and superstitions. In 1900 many in the Western

---

[1] Margalit Fox, "José Argüelles, New Ager Focused on Time, Dies at 72," *New York Times*, April 2, 2011, https://www.nytimes.com/2011/04/03/us/03arguelles.html.

Christian community believed non-Christian religions would soon collapse. Enlightenment philosophers expected all religions, including Christianity, to fade away during the twentieth century.[2] Neither were correct; religion remains strong.

Christianity presents as a missionary religion, its founder stating, "I am the way, the truth, and the life. No one comes to the Father except through me."[3] After Jesus's death, burial, and resurrection, Christ commissioned his apostles and their successors to take this gospel message and disciple the nations. Implicit in this command was the assumption Christianity would win adherents from other faiths and, by inference, these belief systems were false. George Braswell defines religion as "that part of some people's lives that involves rituals, beliefs, organizations, ethical values, historical traditions, and personal habits and choices, some of which refer to the transcendent."[4]

Christianity assumes Judaism. In other words, neither Jesus nor his disciples ever claimed Judaism was false. On the contrary, Christianity purports to fulfill Judaism and rightly interprets (some would say reinterprets) the Old Testament Scriptures in light of Christ's teachings. Biblical Christianity considers all other faiths as false in varying degrees and therefore the proper object of missions. In order to win the adherents of other religions to Christ, believers must understand the beliefs and faith practices of their religions. In his day, William Carey studied world religions, constructing charts showing the predominant faiths in the nations of the world in order to reach them.[5] Today's generation of missiologists should do no less.

TRADITIONAL RELIGION

Although the first religion began with the faith of Adam and Eve and their children worshipping the one true God, unfortunately, idolatry and paganism

---

[2] Michael Pocock, Gailyn Van Rheenen, and Douglas McConnell, *The Changing Face of World Missions: Engaging Contemporary Issues and Trends* (Grand Rapids: Baker Academic, 2005), 81.

[3] John 14:6.

[4] George W. Braswell Jr., *Islam: Its Prophet, Peoples, Politics and Power* (Nashville: B&H, 1996), 4.

[5] William Carey, "Conversion of the Heathens," in Winter and Hawthorne, *Perspectives on the World Christian Movement*, 315–16 (see chap. 1, n. 30).

quickly developed into the second one, traditional religion. Romans 1:21–23 says, "For though they knew God, they did not glorify him as God or show gratitude. Instead, their thinking became worthless, and their senseless hearts were darkened. Claiming to be wise, they became fools and exchanged the glory of the immortal God for images resembling mortal man, birds, four-footed animals, and reptiles."

The many synonyms of traditional religion include animism,[6] folk religion, popular religion, tribal religion, ancestor worship, indigenous religion, primitive religion, totemism, naturalism, dynamism, fetishism, and primal religion. Speaking of these traditions, Paul Hiebert states, "The failure to understand folk religions has been a major blind spot in missions."[7] David Hesselgrave claims a full 40 percent of the world holds to popular religion.[8] Indeed, this chapter demonstrates the ease with which traditional religion blends with other faiths.

Folk Islam, for instance, intermingles traditional cultural beliefs with orthodox Muslim doctrine. Many Americans practice a kind of "folk Christianity." A survey reported that 22 percent of American Christians believe in reincarnation.[9] Some rural churches in the South practice snake handling in their services.[10] Much of the New Age Movement blends naturistic beliefs and practices with elements of one or more of the major world religions. Most in this movement accept pantheism and reincarnation. John Newport writes:

> All New Age religion has been defined as a criticism of dogmatic Christianity as well as criticism of rational and scientific ideologies. . . . The solution, they say, is a "third option" which does not reject religion and spirituality or science and rationality, but combines

---

[6] John Mbiti, speaking of African religions and against using the term "Animism," says, "Animism is not an adequate description of these religions and it is better for that term to be abandoned once and for all. It needs to be emphasized, that African religions are historically older than both Christianity and Islam." John S. Mbiti, *African Religions and Philosophy*, 2nd ed. (Oxford: Heinemann International, 1989), 8.

[7] Paul G. Hiebert, R. Daniel Shaw, and Tite Tiénou, *Understanding Folk Religion: A Christian Response to Popular Beliefs and Practices* (Grand Rapids: Baker, 1999), 29, 74.

[8] David J. Hesselgrave, *Communicating Christ Cross-Culturally: An Introduction to Missionary Communication*, 2nd ed. (Grand Rapids: Zondervan, 1991), 223.

[9] William Wan, "Americans Mix, Match Religion," *Kansas City Star*, December 10, 2009.

[10] Bob Smietana, "Snake Handler Sheds the Law: Grand Jury Declines to Indict Tennessee Pastor on Snake Handling Charges," *Kansas City Star*, January 11, 2014.

them. . . . Its worldview is one of occult mysticism spelled out in secular terms—an ancient wisdom updated and expressed with modern vocabulary. . . . The movement places more importance on experience than it does on beliefs. Beliefs last only as long as they are functional and helpful.[11]

African Traditional Religion (ATR) constitutes a subset of Traditional Religion (TR). Byang Kato says African Traditional Religion represents the most comprehensive title for the religions of Africa.[12] Ambrose Moyo summarizes the beliefs of traditional religions the world over, writing, "The following religious phenomena seem to be basic and common to most of them: (a) belief in a supreme being, (b) belief in spirits/divinities, (c) belief in life after death, (d) religious personnel and sacred places, and (e) witchcraft and magic practices."[13]

I served as a missionary to Tanzania and worked with the Sukuma tribe, the largest in the nation. Sukuma ATR consists of a loose set of private practices that include magic, divination, witchcraft, ancestor veneration, and reverence for deities and subdeities. Like most ATR ethnicities, the Sukuma perform rituals to contact the supernatural and to solve everyday problems.[14]

Formal religions such as Christianity, Islam, and Buddhism focus on eternal destiny questions and possess complicated theologies, treatises, and elaborate hierarchies.[15] Traditional Religion, on the other hand, concentrates on the here and now, often posing causation questions that begin with the interrogative, "Why?" These inquiries often seek answers to questions about infertility, disease, misfortune, and premature death. TR regards calamities such as accidents, disability, or natural disasters as possessing supernatural causes. Nothing "just happens" in the ATR world. In fact, even good fortune in the form of wealth, power, or tranquility must be obtained by sacrifice or divination. As Gailyn Van Rheenen says, "Animists perceive the world as so pervaded

---

[11] John P. Newport, *The New Age Movement and the Biblical Worldview: Conflict and Dialogue* (Grand Rapids: Eerdmans, 1998), 2–4.

[12] Byang Kato, *Theological Pitfalls in Africa* (Kisumu, Kenya: Evangel, 1975), 24.

[13] Ambrose Moyo, in *Understanding Contemporary Africa*, 3rd ed., ed. April A. Gordon and Donald L. Gordon (Boulder, CO: Lynn Reiner, 2001), 301.

[14] Frans Wijsen and Ralph Tanner, *"I Am Just a Sukuma": Globalization and Identity Construction in Northwest Tanzania*, Church and Theology in Context (Amsterdam: Brill Rodopi, 2002), 56.

[15] Hiebert, Shaw, and Tiénou, *Understanding Folk Religion*, 73.

by spirits and forces that human beings have little free will. Fears pervade life where freedom in Christ should reign."[16]

One of the largest traditional religion communities resides, not in Africa, but in China. Chinese Traditional Religion adherents venerate ancestors, practice divination, and consult spirit mediums. Chinese popular religion holds that almost all of the gods, both good and bad, are the deified spirits of previously alive humans.[17] Chinese Traditional Religion seamlessly mixes elements of Confucianism, Taoism, and Buddhism to such an extent it is difficult to discern where one ends and the other begins. The Chinese folk practice of feng shui (wind and water) illustrates the point. Many buildings in China are constructed to supposedly maximize the assistance of cosmic forces by positioning them according to the landscape and horizon.[18]

Since TR adherents accept the spiritual view of life, this religion has usually been receptive to the gospel message. In Acts 13, although opposed by a Jewish false prophet and magician, Barnabas and Paul successfully won the proconsul of Cyprus. After healing a lame man in Lystra in Acts 14, the crowd identified Barnabas with Zeus and Paul as Hermes, even attempting to offer sacrifices to them. After Paul and his companions successfully won a number of converts in Ephesus, the silversmith Demetrius, who made idols for worship of the goddess Artemis, organized opposition to the apostles. He said to his compatriots, "You see and hear that not only in Ephesus, but in almost all of Asia, this man Paul has persuaded and misled a considerable number of people by saying by saying that gods made by hand are not gods."[19]

Paul Hiebert notes that Western society has mostly overlooked "the middle level of the supernatural."[20] This he called the Flaw of the Excluded Middle. Folk religions, especially traditional religion, worry about middle-level concerns like safety, luck, chance, and forces that impact these issues. Hiebert says Western society is flawed in ignoring the apprehensions that folk religions

---

[16] Gailyn Van Rheenen, *Communicating Christ in Animistic Contexts* (Pasadena: William Carey Library, 1991), 98.

[17] Daniel L. Overmyer, *Religions of China: The World as a Living System* (Long Grove, IL: Waveland Press, 1998), 51–52.

[18] Overmyer, 12.

[19] Acts 19:26.

[20] Paul G. Hiebert, quoted in Gailyn Van Rheenen, *Missions: Biblical Foundations and Contemporary Strategies*, 2nd ed. (Grand Rapids: Zondervan, 2014), 203.

have about the middle level between the natural and the supernatural. Hiebert proposes a third way between the two that he calls *Critical Realism*.[21] He says Critical Realism "affirms the presence of objective truth but recognizes this is subjectively apprehended."[22] This assists the church in addressing the apprehensions of the supernatural and natural worlds.

WESTERN RELIGIONS

Judaism

At less than .5 percent of humanity's population, Judaism stands as the smallest of major world religions.[23] Despite its small size, Judaism has greatly influenced the world, especially Christianity and Islam. Both Christians and Muslims claim Abraham as part of their faith's lineage. Islam and Christianity accept Judaism's prophets as their own. Jesus, Paul, the twelve apostles, and most of the early followers of Christ were Jews. Christianity includes most of the Hebrew Scriptures as part of the Christian canon. Although evangelical Christianity accepts the Old Testament as truth without mixture of error, it reinterprets the Jewish writings in ways that are unacceptable in any of the branches of Judaism. Irving Hexham states some of the problems in defining Judaism:

> Finally, it needs to be noted that talking about Judaism is problematic because many Jews dispute the term almost as much as they dispute what it means to be Jewish. The problem here is that Jews belong to an identifiable ethnic group which is neither a religion nor a race. Hence, it is possible to have nonreligious Jews who practice Jewish rituals as a means of affirming their identity. Historically, Jews originated with the family of Abraham, but over time incorporated

---

[21] Pocock, Van Rheenen, and McConnell, *Changing Face of World Missions*, 124.

[22] Paul Hiebert, quoted in Pocock, Van Rheenen, and McConnell, 124.

[23] John L. Esposito, Darrell J. Fasching, and Todd Lewis, *World Religions Today*, 3rd ed. (Oxford: Oxford University Press, 2009), 75.

people from many other families—what we now call nations and races—making any definition of Jewishness exceptionally difficult.[24]

Jewish History. There are various ways to divide Jewish chronology. Winfried Corduan segments their history into three parts: (1) the First Jewish Commonwealth, (2) the Second Jewish Commonwealth, and (3) a third commonwealth: the State of Israel.[25]

The First Jewish Commonwealth. Christians and Muslims usually view the beginning of Judaism in the person of Abraham. Jews, on the other hand, see the inauguration of the Torah in Exodus 19 as the central event in their history. Hexham says, "The divine revelation that took place at Sinai plays as a role in Judaism similar to the role of the crucifixion in Christianity."[26] Evangelical Christians are somewhat familiar with the extensive Jewish history recorded in the Hebrew Old Testament.

Israel's history begins with the story of the patriarchs, which includes their captivity in Egypt. After Moses leads the children of Israel out of Egypt, the First Jewish Commonwealth begins with Moses's giving of the law and extends until the end of the Babylonian captivity. These historical events include Joshua's conquest of the land of Canaan; the period of the judges; the United Kingdom period under Saul, David, and Solomon; followed by the Divided Kingdoms of Israel and Judah. When the northern tribes of Israel were conquered by the Assyrians in 722 BC, most of their inhabitants disappeared forever within the empire of the victor. The Southern Kingdom, composed of members of the tribe of Judah,[27] continued in the land until Judah fell to the Babylonians in 587 BC.

The Second Jewish Commonwealth. After seventy years of captivity in Babylon, the Jews, as they were now called, returned to their tribal land. Cyrus of Persia, the conqueror of the Babylonians, allowed Ezra and Nehemiah to

---

[24] Irving Hexham, *Understanding World Religions: An Interdisciplinary Approach* (Grand Rapids: Zondervan, 2011), 253.

[25] See Winfried Corduan, *Neighboring Faiths: A Christian Introduction to World Religions*, 2nd ed. (Downers Grove, IL: InterVarsity Press, 2012), 63–64, 67, 86.

[26] Corduan, 255.

[27] The tribe of Benjamin resided near Judah and was considered part of the Southern Kingdom. The priestly tribe, the Levites, lived interspersed within both the Northern and Southern kingdoms.

rebuild Israel and their temple. Although under the suzerainty of the Persians and later Alexander the Great and his successors, the Jewish state enjoyed some freedom and autonomy. When Antiochus IV[28] attempted to culturally absorb the Jews and sacrificed a pig on the temple altar, the Maccabees successfully rebelled, installing the Hasmonean priestly dynasty on the kingdom's throne. Subsequently, during the intertestamental period, the Romans removed the Maccabees from power and installed a series of puppet rulers over the kingdom of Israel—one of these was Herod the Great of the New Testament. The troublesome Jewish kingdom caused the Romans consternation for hundreds of years, finally culminating with the destruction of Jerusalem and the temple in AD 70.[29]

During the Second Commonwealth, a number of important groups emerged. The Sadducees, Herodians, Essenes, Zealots, and Pharisees were all prominent during New Testament times. All but the Essenes, a desert-dwelling monastic group, are mentioned in the Bible. The Herodians appear in the New Testament[30] but it is unclear what they believed. Some suppose they favored the restoration of the Herodian dynasty, while others suggest they are another name for the Essenes.[31] The Sadducees, the party of the priests, and the Zealots, a society of revolutionaries, either disappeared or were disbanded when Rome ended the Second Commonwealth in AD 70. This left the Pharisees as the sole repository for Jewish life. During the first century, the Pharisees had become the teachers or rabbis of Israel. Thus, Rabbinic Judaism became the standard for the Jewish faith from the beginning of the Diaspora[32] until the present day.[33] Some of the historical events that transpired during the Diaspora will be covered in a subsequent section.

The Third Jewish Commonwealth: The State of Israel. On May 14, 1948, the state of Israel was established and joined the United Nations soon afterwards.

---

[28] Also called Epiphanes.

[29] Michael Brenner, *A Short History of the Jews* (Princeton: Princeton University Press, 2010), 49–53.

[30] Matt 22:16; Mark 3:6, 12:13; see also Mark 8:15; Luke 13:31–32; and Acts 4:27.

[31] Corduan, *Neighboring Faiths*, 69.

[32] The Diaspora, or dispersion, originally spoke of Jews outside of Palestine living in the Roman Empire. When their homeland was conquered and destroyed in AD 70 by the Roman legions, most Jews fit this category.

[33] Corduan, *Neighboring Faiths*, 68–69.

For the first time in almost 2,000 years, the Jewish people inhabited a home-land all their own. "Zionism," a term coined in 1893, embodies the aspiration of the Jewish people to return to their ancestral home. Although connected to the biblical narrative, Zionism stands apart from religious Judaism. Initially opposing the idea, the horrors Jews experienced in the Holocaust[34] during World War II at the hands of Nazi Germany convinced many Orthodox, Reformed, and Socialist Jews that a Jewish homeland was the only solution to 2,000 years of religious persecution at the hands of Gentile nations.[35] Once their country was established, the nation of Israel fought wars in 1948, 1967, and 1973 to keep their freedom. Today Israel consists of an uneasy alliance of competing ideologies and parties committed to democracy and independence.

Jewish Beliefs and Practices. What is a Jew? Addressing this key question, Irving Hexham writes, "According to Orthodoxy, the only true Jew is someone born of a Jewish mother. Some groups argue that because of this it is impossible to convert to Judaism. Most, however, make some allowance for conversion."[36] Rabbi Morris Kertzer says, "A Jew is therefore a member of a people, by birth or by conversion, who chooses to share a common cultural heritage, a religious perspective, and a spiritual horizon derived uniquely from Jewish experience and Jewish wisdom."[37]

With the destruction of their temple and capital in AD 70 and the loss of their homeland in AD 136,[38] the Jews of the Diaspora developed beliefs and practices to stabilize their society after losing their nation's real estate. The Jewish synagogue filled this vacuum and became the center of Jewish life with the rabbi as its de facto leader. This meant that wherever Jews migrated or fled, they were able to maintain their identity.

---

[34] *Holocaust* means "burnt offering" in Hebrew and represents for Jews the six million Jews exterminated by Adolf Hitler's Germany during World War II—many of them by the ovens and gas chambers of the Nazi Party.

[35] Esposito, Fasching, and Lewis, *World Religions Today*, 125–29.

[36] Hexham, *Understanding World Religions*, 308.

[37] Morris N. Kertzer, *What is a Jew? A Guide to the Beliefs, Traditions, and Practices of Judaism That Answers Questions for Both Jew and Non-Jew*, rev. Lawrence A. Hoffman (New York: Touchstone / Simon & Schuster, 1996), 8.

[38] A Zealot renewal attempted a second Jewish rebellion from AD 132 to 136. Thought by some to be the Messiah, Bar Kochba and his followers were soundly defeated by the Romans. This time the Jews who remained in Palestine for the most part had to leave. See Corduan, *Neighboring Faiths*, 70–71.

Rabbinic Judaism, which began during the first century AD, soon divided into two doctrinal schools, Hillel and Shammai. Rabbi Hillel represented the more lenient perspective and Rabbi Shammai the stricter stand. Over the years the former view prevailed and the Hillel interpretation became the standard. The Jewish Bible or Tanak,[39] represents an acronym for the Torah, or teachings; the Nevi'im, or prophets; and Ketuvim, or writings.[40]

Twenty years after the Romans destroyed Jerusalem in AD 70, rabbinic leaders met in Tiberius and pondered what constituted holy writing in Judaism. The books Christians accept as the Old Testament resulted from this deliberation. By AD 200 another group of Jewish scholars collected all the interpretations and applications in the Tanak. This was called the Mishnah. As the Jews dispersed across the world, more commentaries emerged, so that by the sixth century another body of more recent interpretations of the Scripture was compiled, called the Gemara. The Mishnah and the Gemara were combined into one body of sacred Jewish writings known as the Talmud.[41] Esposito, Fashching, and Lewis, writing about the Talmud, say:

> The genius of the Talmud is in preserving the oral character of the material in written form. To appreciate the uniqueness of the Talmud one really has to look at it and see how its pages are constructed. A typical page is made up of diverse and distinct parts, coexisting on the same piece of paper. These parts express the voices of the rabbis throughout the ages, and teachings about the same subject juxtaposed on the same page.[42]

Even though the various divisions and sects of Judaism hold different beliefs and follow diverse practices, all encourage reading the Tanak and studying the Talmud. This even includes branches of Judaism that believe the former to be composed of myths and the latter to be old-fashioned. These ancient writings, however, provide a sustained rallying point for all Jews to celebrate their identity.

---

[39] Since Hebrew, like Arabic, has no vowels in the original script, vowels have to be added mentally when reading or reciting the text. Therefore "TNK," the first letters of Torah, Nevi'im, and Ketuvim, become TaNaK, or Tanak when transliterated as an acrostic into English.

[40] Esposito, Fashching, and Lewis, *World Religions Today*, 97.

[41] Corduan, *Neighboring Faiths*, 71–72.

[42] Esposito, Fashching, and Lewis, *World Religions Today*, 99.

These writings proclaim the uniqueness of the Jewish God and his chosen people. Judaism believes that God is holy and he entered into a covenant with the Jewish people. An important part of this covenant lies in keeping God's laws, especially honoring the Sabbath. Jews believe that no living thing approximates the divine state. Judaism designates idolatry as one of mankind's most serious sins. Judaism places a high value on human dignity, and as a result cremations and autopsies are forbidden. Paradoxically, many Jews contend that their faith does not believe in an afterlife.[43]

Jewish Sects. As with any religion, differences and controversies emerged in interpreting the interpretations. These resulted in sects, schisms, and divisions within Judaism.

Kabbalah Judaism. Inheriting a tradition of mystical Judaism present in the days of Jesus, Kabbalah Judaism emerged in the seventh century and flourished through the Middle Ages. Adherents see spiritual significance in Ezekiel's chariot, sometimes experiencing "ecstasy, visions, and out-of-the-body experiences."[44] Kabbalah theory derives inspiration from the great Jewish philosopher Moses Maimonides (1135–1204), who argued for an inner spiritual faith accessible through Aristotelian logic.

During the sixteenth century in the city of Safed, Israel, Isaac Luria founded the new mystical school of Lurianic Kabbalah. Its emphasis on Messianism soon produced a colorful figure, Shabbetai Zevi (1626–1676), who proclaimed himself the Messiah. Followers were disappointed, however, when under threat of death by the Ottoman Sultan, Shabbetai converted to Islam. Despite this defection, many of Shabbetai's Kabbalah supporters remained faithful, believing their "Messiah" had entered the realm of evil to retrieve "divine sparks" and obtain redemption for the world. Kabbalists use mystic cosmic theory to explain the exile and Diaspora of the Jews. They argue that during creation a cosmic accident poured some of God's energy into a chasm in the universe. They believe good will not triumph finally until God's energy sparks are returned from the abyss.[45]

---

[43] Hexham, *Understanding World Religions*, 299–302.
[44] Hexham, 295.
[45] Brenner, *Short History of the Jews*, 144–48.

Kabbalah followers develop their spirituality by employing music and meditation to enter a trance.[46] As will be observed in the next section, it has more in common with Islamic Sufism than Judaism. For instance, a modern adherent says:

> The nature of *Kabbalah*, which after all means "receiving," is a cultivation of a deeper awareness of a world beyond ourselves.... We must learn to recognize our interconnectedness—our oneness—with the universe.... Recognize the concept of the divine sparks, with respect to our own souls. Sparks from the primordial explosion have indeed landed in us, and our task is to find an internal harmony with those pieces of the divine presence.[47]

Hasidic Judaism. Hasidic Judaism owes its spiritual lineage to its kabbalist forebears. Founded by Israel ben Eliezer in the eighteenth century, Hasidism sought to reform the faith of Abraham. Eliezer taught that God is found in singing, dancing, and expressions of joy, not in studying the law. Some Hasidic rabbis could heal the sick and foretell the future. Furthermore, Eliezer advocated wearing modern clothing and allowed adherents to adapt to the local culture where they lived. Hasidic Jews today retain the black coat and hat of a Polish gentleman of the 1700s as well as the European customs of the day.[48] Although Hasidic Judaism is considered a part of orthodoxy today, it was viciously attacked in the 1770s for its heretical emphasis on experientialism.[49]

Orthodox Judaism. Before the development of higher criticism religious thought in the nineteenth century, all Jews were of the Orthodox persuasion. Reform Judaism, beginning in Germany, decided to update Judaism to reflect a more modern outlook. Orthodox Jews resisted this challenge and maintain their ancient ways. Of course, there are different kinds of Orthodox Jews. The most conservative of them may not even recognize the state of Israel because it was established by man. Other Orthodox Jews have made concessions to the modern world. Only about 5 percent of America's six million Jews are

---

[46] Kertzer, *What Is a Jew?*, 59.

[47] Kenneth Hanson, *Kabbalah: The Untold Story of the Mystic Tradition* (San Francisco: Council Oak Books, 2004), 247, 249–50.

[48] Corduan, *Neighboring Faiths*, 76–77.

[49] Joseph Dan, *The Teachings of Hasidism* (West Orange, NJ: Behrman House, 1983), 14.

Orthodox.[50] For Orthodoxy, God has spoken through his law with finality and Judaism should not change with the times.

Reform Judaism. Reform Judaism allows adherents to maintain their faith, while choosing what parts of Judaism are appropriate for the modern world. Dietary laws are optional and women may serve as rabbis. Innovations in the synagogue include sermons, choirs, modern decorations, and using local languages. Reform Judaism sees the Torah as a moral guide but also believes other truths are important. About half of American Jews follow this tradition.

Conservative Judaism. Conservative Judaism stands between the Orthodox and Reform positions. Uncomfortable with the total accommodation the latter made with modernity, Conservative Jews follow the Jewish law. Esposito, Fasching, and Lewis comment, "Conservative Judaism arose among Jews who were deeply committed to the Orthodox way of life, yet sympathetic to the 'modern' intellectual worldview of Reform Judaism. The message of Conservative Judaism, 'Think whatever you like but do what the Law requires.'"[51] Just over a majority of American Jews follow this path.[52]

Reconstructionist and Secular Judaism. During the first half of the twentieth century, Rabbi Mordecai Kaplan taught that Judaism was a civilization that was progressing through the ages. Originally a follower of Conservative Judaism, he believed Judaism had to be reconstituted for American society. Kaplan desired secular Judaism to have a place at the table in the discussion of the essence of Judaism. Although adherents of Reconstructionist Judaism are less than 2 percent, their ideas give voice to the many more secular Jews who do not fit into any category.

Islam

Muslims number over 1.6 billion persons globally, making Islam the earth's second largest religion.[53] "Islam" means "submission" and signifies complete

---

[50] Kertzer, *What is a Jew?*, 9–10.
[51] Esposito, Fasching, and Lewis, *World Religions Today*, 120.
[52] Esposito, Fasching, and Lewis, 120
[53] "The Future of World Religions: Population Growth Projections, 2010–2050: Why Muslims Are Rising Fastest and the Unaffiliated Are Shrinking as a Share of the World's

surrender to the will of God.[54] Muslims believe every human being becomes a Muslim at birth,[55] but the parents of non-Muslims lead their offspring into becoming Christians, Jews, or polytheists.[56] *Understanding Islam,* a text composed by the Saudi Arabian government for foreigners, comments on the Five Pillars of Islam. These include (1) repeating the ritual affirmation of faith, (2) praying five times a day toward Mecca, (3) offering 2.5 percent of one's income, (4) fasting during the month of Ramadan, and (5) the pilgrimage to Mecca once during one's lifetime.[57]

Besides the Five Pillars of Islam, there are also five to six beliefs or principles, depending on the source of the list. George Braswell mentions: (1) the nature and characteristics of the one God to whom all submit; (2) the role of God's messengers, the angels; (3) the status of God's prophets; (4) the importance of the sacred writings (the Qur'an, the Gospels, the Psalms, Torah, and the Hadith); (5) belief in the resurrection, judgment, heaven, and hell.[58] Hammudah Abdalati adds several other beliefs, including predestination and the assertion that every Muslim enters this world free of original sin.[59]

Orphaned at age six, Muhammad (AD 570–632) lived first with his grandfather and then with his uncle Abu Talib.[60] Muhammad's reputation as

---

Population," Pew Research Center, April 2, 2015, https://www.pewforum.org/2015/04/02/religious-projections-2010-2050/.

[54] Islamic Affairs Department, *Understanding Islam and the Muslims* (Washington, DC: Embassy of Saudi Arabia, 1989), 5–7.

[55] Hammudah Abdalati, *Islam in Focus,* 2nd ed. (Indianapolis: American Trust Publications, 1993), 16.

[56] Georges Houssney, *Engaging Islam* (Boulder, CO: Treeline Publications, 2010), 106.

[57] They are the framework of the Muslim life: faith, prayer, benevolence, self-purification, and the pilgrimage to Makkah. **1. FAITH.** There is no god worthy of worship except God and Muhammad is his messenger. This declaration of faith is called the *Shahada.* **2. PRAYER.** *Salat* is the name for the obligatory prayers which are performed five times a day, and are a direct link between the worshipper and God. **3. THE "*ZAKAT.*"** The word *zakat* means both "purification" and "growth." Each Muslim calculates his or her own *zakat* [2.5 percent offering] individually. **4. THE FAST.** Every year in the month of Ramadan, all Muslims fast from first light until sundown, abstaining from food, drink, and sexual relations. **5. PILGRIMAGE** (*Hajj*). The annual pilgrimage to *Makkah*—the *Hajj*—is an obligation only for those who are physically and financially able to perform it. The rites of the *Hajj,* which are of Abrahamic origin, include circling the *Ka'ba* seven times. Islamic Affairs Department, *Understanding Islam,* 13, 16–17, 20.

[58] Braswell, *Islam,* 43.

[59] Abdalati, *Islam in Focus,* 12, 15.

[60] Seyyed Hossein Nasr, *Islam: Religion, History, and Civilization* (New York: Harper Collins, 2003), 48.

Al-Amin (الأمين, "the honest one") brought him to the attention of Khadija, a wealthy widow who owned trading caravans. Although he was fifteen years her junior, they were married. Khadija bore Muhammad six children and became his first convert to Islam.[61] When Muhammad attained the age of forty (AD 610) he experienced visions during visits to the cave of Hira. These revelations, purportedly from the angel Gabriel, occurred over a twenty-year period and resulted in the Qur'an.[62] Many in the city of Mecca opposed his monotheistic preaching against idolatry. This caused the small group of Muslims to flee to the city of Medina. This *Hijra* (هِجْرَة, "departure") in 622 from Mecca to Medina marks the first year on the Muslim lunar calendar. Muhammad ruled the city Medina, the first Muslim community, establishing Qur'anic rules for an ideal society.[63] The Muslims seized Mecca without a fight shortly before his death. Upon the Prophet's passing in 632, the first four "Rightly Guided" Caliphs of united Islam (AD 632–661), Abu Bakr, Umar, Uthman, and Ali, spread Islam from Spain as far as Persia.[64]

Khalid Duran counts seventy-three different sects among Muslims.[65] Marshall, Green, and Gilbert say, "For simplicity's sake, however, Islam can be divided into *three fundamental groups, the third generally being part of either of the first two*."[66] These three sects include the Sunni, the Shi'a, and the Sufi.

Representing orthodoxy in Islam, George Braswell estimates that Sunnis compose 90 percent of all Muslims,[67] while other writers number them from 80 to 85 percent of the total.[68] In the ninth century, Muslim theologian Shafi'i revised Islamic law, developing what became known as the Sharia, [شريعة].[69]

---

[61] Akbar S. Ahmed, *Islam Today: A Short Introduction to the Muslim World* (London: I. B. Tauris, 1999), 15–16.

[62] Abdalati, *Islam in Focus*, 18.

[63] Braswell, *Islam*, 15.

[64] Ahmed, *Islam Today*, 55.

[65] Paul Marshall, Roberta Green, and Lela Gilbert, *Islam at the Crossroads: Understanding Its Beliefs, History, and Conflicts* (Grand Rapids: Baker, 2002), 27.

[66] Marshall, Green, and Gilbert, 27. Emphasis added.

[67] Braswell, *Islam*, 90.

[68] John Esposito and Dalia Mogahed, *Who Speaks for Islam? What a Billion Muslims Really Think* (New York: Oxford University Press, 2007), 2; Marshall, Green, and Gilbert, *Islam at the Crossroads*, 27. Patrick Sookhdeo has the lowest figure, placing Sunnis at about 80 percent of Muslims. Patrick Sookhdeo, *Global Jihad* (McLean, VA: Isaac Publishing, 2007), 216.

[69] Malise Ruthven, *Islam in the World*, 3rd ed. (New York: Oxford University Press, 2006), 133.

Shafi'i claimed "it was not the Qur'an alone, but the Qur'an plus the Prophet's Sunna [سُنَّة], as recorded in the hadiths [حديث], that must guide the Muslims."[70] This Islamic hermeneutic became known as Sunni [سُنِّي] Islam.

Legal schools of thought abound within Sunni Islam, including the *Ashari*, *Maturidi*, and *Hanbali*.[71] A puritanical Sunni subsect founded in Arabia in the eighteenth century, however, emerged as the pure strand of Islam.[72] *Wahhabism*, desiring a strict interpretation of the Qur'an, hadith, and enforcement of Sharia, has become the face of orthodox Islam.[73] The Saudi government, though, has moderated Wahhabism's militaristic jihad[74] in recent years.[75] Esposito and Mogahed place the percentage of "politically radicalized" Muslims at about 7 percent.[76]

Shi'a[77] Muslims compose a significant minority within Islam, numbering about 10 to 20 percent of the total. After Muhammad died in 632 a sequence of four *caliphs*[78] were chosen from the *Quraysh* tribe in Arabia to lead the movement during its early days.[79] The divide between Shi'as and Sunnis initially occurred over the issue of succession to the Prophet Muhammad[80] and who would succeed Ali, the fourth caliph.[81] Ali desired his sons Hassan and Hussein to follow him, but the majority demanded the selection to be based on merit, not blood lineage. As Muhammad's cousin and father of his grandchildren, Ali was both the fourth caliph of the Sunnis and the first imam of the Shi'ites and is claimed by both groups.[82] Shi'ites believe Ali inherited the

---

[70] Ruthven, 134.

[71] Bill Musk, *Kissing Cousins? Christians and Muslims Face to Face* (Oxford: Monarch Books, 2005), 23.

[72] Ruthven, *Islam in the World*, 368–69.

[73] Marshall, Green, and Gilbert, *Islam at the Crossroads*, 97.

[74] *Jihad* is an Arabic word meaning "struggle" or "strive." John J. Donohue and John Esposito, eds., *Islam in Transition* (New York: Oxford University Press, 2007), 393. In Islam this can involve one's personal struggle for holiness against sin, known as greater jihad, or it references a "holy war" on God's behalf against the enemies of the faith, known as lesser jihad. Some refer to jihad as the sixth pillar of Islam. Braswell, *Islam*, 71.

[75] Braswell, 99.

[76] Esposito and Mogahed, *Who Speaks for Islam?*, 70.

[77] The meaning of *Shi'ite* is "partisan to Ali." Braswell, *Islam*, 90.

[78] The word *Caliph* means the deputy of the Messenger of God. Braswell, 23.

[79] Braswell, 90.

[80] Sookhdeo, *Global Jihad*, 216.

[81] Marshall, Green, and Gilbert, *Islam at the Crossroads*, 276.

[82] Marshall, Green, and Gilbert, 91.

Prophet's infallibility in leadership and Qur'anic interpretation, which would then pass to his descendants in the form of a hereditary imamate.[83] The martyrdoms of Ali (661), and his sons, Hassan (680) and Hussein (680), by Kharijite[84] and Sunni adherents caused a schism in Islam that continues to this day.[85]

Like their Sunni counterparts, Shi'a Islam also has subgroups. Ninety percent of Shi'ites hold that a series of twelve imams descended from Ali. In 878, the twelfth imam following Ali, Muhammad al-Mumtazzar,[86] was born and proclaimed to be the expected Mahdi.[87] When he disappeared at age nine, Twelvers developed the "hidden imam" doctrine that believes Muhammad al-Mumtazzar is in hiding and will return later. Today, Twelvers follow a series of ayatollahs, or living imams, who guide Shi'a Islam while the twelfth imam tarries in his hiding place.[88]

The remaining 10 percent of Shi'ites are divided between the Seveners and the Zaidis. Dominating in Yemen and the Caspian Sea, Zaidis hold any descendant of Ali can become the imam, not just those from the lineage of Ali and Fatima, Muhammad's daughter.[89] Known also as Isma'ilis, the Seveners acknowledge only seven of the twelve imams venerated by the Twelvers. Led by the Aga Khan, the Isma'ilis compose only 1 percent of all Muslims but have great influence due to their leader, the Aga Khan,[90] and the wealth of their

---

[83] Marshall, Green, and Gilbert, 90–91.

[84] The *Kharijites* were another sect that repudiated both Ali and his Sunni successor, Mu'awiyya. Upon Ali's assassination by a Kharijite, Sunnis installed Mu'awiyya as the fifth caliph, rejecting Ali's sons (and Muhammad's grandsons), Hassan and Hussein. Sookhdeo, *Global Jihad*, 216. Kharijites (literally, "seceders") continue in small communities in North Africa, persisting in their rejection of Sunni and Shi'a Islam. Braswell, *Islam*, 95–96.

[85] Sookhdeo, *Global Jihad*, 131–32.

[86] *Al-Mumtazar* means "the best" or "the excellent" in Arabic.

[87] Muslims believe the Mahdi will be a messiah-like figure who returns at a time of tumult and corruption to bring tranquility and justice to the world. Ruthven, *Islam in the World*, 9. Sunnis, Shi'ites, and Sufis all embrace the doctrine of a coming Mahdi and this messianic concept plays a significant role in popular Islam. Sookhdeo, *Global Jihad*, 129. Shi'ites believe he will return to Kufa, Iraq, while Sunnis hold the Mahdi will move the Ka'ba from Mecca to Jerusalem and rule from there. There are other differences between the Sunni and Shi'a versions of the Mahdi. Sookhdeo, *Global Jihad*, 138–39.

[88] Braswell, *Islam*, 95.

[89] Ahmed, *Islam Today*, 48.

[90] Ahmed, 48.

members.[91] They are widely scattered throughout the Muslim world, living in Pakistan, India, Syria, China, and East Africa.[92]

Shi'as and Sunnis are divided by more than just their differences over succession to the Prophet. Malise Ruthven says Shi'a Islam has set up a quasi-sacerdotal[93] role for the leader by which the sheikh becomes something like a priest in Roman Catholicism.[94] Speaking of the difference between Sunnis and Shi'as, Seyyed Nasr writes:

> The problem was, however, more profound than one of personalities. It also concerned the **function** of the person who was to succeed the Prophet. The Sunnis believed that the function of such a person should be to protect the Divine Law, act as judge, and rule over the community, preserving public order and the borders of the Islamic world. The *Shi'ites* believed that such a person should also be able to **interpret the Qur'an** and the Law and in fact **possess inward knowledge**. . . . Although such a person did not share in the Prophet's prophetic function (*nubuwwah*), he did receive the **inner spiritual power** of the Prophet (*walayah/wilayah*).[95]

This inner power manifests itself through the doctrine of "divine light" (*nur*). Shi'ites believe it passes from imam to imam, rendering each sinless and infallible.[96] They also hold that Muhammad was sinless and this state was passed down through Ali and today's imams.[97] Furthermore, in Shi'a Islam, shrines to departed holy men have been erected with pilgrimages similar to the hajj to Mecca, complete with mourning and self-flagellation.[98]

Sufism is the third major sect of the Muslim faith and represents a template or overlay on Islam, as well as a subsection of the faith. Many orthodox Muslims see Sufi practices as superstitions that pervert the true religion.[99]

---

[91] Ruthven, *Islam in the World*, 209.

[92] Nasr, *Islam*, 13.

[93] "Excessive reliance on a priesthood." *Webster's New World Dictionary of the American Language*, 2nd college ed. (1970), s.v. "sacerdotal."

[94] Ruthven, *Islam in the World*, 196.

[95] Nasr, *Islam*, 11–12. Bold added.

[96] Braswell, *Islam*, 92.

[97] Vali Nasr, *The Shia Revival: How Conflicts within Islam Will Shape the Future* (London: W. W. Norton, 2006), 39.

[98] Sookhdeo, *Global Jihad*, 271.

[99] Carl W. Ernst, *The Shambhala Guide to Sufism* (Boston: Shambhala, 1997), xvii.

Despite this, Carl Ernst estimates about half of all Muslims today practice a form of Sufism.[100] Most identify by their order such as *Qadiriyyas* or *Jilanadias* rather than by the name Sufi.[101] Sufis are often called the mystics of Islam and come from both the Sunni and Shiʻa worlds.[102] In other words, a Sunni or Shiʻa Muslim is often a Sunni Sufi or a Shiʻa Sufi. All Sufis belong to either the Sunni or Shiʻa sects. In other words, there are no Sufi Sufis, as all Sufis are either Sunnis or Shiʻites.

Sufis, the charismatics of Islam, brought mysticism, feelings, and emotions to the faith.[103] As charismatic Christians populate all denominations, so Sufism permeates the ranks of Shiʻites and Sunnis. There are two principle kinds of Sufis: (1) God-intoxicated, and (2) contemplative.[104] The former often exhibit the ecstatic behavior of the whirling dervishes, while the latter emphasize a quiet devotional life. Early Sufis such as al-Muhasibi (781–837) and his pupil and contemporary, Junayd, combined asceticism, mysticism, and Sharia observance.[105] Sufis hold God's path follows feeling, experience, and introspection rather than doctrine.[106]

Abu Hamid al-Ghazali (1058–1111) brought Sufism more into mainstream Islam. Attempting to reconcile mysticism with orthodox Islam,[107] al-Ghazali taught the necessity of both ritual observances and feeling,[108] believing religious certainty depends on religious experience.[109] Al-Ghazali is called the *mujaddid*, or renewer, of Islam[110] and "the greatest Muslim after

---

[100] Ernst, xiii.

[101] *Sufi*, a German word, is a term of recent vintage coined in 1821. Idries Shah, *The Way of the Sufi* (London: Penguin, 1968), 13. Ruthven says the word comes from *suf* or "wool," because of the woolen clothes of Muhammad's disciples. Ruthven, *Islam in the World*, 221–22. Ernst suggests the term came from the Arabic *suffa* ("bench" or "sofa") because the poor followers of Muhammad slept on a bench. Ernst, *Shambala Guide to Sufism*, 22.

[102] Marshall, Green, and Gilbert, *Islam at the Crossroads*, 28; Braswell, *Islam*, 97; Sookhdeo, *Global Jihad*, 45.

[103] Braswell, *Islam*, 97.

[104] William C. Chittick, *Sufism: A Short Introduction* (Oxford: Oneworld, 2000, repr., 2005), 29. Citations refer to the 2005 edition.

[105] Ruthven, *Islam in the World*, 227.

[106] Braswell, *Islam*, 97.

[107] Braswell, 98.

[108] Ruthven, *Islam in the World*, 233.

[109] Braswell, *Islam*, 98.

[110] Esposito, Fasching, and Lewis, eds., *World Religions Today*, 252.

Muhammad."[111] Sufism became less and less orthodox,[112] and constitutes one of the major streams of folk Islam.[113]

There are three major themes in ancient Islamic teaching: (1) submission, (*Islam*, السلم), (2) faith (*Iman*, إيمَان), and (3) doing the beautiful (*Ibsan*, ابصان).[114] Sufism views the latter as its "special domain."[115] The essence of Sufi worship is *al-dhikr* (remembrance).[116] In the al-dhikr (لَذِكّر) ritual, the Sufi repeats the ninety-nine names of God, producing a spiritual state.[117] The recitation of the ninety-nine names of God in this fashion is compulsory.[118] Although Sufism began in asceticism, it developed a strong emphasis on devotion and love.[119]

Al-Sanusi compiled a list of the forty traditional Sufi orders[120] that are still prominent all over the world.[121] New Sufi brotherhoods, however, can be founded as individuals receive new commissions from the Prophet.[122] The local Sufi order is led by a sheikh and belongs to various divisions called tariqas.[123] Sufis exhibit a strong master-disciple ethos with each Sufi required to submit to a sheikh.[124] Sufis like to quote the aphorism, "He who has no Shaykh, his Shaykh is Satan."[125] New members, including women, enter the Sufi orders

---

[111] Ruthven, *Islam in the World*, 35.

[112] Braswell, *Islam*, 97.

[113] Phil Parshall, *Bridges to Islam: A Christian Perspective on Folk Islam* (Grand Rapids: Baker, 2007), 4.

[114] William C. Chittick, *Sufism: A Short Introduction* (Oxford: Oneworld Publications, 2000), 4.

[115] Chittick, 5.

[116] Nasr, *Islam*, 81.

[117] Ahmed, *Islam Today*, 50.

[118] Chittick, *Sufism*, 57.

[119] Chittick, 61.

[120] Ernst, *Shambhala Guide to Sufism*, 112–13.

[121] Laleh Bakhtiar, *Sufi: Expressions of the Mystic Quest* (New York: Avon, 1976), 7.

[122] Georgio Ausenda, "Leisurely Nomads: The Hadendowa (Beja) of the Gash Delta and Their Transition to Sedentary Village Life" (PhD diss., Columbia University, 1986), 444.

[123] *Tariq* or *tarik* is the Arabic word for "way, road, highway, trail, track, path, track, or path." *Tariqa* or *tarika*, is a derivative of *tariq* and means "manner, mode, means, way, method, procedure, system, creed, faith religion, religious brotherhood, or dervish order." Hans Wehr, *Arabic-English Dictionary: The Hans-Wehr Dictionary of Modern Arabic*, ed. J. Milton Cowan (Urbana, IL: Spoken Language Services, 1994), 559.

[124] Ernst, *Shambhala Guide to Sufism*, 29–30.

[125] Abu Yazid al-Bitami, quoted in Ali Salih Karrar, *The Sufi Brotherhoods in the Sudan* (Evanston, IL: Northwestern University Press, 1992), 126.

individually, taking an oath of allegiance to God, Islam, and their sheikh, often receiving a "cloak of blessing" at the ceremony to mark their submission.[126]

Like Shi'ites, Sufis believe in the concept of sainthood (*wilaya*).[127] The power of the departed holy men is called baraka.[128] Adherents also believe the power of baraka assists Sufi saints in the performance of miracles (*karamat*) such as "thought-reading, healing the sick, reviving the dead, controlling the elements and animals, flying, walking on water, shape-shifting, and bilocation."[129] These unusual folk practices of Sufis and Shi'ites continue to annoy some Sunnis and infuriate others.

Two main streams feed into folk Islam: (1) traditional religious practices, including African Traditional Religion (ATR), Arabian traditional religion, or Asian traditional religion and (2) Islamic influences, especially Sufism. John Mbiti comments about those who converted to Islam but retain many ATR practices: "This survival of African Religion in predominantly Muslim areas is in the form of beliefs, rituals, magic and medicine. African traditional ideas and practices have been mixed with those of Islam to suit the requirements of the people concerned, so that they get the best out of both religions."[130] Traditional Religion (TR) profoundly influences the practice of Islam. Samuel Zwemer wrote, "Islam and Animism live in neighborly fashion, on the same street in the same mind."[131]

This blending of TR and Islam produces a myriad of traditions across the world known as folk or popular Islam. Ruthven describes how easily Islam absorbed the faith of traditional religion: "The supreme deities which exist in many pagan traditions could be assimilated to Allah. Lesser local deities could be Islamicized or explained away as vernacular terms for God's attributes, or as the jinns or spirits of Quranic folklore."[132] Many of the Beja tribe

---

[126] Ernst, *Shambhala Guide to Sufism*, 144. Some see the multicolored cloak as a reference to Joseph's coat of many colors.

[127] Ernst, 30.

[128] Hiebert, Shaw, and Tiénou, *Understanding Folk Religion*, 136.

[129] Hiebert, Shaw, and Tiénou, 68.

[130] John S. Mbiti, *Introduction to African Religion*, 2nd ed. (Oxford: Heinemann Educational Foundation, 1991), 188–89.

[131] Samuel M. Zwemer, *The Influence of Animism on Islam: An Account of Popular Superstitions* (New York: Macmillan, 1920), 207.

[132] Ruthven, *Islam in the World*, 259.

of Sudan, Egypt, and Eritrea practice ATR covered only by a thin Islamic veneer. Kapteijns describes the Beja as "'mixers' who retain many non-Islamic practices."[133] I. M. Lewis states, "Islam does not ask its new adherents to abandon their accustomed confidence in all their mystical forces. Far from it. In the voluminous Qur'anic storehouse of angels, jinns, and devils, whose number is legion, many of these traditional powers find a hospitable home; and passages from the Qur'an are cited to justify their existence as real phenomena."[134] The faki is akin to a shaman or witch doctor, while the Zar doctor is a spirit medium. The faki sometimes employs herbal remedies, but usually the treats patients through the agency of the Qur'an. Treatments include reading, wearing, eating, or drinking Qur'anic verses as magical charms or potions. A common cure consists of whispering Qur'anic verses over the affected parts of the body.[135]

Bahaism

In 1844 Persian merchant Siyyid Ali Muhammad Shirazi traveled to Mecca and proclaimed himself the Mahdi, the twelfth imam of Shi'ite Islam. He called himself the "Bab," or door. The Shi'ites did not accept his imamate and executed him and other followers six years later. Before dying, Shirazi prophesied that Allah would send another messenger. Indeed, a few years later Mirza Husayn Ali Nuri pronounced himself to be this messenger, adopting the name Baha'ullah, the "glory of Allah." His followers, known as Baha'is, number about 300,000 today in Iran and 7 million globally.[136] The majority Shi'ites continue to persecute them as a deviant sect. Bahaism has spread across the world with its central shrine located in Haifa, Israel.

Baha'is claim successive prophets, called Babs, or doors, brought God's revelation to mankind. Holding to a form of progressive revelation, adherents

---

[133] Lidwien Kapteijns, "The Historiography of the Northern Sudan from 1500 to the establishment of British Colonial Rule: A Critical Overview," *International Journal of African Historical Studies* 22, no. 2 (1989): 254.

[134] I. M. Lewis, ed., *Islam in Tropical Africa*, 2nd ed. (London: Hutchinson University Library for Africa, 1980), 60.

[135] Frode F. Jacobsen, *Theories of Sickness and Misfortune Among the Hadendowa Beja of the Sudan: Narratives as Points of Entry into Beja Cultural Knowledge* (London: Kegan Paul, 1998), 105, 154.

[136] Robert Spencer, *The Complete Infidel's Guide to Iran* (Washington, DC: Regnery, 2016), 256–57.

believe nine men—Abraham, Krishna, Moses, Buddha, Zoroaster, Jesus, Muhammad, Shirazi, and Baha'ulluah—were prophets and manifestations of God for their time.[137] Baha'ullah, the ninth prophet, brought the final revelation that separated from its parent faith, Islam. Baha'is claim the unity of all religions and mankind and that all faiths teach basically the same message. They preach the necessity of a universal global language accompanied by a one-world government, which would lead to world peace.

The numbers nine and nineteen receive prominence in Baha'i thought. God revealed nine prophets and each Baha'i temple contains nine entrances. The Baha'is observe their own lunar calendar composed of nineteen months, each having nineteen days, although a few days must be added to complete the 365-day Julian calendar.[138] Like Muslims, Baha'is fast during one of the months in their religious calendar. Most Baha'is hold services in their homes, as only eight Baha'i temples presently exist in the world. There are no ministers and few rituals in Bahaism. Adherents specialize in social action, especially medical missions overseas.[139]

Zoroastrianism

Zoroaster (or Zarathustra) lived approximately from 628 BC to 551 BC near the present-day border of Northern Iran and Afghanistan. A contemporary of Jewish prophets Daniel and Jeremiah,[140] Zoroaster established a monotheistic religion centered around the one god, Ahura Mazda (now called *Ohrmazd*), the "Wise Lord." He believed this god operates according to the *Spenta Mainya*, the "bounteous principle," set down in the holy book of the Zoroastrians, the Avesta.[141] This monotheistic religion prohibits the slaughtering of animals for sacrifices. After the founder's death, the religion adopted some polytheistic

---

[137] Benjamin Schewel, "Religion in an Age of Transition," in *Religion and Public Discourse in an Age of Transition: Reflections on Baha'i Practice and Thought*, ed. Geoffrey Cameron and Benjamin Schewel, Baha'i Studies (Ontario: Wilfrid Laurier University Press, 2018), 13–14.

[138] William S. Hatcher and J. Douglas Martin, *The Baha'i Faith: The Emerging Global Religion* (Wilmette, IL: Baha'i Publishing, 2002), 154.

[139] Corduan, *Neighboring Faiths*, 172, 175–76.

[140] Corduan, 188.

[141] Jenny Rose, *Zoroastrianism: An Introduction* (London: I. B. Taurus, 2011), 103.

tendencies. Zoroastrians today believe themselves to be descendants of the magi who visited the Christ-child in Matt 2:1–12 at the nativity.[142]

Worship for Zoroastrians centers around the sacred fire ceremony. Zoroastrian temples burn a fire twenty-four hours a day, seven days a week. Hereditary priests cite passages from the Videvdat (part of the Avesta) from midnight to dawn in order to dispel evil spirits. Many adherents visit a temple daily, but attending once every four months is the minimum requirement. Additionally, devotees maintain sacred fires in their homes.[143] Worshipers must wash upon entering a fire temple, repeat mantras to protect them from evil spirits, and then receive ashes from the eternal fire on their eyelids and forehead.[144]

Numbering only about 35,000 persecuted people in Iran, pockets of Zoroastrians survive in Persia and especially India, where they are known as the Parsees. Estimates of their number worldwide vary widely—from 200,000 to 2 million people.[145] Although mentioned as an acceptable religion by the Qur'an as "people of the book," Zoroastrians are mercilessly persecuted by the Muslim majority in Iran, who call them corrupt and sinful animals. Surprisingly, Zoroastrianism has become attractive to the Iranian younger generation as a subtle vehicle for protesting Islamic fundamentalism.[146] In India, the Parsees continue to decline because this brand of Zoroastrianism does not allow outsiders to convert to their religion.[147]

EASTERN RELIGIONS

Hinduism

Hinduism defies easy description or definition for several reasons. For starters, even the word "Hindu" generates controversy. The Greeks borrowed the term from the Persians who called the Sindhu River (now Indus River) the Hindu River. This designation became the name of the land between the Indus and

---

[142] Spencer, *Infidel's Guide to Iran*, 144.
[143] Hexham, *Understanding World Religions*, 236.
[144] Corduan, *Neighboring Faiths*, 199.
[145] Corduan, 182.
[146] Spencer, *Infidel's Guide to Iran*, 258–59.
[147] Hexham, *Understanding World Religions*, 237.

Ganges.[148] Later the British colonialists called all of South Asia (India, Pakistan, Bangladesh, and Nepal) India. Although Indian intellectuals reject the term *Hinduism* in favor of "the Hindu religious tradition," most Hindus inside India increasingly use the word.[149] Hinduism is the third largest religion in the world and refers to a blend of many sacred practices in South Asia.[150] Of all the major religions, Hinduism resembles traditional religion more than any other faith. Ainslie Embree calls the beliefs of the Indian common people "Popular Hinduism." Idol worshippers in India fall into this category, whereas scholarly Hindus focus on the intellectual abstractions in the Vedas.[151] Diane Morgan says:

> Hinduism is unique among the major religions of the world. It has no founder. It has no dogma. It has no central authority, no pope, and no ecclesiastical council to decide what Hindus must or must not believe. The result is a bewildering, glorious medley of competing philosophies, disparate religious practices, and divergent lifestyles. . . . A devout Hindu can be a monotheist, a polytheist, or a non-theist. He can worship at shrines or worship at home. Or not worship at all. He can renounce the world or conquer it. He can give up sex or raise a large family. There is no creed to recite, only paths to follow. The choice of those paths is completely up to the seeker.[152]

The historical era of the subcontinent began in the second millennium BC when Aryans from the West invaded and conquered the Dravidian-speaking indigenous people.[153] This epoch in Indian history (1500–500 BC) is called the Vedic era. Originally orally transmitted, the Vedas are considered of divine origin, eternal, without beginning, existing in the "perfect language" of Sanskrit. Deepak Sarma writes, "The Vedas are comprised of four traditions, the *Ṛg, Yajur, Sāma,* and *Atharva.* These are further divided into four categories of texts:

---

[148] Ainslie T. Embree, *The Hindu Tradition: Readings in Oriental Thought* (New York: Vintage Books, 1972), vii.

[149] Hexham, *Understanding World Religions,* 117–18.

[150] Esposito, Fasching, and Evans, *World Religions Today,* 304.

[151] Embree, *Hindu Tradition,* 227.

[152] Diane Morgan, *The Best Guide to Eastern Philosophy and Religion* (New York: St. Martin's, 2001), 14.

[153] Hexham, *Understanding World Religions,* 118.

the *Saṃhitas, Brāhmaṇas, Āraṇyakas,* and *Upaniṣads.*[154] Most scholars call the religion of this period "Brahmanism," as proper Hinduism had not yet developed.[155] What came to be known as Hinduism gradually developed out of the concluding section of the Vedas, the Upaniṣads. Philosophical commentaries on the hymns and poems of the Vedas, the Upaniṣads are said to be the oldest metaphysical creations, predating ancient Greek philosophy.[156] The all-male gods of the Vedic period include Agni, the god of fire; Indra, the warrior god; Soma, a god of power; and Varuna, the god of moral order on earth. These gods became minor deities as Hinduism developed in later years.[157]

The doctrines normally associated with Hinduism developed within the Upaniṣads after 1000 BC. Speaking about them, Esposito, Fasching, and Lewis say:

> The central idea they introduced is that of **samsara**, "the world," in which all phenomena are really only secondary appearances. But blinded by illusions (*maya*), humans act foolishly and thereby suffer from *samsara's* "fire," its pains and privations. These last until the realization dawns that the underlying reality is everywhere the same, and it is the unchanging spirit (**Brahman**). The individual soul (*atman*) wanders from birth to death again and again until it finds release from the cycle by realizing that it is nothing other than *Brahman*. An individual's destiny in *samsara* is determined by actions (deeds and thoughts) the person performs.... This natural law, which operates throughout *samsara* and affects the destiny of the *atman* is called **karma**, a complex term whose meaning is often oversimplified. It is important to note that all the world religions that emerged in India accept the *samsara* paradigm.... [E]ach advocates specific yoga practices designed to realize the highest truth and achieve *moksha*, release from further reincarnation.[158]

---

[154] Deepak Sarma, *Hinduism: A Reader* (Oxford: Blackwell, 2008), 5.

[155] Embree, *Hindu Tradition*, 7.

[156] Suren Navlakha, *The Thirteen Principal Upanishads*, trans. Suren Navlakha (London: Wordsworth Editions, Ltd., 2000), X–XI.

[157] Esposito, Fasching, and Lewis, *World Religions Today*, 310–12.

[158] Esposito, Fasching, and Lewis, 312.

Many of these doctrines appear in the Bhagavad Gita, the most important text to arise out of India and the most important of the Upaniṣads.[159] In this poem, a charioteer named Arjuna seeks the advice of Lord Krishna, simultaneously an avatar of Vishnu and unexpectedly, also the god within the warrior.[160]

After the Vedic period, gods increased and decreased with the number thirty-three symbolically representing them. During this time three primary gods emerged: Brahma, the personal god and creator; Vishnu, the preserver of the universe and its order; and Shiva, the destroyer of the universe. All three are but expressions of the Brahman, "the impersonal and pantheistic form of God, which took on prominence in the Upanishads."[161] Other gods in the Hindu pantheon, numbering some 330 million,[162] consist of avatars of the primary deities. Hindus worship cows and prohibit slaughtering them because one Hindu text states all divinities dwell in the cow, while another scripture sees the animal as the incarnation of a goddess.[163] Since Hindus believe only Brahman, the unbounded Consciousness, constitutes reality, the worship of other deities (puja) assists devotees in crystalizing a concept of the divine, facilitating their devotion.

According to Alistair Shearer, an ordinary Hindu usually worships three kinds of gods: the local deity, the family god, and a personal divinity. He says, "According to Hinduism, life is a continuing process of spiritual alchemy whereby the individual being, through countless incarnations, is gradually purified in the fire of experience to the point where he or she can consciously reunite with Brahman, the matrix of all life. . . . In truth, the universe is nothing more or less than the Divine playing an elaborate game with itself."[164]

Another concept important in Hinduism regards the syllable *Aum*, composed of the three Sanskrit letters *a, u, m*—they represent the first letters of the three primary deities, Brahma, Shiva, and Vishnu. The letters also denote, respectively, the wakeful state, dreamful sleep, and dreamless sleep. Taken

---

[159] Ravi Ravindra, *The Bhagavad Gita: A Guide to Navigating the Battle of Life* (Boulder, CO: Shambhala, 2017), 1.

[160] Ravindra, 9–10.

[161] Corduan, *Neighboring Faiths*, 272–73.

[162] Morgan, *Eastern Philosophy and Religion*, 81.

[163] Esposito, Fasching, and Lewis, *World Religions Today*, 357.

[164] Alistair Shearer, *The Hindu Vision: Forms of the Formless* (London: Thames & Hudson, 1993), 6–7.

together and by repeating the three letters at once, the syllable *Aum* ushers in the "fourth state," a blissful condition of peace and tranquility.[165]

The influence of the Vedas becomes manifest in the fact that the caste system comes from the most important of all the Vedic hymns, the Purusa-Sukta 10.90. This hymn depicts a cosmic sacrifice that provides a theological justification for the social structure of the four-level caste (varna) system: Brahmanas, or priestly class; Ksatriyas, or warrior class; Vaisyas, or merchant class; and Sudras, or laboring class.[166] The first three castes constitute "twice-born" castes, while a fifth group, the Dalits, or outcastes,[167] remain outside of society altogether. Over time, thousands of subcastes have multiplied within each of the major four groups.[168] For instance, there is a launderers caste within the Sudras, which prescribes that laundry not washed at home be performed by this caste.

Closely connected to the caste system are the obligations of the three "born-again" castes that correspond to the four stages (ashramas) of life. These consist successively of the student, the householder, a forest hermit, and homeless wanderer. The student learns from his teacher, the householder raises a family, the hermit contemplates the scriptures, while the wanderer strives to achieve the exalted state by giving up family, home, and possessions.

These stages of life are linked to the four aims of life. These include duty (Dharma), material gain (Artha), physical pleasures (Kama), and salvation (release or Moksha).[169] The fourth stage of life requires the ascetic to attempt his release from the transmigration cycle. The eight stages of yoga, both the physical exercises and the mental meditations, compose the vehicle that accomplishes a release from the Karmic cycle.[170] Yoga, the origin of the English term "yoke," spiritually links each person's true self, Atman, with the cosmic

---

[165] *The Thirteen Principle Upanishads*, trans. F. Max-Muller, notes, introduction and revision by Suren Navlakha (Ware, Hertfordshire, UK: Wordsworth Editions, 2000), xxi–xxii.

[166] Sarma, *Hinduism*, 6.

[167] Outcastes compose 15 percent of the population of India. "Untouchability" was outlawed in 1948, but the stigma of discrimination persists. Morgan, *Eastern Philosophy and Religion*, 51. Untouchables are also known as Dalits.

[168] Embree, *Hindu Tradition*, 75–76.

[169] Embree, 75–78.

[170] George W. Braswell Jr., *Understanding World Religions: Hinduism, Buddhism, Taoism, Confucianism, Judaism, Islam*, rev. ed. (Nashville: Broadman and Holman, 1994), 33.

self, Brahman. The aim of yoga is Moksha, which liberates the Hindu from their bodily existence and awakens the self to realize its cosmic consciousness.[171] Although Westerners often consider yoga exercises harmless, there is more to it than meets the eye. Ravi Ravindra, a Hindu writer, says, "Yoga cannot be accomplished without *yajna*, an activity involving a collaboration between human beings and the devas, subtle energies inside and outside ourselves, requiring sacrifice of the attachment to one's usual level of being."[172]

Conceptualizing Hinduism challenges the mind. Alistair Shearer declares, "The system operates like a vast hologram, any individual part of which contains the image of the whole and is imbued with the energy of the whole."[173] This is due primarily to the doctrine of Maya (illusion) perpetrated by the great Hindu thinker Shankara (788–838). He founded about AD 800 the Advaita, non-dualistic school called Vedanta. This Hindu philosophical discipline answers the question of why each human being feels that he or she is an individual and not part of the one divine reality. The doctrine of Maya states that humans stand in unity with the universal Brahman but are trapped by an illusion to the contrary.[174] As Randal Nadeau observes, "In Hindu mystical philosophy, what we see is not truly real; what is truly real is unseen."[175]

Another school of thought in Hinduism, Sankhya, stands in almost polar opposition to the unified cosmos of Shankara, postulating a dualistic universe. Although admitting the reality of gods, the Sankhya school (c. fifth century AD) denies the reality of a transcendent deity. Furthermore, this school holds that both matter and spirit are eternal, in opposition to Shankara, who saw all matter as an illusion.[176] Striking in almost a middle position, Ramanuja (1025–1137) taught that each person exists as a fragment of Vishnu. This scholar said, however, that individuals do not merge with Brahman but maintain a "separate nondifference" even after achieving Moksha.[177] Furthermore, Ramanuja

---

[171] Randall L. Nadeau, *Asian Religions: A Cultural Perspective* (Oxford: John Wiley & Sons, 2014), 109, 110, 120, 122.

[172] Ravindra, *Bhagavad Gita*, 10–11.

[173] Shearer, *Hindu Vision*, 9.

[174] John Y. Fenton et al., *Religions of Asia*, 2nd ed. (New York: St. Martin's, 1988), 87.

[175] Nadeau, *Asian Religions*, 122.

[176] Esposito, Fasching, and Lewis, *World Religions Today*, 327.

[177] Esposito, Fasching, and Lewis, 128–29.

believed the physical world, a sense of self, and Brahman are real.[178] Finally, Ramakrishna (1836–1886) and his follower Vivekanda (1863–1902) adapted the philosophy of Shankara to Western thought. Blending Hegel with Shankara, they teach that behind the physical world stands an unseen reality. The two teachers also insist mankind is one in Brahma, Shiva, and Vishnu.[179]

Ramakrishna and Vivekanda popularized Hinduism to the extent that Westerners began to incorporate some of its principles. The Theosophy movement of Helena Blavatsky (1831–1891), the Christian Science Church of Mary Baker Eddy (1821–1910), the Transcendental Meditation movement of Maharishi Mahesh Yogi (1917–2008), and countless other new religious movements incorporate Hindu theology and practices.[180]

Yoga has become quite popular and is even being practiced by some Christians and sponsored inside churches. Yoga instructor Kerri Verna says, "I've had Christians ask if this is Okay. But yoga is not what it was 20 years ago. It used to be a form of religion; now it's evolved into just a form of exercise."[181] Al Mohler, speaking about yoga, disagrees. He claims "the stretching and meditative discipline derived from stretching exercises is not a Christian pathway to God. Mohler says he 'objects to the idea that the body is a vehicle for reaching consciousness with the divine. That's just not Christianity.'"[182] I agree with Mohler and believe that contextualizing yoga for Christians is not appropriate.

Buddhism

Although scholars question the date of his birth, Gautama Siddhartha, also known as Shakyamuni (560–480 BC or 460–380 BC), was born on the Nepalese side of the border with India.[183] Living the life of an affluent prince, Shakyamuni married Yashodhara (Honorable Lady), winning her hand against

---

[178] Hexham, *Understanding World Religions*, 156.

[179] Hexham, 158.

[180] Nadeau, *Asian Religions,* 134–35.

[181] Lois K. Solomon, "Yoga—with Bible Verses: A Thriving Exercise Movement Blends Christianity with Hindu Practices," *Los Angeles Times*, May 10, 2010, E-7.

[182] Dylan Lovan, "Baptist Leader Won't Bend on His Anti-Yoga Stance," Associated Press in the *Kansas City Star*, October 9, 2010.

[183] Yasuji Kirimura, ed., *Outline of Buddhism* (Tokyo: Nichiren Shoshu International Center, 1981), 3–4.

other suitors in an archery contest.[184] After a number of years of domestic life, including having a son named Rahula, Siddhartha became curious about the outside world. According to the well-known story, Shakyamuni ventured out of his palace and saw four disturbing sights during four separate excursions: an old man, a sick person, a corpse, and an ascetic. These scenes led Shakyamuni to ponder the reason for suffering in life, causing him to renounce the world, and begin a quest for truth.[185] Shakyamuni sought assistance from two Hindu Brahmin teachers, studied the Vedas, and practiced meditation with them for a time. Not finding fulfillment in meditation, he joined five young men who were also interested in following an ascetic path. After six years he left his five companions when he discovered these practices did not bring him to the truth.

At the age of thirty-five (some say thirty) while sitting under a pippala tree (later called Bodhi), Shakyamuni attained enlightenment and became a Buddha, an "enlightened one." After forty-five days of bliss, Siddhartha's companions rejoined him and were enthralled at his new teaching. Buddha's enlightenment was threatened by Mara (illusion) and his demon forces, but Siddhartha was able to defeat them by conquering his desires (*kleshas*),[186] retaining his enlightenment.[187] The Buddha explained his insights by describing their three characteristics. First, Siddhartha taught the Middle Way. The Buddhist should live a life of moderation, not practicing asceticism or embracing indulgence. Second, he revealed the Four Noble Truths of Buddhism and

---

[184] Gabriel Mandel Khan, *Buddha: The Enlightened One* (San Diego: Thunder Bay Press, 2005), 23.

[185] Huston Smith and Philip Novak, *Buddhism: A Concise Introduction* (New York: Harper-Collins, 2003), 5–6.

[186] Yasuji Kirimura writes, "The Buddhist term 'earthly desires' (*bonno*) originates from the Sanskrit (*Klesha*) which is sometimes translated. It is a collective term for various mental functions which disturb one physically and spiritually." Yasuji Kirimura, ed., *Outline of Buddhism* (Tokyo: Nichiren Shoshu International Center, 1982), 165–66. When the Buddha achieved enlightenment, he was still a reform-minded Hindu, thus the Sanskrit word. As Buddhism separated from Hinduism it left the Sanskrit-Indian world. Other words describing similar feelings were brought in from other cultures and their languages. On the other hand, Thich Nhat Hanh writes, "In the Discourse on Turning the Wheel of the Dharma, the Buddha did say that craving [*trishnas*] is the cause of suffering, but he said this is because craving is the first on the list of afflictions (*Kleshas*)." Thich Nhat Hanh, *The Heart of the Buddha's Teaching: Transforming Suffering into Peace, Joy, and Liberation* (New York: Broadway Books, 1999), 22.

[187] Khan, *Buddha*, 31.

third, the Eightfold Path.[188] Buddhism teaches that mankind's desires cause suffering. Conquering these desires by meditation leads to Nirvana, a state of bliss but not an actual place.[189] Achieving insight (prajna) allows one to enter Nirvana and become enlightened.

The Four Noble Truths are axiomatic to Buddhism. The first claims that life involves suffering.[190] The second states that desire causes the suffering. The third calls for putting away these offending desires.[191] The fourth Noble Truth urges the Buddhist to follow the Eightfold Path. The Eightfold Path prescribes a cure for the ill effects of suffering. Gabriel Khan says, "The Buddha offered the Eightfold Path in his first Dharma talk, he continued to teach the Eightfold Path for forty-five years... right faith, right thinking, right speech, right action, right livelihood, right diligence, right mindfulness, and right concentration."[192]

The heavenly god Bonten (Brahman) urged the young Buddha to preach his new knowledge far and wide. During the next forty-five years of his life, the faith grew rapidly. After a time, his son was converted, as was his sister, who became the first Buddhist nun.[193] Shakyamuni died at the age of eighty from eating spoiled boar's flesh.[194]

Representing orthodoxy in original Buddhism, Theravada Buddhists later received the name Hinayana, "Lesser Vehicle," by their detractors, the Mahayana Buddhists. The latter call themselves the "Greater Vehicle" because they believe all Buddhists, including women, have the potential for enlightenment, not just the clergy. Laymen among the Mahayana sect began venerating relics of the Buddha and building stupas to house them.[195] Theravadas believe in self-effort while downplaying ritual and spirituality. Mahayana Buddhists, on the other hand, emphasize the ritual, compassion, and the supernatural.[196]

Mahayana Buddhism subsequently subdivided into a number of sects, including the Pure Land school, which worships five successive historical

---

[188] Hanh, *The Heart of the Buddha's Teaching*, 6–8.
[189] Overmyer, *Religions of China*, 41–42.
[190] Smith and Novak, *Buddhism*, 32.
[191] Nhat Hanh, *Heart of the Buddha's Teaching*, 9.
[192] Nhat Hanh, 49.
[193] Kirimura, *Outline of Buddhism*, 9–11.
[194] Smith and Novak, *Buddhism*, 12.
[195] Kirimura, *Outline of Buddhism*, 32, 35. A *stupa* is a building that houses relics.
[196] Smith and Novak, *Buddhism*, 71.

incarnations of the Buddha. The Pure Land school (Chan) spread throughout China, but became Zen Buddhism upon arriving in Japan. The Pure Land school emphasizes meditation but in Japan developed a more militaristic tone when Zen was adopted by the Samurai warrior class. Tibetan Lamaism, another offshoot of Mahayana Buddhism, developed Tantric , which practices sex during some of its rituals.[197]

Although originating from the Mahayana sect, Vajrayana Buddhism (Diamond Thunderbolt) became the third major Buddhist division. Extant in Tibet and Central Asia, Vajrayana Buddhism developed many mystical ideas and practices. Like some Mahayana adherents, the Vajrayana believe in the Cosmic Buddha—something akin to the spirit of the universe. Speaking about the Thunderbolt Vehicle (eighth century AD), Gabriel Khan says, "The autonomous form of Buddhism that came into being considered possible control of the elements, levitation, telepathy, teleportation, resistance to intense cold, and other wonders obtained through knowledge of the way and the use of symbolic hand gestures (*mudras*), ritual words (*mantras*), symbolic diagrams (*yantras*), and painted cosmologies (*mandalas*)."[198]

Buddhism began as a reform movement in Hinduism. Smith and Novak call it "Indian Protestantism."[199] Siddhartha envisioned Buddhism more as a philosophy to solve the riddle of suffering than a religion by which to attain salvation. Rather, Buddhism strives to achieve insight (Prajna), enlightenment, and Nirvana. Later, as with Confucius, the Buddha assumed godhood in popular thought, especially among the Mahayana.

The indigenous people of Southeast Asia blend their folk practices with Buddhism. For example, the people of Myanmar worship the Nat spirits of Burmese folk religion alongside the Buddha in their temples. The popular religion of the common Buddhist people coupled with the mystical practices of the Tantric and Thunderbolt divisions seem to be leading Buddhism into an increasingly folk Buddhist direction.

---

[197] Corduan, *Neighboring Faiths*, 290, 292,346.
[198] Khan, *Buddha*, 82, 84–85.
[199] Smith and Novak, *Buddhism*, 21.

Jainism

Nataputta Vardhamana (599–527 BC) founded Jainism. After the death of his parents by assisted suicide when he was thirty, Vardhamana began preaching about the sacredness of all life and nonviolence. Soon he was given the name Mahavira Jina, "the great victor" or "the great hero." Beginning as a Hindu reform movement, Jainism accepts the Samsara paradigm but insists all life is sacred, including insects. According to Jains, the practice of fourteen difficult stages of meditation leads to Nirvana.[200] Mahavira also taught that although matter and spirit are eternal, no creator god exists. Secular writer Diane Morgan calls Jainism "an explicitly atheistic religion."[201]

Despite not believing in a god, Jains hold to a spiritual cosmology of three levels with metaphysical dimensions, offer prayers, and practice meditation to achieve peace.[202] The lowest realm consists of 8.4 million hells, which punish miscreants for their mistakes during previous lives. The middle level constitutes the abode where humans now live. The highest level is reserved for those who have attained the celestial bliss of moksha (release). Jains count rosaries numbering 108 beads as they pray. The swastika is their religion's symbol.[203] Mahavira taught that liberation from the cycle of birth and rebirth comes through right knowledge, correct practice, and severe asceticism. Jain monks renounce family, clothing,[204] possessions, and food, often starving themselves to death to reach true spiritual liberation.[205] This state of enlightenment is called Kaivalya.

Jains reject the universal soul and impermanence of Hinduism and the emptiness doctrine of Buddhism, but subscribe to the Samsara paradigm. Instead they strive to hold to the "triple gems of Jainism": right faith, right knowledge, and right conduct. Jainism sees religion as basically an exercise in self-effort. The five vows for the monks of Jainism are: (1) Ahimsa—no harm to anything living; (2) telling the truth—misleading nobody; (3) not stealing—not owning anything; (4) abstinence—no sexual relations or entertainment,

---

[200] Khan, *Buddha*, 18–19.
[201] Morgan, *Eastern Philosophy and Religion*, 265.
[202] Mahaveer Raj Gelra, *Jainism: In 13 Chapters* (Create Space, 2017), 26.
[203] Fenton et al., *Religions of Asia*, 3, 286. The Swastika of Jainism is unrelated to the Nazi Swastika.
[204] Jain monks are often "sky clad," that is, nude.
[205] Hexham, *Understanding World Religions*, 234.

with limited food and drink; and (5) detachment from the world.[206] Laypersons live austere lives but not to the extent of their clergy. Jains number about four million worldwide.[207] Although Jainism ranks as the smallest of the world's major religions next to Judaism, its influence far surpasses its size.

> Perhaps the biggest (and undoubtedly the most surprising) influence Jainism has had on the world at large is in how we eat. Today vegetarianism has become a viable option for millions worldwide and much of the reason behind this is due to Jainism and its high ideal of not eating animals. Of course, most Europeans and Americans are almost completely unaware of Jainism and its doctrine of ahimsa, but it has had a profound impact on the ever growing vegetarian movement. Coupled with Buddhism and Hinduism (which advocate, to some degree, abstaining from eating animals), Jain philosophy has touched many people who are interested in alternative lifestyles, even if they may be unaware of Indian ethical systems per se.[208]

Sikhism

Sikhism, a derivation of the word for "disciple" in the Punjab language,[209] owes its existence to the religious events in India at the time of its beginnings. Guru Nanak's (1469–1539) new religion constituted an indigenous response to both Hinduism and Islam. Like Islam, Sikhism believes in one god, while denying the caste system and the authority of the Vedas. Like Hinduism, the Sikhs accept the Samsara paradigm, including karma and reincarnation. Similar to his contemporaries Martin Luther (1483–1546) and John Calvin (1509–1664), Guru Nanak saw himself as the reformer of religion in India. His mantra was, "There is no Hindu, there is no Mussalman."[210]

---

[206] Corduan, *Neighboring Faiths,* 360–61.

[207] Corduan, 358.

[208] Andrea Diem-Lane, *Ahimsa: A Brief Guide to Jainism* (Walnut, CA: Mt. San Antonio College Philosophy Group, 2016), 37.

[209] Eleanor Nesbitt, *Sikhism: A Very Short Introduction,* 2nd ed. (Oxford: Oxford University Press, 2016), 2.

[210] Guru Nanak, quoted in Patwant Singh, *The Sikhs* (New York: Doubleday, 1999), 18.

Sikhism focuses on achieving *anand* (bliss), not arguing about doctrine or performing rituals.[211] Although Guru Nanak attempted reform, the tenth guru after him, Guru Gobind Singh (1676–1708) established Sikhism as a religion separate from both Islam and Hinduism. The Khalsas (the pure ones) were baptized[212] into the new faith and identified by five distinctions, each beginning with the letter *K*. According to Patwant Singh:

> These were *kesh* (long hair), *kanga* (comb), *kara* (steel wristband), *kachh* (short breeches) and *kirpan* (short sword). . . . As a final stamp of distinction and dedication, Guru Gobind Singh gave each *Sikh* the surname *Singh*, or Lion—a fitting tribute to a people who had been fighting for identity for almost 230 years. And because of the distinctive turban which *Sikh* men tie around their hair every day, they stand out in a crowd and are easy to identify.[213]

Shortly before his death, Guru Gobind Singh proclaimed that an eleventh guru would not be necessary. He said his teachings and the teachings of the previous nine gurus would comprise a text called the Guru Granth Sahib. In other words, the eleventh guru would be a book and not a person. This text is comparable to the Bible or the Qur'an for the Sikhs.[214] Guru Gobind Singh says, "Wherever there are five Sikhs assembled who abide by the Guru's teachings, . . . know that I am in the midst of them. . . . Read the history of your Gurus from the time of the Guru Nanak. Henceforth the Guru shall be the Khalsa and Khalsa the Guru. I have infused my mental and bodily spirit into the Granth Sahib and the Khalsa."[215] Sikhs also share a daily communal meal called a *langar* in either their homes or meeting places that are open to all.[216] Sikhs number about 23 million worldwide.[217] Most Sikhs trace their lineage to the Punjab area of India.[218]

---

[211] Jasprit Singh and Teresa Singh, *Style of the Lion: The Sikhs* (Ann Arbor, MI: Akal Publications, 1998), 12, 16.

[212] *Sikh* baptism is performed with water mixed with sugar and stirred with a double-edged sword. P. Singh, *The Sikhs*, 56.

[213] P. Singh, *The Sikhs*, 53–54.

[214] Singh and Singh, *Style of the Lion*, 12.

[215] P. Singh, *The Sikhs*, 68.

[216] Singh and Singh, *Style of the Lion*, 97.

[217] Corduan, *Neighboring Faiths*, 373.

[218] Nesbitt, *Sikhism*, 8.

Confucianism

Confucius (551–479 BC) grew up in a humble family in the small Chinese state of Lu.[219] He developed a philosophy of life called *li*, desiring to follow a balanced and harmonious path. This way included right relationships between ruler and subject, parent and child, husband and wife, and friend and friend. Although dismissive of Chinese folk religion's divination and shamanism, Confucius affirmed the divine. Confucius denied originality in his philosophy but claimed to be one who organized the wisdom of the ancients in order to reform the world. Confucius urged leaders to lead in an ethical, empathetic, and compassionate way.[220]

Confucians revere education as the primary means to improve the ability and character of their adherents. Furthermore, the religion trusts in the ability of administration, organization, rules, policies, and procedures to cure mankind's ills.[221] Confucius's prescriptions for society were reduced to written form by his disciples in a book titled *Discourses and Sayings (Lun-yu)*.

Confucianism languished in China for over a thousand years before experiencing a revival in the twelfth century AD. New Confucians like Zhu Xi (1130–1200) "taught that everything in the world is composed of 'vital substance' (*qi*), which is shaped into different forms according to 'ordering principle' (*li*). . . . All things are united by the supreme ordering principle of the whole universe which Zhu Xi call the *tai-ji*, 'the great ultimate.'"[222] Therefore, Confucianism, which began as a philosophy, developed into a religion as the founder became a deity in Chinese popular religion. Confucianism also gained increasing popularity with governments that approved of Confucianism's affirmation of the established order and submission to authority. Although Confucianism waned in the nineteenth century under colonialism and in the twentieth century under Communism, it is presently experiencing a revival in China.

---

[219] C. Alexander Simpkins and Annellen Simpkins, *Simple Confucianism: A Guide to Living Virtuously* (Boston: Tuttle, 2000), 9.
[220] Overmyer, *Religions of China*, 28.
[221] Simpkins and Simpkins, *Simple Confucianism*, 76–77.
[222] Simpkins and Simpkins, 49.

Taoism (Daoism)

Although some doubt his existence, *Lao Tzu* (c. fourth century BC), "the Old Master," reportedly composed the Tao Te Ching (I Ching). This book trails only the Bible and Hinduism's Bhagavad Gita as the most translated book in the world.[223] Purportedly a government archivist, Lao Tzu supposedly instructed Confucius. Most scholars, however, doubt they were contemporaries. Tao Te Ching speaks of the "Dao as the formless and ineffable Way that is the wellspring of creative power for a universe of constant transformation. The Dao is the mother of heaven and earth and is the spontaneously self-generating life of the universe. Everything in the universe has its own virtue or power (*de* or *te*) which, if permitted to flourish, brings a natural order and harmony to the world."[224]

Whereas Confucianism stresses self-improvement, Taoism emphasizes the natural way. The former stresses order and exactness, while the latter emphasizes spontaneity and freedom.[225] Crucial to Taoism is the yin-yang concept. These opposites describe a world of heaven and earth, male and female, good and evil. Taoism strives to sometimes foster one over the other, blend the two, or transcend both. The Tao Te Ching assists the adherent in balancing life's opposite pulls so he can exist "being beyond the world while living in the world."[226]

Like Confucius, by the second century AD, Chinese traditional religion had deified Lao-Tzu and worshiped him as the creator of the world. By the fourth century AD, Taoism had developed a priesthood, replete with divination and magical rites to tell the future and influence the supernatural.[227] Statues of both Confucius and Lao-Tzu appear in most Chinese temples around the world. Devotees pray to them daily. Although folk Taoists concern themselves with deliverance from demons by a spirit medium or Taoist priest,[228] philo-

---

[223] Victor H. Mair, preface to *Tao Te Ching* by Lao Tzu, trans. Victor H. Mair (New York: Bantam, 1990), xi.

[224] James Miller, *Daoism: A Beginner's Guide* (Oxford: Oneworld, 2003), 5–6.

[225] Eva Wong, *Being Taoist: Wisdom for Living a Balanced Life* (Boulder, CO: Shambhala, 2015), 17.

[226] Liu I-Ming, commentary in *Understanding Reality: A Taoist Alchemical Classic* by Chang Po-tuan, trans. Thomas Cleary (Honolulu: University of Hawaii Press, 1987), 3–4.

[227] Overmyer, *Religions of China*, 35.

[228] Overmyer, 52.

sophical Taoists are preoccupied with balancing the yin-yang dilemma by following the Celestial way.

The Taoist scriptures, Tao Te Ching, consist primarily of paradoxical aphorisms such as "The sage knows without journeying, understands without looking, and accomplishes without acting."[229] Taoism teaches that if mankind follows the natural heavenly order that comes innately to each person, all would transpire as it should. Lao Tzu writes:

> When you wish to contract something, you must momentarily expand it; When you wish to weaken something, you must momentarily strengthen it; when you wish to reject something, you must momentarily join with it; When you wish to seize something, you must momentarily give it up. This is called "subtle insight." The soft and weak conquer the strong.[230]

CONCLUSION

It is quite evident that the adherents of the religions discussed in this chapter exhibit admirable sincerity and commitment to their faiths. Additionally, many of the founders of these religions and their adherents exhibit some excellent qualities. It is also clear that the originators of each of these religions lived and died as ordinary mortals. Although some of these religions claim a miraculous birth for their founder, none assert either a resurrection or bodily ascension to a heavenly place. This fact renders Christianity exceptional among the world religions. Christianity must fervently press its claims of uniqueness and exclusivity *vis-à-vis* the other religions. This is because Jesus said in John 14:6, "I am the way, the truth, and the life. No one comes to the Father except through me." The missionary must learn the culture and religion of each society and contextualize it to the gospel. However, at the end of the day, each person from other faiths must be asked to turn from that belief system and follow Christ.

---

[229] Lao-Tzu, *Tao Te Ching*, 15.
[230] Lao-Tzu, 103.

READING FOR FURTHER STUDY

Chittick, William C. *Sufism: A Short Introduction*. Oxford: Oneworld, 2005.

Corduan, Winfried. *Neighboring Faiths: A Christian Introduction to World Religions*, 2nd ed. Downers Grove, IL: InterVarsity Press, 2012.

Hexham, Irving. *Understanding World Religions: An Interdisciplinary Approach*. Grand Rapids: Zondervan, 2011.

Ruthven, Malise. *Islam in the World*, 3rd ed. New York: Oxford University Press, 2006.

Zwemer, Samuel M. *The Influence of Animism on Islam: An Account of Popular Superstitions*. New York: Macmillan, 1920.

6

Culture and Worldview

I learned of the deficit of my cultural knowledge during my first term of service as a missionary in Africa.

The Baptist Mission house in Mwanza stood on the outskirts of the second largest city of Tanzania. In the cliffs behind our dwelling lived a family of owls (and a leopard). One day my four-year-old son and seven-year-old daughter brought to me an adolescent owl with a broken wing, pleading that we nurse it back to health. Being a compassionate father, I carried the owl to the local veterinarian, who formed a cast for the wing. Dutifully, I brought the owl a kilo of meat each day to supply it proper nourishment. One day several Tanzanian pastors said there was some grumbling in the local Baptist church about my ministering to an owl. I discovered that in the Sukuma African Traditional Religion (ATR), owls serve as sorcerers' assistants and summon witch doctors and witches to their coven meetings.[1] The Tanzanian Christians wondered if their missionary might be a witch doctor since I had tamed such an obvious messenger of evil.

---

[1] Piet van Pelt, *Bantu Customs in Mainland Tanzania*, rev. ed. (Tabora, Tanzania: Tanganika Mission Press, 1982), 74.

INTRODUCTION

Despite some instruction in missionary orientation about the culture and the worldviews of other societies, I was not prepared for how Sukuma thinking differed so much from the Western perspective. Although the concepts of society and worldview appear easily mastered subjects at first glance, cultural acquisition requires much more than meets the eye. Today North Americans mix with other nationalities, listen to the diverse languages, taste exotic food, and observe colorful native dress. Noticing, accepting, and appreciating other societies, however, differs significantly from understanding them foundationally. Unfortunately, language, food, and clothing represent only the external levels of culture and worldview. The underlying presuppositions, thought patterns, and mental constructs present by far the greatest challenges.

Early missionaries achieved some cultural acquisition, and as a rule, exceed today's missionaries in their language acquisition. Without the linguistic training of today, William Carey, Robert Morrison, and Henry Martyn produced remarkable Bible translations while also preaching the gospel. Hudson Taylor's missionaries donned ordinary Chinese dress in order to ease some of the foreignness in their appearance. In Burma, Adoniram Judson erected a Buddhist-style zayat[2] to preach the Bible to passing crowds—quite innovative in the nineteenth century.

Although founded as academic disciplines in the nineteenth century, the social sciences were not significantly harnessed by missionaries until the twentieth century. The mastery of anthropology, sociology, psychology, and linguistics assists the missionary in cultural acquisition, thereby reducing errors in their understanding of the society's worldview.

CULTURE

Paul Hiebert defines culture as "the more or less integrated systems of ideas, feelings, and values and their associate patterns of behavior and products shared

---

[2] "It was a small hutlike building not quite thirty feet long and twenty feet wide, and the front ten feet of the length consisted of the thatched bamboo porch where Adoniram planned to sit and exhort passers-by." Anderson, *To the Golden Shore*, 220 (see chap. 4, n. 118).

by a group of people who organize and regulate what they think, feel and do."[3] Essentially, one's family and the broader society serve as cultural tutors for children and adolescents. Sherwood Lingenfelter observes:

> A human being is completely helpless at birth and lives through a period of near-total dependency on others that lasts almost six years. During this time, a child is subjected to the intensive influence of parents and a few other adults. During this intensive interaction, parents seek to teach the child certain forms of behavior, values, and modes of living.... Furthermore, every individual goes through a lifelong process of learning or what anthropologists call encultura-tion. This larger process is the means by which an individual acquires the cultural heritage of a larger community.[4]

Humans absorb their unconscious presuppositions rather than ponder their significance. Societal practices develop as unquestioned "givens" to those growing up in the culture. For instance, instead of throwing rice at weddings like Westerners, the Beja people of Egypt, Eritrea, and Sudan toss camel dung the couple's way to insure fertility for the marriage and their livestock. Maori warriors in New Zealand extend their tongues in order to intimidate their enemies,[5] while Chinese do so only when embarrassed. As L. C. Brown states, "No custom is 'odd' to the people who practice it."[6] Indeed, to them it is normal and unquestioned.

The word "culture" originates "from the German *Kultur*, meaning to develop or grow."[7] The concept emerged about the same time in the early nineteenth century as the related German idea *Weltanschauung* (worldview). For German philosophers and historians such as Emanuel Kant, worldview describes one's view or perspective on the world, including imbedded cultural patterns.[8] The

---

[3] Paul G. Hiebert, *Anthropological Insights for Missionaries* (Grand Rapids: Baker, 1985), 30.

[4] Sherwood G. Lingenfelter and Marvin K. Mayers, *Ministering Cross-Culturally: An Incarnational Model for Personal Relationships*, 2nd ed. (Grand Rapids: Baker Academic, 2003), 19.

[5] James Gruber et al., "The Hands, Head, and Brow: A Sociolinguistic Study of Māori Gesture," accessed April 17, 2018, https://ir.canterbury.ac.nz/bitstream/handle/10092/11914/12653830_handsheadbrow-Maori-toappear.pdf?sequence=1.

[6] L. C. Brown, quoted in van Pelt, *Bantu Customs*, 17.

[7] Brian M. Howell and Jenell William Paris, *Introducing Cultural Anthropology: A Christian Perspective* (Grand Rapids: Baker, 2011), 27.

[8] Paul G. Hiebert, *Transforming Worldviews: An Anthropological Understanding of How People Change* (Grand Rapids: Baker Academic, 2009), 13–14.

more comprehensive concept of worldview, which will be discussed later in this chapter, includes culture. Briefly, however, worldview can be said to describe the big picture, whereas culture supplies the details therein. James Plueddemann says, "The *worldview* of a culture describes deep philosophical assumptions about the purpose of life and the nature of reality. Cultural *practices* are the externals, the things we can see, hear, smell, taste or touch: architecture, music, food, clothing, language, transportation and hair style."[9]

The vantage point of the cultural observer matters greatly. Society may be viewed from either the "emic" or "etic" perspective.[10] The insider, the emic viewpoint, sees the culture as an unconscious "given," the normal state of affairs. The insider may disapprove of some of their society's practices but these do not strike the individual as strange, only wrong. An insider often views his culture as preeminent. Although every society admires their society's laudable aspects and unique contributions, an extreme preoccupation with its superiority leads to ethnocentrism. Ethnocentrism represents a feelings-based reaction to another culture, which finds the foreign society wanting by comparison. Once a Brazilian told me he disliked America because the country lacked sufficient crowds. He enjoyed people constantly pressing around him and felt lonely and isolated in America's wide-open spaces.

The outsider perspective, the etic outlook, views another culture from the vantage point of a foreigner. The outsider may be a tourist, traveler, missionary, businessperson, immigrant, or long-term resident. Focusing on cultural differences rather than the similarities characterizes this perspective. Sometimes the differences are positive. I lived in Brazil for six and a half years. The city of Campinas collects trash every day, quite a nice custom. In America, weekly rubbish pickup is the norm.

An outsider's perspective on American culture might surprise the reader. I asked a seminary class that included several Africans their impression upon arriving in America. A Kenyan shared being taken aback by the immigration official when he landed in the US. The student said the bureaucrat lifted his hand, calling each person in line forward, repeating the same word, "Next, next,

---

[9] James E. Plueddemann, *Leading across Cultures: Effective Ministry and Mission in the Global Church* (Downers Grove, IL: IVP Academic, 2009), 71.

[10] Hiebert, *Anthropological Insights*, 94–96.

next." The Kenyan commented, "I was very offended. In Africa, we would only address a child this way."

Speaking of culture, Richard Niebuhr says:

> Culture is the artificial secondary environment which man superimposes on the natural. It comprises the language, habits, ideas, beliefs, customs, social organizations, inherited artifacts, technical processes, and values...Though we cannot venture to define the "essence" of this culture, we can describe its chief characteristics. For one thing, it is inextricably bound up with man's life in society: it is always social.[11]

Several metaphors describe the concept of culture well. Some portray culture as being like water to a fish,[12] while others refer to it as a set of lenses through which one sees the world.[13] In the first analogy, a fish immersed in the water probably does not comprehend the concept of wetness. Water represents the natural, known world to aquatic creatures. The second comparison, a set of lenses, describes varying kinds of glasses. The glasses may be clear, colored, distorted or broken, but they provide different visual experiences. The apostle Paul wrote in 1 Cor 13:12, "For now we see only a reflection as in a mirror." Our culture constitutes our lens for viewing the world and other societies.

The concept of a map provides another useful metaphor. Cultural cartography assists individuals, quite unconsciously, to navigate their societies. Acquiring these societal maps during childhood, insiders know whether to eat with their hands, silverware, or chopsticks; whether to look at a stranger in the eye or gaze in another direction; and whether to greet others by shaking hands, hugging, kissing on the cheek, or bowing. Insiders know which gestures and words are obscene, whereas outsiders often make embarrassing mistakes. There are no cultural GPS devices available to outsiders except observation, and imitation by trial and error. Societal maps must be learned and committed to memory. Anthropologists have developed a helpful taxonomy for different

---

[11] H. Richard Niebuhr, *Christ and Culture* (New York: Harper & Row, 1975), 32.

[12] Judith N. Martin and Thomas K. Nakayama, *Experiencing Intercultural Communication*, 2nd ed. (Boston: McGraw-Hill, 2005), 27.

[13] Howell and Paris, *Introducing Cultural Anthropology*, 38–39.

kinds of cultures and their practices. These include band, tribal, peasant, and urban societies.[14]

Band Societies

Anthropologists define band societies as small groups of blood-related people, numbering between 50 and 500 individuals. Although few of these entities remain in the world, band societies are the most basic communal unit historically. Reflecting these communities' extremely individualistic and egalitarian nature, marriage is based on love, with some input from family. Although there is often a headman or a shaman for a band, apart from these informal offices, little hierarchy occurs. Consensus, usually by older males, governs decision-making. Band societies exist without laws, courts, military, police, or jails. Bands live in face-to-face communities with an orientation toward the present. These societies favor oral communication, prizing storytelling and the retelling of cultural myths. Some call these societies "hunter-gatherers" because they lack agriculture and usually work less than four hours a day. Although some might consider such cultures ideal, bands are subject to drought, floods, fires, disease, wild animal attack, and assault from outsiders.[15]

While touring a rural area of Paraguay with some missionaries, I spotted a band of about forty men, women, and children walking quickly through the forest. The missionaries informed me this small group constituted a separate people group, living on the fringes of the tribal area of the majority Guarani ethnicity. Although rare, band societies like this persist in the frontier regions of missions.

---

[14] Paul G. Hiebert and Eloise Hiebert Meneses, *Incarnational Ministry: Planting Churches in Band, Tribal, Peasant, and Urban Societies* (Grand Rapids: Baker, 1995), 46. In *Incarnational Ministry*, coauthored by his daughter, Paul Hiebert lists four major societies. In Hiebert's capstone work, *Transforming Worldviews*, published after his death, his children collapse the band and tribal categories into "small-scale oral societies" and expand urban societies into three categories; modern, post-modern, and glocal. See chapters 5–9 of *Transforming Worldviews* by Paul G. Hiebert.

[15] Hiebert and Meneses, *Incarnational Ministry*, 62–68.

Tribal Societies

John Friedl calls a tribe, "a confederation of groups who recognize a relationship with one another, usually in the form of common ethnic origin, common language, or strong pattern of interaction based on intermarriage or presumed kinship."[16] A tribe may number from 500 to 35 million people.[17] Although ethnicity forms the most important link within a tribal group, language and culture are also important. Some tribes remain small, while others have grown extremely large, like the Somalis. This ethnicity has developed many subtribes and clans within their divisions. Sometimes a tribal group spans several nations, such as the Kurds who dwell in parts of Turkey, Iraq, Syria, and Iran, and the Beja of Egypt, Eritrea, and Sudan.

In tribal societies, marriage fulfills social responsibilities for the group rather than happiness for the individual. Therefore, in traditional tribes love seldom enters into the equation in regard to the choice of a marriage partner. Often, polygamous and sometimes polyandrous (plural husbands) matrimony characterizes the husband-and-wife relationship. Tribal members remain loyal to their family, clan, subtribe, and tribe. Gender and age-based associations, as well as tribal secret societies, provide further cohesion. Economically, tribal societies usually pursue horticultural, pastoral, or fishing occupations. For instance, the Beja tribe raise camels, sheep, and goats. Interestingly, although living along the Red Sea coast, they observe a taboo that forbids consuming any seafood. Seminomadic horticultural peoples employ a type of slash-and-burn agriculture called swidden as they follow the rains. Similarly, nomadic pastoral tribes chase any moisture they can locate in order to feed their livestock. Despite the absence of police, jails, or the military in tribal societies, chiefs, clan leaders, elder councils, and village headmen enforce unwritten cultural rules. Like band societies, tribal life trends holistically with scientific knowledge limited to concrete thinking and solving practical problems.

A tribal society normally follows a specially tailored version of traditional religion that includes belief in ancestors, ghosts, magic, deities, and the power of shamans. Bands and tribes see a causal link between life's calamities and the disfavor of the spirit world. Although band societies view land ownership as

---

[16] John Friedl, quoted in Hiebert and Meneses, *Incarnational Ministry*, 85.

[17] There are fifteen million Somalis and approximately thirty-five million Kurds.

of minimal importance, tribal cultures highly value their ethnic homelands. A Luo tribesman living in Nairobi, Kenya, outside the tribal domain must return to the land of his ancestors along Lake Victoria for burial so his soul may rest in peace. Lately, most tribal people have entered the modern world due to the rise of nation states. Despite this reality, the culture of the tribe still prevails among a significant number of its members. One writer reports that Beja culture (eastern Sudan, southern Egypt, and northern Eritrea) has changed little during the last thousand years and their religion has been minimally impacted by Islam over the last five hundred.[18]

Peasant Societies

Peasant societies represent the third type of culture in this anthropological taxonomy. Large populations in countries like China, India, and Russia live in multiethnic peasant societies. Hiebert says:

> The distinction between tribal and peasant societies is not a sharp one. Tribal societies, too, are not isolated. They often have symbiotic economic and ritual relationships with one another and with peasant communities. The primary distinction is not the degree of outside involvement but the character of that involvement. Tribal societies are more or less politically and economically autonomous. . . . Peasants are subject to outside rulers who tax their surplus production to maintain courts, cities, armies, and a ruling elite. . . . Peasants differ from city dwellers, however, because they are tied to the land and produce their own food.[19]

Whereas band and tribal cultures form largely classless communities, castes and class differences markedly divide peasant cultures. Many castes specialize in particular jobs that can only be performed by members of that caste or subcaste. For instance, some years ago I encountered a special launders' caste in Calcutta, India. In the same city, I observed someone cleaning the wax out of the ear of a passersby. The missionary explained the "ear-picker's" caste earns their living in this fashion.

---

[18] B. A. Lewis, "Deim el Arab and the Beja Stevedores of Port Sudan," *Sudan Notes and Records* [SNR] 43 (1962): 37.

[19] Hiebert and Meneses, *Incarnational Ministry*, 186.

Peasant societies have largely inherited the feudal hierarchies of the serf, merchant, and nobility classes. The divide between castes and classes in peasant society often present as racially or ethnicity based. Peasants remain tied to the land as agriculturalists or pastoralists, with survival as their main goal. Large-scale farms, plantations, and ranches often employ peasants as laborers. The patron-client relationship serves as the most important political bond between individuals. In this system, the patron-elite protect their client-workers with just enough sustenance to keep them loyal and above the poverty level.

Within peasant societies the concept of nation states developed, including the institutionalization of governments in the form of monarchies and dictatorships. Because of their multiethnic and multilingual natures, peasant societies value cultural pluralism. Additionally, written communication becomes more important than oral communication. Although the peasants themselves survive by bartering, peasant societies demand a monetary system to facilitate the exchange of goods and services within the larger economy.

The members of peasant societies generally belong to one or more of the major formal religions rather than a traditional religion. The peasants themselves, however, often blend folk religion with the high religion of the nation. Whereas band societies remain indifferent to land ownership, and tribal societies try to possess it, the state controls the land in most peasant societies. Since possessions impede the travel of nomadic bands and tribes, wealth accumulation stagnates in those societies. In peasant communities, however, the accumulation of wealth advances as an important cultural value. This led peasant societies to unconsciously adopt the concept of the limited good. This belief holds that only so much wealth exists within any culture. Therefore, if one's neighbor prospers then it has been at the expense of others. George Foster explains: "If 'Good' exists in limited amounts which cannot be expanded, and if the system is closed, it follows that an individual or family can improve a position only at the expense of others."[20] Such attitudes disincentivize risk taking and encourage the maintenance of the status quo.

---

[20] George Foster, quoted in Hiebert and Meneses, *Incarnational Ministry*, 219.

Urban Societies

Urban societies often defy definition due to their ethnic diversity, sprawling size, and large populations. In Paul Hiebert's *Transforming Worldviews*, the "Urban Society" category of his earlier work, *Incarnational Ministry*, becomes the "Glocal Worldview." In his earlier work, Hiebert writes:

> The city is culture par excellence; the epitome of human creation. Nature surrounds the tribesman and the peasant. Humans create the environment of city folks. It is bricks, steel, mortar, and cement; streets, sidewalks, bridges, and tunnels; and elevators, cars, buses, trains, and airplanes.... The city never sleeps. The city is also the climax of human culture because it contains in it the riches of many cultures.... Its libraries and computers store the accumulated knowledge of humankind down through the ages.[21]

Cities also provide the museums, concert halls, opera houses, sports stadiums, airports, courts, shopping centers, train stations, universities, trade schools, and stock markets for the nation or surrounding area. Urban culture affords its population the opportunity to exercise the city's cardinal cultural values—individualism, diversity, and consumerism. In an urban area, nobody must conform as strictly to the cultural norms enforced in band, tribal, and peasant societies. Classes exist in the city but are not usually based upon ethnicity or caste. Stratification develops due to urban occupational specialization, resulting in some jobs receiving more remuneration than others.

Despite these realities, the individual possesses multiple lifestyle options in the city. The city dweller can express his or her individualism in a multitude of ways. A missionary in Cairo told me that a Muslim can more easily decide for Christ inside the anonymity the city provides. Difficulties abound for such seekers in the villages and countryside, where everyone is known. Cities certainly manifest local and regional personalities—Baltimore differs from Bangkok, Atlanta from Algiers, Milwaukee from Moscow, and Chicago from Cape Town—but all enjoy urban similarities.

Additionally, cities reflect tremendous diversity, not just culturally but because of their many choices. I served as pastor of a church in Los Angeles

---

[21] Hiebert and Meneses, *Incarnational Ministry*, 308–9.

County in the first Chinese-majority city in the United States (Monterey Park). One could choose from over forty-five Chinese restaurants in a seven-and-a-half-square-mile area. With such diversity comes the necessity of toler-ating conflicting cultural tastes. I now reside in a neighborhood of Kansas City with a neighborhood association. The association prohibits boats, recreation vehicles, and cars without license plates from occupying the neighborhood's driveways and streets. Although the neighborhood association bans "inappro-priate" and "unsightly" statuaries, it tolerates large figures of the Buddha, Shiva, and the Virgin Mary in a nod to cultural diversity.

Most of all, cities project a culture of consumerism. Big-box discount stores, malls, and shopping centers dot the landscape of metropolises around the world. Most goods and services originate in urban areas. Paul Hiebert says urbanization has generated a popular culture that is global in nature, creating a transcultural elite who move easily about the world.[22] *Cultural lift* occurs as country people move to the city and become affluent. Donald McGavran says cultural lift can take place when educational, medical, and agricultural improvements impact a society.[23] Additionally, lift may happen when the lost are redeemed and turn to Christ. The new believers no longer drink, gamble, or beat their wives but have been "lifted" by redemption into a new kind of Christian culture. Although this represents a favorable outcome, McGavran says the challenge is for new believers to change their lifestyles while simul-taneously maintaining their relationships with lost friends, relatives, and co-workers.[24] Failure to do so halts church growth because the new believers have been "lifted" out of the culture of their receptive friends.

At the other end of the spectrum, in many second- and third-world cit-ies, band, tribal, and peasant people resist integration into urban society. After studying Beja culture along the Red Sea, Frode Jacobsen reached some import-ant conclusions about peasant integration in cities:

> Although living in a town clearly has some impact on rural people moving in, the towns themselves may also be changed in the process.

---

[22] Hiebert, *Transforming Worldviews*, 245–46.
[23] Donald A. McGavran, *Understanding Church Growth*, 2nd ed. (Grand Rapids: Eerdmans, 1980), 295.
[24] McGavran, 296–97.

> Instead of echoing the usual point of view that the people of the Red
> Sea Hills are getting increasingly urbanized, one might state that the
> towns in some senses may be becoming increasingly ruralized. . . . I
> am inclined to argue, however, that the tribal traditions are not weak
> in the towns. They may even grow in importance as the towns get
> increasingly "tribalized."[25]

Jacobsen makes the point that often rural people import their lifestyles, beliefs, and practices from the countryside into the cities. Urban life often impacts the rural person more than vice versa, but sometimes the opposite is true.

WORLDVIEW

In his capstone work, Paul Hiebert defines worldview as "the 'fundamental cognitive, affective, and evaluative presuppositions a group of people make about the nature of things, and which they use to order their lives.' Worldviews are what people in a community take as given realities, the maps they have of reality that they use for living."[26] The cognitive dimension describes how people think and provides the intellectual content of the culture. This dimension addresses societal knowledge, logic, and wisdom. For instance, although the Burmese in Myanmar are Buddhists, "everyone knows" the Nat spirits control everyone's destiny. On the contrary, in the West, most people believe life's events occur without direct supernatural causation.

Societies create difficult-to-discard traditions. I attempted to introduce solar ovens as a development project to several North African people groups. These devices cook food efficiently without burning scarce and expensive firewood. After repeated unsuccessful attempts to convince the nationals of the value of solar cooking, one woman explained, "If we use this thing, it is true, we will not have to gather firewood or cook over the fire three times a day—but our husbands will say we are lazy and beat us because we are doing nothing."

The affective dimension of worldview relates to feelings and attitudes. Matters of taste surface in this dimension. For instance, in Western culture a beautiful or handsome individual must be thin. Conversely, in sub-Saharan

---

[25] Jacobsen, *Theories of Sickness*, 44–45 (see chap. 5, n. 136).
[26] Hiebert, *Transforming Worldviews*, 15.

Africa a plump person radiates health, while the slim individual is viewed as sickly. Greek, Turkish, and Italian societies allow for the venting of feelings, while in sub-Saharan Africa and India losing one's temper constitutes a grave sin. The affective dimension also governs the aesthetics of a society. For instance, Brazilians bathe three times a day and are repulsed by unclean Americans who bathe only once daily.

The Tanzanian government requires expatriates to secure stamps in their passports, certifying they have paid their income taxes. Once while waiting in the Mwanza revenue office, I engaged a Japanese foreign-aid worker in conversation. Since I spoke no Japanese and the Asian man no English, the discussion took place in Swahili. When I asked the nature of his work, the Japanese employee said his horticulturalist job consisted of planting flowers in the traffic circles of the city. When asked why the government of Japan would send someone all the way to Africa to plant flowers, he proudly replied that Japan desired to beautify the country. Such an aesthetically pleasing project, he continued, would bring harmony, good feelings, and peace to the nation. Although Tanzanians like flowers, when the Japanese aid worker departed all the flowers died. Japanese Buddhist philosophy believes achieving a balance between mankind and nature brings harmony in the universe. Although most Westerners and Africans appreciate floral aesthetics, their admiration does not extend that far.

The third dimension of worldview involves choices concerning right and wrong, moral and immoral, and true and false. The evaluative dimension subconsciously superintends societies as they determine cultural decisions. For instance, Brazilians abhor Westerners who "pick their teeth" without covering their mouths. Brazilians also chafe at foreigners who touch their food with their hands for "everyone knows" one does not touch what enters one's mouth. Similarly, even Christian women in Brazil dress in attire that appears skimpy or provocative to Westerners. Brazilians consider most Americans prudish in regard to sexual mores.

Another example of the evaluative dimension transpired during my first term as a missionary in Tanzania. A famine occurred due to the severe drought and as a result, the Baptist missionaries requested hunger-relief funds from their mission agency. The freight office in America purchased several shipping containers of corn meal, the staple food of East Africa. As my colleagues and I began to distribute the rations, the recipients exclaimed in surprise and revulsion, "This is yellow corn meal. We eat white corn meal." We asked, "What's the difference?" The nationals replied, "Everyone knows yellow corn meal makes you sterile." Despite the drought and food shortage, nobody would consume the corn meal. Later the commodity became animal feed.

Missionary anthropologists have developed several other worldview scaffoldings. Although Paul Hiebert, Tite Tiénou, and Daniel Shaw first pointed out the worldview concepts of guilt-innocence, shame-honor, and fear-power in *Understanding Folk Religion*, Roland Muller significantly expanded the concepts in his subsequent book, *Honor and Shame*. Muller notes that all cultures constitute a mix of societies:

> The problem comes when we want to simplify cultures into these three basic classifications. They do not easily fit, because they are made up of blends of all three. Thus, when analyzing a culture, one must look for the primary cultural characteristics, and then the secondary ones.[27]

Most Westerners hold to a guilt-innocence worldview and subsequently craft their gospel presentations correspondingly. The Westerner thinks from the perspective of either good or bad or right and wrong. Their presentations rely on clear-cut propositional truths that often fall on deaf ears in the Islamic world because most Muslims hold a different worldview. Once I was traveling off-road in the Horn of Africa with a national partner. The national flagged down a nomad on a camel who stopped to speak with him. The Christian worker, trained in Western propositional thinking, drew a bridge in the sand with a stick, explaining how Christ bridged the chasm of sin and reconciled mankind to God—an improvised rendition of the "Bridge to Life" gospel presentation tract, common in North America. Unfortunately, the nomad had never seen a bridge nor could he understand how a sand drawing could represent something supernatural.

A majority of Muslims follow a shame-honor worldview perspective. Raphael Patai says, "One of the important differences between the Arab and

---

[27] Roland Muller, *Honor and Shame: Unlocking the Door* (Bloomington, IN: Xlibris, 2000), 20.

Western personality is that in Arab culture, shame is more pronounced than guilt."[28] A shame-honor culture holds relationships, reputation, and honor above other values. For example, the shame-honor worldview esteems "saving face" over forthrightness. In Tanzania, villagers will slaughter a prized goat or their last chicken in order to provide a visitor with an honorable meal—even if the gesture plunges them further into poverty. Societies possess culture-specific etiquettes that navigate their worldview pitfalls. For instance, many tribes in the Horn of Africa perform a coffee ceremony when guests come to call. Depending on the tribe, two, four, or five cups of coffee are consumed by everyone during the visit. The ceremony of roasting and grinding the coffee beans, brewing, and consuming the coffee takes exactly one hour. At the end of the time period, "everyone knows" it is time for the guests to leave. The coffee ceremony represents a culturally appropriate way of coaxing guests to depart. Western society, unfortunately, lacks such a helpful manner of convincing visitors not to overstay their welcome.

The fear-power worldview is the most widely held perspective of those from traditional, folk religious backgrounds. Fear of evil spirits and dark forces contributes to this point of view. Popular religion employs spells, potions, and rituals to avoid misfortune and foil evil spirits. In Tanzania, traditional Sukuma fear the water monster Ngassa.[29] This god appears in the form of a large fish, crocodile, or hippopotamus and lives in Lake Victoria.[30] Another deity, Katabi, commands the reverence of a dedicated spirit-possession society.[31] Other minor evil spirts cause storms, floods, and droughts. The improper veneration of ancestors causes these disasters, but Sukuma believe the high god, Liwelelo, actually sends the misfortunes through his evil spirits.[32]

I postulate a fourth worldview perspective observable in societies around the world. The existential-transcendent worldview exalts religious experience

---

[28] Raphael Patai, *The Arab Mind*, rev. ed. (New York: Hatherleigh, 2002), 113.

[29] Also called Mugassa. Sukuma and even some of the Arabs offer a sacrifice to the lake deity to insure safe passage. Berta Millroth, *Lyuba: Traditional Religion of the Sukuma* (Uppsala, Sweden: *Studia Ethnographica Upsaliensia*, 1965), 110.

[30] Millroth, *Lyuba*, 107; Evie Adams Welch, "Life and Literature of the Sukuma in Tanzania, East Africa" (PhD diss., Howard University, 1974), 183.

[31] R. G. Abrahams, *The Nyamwezi Today: A Tanzanian People in the 1970s* (Cambridge: Cambridge University Press, 1981), 78.

[32] Welch, *Life and Literature*, 177.

above all else. For instance, Muslim Sufis prize the ecstatic feelings they receive from their ritual dances or reciting Allah's ninety-nine names. Sufis consider these actions and emotions more important than Islam's doctrine or praying five times a day. When Buddhist and Hindu yoga practitioners achieve altered states during their devotions, it trumps other worldview perspectives in their culture. The existential-transcendent worldview centers around the emotions and the supernatural, prizing feeling and experience above all else.

Martin and Nakayama postulate another worldview scaffolding system. They note Western culture places a high value on "doing." Industriousness and productivity, therefore, receive acclaim from Americans. "What do you do for a living?" typifies one of the first questions strangers ask when they meet. Latin American society admires "being," that is, experiencing life. Such cultures enjoy "living in the moment" and "self-actualization." In a third perspective, many Asian nations exhibit a "growing" mentality. These societies value educational, esthetical, and spiritual development.[33] American missionaries are often perplexed that their host society does not share their "doing" worldview.

To understand other cultures and worldviews, Westerners should understand their own perspective and presuppositions. Paul Hiebert describes these in one of his earlier books, *Anthropological Insights for Missionaries*. In this text, he describes the worldview of European and North America missionaries that often clashes with their host cultures. Western cultural assumptions include a belief in (1) a real and rational world, (2) an analytical approach, (3) a mechanistic worldview, (4) individualism, (5) equality, (6) a priority of time over space, and (7) an emphasis on sight.[34]

Westerners naturally assume humans live in a real and rational world. For this reason, Americans rely on the physical sciences for medical procedures and the social sciences to understand and predict human behavior. On the contrary, the Beja people believe in "spirit spiders" who leave both a physical and spiritual mark on their victims. Hindus in South Asia assume the perceivable world is an illusion. Since Westerners presume the natural realm can be managed, much of the activities of governments, aid organizations, and missionary humanitarian work involves technology and development projects. Americans

---

[33] Martin and Nakayama, *Experiencing Intercultural Communication*, 38–39.
[34] Hiebert, *Anthropological Insights*, 113–36.

assume the recipients of their mission work share their aspirations. I overheard two older Tanzanian men discussing the poor electrical service in the city of Mwanza. Ephraim said to his friend, "Electricity isn't necessary. It's necessary for Wazungu,[35] but not for us."

Westerners assume an analytical approach best solves problems. Westerners imagine every obstacle can be overcome and every dilemma has a solution. This perspective causes missions agencies to require their representatives to formulate goals, objectives, and long-range plans. Such sophisticated systematic methodologies may overwhelm the nationals. A number of years ago, I convinced my mission agency to build a hafir[36] in a remote desert region in the Horn of Africa. I brought a retired engineer from the US Bureau of Reclamation to construct the earthen dam. I also purchased a used dump truck and secured a large earth mover from a Muslim friend. Unfortunately, a national worker stole the truck and drove it across an international boundary and then a war broke out between the two countries. The hafir was never built and the nomads watched as another Western development project floundered.

Westerners automatically assume a mechanistic worldview. Somewhat similar to the analytical approach, this category holds that reality can be quantified, systematized, and reduced to a few theories. Paul Hiebert explains "reductionism" in this way:

> Here all insights are noted but ultimately reduced to a single explanatory system. Religious truths are reduced to cultural beliefs, cultural beliefs to social constructs, societies to aggregates of individual humans, humans to animals, animals to chemical reactions, chemical reactions to atomic particles, and atomic particles to quantum particles. In the end, there is nothing but masses of vibrating strings. All the rest, including humans, is epiphenomenal.[37]

Western missionaries acknowledge the leading of the Holy Spirit in their work, but they nonetheless formulate best-practice solutions, systematize their

---

[35] The Swahili word, *Wazungu* (singular, *Mzungu*) refers to a European or North American. The actual meaning of the word is "those who come (or go) around," a fitting description of a Westerner.

[36] Arabic term for an "earthen dam."

[37] Paul G. Hiebert, *The Gospel in Human Contexts: Anthropological Explorations for Contemporary Missions* (Grand Rapids: Baker Academic, 2009), 128–29.

evangelism approaches, and quantify the progress of church planting through sociological and statistical analysis. Although some of these Western methods obviously possess value, the rest of the world does not share this cultural assumption.

Individualism ranks as the most prevalent worldview presupposition among Westerners. Americans assume the rest of the world possesses the same choices as Westerners. In most parts of the globe daughters must secure the permission of their families in order to marry. Fathers, in Muslim societies, determine the parameters for family behavior. While living in a Muslim country in the Horn of Africa, I visited the business office of some national friends with my thirteen-year-old daughter. The receptionist, dressed in conservative Muslim garb, asked a pointed question; "Why don't you love your daughter?" I replied, "I certainly love my daughter very much. Why don't you think I love her?" She replied, "If you loved your daughter, she would be wearing long sleeves and a head covering. You must not love her."

Similarly, village elders make decisions by group consensus without much consideration of the individual. Westerners value self-reliance and self-actualization, while many other societies do not. Within the category of individualism, humanitarianism surfaces as an important corollary value. Since Americans believe every human possesses intrinsic worth, assisting others in need is an important worldview assumption. Sometimes missionaries believe their compassion for the needy will cause those from other religions to come to Christ. This is not always the case. When I lived in the Horn of Africa, I partnered with the aid organization Fellowship of African Relief. Colin Adams shared about overhearing two old nomads describing in Arabic their reaction to the hunger relief his organization was providing. From behind the driver in the back of a lorry, one Muslim tribesman said to the other, "Yes, the food is good. You see, Allah has tricked the infidels into feeding us."

The preamble to the United States Declaration of Independence[38] proclaims that all men are created equal. Equality represents a cultural value not

---

[38] "We hold these truths to be self-evident, that all men are created equal, that they are endowed by their Creator with certain unalienable Rights, that among these are Life, Liberty and the pursuit of Happiness." "Declaration of Independence: A Transcription," National Archives: America's Founding Documents, accessed April 29, 2018, https://www.archives.gov /founding-docs/declaration-transcript.

shared by much of the world. Many societies, on the contrary, believe people are born into this world very much unequal. Cultures with the caste system suppose the sins individuals commit during their past lives condemn that person to the lower sections of society. Additionally, the Western worldview assumption of equality breeds a cultural value of informality. Inconceivable in many countries, most North American organizations place their employees on a first-name basis with each other. Of course, unspoken rankings of wealth, power, and income belie existing social divisions, but the cultural value of informality persists in American society. While Westerners joke with friends and coworkers, other societies maintain a mode of decorum and become uneasy with the informality exhibited by Americans. Furthermore, most Westerners lean toward frankness, directness, and forthrightness in dealing with others. Other societies, however, prefer to solve interpersonal problems through a third party or behind the scenes. When the American missionary insists on "having it out" or "insisting on their rights," those in shame-honor societies feel slighted and nationals from fear-power cultures are offended by the anger that surfaces in such conflicts. One Baptist missionary became tired of waiting in the long lines at the only bank in Mwanza, Tanzania. Instead of using the culturally acceptable choice of pushing ahead of others, this Christian worker mounted the counter and lay prone on top of it. Instead of arresting the culprit, the kind and patient Tanzanians convinced him to use a less direct approach. Behind the scenes, however, the local municipality informed the mission that this foreigner's residence visa would not be renewed.

Americans place a high priority on time over space. For Westerners time progresses in a straight line and divides their days into segments of time devoted to work, family, leisure, and attending to errands. North Americans believe in time management and deplore wasting it. Other societies do not view time as a manageable commodity but rather remain in the moment. My Oxford-educated African friend remarked that it was odd that I would carry a book or magazine to read while standing in lines in Africa. He said, "We don't mind wasting time." Additionally, since other societies value relationships over arbitrary deadlines, punctuality suffers. In many communities along the Amazon River it rains every afternoon. Nationals will often set up appointments, saying, "I'll meet you tomorrow after the rains." In the West, if one is more than five or ten minutes late, an excuse is needed. In Africa, on the other hand, one is not late until an hour has passed. South American culture splits the difference. Paul Hiebert says:

> Time in many parts of the world is not a commodity nor is it linear. In much of Africa, for instance, it is episodic and discontinuous. There is no absolute "clock" or single time scale. Rather, there are many kinds of time—mythical time, historical time, ritual time, agricultural time, seasonal time, solar time, lunar time, and so on. Each of these has a different duration and quality. . . .
>
> In some tribes time is almost like a pendulum, going back and forth. People in these cultures speak of going back in time, or of time "stopping."
>
> In South Asia time is both cyclical and linear. Thus, humans are born and reborn in an endless series of lives, but these cycles are part of the greater life of a god, which has a beginning and an end.[39]

Western society focuses on the future and is youth oriented. Other cultures around the world, however, respect and honor older persons and consult them about major decisions. Problems occur overseas because the majority of missionaries come from the younger generation. Mission agencies send young missionaries to disciple and train men and women much older than themselves. Western society values private property ownership, but not to the extent of other cultures. Other societies see the land as sacred.

Paul Hiebert says, "Another fundamental theme in the North American world view is our emphasis on sight rather than sound, touch, taste, or smell. This is seen in our choices of such phrases as 'world view,' 'I see,' and 'Let's look at the situation.' This Western emphasis on a visual world has its roots in Greek philosophy. . . . The crowning achievement of this view was literacy and the printed word."[40] The written-word paradigm has produced the storage of written information, an emphasis on data-based knowledge, theoretical thinking, and systematized educational disciplines replete with multiple abstract concepts. Face-to-face oral societies deal in the here and now of life, not in the hypothetical, speculative, or figurative. They are often perplexed at the

---

[39] Hiebert, *Anthropological Insights,* 131.
[40] Hiebert, 134.

thought processes and mental constructs of Westerners. Boureima, a Fulani tribe member, says the standard initial greeting between males in his society is "How are your cattle?" The welfare of one's family and health comes after this important salutation.

In *Transforming Worldviews*, Hiebert presents another (but related) model for worldview analysis. The synchronic model looks at a culture's structure of reality. Conversely, a diachronic model looks at a society's cosmic stories. The former could be called world-map constructs, while the latter can be viewed as world myths.[41]

Although Hiebert's categories and insights are helpful, David Hesselgrave writes:

> Some students of culture themselves would disagree with Hiebert— at least partially. As early as 50 years ago, E. Perry, F. H. Smith, and E. R. Hughes developed a trinary understanding of cultural epistemology based on a study of Indian and Chinese thinking on one hand and the thinking of Western cultures on the other. They found differences in cultural thinking to be more a matter of priority than of kind. According to them, *all peoples think in three ways—conceptual postulationally, concrete relationally and psychically intuitionally*. The difference between cultures is not one of kind but of the assignment of differing priorities to each of the three ways of thinking. Westerners assign priority to "conceptional/postulational thinking"; Chinese (and, I would add, most tribals as well) give priority to "concrete relational/pictorial thinking"; and Indians prioritize "psychical/intuitional thinking" considering it the highest form of knowing. To the extent that Perry, Smith, and Hughes are correct: Western rational thinking is not simply Western; it is also Chinese and Indian, though not to the same degree. This understanding is in accordance with that of those Christian scholars who believe that, however identified, *Western thinking ("logic") is not unique to Western culture*.[42]

---

[41] Hiebert, *Transforming Worldviews*, 335. Synchronic elements include cognitive, affective, and evaluative as well as the epistemological foundations of a worldview. Conversely, Diachronic themes include stories, dramas, and metanarratives.

[42] David J. Hesselgrave, "Conclusion: A Scientific Postscript—Grist for the Missiological Mills of the Future," in Hesselgrave and Stetzer, *MissionShift*, 284–85 (see chap. 4, n. 97). Emphasis added.

Although Hiebert's categories are helpful, the insights of Perry, Smith, and Hughes explain why missionaries find systematic, logical thinkers in every society—even in so-called primitive ones. It might also explain why many North Americans do not think logically, even though they reside in the purported advanced West. At best, cultural scaffoldings provide models for understanding the outside world.

CONCLUSION

Paul Hiebert states, "Two of the greatest problems faced by missionaries entering new cultures are misunderstandings and premature judgments."[43] Upon moving to South America, I noticed some cultural practices that differed from the societies of either America or Africa. Shortly after arriving in Brazil, I questioned several missionaries why they passed emergency vehicles whose lights were flashing. They explained that in Brazil police cars, fire trucks, and ambulances announce their presence by flashing their lights when no emergency exists. When an emergency occurs, however, first responders deactivate their lights and sirens.

Worldview and culture represent the portal through which one enters a mission field. Neither the proclaimer nor the receiver is a blank slate, rather each unconsciously puts their own presuppositions, prejudices, and biases as an overlay upon the world. As the missionary presents the gospel and the national listens to the presentations, each does so through their own culture and worldview prism. How this occurs is the subject of the next chapter.

READING FOR FURTHER STUDY

Hiebert, Paul G. *Transforming Worldviews: An Anthropological Understanding of How People Change.* Grand Rapids: Baker Academic, 2009.

McGavran, Donald A. *Understanding Church Growth*, 2nd ed. Grand Rapids: Eerdmans, 1980.

Muller, Roland. *Honor and Shame: Unlocking the Door.* Bloomington, IN: Xlibris, 2000.

---

[43] Hiebert, *Anthropological Insights*, 111.

Patai, Raphael. *The Arab Mind*. Revised ed. New York: Hatherleigh, 2002.

Plueddemann, James E. *Leading across Cultures: Effective Ministry and Mission in the Global Church*. Downers Grove, IL: IVP Academic, 2009.

7

Contextualization

The following story, describing an experience I had in Kenya, appeared in a journal article a few years ago.

> While living in North Africa, I travelled down to East Africa with my family to visit . . . a couple ministering to the *Samburu* tribe near Maralal in northern Kenya. The nomadic *Samburu* wear traditional red robes, herd cattle and live in mud dwellings. [Missionary Don] Dolifka asked me to preach a message to a group of twenty men seated on boulders beneath a grove of trees on Sunday morning. I spoke in Swahili while a young *Samburu* college student translated into the local language.
>
> Since these men had never attended a church service nor listened to a message from the Bible, I decided to speak on a simple passage—the woman at the well in John 4:3–42. I began by asking, "How would you like it if a man came to your village and asked for water from one of your women?"
>
> Surprisingly, the men rose from their rocks and began discussing my query in a small circle. Since the question was asked rhetorically I was not prepared for the interruption. The missionary and Seth, my ten-year-old son, observing my discomfort, watched with amusement. After five minutes the men resumed their positions. The oldest stood up and spoke for the group, "We would not like it. We do not want anyone speaking to our women, not even Jesus."

Surprised and perplexed, I realized this sermon was going to be more difficult than I had imagined. I decided to go a different direction. As the message progressed I made the mistake of asking another rhetorical question. As I presented the Gospel of Christ and spoke of the death, burial and resurrection of Jesus, I asked, "How many of you have ever heard of someone who died and came back from the dead after three days?"

Once again the men stood from their rocks and began discussing my question. I thought, "What could they be talking about this time?" After about five minutes everyone sat down again on the rocks. The oldest said with great gravity, "One man here knows someone who died and came back after two days, but none of us has ever heard of anyone who came back after three."[1]

INTRODUCTION

When this event transpired, I had served as a missionary for eight years and considered myself fairly competent in cross-cultural communication. Unfortunately, unseen cultural impediments blocked a smooth transfer of meaning. This incident highlights the need for extensive training for those ministering in other societies. Although modern technological advances have removed many obstacles, David Hesselgrave claims, "The cultural barriers are the most formidable."[2]

As one of the most important concepts in missions, definitions of contextualization abound. Gailyn Van Rheenen says, "Models emphasizing scripture usually define contextualization as the translation of biblical meanings into contemporary culture."[3] The term emerged in the middle of the twentieth century in a 1957 publication of the International Missionary Council (IMC).[4] Originators of the term initially designed it to describe their desire to incorporate

[1] Robin Dale Hadaway, "For Tropical Preaching: Proclaiming Biblical Truth Cross-Culturally," *Midwestern Journal of Theology* 14, no. 1 (2015): 1–2.

[2] Hesselgrave, *Communicating Christ Cross-Culturally*, 96 (see chap. 5, n. 8).

[3] Gailyn Van Rheenen, "Syncretism and Contextualization: The Church on a Journey Defining Itself," in *Contextualization and Syncretism: Navigating Cultural Currents*, Evangelical Missiological Society Series (Pasadena: William Carey Library, 2006), 3–4.

[4] This organization joined the World Council of Churches (WCC) in 1961.

the needs, aspirations, and desires of contemporary national believers into set biblical and church traditions.[5] This paralleled the WCC's steady drift toward focusing less on missions and evangelism and more on experimental theologies, gender issues, and social justice. In other words, contextualization began as an effort to ground theological education and the church closer to contemporary society while deemphasizing the Scriptures. Evangelicals, however, harnessed the term to describe how the gospel could be proclaimed with cultural sensitivity. David Hesselgrave lists three evangelical definitions of contextualization in his book on the subject:

1. "We understand the term to mean making concepts or ideals relevant in a given situation" (Byang Kato).

2. "[Contextualization is] the translation of the unchanging content of the Gospel of the kingdom into verbal form meaningful to the peoples in their separate culture and within their particular existential situations" (Bruce J. Nicholls).

3. "Contextualization properly applied means to discover *the legitimate implications* of the gospel in a given situation. It goes deeper than application. Application I can make or need not make without doing injustice to the text. Implication is *demanded* by the proper exegesis of the text" (George W. Peters).[6]

Hesselgrave says, "There is not yet a commonly accepted definition of the word *contextualization*, but only a series of proposals, all of them vying for acceptance."[7] Despite this lack of agreement, missiologists favor the concept as the best descriptive term available.[8] I define Christian contextualization as the correct application of biblical truth using insights from a society's culture and worldview in order to communicate the unchanging gospel to a constantly changing world.

---

[5] David J. Hesselgrave and Edward Rommen, *Contextualization: Meanings, Methods, and Models* (Pasadena: William Carey Library, 2000), 28–29.

[6] Hesselgrave and Rommen, 33–34.

[7] Hesselgrave and Rommen, 35.

[8] According to David Hesselgrave, "Acceptable contextualization is a direct result of ascertaining the meaning of the biblical text, consciously submitting to its authority, and applying or appropriating that meaning to a given situation." Hesselgrave and Rommen, 202.

TYPES OF CONTEXTUALIZATION

Non-Contextualization

Most mission volunteers and new missionaries initially practice this kind of contextualization. If translated by a competent interpreter, Westerners believe their messages will be understood by everyone. This "just go and preach the gospel" mentality Paul Hiebert calls "positivism." Theological positivism holds that the visitor's worldview, communication method, and concept of Christianity corresponds one-to-one with the Westerner's culture, idea of objective truth, and their interpretation of the Bible.[9] Unfortunately, this seldom, if ever, proves to be true.

As a young missionary, I attended a national evangelism conference in Dar es Salaam, Tanzania. Harry Mwasanjala, president of the Baptist Convention of Tanzania, translated for his counterpart, the president of a Baptist state convention in the US. Harry spoke English fluently but the colloquial expressions of the speaker proved too much of a challenge. About halfway through his message to the Tanzanians and missionaries, the American said, "Sometimes, you just wake up and have a 'Blue Monday.'" Stunned, Mwasanjala looked at the pastor and walked off the stage. Spotting an older missionary, Harry said, "Here, you translate. I've had enough." Non-contextualization generally occurs innocently; however, missionaries have the responsibility to widen their perspectives to include the concepts of other cultures.

Cross-Cultural Communication

Seba Eldridge defines communication as "the transfer of meaning through the use of symbols."[10] Cross-cultural communication constitutes a form of contextualization because these symbols must be encoded by the source, transmitted as a message, and decoded by the recipient. The idea may be conveyed contextually through an accurate translation or delivered without one. The originator of the message may contextualize (or non-contextualize) their language, dress,

---

[9] Hiebert, *Gospel in Human Contexts*, 19–20 (see chap. 6, n. 37).
[10] Seba Eldridge quoted in Hesselgrave, *Communicating Christ Cross-Culturally*, 55.

and manner of speaking. Finally, the recipients decode the message through their own cultural lenses.

David Hesselgrave describes the missionary problem as "communicating Christ across cultural barriers to the various people of the world."[11] Whereas translation involves the transfer of meaning from one language to another, the ancient academic discipline of rhetoric describes the oral delivery process. Aristotle divided the conveyance of spoken messages into three categories: (1) the speaker, (2) the speech, and (3) the audience. Other writers use similar terms, including (1) the source, (2) the message, and (3) the respondent.[12] Eugene Nida's three-culture model provides a valuable scaffolding for examining the different aspects of communication. The paradigm consists of (1) the missionary culture (source), (2) the Bible culture (message), and (3) the mission field culture (respondent).[13]

The Missionary Culture

The previous chapter describes how the worldview and culture of Westerners color their gospel presentations. Craig Skinner says, "Any speaker who assumes that his audience thinks and feels exactly like he does will always be wrong."[14] Since Americans understand their own culture, they apprehend other societies through this prism. Former United States Department of Defense Secretary Donald Rumsfeld famously said, "There are known knowns. There are things we know that we know. There are known unknowns. That is to say, there are things that we now know we don't know. But there are also unknown unknowns. There are things we do not know we don't know."[15]

These observations certainly apply in missions. One arrives in a new society fairly ignorant of cultural norms, practices, and traditions quite obvious to everyone else. I visited many villages in Tanzania for years before learning the reason for the strategic placement of small, beehive-like, wicker structures

---

[11] Hesselgrave, *Communicating Christ Cross-Culturally*, 26.

[12] Hesselgrave, 41.

[13] Hesselgrave, 107.

[14] Craig Skinner, *The Teaching Ministry of the Pulpit* (Grand Rapids: Baker, 1981), 32.

[15] Donald Rumsfeld, quoted in David C. Logan, "Known Knowns, Known Unknowns, Unknown Unknowns and the Propagation of Scientific Enquiry," *Journal of Experimental Botany*, 60, no. 3 (March 2009): 712, https://doi.org/10.1093/jxb/erp043.

outside many of the dwellings. "Everyone knew"—except the new mission-ary—these edifices housed departed ancestral spirits.

The Bible Culture

Scott Moreau says, "Contextualization means the message . . . is defined by Scripture but shaped by culture."[16] Understanding the Bible requires an aware-ness of the life and times of the Old and New Testaments. Translation con-textualizes the Scriptures by rendering them from their original languages into the local vernacular. This requires careful exegesis by the Bible translator in order to decipher the true meaning. For instance, early translators rendered the often-mentioned Old Testament phrase "ships of Tarshish" incorrectly (Isa 60:9). Research later demonstrated that a "Tarshish ship" was a particular class of boat, such as a clipper ship.

Contextualization occurs in both written and oral forms. My daughter-in-law works as a professional, simultaneous, Russian-English translator. In this most difficult linguistic conversion, the translator instantly analyzes the mean-ing, emphasis, and cultural appropriateness of each term and renders it rapidly and seamlessly into another language. Although phrase-by-phrase translators receive more time for their responses even these occasions present difficulties.

A Baptist mission group in South America annually attempts to evangelize the two million people who gather on the streets of Salvador during *Carna-val*, the Brazilian Mardi Gras. Brazilian nationals, missionaries, and volunteers erect evangelism platforms just off the parade route. When short of translators for their visitors one year, the organizers pressed into service a sixteen-year-old missionary kid (MK). At the completion of the ten-minute message, the volunteer exhorted the crowd to "commit" their lives to Christ. The MK, more accustomed to "street Portuguese" than religious terminology, translated the word "commit," as in "commit a crime," rather than the preferred, "commit your life" to Christ.

Bible translation is both an art and a science. Translation contextualization occurs when a linguist chooses one word over another in the vernacular. With

---

[16] A. Scott Moreau, *Contextualization in Missions: Mapping and Assessing Evangelical Models* (Grand Rapids: Kregel, 2012), 35.

more than 6,000 languages spoken in the world,[17] each with its own unique expressions, this represents a daunting task. Some religions, however, forbid the translation of their holy books. For instance, Muslims believe the Qur'an cannot be converted into another language. Believing the Arabic script of the Qur'an represents Allah's exact words, Islam holds these cannot be captured faithfully by another language. Consequently, for Muslims a "translation" of the Qur'an is impossible but becomes an "interpretation" and no more.[18]

Translations transfer meaning from one language to another. John Beekman and John Callow write about the contextualization obstacles in choosing literal over idiomatic translations.

> Translations tend to cluster around two basic types—literal and idiomatic. . . . They . . . are scattered at varying points on the continuum between these two opposite poles. . . . A literal translation is characterized by a high transference of the linguistic *form* of the source language into the receptor language. . . . On the other hand, an idiomatic translation aims at high transference of *meaning* from the source language into the receptor language.[19]

Language communicates meaning through vocal sounds composed of vocabulary, grammar, and phonology. Katharine Barnwell says that while "meaning is universal, form is different for each language."[20] A faithful translation transfers the meaning and dynamics of the original as clearly and idiomatically correct as possible.[21] The process involves deriving the exact meaning of the text of the receptor language (exegesis) and re-expressing that message in the receptor language (restructuring). A good translation should be accurate, clear and natural.[22] Since missionaries, volunteers, pastors, and laypeople de-

---

[17] Richard Blight, *Translation Problems from A to Z* (Dallas: Summer Institute of Linguistics, 1992), 5.

[18] Abdalati, *Islam in Focus*, 3n2.

[19] John Beekman, "Idiomatic versus Literal Translation," *Notes on Translation* 18 (1965): 1–15, quoted in Mildred Larson, *A Manual for Problem Solving in Bible Translation* (Dallas: Summer Institute of Linguistics, 1975), 17.

[20] Katharine Barnwell, *Introduction to Semantics and Translation: With Special Reference to Bible Translation*, 2nd ed. (Horsleys Green, UK: Summer Institute of Linguistics, 1980), 8.

[21] John Beekman and John Callow, *Translating the Word of God* (Grand Rapids: Zondervan, 1974), 31, 32, quoted in Larson, *Problem Solving in Bible Translation*, 21–22.

[22] Barnwell, *Semantics and Translation*, 15.

sire to communicate the gospel, contextualizing the Scriptures represents an important first step in the process.

A particularly sticky issue has been how to translate divine filial terms, especially the phrase, "Son of God." Some Bible translators and practical missiologists have argued that this biblical phrase suggests sexual relations in many languages. Therefore, some field translators have tried to soften the force of "Son of God" by translating the phrase something like "Beloved of God" or "God's favored one." David Hesselgrave counters:

> If the very words of Scripture are *God-breathed*, then textual accuracy is more important than supposed cultural relevance. In fact, when it comes to the biblical text, accurate translation and interpretation will, by definition, be culturally relevant. Accurate text will be free to speak, confirming or correcting cultural values and practices.[23]

This controversy caused Wycliffe/SIL to seek counsel from the World Evangelical Alliance (WEA) concerning Bible translation procedures. The WEA adopted recommendations that Wycliffe/SIL received and implemented concerning how to translate divine filial terms. The translation guidelines were formulated to insure that terms like "Son of God" would be translated with the meaning the New Testament intended.[24]

The Respondent Culture

Understanding the respondent culture presents special challenges for the missionary. A seminary colleague, Thomas Johnston, taught for a semester at the

---

[23] Hesselgrave, *Paradigms in Conflict*, 236 (see chap. 3, n. 31).

[24] The World Evangelical Alliance released an eighty-eight-page document titled "Divine Familial Terms Translation Procedures," as well as a four-page executive summary of that document. The summary statement says, "This document, Divine Familial Terms Translation Procedures, guides translators, translation consultants, and other translation program personnel in the technical decision-making processes for the selection and testing of appropriate terms for "father" and "son of God" in Muslim contexts. This document and the processes explained therein were developed in accordance with the recommendations of the panel named by the World Evangelical Alliance (WEA) and are approved by the WEA Oversight Group (December 2016). Please refer to the Executive Summary for an overview or to the complete document for the detailed procedures. World Evangelical Alliance, "WEA Divine Familial Terms Oversight Group Affirms Wycliffe and SIL's Bible Translation Guidelines," press release, February 20, 2017, http://worldea.org/news/4742." Links to the complete report and to the executive summary can be found in the press release.

Baptist seminary in Togo during a teaching sabbatical. During class a pastor asked Johnston a very unusual question. The ministerial student queried, "What do you do when your church is full of sorcerers?" Such a question seldom surfaces in American seminary classrooms.

This incident highlights the issue of cultural distance in missions. David Hesselgrave says:

> At Lausanne in 1974 Ralph Winter categorized cross-cultural evangelism as being E-1, E-2, and E-3 evangelism (later the category of E-0 evangelism was added). These categories denote differences based on the degree of "cultural distance" between the evangelist or missionary and respondents in another culture. The difficulty encountered in any particular instance of evangelism (or communication more widely conceived) is directly proportional to the degree of difference between the two cultures involved.[25]

These distinctions apply, not only in America, but throughout the world. A pastor speaking to his own congregation encounters a cultural distance between source and respondent of E-0. When, however, the same pastor preaches outside his church but within his own society, the E-1 cultural distance category applies. Western missionaries in Europe or Chinese missionaries in Asia must bridge a cultural distance gap of E-2. The greatest challenge, however, involves spanning the E-3 cultural chasm when missionaries ministers in a society very unlike their own.

James Engel and Wilbert Norton claim the apostle Paul "was both message and audience centered."[26] Modern missionaries should be as well. Cultural contextualization should not dominate the Christian message but should focus on transmitting gospel content. On the other hand, the cultural relativist position claims, "any cultural behavior can be judged only within the cultural context in which it occurs."[27] Evangelicals reject this position, however, contending that properly contextualized cross-cultural communication respects the local society without sacrificing biblical truth.

---

[25] Hesselgrave, *Communicating Christ Cross-Culturally*, 169.

[26] James F. Engel and Wilbert Norton, *What's Gone Wrong with the Harvest?* (Grand Rapids: Zondervan, 1982), 24.

[27] Martin and Nakayama, *Experiencing Intercultural Communication*, 19 (see chap. 6, n. 12).

Contextualization from the Bible

Missiologists often point to a number of Scriptures in order to justify various kinds and levels of contextualization. The most prominent of these passages include the "Unknown God" of Acts 17:16–34 and the "All things to all people" section of 1 Cor 9:11–23.

Acts 17:16–34 (The Unknown God). During his second missionary journey, Paul and his companions traveled through Asia Minor, Macedonia, and Greece, experiencing both persecution and response. Silas and Timothy left Paul in Athens, the most advanced culture of the ancient world.[28] Before the court of the Areopagus Paul began his contextualized gospel presentation. Paul discovered an altar inscription "To an Unknown God." F. F. Bruce says, "According to Diogenes Laertius, the Athenians during a pestilence sent for Epimenides the Cretan who advised them to sacrifice sheep at various spots to commemorate the occasion, altars to unnamed gods were set up."[29] Like a laser Paul zeroed in on this point of disquietude and made the connection. Cultural points of contact differ in every culture.

Howard Norrish served as a vice president for a mission agency that operates in some of the most resistant countries in the Levant. When I asked him, "What's the toughest people group to witness to?," Norrish said, "The British. My culture is the most difficult." He continued, "It's not socially acceptable to speak to someone on the street in Great Britain. You can talk to anybody though if you are walking a dog. Therefore, I bought a dog so I could meet neighbors on the street and speak to them about the Lord." This exemplifies contextualization.

Quickly making the association between Athenian traditional religion and Christianity, Paul pronounced, "Therefore, what you worship in ignorance, this I proclaim to you" (Acts 17:23b). This association is an example of contextualization that replaces or reinterprets non-Christian concepts with Bible truths.

---

[28] Although Corinth was the capitol of Achaia, Athens was the "cultural capital of the whole ancient world," according to Charles W. Carter and Ralph Earle, *The Acts of the Apostles* (Grand Rapids: Zondervan, 1973), 252. See also Frederick F. Bruce, *The Acts of the Apostles* (Grand Rapids: Eerdmans,1949), 331, where he states, "The sculpture, literature and oratory of Athens in the 5th and 4th Centuries BC have never been surpassed. In Philosophy too . . . being the native city of Socrates and Plato and the adopted home of Aristotle, Epicurus, and Zeno."

[29] Bruce, *Acts of the Apostles*, 336.

Paul used their pagan concept of god as a point of departure for preaching, not as a theological statement that their Unknown God equals the Christian God in a one-to-one equivalency. Instead, the apostle filled their limited notion of god with correct concepts about God's true nature. What concepts did Paul communicate to the Athenians in Acts 17:16–34?

The connection Paul made was selective. Negatively, Paul informed the Athenians that God is neither a temple dweller (v. 24), served by man (v. 25), nor a piece of art (v. 29). Furthermore, Paul did not appeal to the Athenians through the Old Testament, as he did with the Jews in Pisidian Antioch in Acts 13. Paul omits Jewish history from his presentation because the Council of the Areopagus was composed of Greeks. Here the apostle engages Greek philosophy and mythology, leading them to the cross.

Positively, Paul described God as the creator of the world (17: 24a), mankind, and ethnicities (v. 26). In verse 28, Paul notes, "as even some of your own poets have said, 'For we are also his offspring.'"[30] According to the apostle, God is the Existing One, "for in him we live and move and have our being" (v. 28). Here Paul references a poem about Zeus by his son Menos in a poem by Epimenides, using a brief secular source as a bridge to the gospel.

In this way, Paul demonstrated the acceptability of using a citation from another religion's writings for illustrative purposes. Paul's use of secular sources avoids the pitfall of the example becoming the message. Judicious, profound, and brief, the apostle's digression into Greek moral philosophy makes the connection and moves on. As Gerhard Friedrich says:

> In his preaching at Athens, Paul makes use of the pantheistic sense of God common to the Greeks, and attempts on this basis to open up to them the way to a full belief in God. . . . Hence this statement is to be regarded merely as an acknowledged starting point for his missionary preaching, not as a confession of his own theological convictions.[31]

Contextualized bridges to the gospel should not detract from the message, become entangled in the illustration, or supplant their referent. The older film

---

[30] Here, Paul quoted the Greek poet Aratus.
[31] Gerhard Friedrich, "κινέω (*kinaio*)," in *TDNT*, vol. 3.

The Bridge on the River Kwai features a British colonel who has been captured and taken to a Japanese prisoner of war camp in Thailand. The colonel decides that building a bridge over the river will improve morale and save lives. They successfully construct a spectacular bridge with local materials in record time. The colonel, however, discovers an Allied commando team plans to blow up his beautiful structure. Although the enemy would use the bridge to transport troops and supplies, the officer desires to preserve the bridge. In the film's final scene, the colonel realizes he has been more interested in building a bridge than winning the war. Therefore, he falls on the dynamite charge, sacrificing the beautiful edifice in the interest of achieving the greater goal. Unfortunately, sometimes beautiful contextualized bridges meant to share the gospel become an end in themselves and become more of an impediment than a solution to the original problem.

Paul's contextualized bridge allows him to proclaim, "Therefore, having overlooked the times of ignorance, God now commands all people everywhere to repent, because he has set a day when he is going to judge the world in righteousness by the man he has appointed. He has provided proof of this to everyone by raising him from the dead" (Acts 17:30–31). In these verses, Paul pivots again, using legal terms to address the Council of the Areopagus. The charge is willfully ignoring the true God and the call is to repentance. God can order all men to repent because of the evidence Paul presents:

> The resurrection of Jesus Christ from the dead. The term "raising" [the verb form for *Anastasis*, ἀναστήσας] is interesting; in the papyri . . . the verb is frequent in inscriptions with the sense of "erection" of a monument . . . and for the "setting up" of a statue . . . The narrative in Acts 17 prepares us for the total novelty of the meaning of the "resurrection": it was a perfectly natural use of the word, but the idea itself was new.[32]

The resurrection proves God's plan worked. Proper contextualization includes exegeting the society, bridging that culture to the most important aspects of Christianity, primarily the cross of Christ.

---

[32] Moulton and Milligan, "ἀναστήσας [*Anastasis*]," *Vocabulary of the Greek Testament*, 37–38 (see chap. 2, n. 13).

Paul never allows his cultural bridging to overshadow the gospel message. Because the unknown god was unknown, Paul did not have to empty the concept of elements incompatible with Christianity. On the contrary, he filled the "Unknown God" idea with Christian meaning because no other meaning existed. Paul did not attempt to contextualize Zeus, Thor, or Diana, because the unchristian elements associated with their names were so deeply embedded in them. Conversely, the "Unknown God" could be easily contextualized because the referent was neutral and easily provided with Christian meaning.

In my view, missiologists err when they suggest the god of Islam, Hinduism, or Buddhism can be contextualized in the manner of the apostle Paul in Acts 17. Unfortunately, too many known unchristian concepts exist in each of these religions to illustrate Christian concepts. Paul legitimately connected the Christian God to the "Unknown God" because no elements of Greek mythology were attached to it. On the other hand, identifying Krishna, Buddha, or Allah with the Unknown God presents problems because of these deities' questionable qualities. Finally, an analysis of Acts 17 demonstrates that missionaries can judiciously select certain religious concepts and practices as contextualized bridges for the gospel.

1 Corinthians 9:19–23. (All things to all men). These verses[33] contain one of the most famous and often quoted missions passages in the New Testament. Missiologists employ this text to support a variety of mission methods. Some hold this Scripture teaches missionaries should adopt practices of the receptor population. This would include wearing a white robe when living among Muslims or drinking milk mixed with blood when ministering to African pastoralists. This text has even been used to justify that one could become as a Muslim to reach Muslims, a Hindu to evangelize Hindus, or a Buddhist to witness to Buddhists. Anthony Thiselton says, "This passage is widely known as expounding a principle of missionary 'accommodation and flexibility' on the part of

---

[33] "Although I am free from all and not anyone's slave, I have made myself a slave to everyone, in order to win more people. To the Jews I became like a Jew, to win Jews; to those under the law, like one under the law—though I myself am not under the law—to win those under the law. To those who are without the law, like one without the law—though I am not without God's law but under the law of Christ—to win those without the law. To the weak I became weak, in order to win the weak. I have become all things to all people, so that I may by every possible means save some. Now I do all this because of the gospel, so that I may share in the blessings."

these who proclaim the message."[34] Should one accommodate in missions, and if so, how much?

These verses begin with an introductory sentence in v. 19 and conclude with a summary statement in v. 23. Between these verses Paul lists three classes of people: (1) Jews in v. 20; (2) those without law, likely Gentiles, in v. 21; and (3) the weak in v. 22.

The Jews. Paul makes quite a broad introductory statement in 1 Cor 9:19: "Although I am free from all and not anyone's slave, I have made myself a slave to everyone, in order to win more people." Paul proclaims his total freedom in Christ. He repeats this in the summary statement in 1 Cor 10:23, "Everything is permissible, but not everything is beneficial. 'Everything is permissible,' but not everything builds up." What does it mean to have Christian liberty and freedom? According to Paul, liberty includes the freedom to serve others. Paul said, "I have made myself a slave." The purpose of becoming a slave is that it opens a path to win[35] more to Christ.

The Jews are the first-mentioned subjects of Paul's evangelism efforts (9:20). The difficulty in the passage involves the phrase, "to the Jews I became as a Jew." Since the Bible presents Paul as a Jew, what does it mean when the apostle says, "I became as a Jew"? David Garland dismisses Chrysostom's view that Paul did not become a Jew in reality but in appearance only and with Barrett's interpretation that Paul's Judaism was "a guise he could adopt or discard at will."[36] Garland holds that Paul remaining a Jew cost him dearly:

> The clearest example of what Paul means by becoming "as a Jew" and as "one under the law" is his description of the thirty-nine lashes he suffered at the hands of the Jews (2 Cor. 11:24). . . . Paul's motives for submitting to this discipline are a little more difficult to penetrate, but rulings from the Mishnah may help. The Mishnah lists thirty-six sins, including blasphemy, that warrant being cut off from

---

[34] Anthony C. Thiselton, *The First Epistle to the Corinthians* (Grand Rapids: Eerdmans, 2000), 702.

[35] The word means "to win" an argument, rather than "to conquer or vanquish," the usual meaning. Although the word κερδήσω [*kerdaiso*] has a commercial connotation of material gain, Daube employs it as a technical word for winning a proselyte in Judaism. The verb appears five times in 9:19–21. David Daube, "κερδαινω as a Missionary Term," *Harvard Theological Review* 40, no. 2 (April 1947): 109–120, quoted in Thiselton, *First Epistle to the Corinthians*, 701.

[36] David E. Garland, *1 Corinthians* (Grand Rapids: Baker, 2003), 429.

the people without warning (*m Ker.* 1:1). What is important to note, however, is that flogging averted both a harsher punishment at the hands of God and being cut off from the people (Lev. 18:29). The Mishnah rules, "*And thy brother seem vile unto thee* [Deut. 25:3]—when he is scourged then he is thy brother" (*m. Mak.* 3:15). . . . Paul accepted these penalties to keep open the option of preaching the gospel message in the synagogue.[37]

Paul remaining a Jew cost him greatly as he gave his own body and blood to remain under the law as a Jew.

While living in North Africa, I visited another mission agency's staff meeting on a Saturday morning. Most present were nationals living in the Muslim part of the country. One team had just returned from showing the *Jesus* film in the marketplace of a large Muslim city. One tall tribesman stood and shared his story: "Toward the end of the film some Muslims beat us up, damaged our projector, and dismissed the crowd. However, I believe God wants us to go back there again next week." The attitude of these men recalls that of the apostle Paul, whose witness cost him dearly.

Since the apostle Paul, a Jewish convert, used his Judaism to remain inside Judaism, some missiologists hold one can remain within another major religion while retaining allegiance to Christianity. Those who maintain this opinion point to 1 Cor 9:20. Judaism as it relates to Christianity, however, fits into a special category. A number of years ago, I taught a missions class in Nairobi, Kenya. Discussing this issue, the students were asked, "Can one say, 'To the Muslims, I became as a Muslim' in the same way that Paul said, 'To the Jews, I became as a Jew'?" Russ Bush, the late academic dean of Southeastern Baptist Theological Seminary, answered the question:

> This is the difference. Christianity came out of Judaism. The New Testament emerged from the Old Testament. With Judaism properly interpreted you are dealing with truth. This is not so with Islam. The Qur'an is not a true document, therefore, one cannot use this passage [1 Cor 9:20] and extrapolate that one can be a Christian and observe the tenants of Islam in the same way that Paul could follow parts of the law of Moses and follow Christ.[38]

---

[37] Garland, 430.
[38] June 2005.

According to Russ Bush, 1 Cor 9:20 does not support Christians winning adherents of other belief systems by practicing portions of the other religion's faith. Christians may adopt cultural practices such as dress and diet so as not to offend their hosts. This, however, differs from straddling the fence, and identifying as an adherent of a non-Christian faith. Rather, this passage teaches Christlike servanthood as the preferred method of outreach over arguments designed to convince others that Christianity resembles their faith more than it might appear.

Gentiles. The Gentiles constitute Paul's second category of evangelism efforts. Every commentator believes 1 Cor 9:21 refers to the Gentiles. Garland says:

> He did not become a pagan sinner, but he did give up his zeal for the tradition of the fathers and righteousness earned under the law so that he might live under the grace of God (Gal. 1:13–16). In effect, he became like a Gentile, as one without heritage, without the merit of the fathers, without works of law to set him apart from others or to justify his salvation. Paul lived among the Galatians simply as a Christian, not as a Jew or a Pharisee of Pharisees.[39]

Paul, however, guards against his readers thinking he had become a lawless person, sanctioning antinomianism. Paul declares in Rom 7:12 the law is holy, just, and good, only denouncing its misuse. Richard Hays instructs that "being free from the law does not mean that Paul runs wild with self-indulgence. . . . Instead, he lives with a powerful sense of obligation to God."[40]

Theodore Roosevelt became president of the United States when an anarchist shot President William McKinley on September 14, 1901.[41] Anarchists decry all laws and governments. These radicals were quite active at the turn of the nineteenth century. 1 Corinthians 9:21 does not advocate a spiritual anarchistic position. On the contrary, Christians are not without the law of God but are under the "law of Christ."

---

[39] Garland, 431–32.

[40] Richard B. Hays, *First Corinthians: Interpretation: A Bible Commentary for Teaching and Preaching* (Louisville, KY: John Knox, 1997), 154, quoted in Thiselton, *First Epistle to the Corinthians*, 704–5.

[41] Edmond Morris, *Theodore Rex* (New York: Random House, 2001), 3–4.

Barrett calls this "one of the most difficult sentences in the epistle, and also one of the most important."[42] The phrase "law of Christ" appears only here, Rom 8:2, and Gal 6:2. Garland states this is not the law of Moses nor the teachings Christ gave his disciples. It's a new law redefined and fulfilled by Christ's love.[43] This law assists Christians as they behave differently.

When I lived as a missionary in São Paulo, Brazil, I drove each day to the domestic airport to pick up my mail. On the return trip, suddenly, one vehicle rear-ended another just in front of me. The driver of the first vehicle jumped out of his car and slammed the door. The driver of the second car also leaped from his sedan, shut the door and headed straight for the driver of the first car. Expecting to observe a Brazilian version of road rage, I was surprised when they approached each other and embraced with a hug. They reacted in a way that rarely occurs in America.

1 Corinthians 9:21 advocates contextualization when evangelizing those without law. The text teaches that while Christians may not abandon the law of God (Christian morality), they may use their own judgment on cultural questions and personal appearance issues not covered in Scripture. Christians should follow both the timeless law of God (morality) and the equally ageless law of Christ (love).

The Weak. The third focus of Paul's evangelism ministry is the weak (1 Cor 9:22). According to Stahlin:

> The 1st main meaning [of ἀσθενής, *asthenais*] is "weak" or "weakest" in the physical sense. In the New Testament, however, the words are hardly ever used of purely physical weakness but frequently in the comprehensive sense of the whole man.[44]

The New Testament uses the word more in the sense of spiritual weakness. This seems to be the sense of 1 Cor 8:10–11: "For if someone sees you, the one who has knowledge, dining in an idols temple, won't his weak conscience be encouraged to eat food offered to idols? So the weak person, the brother or sister for whom Christ died, is ruined by your knowledge."

---

[42] C. K. Barrett, *A Commentary on the First Epistle to the Corinthians*, 2nd ed. (London: Black, 1971), 212, quoted in Thiselton, *First Epistle to the Corinthians*, 704.

[43] Garland, *1 Corinthians*, 432.

[44] Gustaf Stahlin, "[*asthenais*] ασθενης," in *TDNT*, vol. 1.

What does 1 Cor 9:22 mean here? John MacArthur sees the weakness as their inability to grasp the gospel.[45] Garland suggests "'weak' may also allude to the theological condition of all humankind as ungodly."[46] Simon Kistemaker, however, sees "a double connotation that refers to both the weak in conscience and the economically weak."[47]

The second part of 9:22 constitutes the crux of the issue, where Paul says, "I have become all things to all people so that I may by every possible means save some." So, was Paul a chameleon guilty of pretense and duplicity? Garland explores this question:

> Did Paul adopt the pose of a flatterer who masquerades as something that he is not in order to ingratiate himself with potential converts? . . . The allegation that Paul was guilty of inconsistency is unjustified. He rebuked Cephas for acting out of fear and wilting under external pressure from the men from James. . . . (Gal 2:11–14).[48]

Donald Carson says, "this is not a licence for unlimited flexibility"[49] and James Moffat claims Paul was not "wishy-washy" here.[50] Paul steadfastly maintained high standards and boundaries, never compromising on biblical truth or on important doctrinal matters.

What are the lessons of this passage? Christians do not have a license to sin, offend, or do as they please. Instead, they have the liberty to love and serve one another. They possess the freedom to give up their rights so people can more easily enter the kingdom of God. Martin Luther wrote about the apostle Paul in his work *On Christian Liberty*. The great Reformer said, "A Christian

---

[45] MacArthur says, "When among those who were weak he acted weak, he stooped to the level of their comprehension. To those who needed simple or repeated presentations this is what he gave them." John MacArthur, *First Corinthians*, MacArthur New Testament Commentary (Chicago: Moody, 1984), 213.

[46] Garland refers to Rom 5:6 as his text: "For while we were still helpless (weak) at the right time Christ died for the ungodly." Many commentators contend "the weak" refers to those weak in faith. Garland, *1 Corinthians*, 433–34.

[47] Simon J. Kistemaker, quoted in Garland, *1 Corinthians*, 433n18.

[48] Garland, *1 Corinthians*, 434.

[49] D. A. Carson, "Pauline Inconsistency: Reflections on 1 Corinthians 9:19–23 and Galatians 2:11–14," *Churchman* 100 (1986), 33, quoted in Garland, *1 Corinthians*, 435.

[50] James Moffat, *The First Epistle of Paul to the Corinthians*, MNTC 7 (London: Hodder & Stoughton, 1938), 123, quoted in Garland, *1 Corinthians*, 435.

man is the most free of all, and subject to none; a Christian man is the most dutiful servant of all, and subject to everyone."[51]

Missionaries may use their Christian freedom to win others but are not free to offend unnecessarily. They are free to creatively contextualize the gospel to reach Jews, Gentiles, and the weak in each society. On the other hand, missionaries are not free to dilute, bend, or alter biblical truth in order to make the message more palatable and less offensive. On the contrary, believers are free to give up their rights, go the extra mile, turn the other cheek, and love their enemies. Becoming "all things to all men" does not give license to blur the differences between Christianity and other religions to make the former more acceptable to the latter. Rather, the missionary should go out of his way to blend in culturally while respectfully promulgating and defending the faith.

Contextualization Issues with Other Religions

Contextualization approaches abound in Christian ministry, especially to Muslims. Non-contextual approaches have been popular with apologists attempting to reach those of other religions. The debate-polemic approach, sometimes known as the "direct method," favors using "proof texts" and argumentation to win adherents. Those currently employing the direct approach encourage courtesy in their presentations but state the matter plainly. Jay Smith says, "The Qur'an has huge errors in it, enormous errors. My goal is to eradicate the whole edifice of Islam so that [Muslims] can then look for the alternative."[52] This non-contextualized approach effectively communicates the gospel without significantly adapting the message to the audience. This approach sometimes works.

In 2002, I traveled to East Africa with the president of the Foreign Mission Board of the Brazilian Baptist Convention. Our traveling party met with a young Brazilian missionary working with Somali refugees in a large city. Describing his ministry in Portuguese, the missionary said he taught automobile

---

[51] Martin Luther, "Treatise On Christian Liberty," (1520). Accessed September 3, 2018. https://history.hanover.edu/courses/excerpts/165luther.html

[52] Jay Smith, quoted in Stan Guthrie, "Deconstructing Islam: Apologist Jay Smith Takes a Confrontational Approach," *Christianity Today*, September 9, 2002, 37, https://www.christianitytoday.com/ct/2002/september9/32.37.html.

mechanics to about fifty Muslim men. Amazingly, over a two-year period he had won seventeen Somali men to Christ. When asked how he had accomplished this feat with such a difficult people group, he replied, "I tell them Muhammad was a false prophet, the Qur'an is from the devil, and they are going to hell if they do not repent and believe in Jesus." Quite amazed, the author asked, "That's your method?" He responded, "I tell them the truth." Fifteen years later at a large Muslim evangelism meeting in Thailand attended by more than 800 people, I by chance ran into this Brazilian missionary again. After being reminded of the meeting years ago, the Brazilian said, "That's my method; I am still using it and it's still working."

Qur'anic Contextualization Methods. Many Qur'anic passages refer to biblical persons and stories. This similarity leads Christians to select verses from the Qur'an to bolster a Christian hermeneutic, despite the fact the Qur'an denies Jesus's divinity (*Sura* 9:30–1) and the Trinity (*Sura* 4:171). Sam Schlorff explains:

> The Qur'an calls Christ "the Word of God" and "a Spirit from Him" (4:171; 3:45). It has Him born of a virgin (19:16–35) and calls Him "Illustrious (*wajiih*) in this world and the next, and among those closest to God" (3:45). He is the only prophet who is said to have created, and to have raised the dead (3:49). And of all the prophets, including Mohammad, Christ is never said to have sinned (see 3:36).[53]

Using the Qur'an as a bridge to the gospel presents some problems. First, when Christians bend Qur'anic verses to match Christian interpretations, Muslims often object. Second, when missionaries spice their presentations with Qur'anic citations, the Christian inadvertently confers some legitimacy on Islam's holy book. Sam Schlorff calls the method of mining Qur'anic truth in order to disclose its deeper meaning in the Bible the "new hermeneutic" in Qur'anic analysis.[54]

To find some middle ground with Islam, many well-meaning missiologists have attempted various approaches to reaching out to Muslims. Geoffrey

---

[53] Samuel P. Schlorff, *Missiological Models in Ministry to Muslims* (Upper Darby, PA: Middle East Resources, 2006), 63–64.
[54] Schlorff, 72.

Parrinder's *Jesus in the Qur'an* claims "the undoubted revelation of God in Muhammad and in the Qur'an."[55] Ralph Winter proposes adopting a non-confrontational attitude, stating, "Cannot we think of the Qur'an as we do the Apocrypha and let it gradually take a back seat to our Bible simply because it is not as edifying intellectually or spiritually?"[56] Another bridging methodology that uses the Christian interpretation of the Qur'an is the "CAMEL" method.

Proponents claim to have developed the CAMEL method while watching Muslim converts in South Asia win Muslims to Christ.

> It soon became clear to us that the shortest bridge available was found in 13 verses of *Surah al-Imran*, chapter 3 of the Qur'an, which spoke of *Isa al-Masih* (Jesus Christ). This passage declared that Jesus would be born of a virgin; that He would do miracles; that He would be a sign to the whole world; that Allah would cause Him to die and raise Him again to heaven. To help us remember the key points in the chapter we used the acronym **C-A-M-E-L**. These letters brought to mind the chapter's key teaching that *Isa*'s mother, Mary, was **C**hosen to give birth to *Isa*; that **A**ngels announced the good news to her; that *Isa* would do **M**iracles, and that He knew the way to **E**ternal **L**ife. In this way, the *Camel* method was born.[57]

This technique mentions Mary, Jesus's mother, in the initial steps of the CAMEL acronym (**C-A**). Introducing Mary brings problems, as the Qur'an replaces the Holy Spirit in the Christian Trinity with Jesus's mother.[58] The third element of the CAMEL acronym (**M**) describes the miracles[59] of Jesus as

---

[55] Geoffrey Parrinder, quoted in Schlorff, *Ministry to Muslims*, 74–75.

[56] Ralph D. Winter, "Going Far Enough?" in Winter and Hawthorne, *Perspectives on the World Christian Movement*, 671 (see chap. 1, n. 30).

[57] Kevin Greeson, *The Camel: How Muslims Are Coming to Faith in Christ* (Arkadelphia, AR: Wigtake Resources, 2007), 16, 41–42. Although *The Camel* claims "missionaries did not invent the Camel method. It is the method we learned from Muslim-background believers," most likely Westerners formulated the **C-A-M-E-L** acronym. The Arabic transliteration of camel would be spelled *jimel*. The Arabic script version would be written from right to left without vowels in the Semitic manner (**L-M-J**).

[58] The Qur'an views the Trinity as Father, Son, and Mary. Braswell, *Islam*, 251 (see chap. 5, n. 4).

[59] *The Camel* quotes Qur'an *Sura* 3:49 in support of Jesus performing miracles: "And (make him) an apostle to the children of Israel: That I have come to you with a sign from your Lord, that I determine for you out of dust like the form of a bird, then I breathe into it and it becomes a bird with Allah's permission, and I heal the blind and leprous and bring the dead to life with Allah's permission." Greeson, *Camel*, 105.

recorded in the apocryphal *Gospel of Thomas*. 'E-L' represents the final step in the acronym and signifies 'Eternal Life'. Reaching this conclusion from *Sura* 3:45[60] involves taking some significant literary license. Kevin Greeson, in *The Camel*, holds this sura refers to Christ's resurrection, although Islamic theology disagrees with such an interpretation.[61]

The four-step CAMEL method and other propositional[62] methods also clash with the literary style of the Qur'an. Islam's holy book communicates in poetic style and through emotion. Although Muslims certainly participate in propositional arguments, biblical interpretations of Qur'anic phrases repel rather than attract. Sam Schlorff advocates a more direct approach:

> The focus is on what Mohammad understood the terms to mean and how his original hearers would have understood him. In practical terms, this means that Qur'anic language may not be interpreted in terms of what one might think similar biblical language might have meant. It cannot be filled with Christian content.[63]

As an example, a believer might say to a Muslim, "The Qur'an mentions '*Isa*[64] in these instances. The Bible calls '*Isa* by the name Jesus Christ. The Scriptures

---

[60] *The Camel* quotes from *Sura* 3:54–55 as the Qur'anic proof text that Jesus is the way to Eternal Life: "And they planned and Allah (also) planned, and Allah is the best of planners. And when Allah said: O *Isa*, I am going to terminate the period of your stay (on earth) and cause you to ascend unto Me and purify you of those who disbelieve and make those who follow you above those who disbelieve to the day of resurrection; then to Me shall be your return, so I will decide between you concerning that in which you differed." Greeson, *Camel*, 105–6 (italics his, bold added). Greeson does not source the interpretation (translation) of the Qur'anic sura (verse).

[61] Greeson, *Camel*, 118, 127, 138.

[62] Propositional methods feature "one, two, three"; "first step, second step, third step"; or "first point, second point, third point" arguments.

[63] Schlorff, *Ministry to Muslims*, 133.

[64] Opinions differ regarding the use of the Qur'anic word for Jesus: '*Isa* as opposed to *Yasuu*', a transliteration of the Greek word *Iesous* (Ἰησοῦς), widely used by Christian Arabs. Forty-two New Testament translations employ the latter, while seventeen (including Henry Martyn's renowned 1814 Persian translation) use '*Isa* [عِيسَى.]. See Schlorff, *Ministry to Muslims*, 36. Some missiologists prefer '*Isa* since Muslims know the term. Others argue that the Qur'anic meaning of '*Isa* differs too radically from the biblical understanding of Jesus. See John Ankerberg and Ergun Caner, *The Truth about Islam and Jesus* (Eugene, OR: Harvest House, 2009), 8. However, Schlorff (37) concludes since both Christians and Christian cults use Jesus with different connotations, evangelicals can safely employ '*Isa* when speaking to Muslims about Christ. The same arguments apply in the question concerning the name of God; J. D. Greear, *Breaking the Islam Code* (Eugene, OR: Harvest House, 2010), 160. This case differs slightly as no good alternative exists for "God" in Arabic apart from Allah الله. Every reputable Arabic Bible translation utilizes

say this about Him." Rather than validating the Qur'an, this reference serves as a jumping-off point.

Muslim society blends the cultural and religious elements of its populace. In the Middle East and North Africa many Muslim men wear long white Islamic robes with caps on their heads. Although most Muslims dress in Western style in the cities,[65] those in the countryside prefer traditional clothing. Contextualizing culture dates back to the nineteenth century.[66] Christian workers today, with some exceptions, appreciate the customs of the places where they serve. Missionaries should be careful, however, about eating or abstaining from certain foods because sometimes these have religious connotations.[67]

Another missionary and I were dining at an outdoor restaurant in the Horn of Africa. After reviewing the Arabic menu, one of the Eastern Orthodox men in the party said, "I do not eat Muslim meat." His religious beliefs demanded that an Eastern Orthodox priest be present when the animal was slaughtered. Therefore, for Abraham, there was nothing in this Muslim restaurant he could consume.

Opinions differ about contextualizing in regard to clothing. Western women cover themselves in some Muslim countries to avoid male harassment. In other Islamic countries, however, women feel comfortable wearing modest Western dress. Male missionaries also face dilemmas about clothing because many Muslims wear European-style clothing in Islamic countries. Sometimes when missionaries contextualize their dress to the culture the results are humorous.

A number of years ago, a Scandinavian missionary wore a flowing, white Islamic garment in an attempt to be culturally appropriate. Only a few foreigners

---

the term, despite the fact that Christian and Muslim concepts of God differ significantly. Christians worship the God of Abraham, Isaac, and Jacob. Muslims worship the Allah of Abraham and Ishmael. In addition, some of the ninety-nine names of God do not reflect a Christian idea of God (e.g., *Al-Qahhar*, the All Compelling Subduer; *Al Khafid*, the Abaser; *Al-Mudhill*, the Giver of Dishonor; *Al Mumit*, the Bringer of Death, the Destroyer; *Al-Mu'akhkhir*, the Delayer; *Al-Wali*, the Patron; *Al-Ghani*, the All Rich, the Independent.

[65] Andrew Wheatcroft, *Infidels: A History of the Conflict between Christendom and Islam* (New York: Random House, 2004), 315.

[66] Hebert J. Kane, *A Concise History of the Christian World Mission* (Grand Rapids: Baker, 1982), 166, 169.

[67] Braswell, *Islam*, 62–63.

lived in the large port city along the Red Sea. When the tall, blond European strolled around the marketplace he attracted a huge crowd everywhere he walked. Rather than blending in with the society, the opposite occurred.

Insider Movements. Generating much debate, the insider movement attempts to contextualize Christianity within Islam.[68] Charles Kraft, appropriating a concept from the field of linguistics, harnessed the notion of "dynamic equivalency"[69] to the discipline of missiology.[70] This version of contextualizing Christianity with Islam favors converts who receive Christ remaining in the Muslim faith. The insider movement[71] points to Hebrew Christians who remain in Judaism and call themselves Messianic Jews.[72] Insider advocate John Travis[73] writes, "In the past four decades tens of thousands of Jews have accepted Jesus as their Messiah yet remain socio-religiously Jewish."[74] In a similar vein, the insider movement believes "Messianic Muslims" may accept 'Isa the Messiah as their Savior while maintaining their Islamic cultural

---

[68] There are insider movements in Buddhism, Hinduism, and other religions in addition to Islam. This chapter on contextualization, however, will concentrate on insider movements within Islam because they are by far the largest.

[69] Eugene Nida coined this term, which describes a translation that attempts to express the meaning of the words rather than a formal equivalence of them. In missiological terms a "dynamic equivalent" cultural practice might be substituted for a biblical one if no suitable form exists in a particular culture. See Hesselgrave, *Paradigms in Conflict*, 260. For instance, if a society lacks bread, then another staple food might be substituted for it during the Lord's Supper.

[70] Charles H. Kraft, "Dynamic Equivalent Churches in Muslim Society," in *The Gospel and Islam: A 1978 Compendium*, ed. Don McCurry (Monrovia: Missions Advanced Research and Communication Center, 1978), 114.

[71] The insider movement advocates staying within Islam while accepting 'Isa as the Messiah. Greear says, "They want to see movements to Jesus *within* Islam rather than *from* Islam. These are called *insider movements.*" Greear, *Breaking the Islam Code*, 153. Rebecca Lewis says, "Insider movements can be defined as movements to obedient faith in Christ that remain integrated with or inside their natural community." Rebecca Lewis, "Insider Movements: Retaining Identity and Preserving Community," in Winter and Hawthorne, *Perspectives on the World Christian Movement*, 673.

[72] Schlorff, *Ministry to Muslims*, 80–81.

[73] John J. Travis "The C-Spectrum: A Practical Tool for Defining Six Types of 'Christ-Centered Communities' Found in Muslim Contexts," in Winter and Hawthorne, *Perspectives on the World Christian Movement*, 664. John Travis is a pseudonym for one of the leading proponents of the insider movement, a missionary I know in Asia who has been involved in contextualized Muslim ministry since 1987.

[74] John J. Travis, "Response One," in "Four Responses to Timothy C. Tennent's *Followers of Jesus ('Isa) in Islamic Mosques: A Closer Examination of C-5 'High Spectrum' Contextualization*," *International Journal of Frontier Missions* 23, no. 3 (2006): 124–25.

distinctiveness.[75] Mark Durie disagrees with contextualizing Islam in the same manner as some Messianic Jews attempt with Judaism. He says:

> Unlike *Muslim*, or the Muslim *Umma*, the terms *Jew* and *Israel* are biblical categories. . . .
>
> To place *Muslim* in the same category as *Jew*, or the *Umma* as analogous to *Israel* raises serious theological difficulties, because the two are not equivalent from a gospel perspective. . . .
>
> A kind of inversion or reversal takes place when people speak of Messianic Muslims, as if this phenomenon was equivalent to Messianic Jews. This reversal is redolent of Islamic supersessionist dogma, in which Islam identifies Judaism and Christianity with itself in order to supplant them, on the grounds that all the patriarchs and prophets were actually Muslims and their religion Islam, so Islam becomes the true Judaism and the true Christianity. If one accepts this (false) premise, then what could be more natural than the concept of "Messianic Muslims," because, after all, Jesus was a Muslim prophet? The problem with this conclusion is that Islamic supersessionism is based on the rejection of the authenticity of the gospels, and thus the Jesus of history. To speak of Messianic Muslims is to attempt to establish a bridge to Jesus on the foundation of Islamic supersessionism.[76]

John Travis's C-Spectrum scale provides a framework for examining issues related to the insider movement. "The C1–C6 Spectrum compares and contrasts types of 'Christ-centered communities (groups of believers in Christ) found in the Muslim world. . . . The spectrum attempts to address the enormous diversity which exists throughout the Muslim world in terms of ethnicity, history, traditions, language, culture, and in some cases, theology," explains Travis.

---

[75] Rick Brown, "Biblical Muslims," *International Journal of Frontier Missions* 24, no. 2 (2007): 65–74.

[76] Mark Durie, "Messianic Judaism and Deliverance from the Two Covenants of Islam," in *Muslim Conversions to Christ: A Critique of Insider Movements in Islamic Contexts*, ed. Ayman S. Ibrahim and Ant B. Greenham (New York: Peter Lang, 2018), 267–68. Durie, a friend of mine, is a linguist, former missionary, and Anglican priest in Australia.

C1–Traditional Church Using Outsider Language. . . . A huge cultural chasm often exists between the church and the surrounding Muslim community. . . . C1 believers call themselves "Christians."

C2–Traditional Church Using Insider Language. Essentially the same as C1 except for language. . . . The cultural gap between Muslims and C2 is still large. . . . C2 believers call themselves "Christians."

C3–Contextualized Christ-Centered Communities Using Insider Language and Religiously Neutral Insider Cultural Forms. . . . Islamic elements (where present) are "filtered out" so as to use purely "cultural" forms. . . . C3 congregations are comprised of a majority of Muslim background believers. C3 believers call themselves "Christians."

C4–Contexualized Christ-Centered Community Using Insider Language and Biblically Permissible Cultural and Islamic Forms. Similar to C3, however, biblically permissible Islamic forms and practices are also utilized. . . . C4 communities comprised almost entirely of Muslim background believers. C4 believers . . . are usually not seen as Muslim by the Muslim community. C4 believers identify themselves as "followers of *'Isa* the Messiah" (or something similar).

C5–Christ-Centered Communities of "Messianic Muslims" Who Have Accepted Jesus as Lord and Savior. C5 believers remain legally and socially within the community of Islam. Somewhat similar to the Messianic Jewish movement. . . . C5 believers are viewed as Muslims by the Muslim community and think of themselves as Muslims who follow *'Isa* the Messiah.

C6–Small Christ-Centered Communities of Secret/Underground Believers. Similar to persecuted believers suffering under totalitarian regimes. . . . C6 believers are perceived as Muslims by the Muslim community and identify themselves as Muslims.[77]

Insider movement proponents focus on eliminating the cultural gap between Christian and Muslim communities. Entry into Christianity without

---

[77] John J. Travis, "The C1 to C6 Spectrum: A Practical Tool for Defining Six Types of 'Christ-Centered Communities' ('C') Found in Muslim Context," Dispatches from the Front, Frontline Missions International, accessed July 31, 2019, https://www.frontlinemissions.info/the-c1-to-c6-spectrum.

sacrificing identity with one's culture is the goal of insider advocates like Rebecca Lewis.[78] John Travis states, "If perhaps the single greatest hindrance to seeing Muslims come to faith in Christ is not a theological one (i.e., accepting Jesus as Lord) but rather one of culture and religious identity (i.e., having to leave the community of Islam), it seems that for the sake of God's kingdom much of our missiological energy should be devoted to seeking a path whereby Muslims can remain Muslims, yet live as true followers of the Lord Jesus."[79]

Encouraging believers in Christ to remain in Islam bothers many. Although an advocate for C4 contextualization, Phil Parshall disagrees with the C5 approach. He believes "Messianic Muslims" remaining in the mosque, participating in prayers, and affirming Muhammad as a prophet presents problems.[80] The main difference between the C4 and C5 categories concerns the believers' *identities*. Timothy Tennent explains, "The crucial issue at stake is *self*-identify. C5 believers are fully embedded in the cultural and religious life of Islam. That is why their presence in the Mosque is referred to as an 'insider movement,' because they really *are* insiders. It is even inaccurate to refer to them (as they often are) as MBBs [Muslim background believers], because, for them, Islam is not in their *background*, it remains as their primary *identity*."[81]

Where C4 Christ followers may retain some Islamic cultural forms, both the society and the believers themselves identify C4 adherents as Christians. Whereas C4 contextualization majors on Muslim culture, many C5 believers practice some Islamic religious forms. Since C5 proponents[82] advocate Muslim believers remaining in Islam, the dispute has centered mainly on this type of contextualization with Islam.

---

[78] Rebecca Lewis, "Insider Movements," in Winter and Hawthorne, *Perspectives on the World Christian Movement*, 674.

[79] John J. Travis, "Must All Muslims Leave 'Islam' to Follow Christ?" in Winter and Hawthorne, *Perspectives on the World Christian Movement*, 672.

[80] Phil Parshall, "Going Too Far?" in Winter and Hawthorne, 666.

[81] Timothy C. Tennent, "Followers of Jesus ('Isa) in Islamic Mosques: A Closer Examination of C-5 'High Spectrum' Contextualization," *International Journal of Frontier Missions* 23, no. 3 (Fall 2006), 104. Tennent is president of Asbury Theological Seminary.

[82] John Travis and most other C5 proponents do not advocate foreign Christian workers becoming Muslims (or saying they are Muslims to reach Muslims). C5 is for those already within Islam who have converted to Christ. Travis, "Must All Muslims Leave," in Winter and Hawthorne, *Perspectives on the World Christian Movement*, 669; Tennent, "Followers of Jesus," 108.

Unfortunately, C5 contextualization assumes Muslim forms can be un-hinged from their Muslim implications.[83] This avoids the fact that meanings and forms flow from agreements by insiders among themselves within the so-ciety.[84] Outsiders reformulating the religious paradigms of others invariably make mistakes. Hiebert sounds this warning:

> When we try to reinterpret symbols used by the dominant society, however, we are in danger of being misunderstood and ultimately of being captured by its definitions of reality. . . . We are not free to arbitrarily link meanings and forms. To do so is to destroy people's history and culture. . . . The greatest danger in separating meaning from form is the relativism and pragmatism this introduces.[85]

This represents the principle danger in the contextualization process—syn-cretism. It is easy for someone seeking to contextualize the gospel to create something new and strange by blending disparate elements into a new mix. This is especially true when Westerners attempt to contextualize practices within Hinduism, Buddhism, and Islam. Westerners suppose that they can innocuously introduce their Christian interpretations into foreign forms. Such accommodation may reduce the potential for persecution and isolation, espe-cially in Islam, but may cause misunderstandings in the host society. Although these steps often make Muslim converts feel more comfortable as they move from Islam into Christianity, such practices may delay a wholehearted com-mitment to the new faith. Sam Schlorff reflects:

> There are no neutral "religious structures" (such as ritual prayer) that may be joined to Christian faith-allegiance without creating serious semantic distortion and theological confusion. This is one reason I reject the intuitive approach suggested by some—contextualization by experimentation.[86]

Most troubling of all are the insider movement nationals who call them-selves Muslim Followers of Christ (MFCs). These believers see themselves as

---

[83] Schlorff, *Ministry to Muslims*, 150.
[84] Hesselgrave, *Communicating Christ Cross-Culturally*, 67.
[85] Paul Hiebert, quoted in Schlorff, *Ministry to Muslims*, 150.
[86] Schlorff, *Ministry to Muslim*, 151.

true Muslims who follow Christ as their Lord.[87] I know a number of MFCs, and they are quite sincere. One told me, "Christianity is our religion but Islam is our culture." Words enjoy subjective meanings that surpass translation. Although the word "Muslim" means "one who is submitted to God," persons who call themselves Muslims attach additional significance to the term. In a sense, MFCs attempt to have it both ways. They hope to remain in the culture by calling themselves Muslims but worship as believers in Christ. Certainly, religions have cultural aspects, but religion is not totally cultural nor culture completely religious. Parshall well asks, "How would we feel if a Muslim attended (or even joined) our evangelical church and partook of communion . . . all with a view to becoming an 'insider'?"[88]

While affirming C4 methodology, J. D. Greear rejects this kind of C5 contextualization.[89] Timothy Tennent[90] and Phil Parshall[91] allow it temporarily for new converts transitioning from Islam to Christianity. These missiologists call into question much of current contextualization, especially the Islamic variety. As Peter Pikkert says, "Even the most contextualized of churches will not look like a mosque. It will not have that 'Muslim flavor' which is supposed to ease entry into Christianity."[92]

Redemptive Analogy

Missionary Don Richardson coined the term "redemptive analogy" due to his work with the Sawi people in Papua, New Guinea. Redemptive analogies are practices, beliefs, or customs that lie dormant within a society and can be used to illustrate aspects of Christ's redemptive work.[93] For the Sawi people, who value treachery over honesty, their culture allowed for a "peace child" to be

---

[87] For a more extensive presentation by a proponent of this view, see Joseph Cummings, "Muslim Followers of Jesus?" in *Understanding Insider Movements: Disciples of Jesus within Diverse Religious Communities*, ed. Harley Talman and John Jay Travis (Pasadena: William Carey Library, 2015), 28.

[88] Phil Parshall, in Winter and Hawthorne, *Perspectives on the World Christian Movement*, 666.

[89] Greear, *Breaking the Islam Code*, 159–60.

[90] Tennent, "Followers of Jesus," 113.

[91] Parshall, in Winter and Hawthorne, *Perspectives on the World Christian Movement*, 666–67.

[92] Pikkert, *Protestant Missionaries to the Middle East*, 187 (see chap. 4, n. 137).

[93] Don Richardson, "Redemptive Analogies," in Winter and Hawthorne, *Perspectives on the World Christian Movement*, 430.

exchanged between warring tribes to reconcile the combatants. Richardson holds that all cultures possess redemptive analogies within their traditions that are waiting to be unlocked.[94] I discovered a redemptive analogy among the Beja people of the Horn of Africa. According to a well-known tribal legend, Gwa'i'alor, a prominent sheikh, sheltered a murderer from vigilantes on his estate. When the blood avengers arrived to take the prisoner, the sheikh protested that giving up a guest in his house would shame him forever. Gwa'i'lor said that the vigilantes could take him instead. After agreeing he would sleep beneath a certain tree that night, the blood avengers waited until dark. That evening the sheikh's oldest son decided that he would give his life for the murderer in place of his father. When the vigilantes discovered the magnanimity of the father and son they relented and did not kill the perpetrator.[95]

All redemptive analogies disintegrate at some point. The peace children in Sawi villages eventually reach adulthood or succumb to childhood diseases. The internecine warfare remedy Richardson discovered lacks the eternal element of the referent. Gwa'i'lor's son did not actually die for the criminal but only planned to do so. Even if the sheikh's son had died, he would have purchased with his blood only one person, not the entire human race. Both these redemptive analogies use cultural traditions as metaphors to describe eternal truths.

Some biblical truths cannot be easily contextualized. David Hesselgrave speaks about the supra-cultural validity of the essential elements of the gospel. The categorical validity of certain aspects of the gospel, such as the death of Christ, his resurrection, faith, redemption, and conversion, must be presented as they appear in the Bible.[96]

Hesselgrave points out that certain biblically enjoined symbols cannot be contextualized. For instance, the scriptural symbol must be used or the meaning becomes irreparably altered. Water must be used for baptism because the liquid forms part of the meaning.[97] The original form of the ordinance posits some limitations on the degree of contextualization that can occur.

---

[94] Moreau, *Contextualization in World Missions*, 147–48.

[95] W. T. Clark, "Manners, Customs, and Beliefs of the Northern Beja," *Sudan Notes and Records (SNR)* 21, no. 1 (1938): 26–27.

[96] Hesselgrave and Rommen, *Contextualization*, 172–73.

[97] Hesselgrave and Rommen, 173.

David Hesselgrave told me the following story, which exemplifies the best in contextualization. He states:

> One night after arriving in Japan in 1950, I happened upon a celebration featuring a number of costumed dancers and instrumentalists. The celebrants were observing the Buddhist festival of *Obon*. Later I discovered *Obon* means to crucify upside down and that the festival grows out of an incident in the life of Buddha and his disciple, Mokuren.
>
> Mokuren's mother had died and he pleaded with the Buddha to let him see how she was doing in the afterlife. The Buddha was reticent, but finally agreed. To Mokuren's shock and sorrow, his mother was being crucified upside down. After that time, it became customary for family members to take a lantern annually, go to the cemetery, and escort dead relatives back home for a time of celebration. I recall a message Hashimoto Sensei, a specialist in world religions, preached in our Gospel Hall in Urawa City during Obon in 1951. Hashimoto retold the story of Mokuren and the Buddha; the background of Obon; and concluded as follows:
>
> "My friends, the truth is that almost two thousand years ago on a cross outside Jerusalem in Palestine the Son of God, Jesus Christ, suffered far more than physical pain. Bearing your sin and mine, he also bore the wrath of God the Father against sin and evil, and suffered the separation from the Father that holiness and justice required. The sad thing about Obon is that, after a short time of respite and celebration with dead parents and loved ones, our Buddhist friends must escort them back to their grave where they will hang upside down on a cruel cross for another year. What a cruel thing to do to one's loved ones! But that is what Buddhism teaches. Friends, the truth is much different. The Bible teaches us that Jesus Christ was crucified and rose again so that you and your loved ones need never suffer either crucifixion or separation from God—neither in time nor in eternity. That is what we Christians term the 'gospel'— good news. And that, indeed, is what it is."[98]

---

[98] David Hesselgrave, conversation with the author, November 6, 2012, during Mission Week at Midwestern Baptist Theological Seminary, Kansas City, Missouri.

Indigeneity and Contextualization

Around the turn of the last century, Rufus Anderson and Henry Venn developed the idea of indigenizing missions. During this era of colonialism, Western missionaries pastored mission churches abroad, directed overseas evangelism efforts, and financially undergirded the work. Henry Venn, however, advocated what became known as "three-self missions." According to this theory, missionary churches should be (1) self-governing, (2) self-supporting, and (3) self-propagating.[99] In the indigenous church scenario, national believers take care of their own affairs. My experience has been that the nationals prefer taking over the governance from the missionaries, the missionaries like passing the financial support to the nationals, and the results are mixed in regard to propagating new churches. In another chapter, the complex problem of subsidy will be addressed.

The cross-cultural contextualizer can take heart that something non-native may become indigenous. For instance, rubber only grows naturally in Brazil, but a British secret agent spirited stolen trees out of South America to Malaysia, where they thrive. Coffee only occurs wild in Ethiopia, but Columbian coffee, transplanted from Africa, has become world famous. Cotton emerged from the Nile Delta and while homemakers all over the world prize Egyptian cotton, the American South also produces this fabric. In the same way, the gospel can be planted in the fertile soils of all the peoples of the world. Each culture can claim Jesus as its own.

CONCLUSION

Paul Hiebert says that both the messenger and the message must be contextualized.[100] Concerning this, Lingenfelter writes:

---

[99] A. Scott Moreau notes that "Alan Tippett suggested a truly indigenous church would have six 'self's,' adding to the existing three-self formula, (i.e., 'self-image' [seeing it as independent of its founding mission]; 'self-functioning' [capable of carrying on all its own functions], and 'self-giving' [knowing the needs of its community and be able to assist meeting those needs." Moreau, *Contextualization in World Missions*, 124.

[100] Hiebert, *Gospel in Human Contexts*, 22.

The challenge is to become what Malcolm McFee (1968) calls a 150-percent person. McFee uses this concept to describe Black Foot Indians who are enculturated into white American society. He argues that they are still 75 percent traditional Black Foot, but they have also learned to adapt to and follow the larger American culture to the point at which some are 75 percent white as well. He calls these people 150-percent persons. Like these Indians, we will never become 100-percent insiders in another culture or subculture. The only way that it is possible is the way Jesus did it, to be born into that other culture and to spend a lifetime in it. However, it is possible to follow his example to be "imitators of God," as Paul commands in Ephesians 5:1, and to "live a life of love" (v. 2) in the culture in which we hope to minister. Our goal should be to become more than we are.[101]

Contextualization theories often focus on the clever, complex, and unusual. Perhaps missionaries should develop self-contextualizing strategies rather than experimenting with novel constructs based on speculative hermeneutics. Furthermore, a measure of grace should be extended to the practitioners of contextualization. It has been my experience that I sometimes view my contextualization as the correct perspective and somebody else's contextualization as syncretism. Only Jesus perfectly contextualized himself. Everyone else travels on a journey to better present the gospel to those across the world.

Currently, contextualization is probably the most important, yet controversial, concept in missions. Missionaries and short-term volunteers make contextualization choices every day. As previously mentioned, choosing certain words over other terms in a Bible translation is contextualization. In an Islamic context, when a male missionary grows a beard or shaves, he makes a contextualization choice. When a missionary woman covers her head or dresses like a Western female, she makes a contextualization decision. When missionaries are willing to sit around a fire and talk endlessly with older men and women, they are on the road to contextualizing themselves to their host culture. It is a long process and challenges the missionary to his core.

---

[101] Lingenfelter and Mayers, *Ministering Cross-Culturally*, 2nd ed., 24 (see chap. 6, n. 4).

READING FOR FURTHER STUDY

Garland, David E. *1 Corinthians*. Grand Rapids: Baker, 2003.

Hiebert, Paul G. *The Gospel in Human Contexts: Anthropological Explorations for Contemporary Missions*. Grand Rapids: Baker Academic, 2009.

Lingenfelter, Sherwood G. *Ministering Cross-Culturally: An Incarnational Model for Personal Relationships*, 2nd ed. Grand Rapids: Baker Academic, 2003.

Moreau, A. Scott. *Contextualization in Missions: Mapping and Assessing Evangelical Models*. Grand Rapids: Kregel, 2012.

Schlorff, Sam. *Missiological Models in Ministry to Muslims*. Upper Darby, PA: Middle East Resources, 2006.

8

Philosophy of Missions

In February 1990 my wife and I met with prominent Christian researcher David Barrett, author of the *World Christian Encyclopedia*.[1] He consulted with each missionary couple at the mission agency's headquarters in Richmond, Virginia, prior to their departure for restricted-access assignments. Barrett pronounced, "Many a Christian worker has traveled to North Africa assigned to reach the Beja, but after a few years of encountering resistance, they moved on to a more receptive group. Only by focusing on the Beja[2] will this tribe ever be reached." Our family moved to the capital of one of the three countries where the Beja reside, serving as strategy coordinator missionaries.[3] During our time there, the first believers and churches emerged and continue to prosper today.

Years later, I worked as the regional leader (director) for the same mission agency in South America. When the home office asked when the region would evangelize the unreached indigenous tribes along the Amazon River,

---

[1] David B. Barrett, *World Christian Encyclopedia: A Comparative Study of Churches and Religions in the Modern World, AD 1900–2000* (Nairobi: Oxford University Press, 1982).

[2] The Beja number about 1.5 million and reside in North Africa. They are almost 100 percent Muslim.

[3] A strategy coordinator directs strategy to evangelize a people group by mobilizing resources from the Christian world regardless of international boundaries. My wife and I were part of an experiment of our mission, the International Mission Board (IMB). Cooperative Services International (CSI) was formed to focus on specific unreached, limited access tribes regardless of geopolitical boundaries.

the area's researcher countered that out of 175 million people[4] in Brazil, only about 185,000 were Native Americans.[5] He pointed out that the largest tribe, the 35,000 Yanomami, had received the attention of other mission boards for years. I declined to move missionaries from the population centers of eastern South America to engage less than one-tenth of 1 percent of the inhabitants of the region.

Over the last thirty years many mission organizations have greatly reduced their work among the majority populations of nations in sub-Saharan Africa and Latin America to focus on smaller people groups in other parts of the world or exit altogether. This change of focus in missions corresponds to a shift in philosophy.

MISSION PHILOSOPHY

The Relationship between Mission Philosophies, Strategies, and Methods

Philosophies, strategies, and methods sometime seem to blend and overlap in missions. This chapter begins, therefore, with a brief description of the meanings and nuances of these concepts. First, a philosophy of missions describes the perspective through which one views the missionary task. The introductory chapter of this book presents several philosophies of missions. For instance, the unreached-people group (UPG) philosophy holds that strategies and methods should be aimed at the least evangelized ethnicities in the world. On the opposite end of the spectrum, church-growth theory advocates channeling resources toward the world's most receptive homogeneous units. Adherents of the spiritual-warfare philosophy of missions view the binding of territorial spirits as the essential first step in missions. In short, one's philosophy of missions answers the question, "What is the missions task?" While UPG advocates yearn to penetrate the last frontier, and church growth supporters aspire to reap

---

[4] Brazil's population is now estimated at just over two hundred million.

[5] The IBGE 2010 Census (Brazil) lists 896,917 native people for the country, but this count includes the *Quilombolas* (descendants of slaves) who are indigenous to another continent and have intermarried with Brazilians of both European and American Indian lineage. Even the larger number amounts to only 0.47 percent of the population of Brazil.

the harvest, spiritual-warfare adherents believe both can be accomplished by defeating Satan first.

Derived from the Roman military, the second term, "strategy," describes an overarching plan for effectively marshalling resources in accordance with a mission organization's philosophy.[6] In other words, a strategy embodies a plan to implement one's philosophy of missions. For example, church-planting strategies work well in both church-growth situations and among unreached peoples. Similarly, human-needs strategies and business-as-mission ventures exemplify options that fit most philosophies of missions.

The third term, "methods," portrays the detailed tactics that accomplish the strategy plans. Winston Crawley says, "Details of missions methods and approaches would be understood as part of missions tactics."[7] Methods within a church-planting strategy would include starting cell churches, house churches, T4T churches,[8] traditional churches, Purpose Driven churches,[9] cowboy churches, surfer churches, and seeker-friendly churches, to name just a few. Church planters employ different evangelism tactics within these methods.

Although missionaries in the nineteenth century, such as William Carey and Hudson Taylor, conducted some cultural and demographic research, Winston Crawley said that until the 1970s, mission agencies planned "without much awareness of 'strategy.'"[10] Missionaries entered new countries by opening hospitals, clinics, orphanages, and schools, while preaching and starting churches. Strategy primarily involved sending missionaries to geographic locations without stipulating what they should do when they arrived.[11] Although some attention was given to researching the ethnicities within those countries,[12] systematizing missions came later. In North America, churches and denominations also largely practiced geographical church founding. In other words,

---

[6] Crawley, *A Story to Tell*, 262 (see chap. 1, n. 45).

[7] Crawley, 262.

[8] *Training for Trainers* or the China house-church method.

[9] Rick Warren, pastor of Saddleback Church in Southern California, developed this method.

[10] Crawley, *World Christianity*, 70 (see chap. 1, n. 26).

[11] Crawley, 9–34. Crawley said in an earlier book, *Global Mission: A Story to Tell* (262), "The Foreign Mission Board did not make formal reference to mission strategy until 1965."

[12] William Carey prepared a chart of the religions of the countries on the continents of his day. See Carey's article in Winter and Hawthorne, *World Christian Movement*, 315–16 (see chap. 1, n. 30).

if a county-seat town did not have a church of a particular denomination, a congregation would be planted by them in that locale. Detailed statistical and demographic research did not enter in to the equation until much until later.

The Two Principle Missions Philosophies

Prior to the last half of the twentieth century, "just preaching the gospel" constituted the prevailing missions philosophy among evangelicals, both overseas and in the Western world. Two pioneer missiologists changed this. Donald McGavran's *The Bridges of God,* published in 1955, postulates that people apart from Western countries usually become Christians within their own strata of society.[13] In his later book, *Understanding Church Growth,* McGavran claims that most nations are not homogeneous but "belong to pieces of a mosaic."[14] Additionally, McGavran writes, "People like to become Christians without crossing racial, linguistic, or class barriers."[15] This homogeneous-unit principle (HUP) postulates "peoples become Christian fastest when least change of race or clan is involved."[16] This emphasis led to customizing strategies for particular ethnic groups—standard practice today. Internationally, the HUP concept birthed the unreached-people-group movement, while domestically the idea led to the development of "seeker-friendly" church strategies, as well as language and ethnic missions.

Ralph Winter, McGavran's colleague at Fuller Theological Seminary, borrowed the HUP concept and named certain smaller homogeneous units "hidden peoples." Later, C. Peter Wagner and Edward R. Dayton began calling unevangelized homogeneous units "unreached peoples."[17] Winston Crawley observes: "Since 1970, attention of the Christian mission enterprise has focused increasingly on people groups, rather than on nations."[18] He adds:

> Winter effectively shifted the main theme of today's missiology
> from church growth to unreached peoples, thereby becoming the

---

[13] Donald A. McGavran, *Bridges of God: A Study in the Strategy of Missions* (Eugene, OR: Wipf and Stock, 2005; London: World Dominion Press, 1955), 1.

[14] McGavran, *Understanding Church Growth,* 3rd ed., 53 (see chap. 1, n. 27).

[15] McGavran, 163.

[16] McGavran, *Bridges of God,* 23.

[17] McGavran, *Understanding Church Growth,* 3rd ed., 51.

[18] Crawley, *World Christianity,* 73.

most influential missiologist of the 1980s and 1990s. It is interesting that McGavran first directed Christian attention to people groups, as a lead-in to his concern for growth; and that he and Winter were colleagues at Fuller—*but their strategy thrusts move in opposite directions*. McGavran wanted major effort to concentrate on *responsive peoples*, where the harvest is ripe, but Winter urges concentration on places where the *gospel seed has not yet been sown*.[19]

The unreached-people-group concept and church-growth theory represent the two most prevalent mission philosophies in the first part of the twenty-first century. These conflicting perspectives turn on different interpretations of the same data. In today's mission milieu, research drives the formation of the theories and strategies that have developed, largely in the direction of UPG missions.

Another important concept of Donald McGavran and receptivity missions is the idea of "people movements." People movements represent individual decisions made in a group setting. McGavran defines the term:

> A people movement results from the joint decision of a number of individuals [whether five or five hundred] all from the same people group, which enables them to become Christians without social dislocation, while remaining in full contact with their non-Christian relatives, thus enabling other groups of that people group, across the years, after suitable instruction, to come to similar decisions and form Christian churches made up exclusively of members of that people.[20]

Many individual members of people groups in the world do not make judgments themselves. They often look to their fathers, elders, or tribal leaders to lead them in their decision-making processes. McGavran says the great growth in the future of missions is likely to be among people movements.[21]

Despite the emphasis on homogeneous units, McGavran acknowledges the existence of the urban exception, writing, "In a few metropolitan centers . . . the fire under the pot has grown hot enough so that homogeneous units are disintegrating . . . . In such cities, some conglomerate Churches are growing

---

[19] Crawley, 74–75. Emphasis added.
[20] McGavran, *Understanding Church Growth*, 3rd ed., 223.
[21] McGavran, 224.

rapidly by conversion. . . . In most cities, however, conglomerate Churches are not growing rapidly by conversion. If congregations increase they do so by transfer growth."[22]

Statistics and Missions

Mark Twain, quoting former British Prime Minister Benjamin Disraeli, famously said, "There are three kinds of lies: lies, damned lies, and statistics."[23] As it became clear that the unreached people groups of the world were being underserved or ignored, mission agencies sought ways to determine which areas were reached or unreached. Maps were composed to show the relative "lostness" and "reachedness" of the world. Sociology and statistics play heavily in these choices.

When I moved from eastern Africa to eastern South America to become the regional leader in the summer of 1997, the IMB was using the 20 percent figure in its statistics. Within a year the percentage was lowered to 12 percent. The following year featured a precipitous drop in the "reachedness" scale. Two percent evangelical believers became the new statistical benchmark for the IMB and most other mission agencies.

Patrick Johnstone, the editor of *Operation World*, Luis Bush of the *Joshua Project* of the AD 2000 Movement, and some others decided that the 20 percent figure was too high.[24] They determined a much lower threshold was appropriate for measuring relative "unreachedness." Johnstone writes:

---

[22] McGavran, *Understanding Church Growth*, 2nd ed., 244 (see chap. 6, n. 23).

[23] Mark Twain, *The Quotable Mark Twain: His Essential Aphorisms, Witticisms & Concise Opinions*, ed. R. Kent Rasmussen (New York: McGraw-Hill, 1998), 264.

[24] Speaking of this 20 percent benchmark, John Mark Terry and J. D. Payne write, "In his renowned work *Diffusion of Innovations* (2003) [Everett M.] Rogers explains that when a new idea, product, or concept is introduced into a society, the spread, or diffusion of that knowledge occurs rapidly and throughout the society when 10 to 20 percent of the population has embraced it. Although Rogers's initial work was conducted in the field of agriculture, missiologists in the 1970s and 1980s applied his finding to the dissemination of the Gospel across any people group." John Mark Terry and J. D. Payne, *Developing a Strategy for Missions: A Biblical, Historical, and Cultural Introduction* (Grand Rapids: Baker Academic, 2013), 188. See also Robin Dale Hadaway, "A Course Correction in Missions: Rethinking the Two-Percent Threshold," *Southwestern Journal of Theology (SWJT)* 57, no. 1 (Fall 2014): 17–28.

> The original Joshua Project editorial committee selected the criteria less than 2% evangelical Christian and less than 5% Christian adherents. While these percentage figures are *somewhat arbitrary*, there are *some that suggest* that the percentage of a population needed to be influenced to impact the whole group is 2%.[25]

This small group of evangelical researchers and missiologists changed the thrust of missions by lowering the statistical benchmark for "unreachedness." Although a 20 percent evangelical population threshold for "reachedness" seems arbitrary, lowering the bar to 2 percent appears quite subjective. Johnstone never identifies the "some" who suggest that 2 percent of a population can influence the majority. The 2 percent threshold continues to serve as the theoretical basis for designating parts of the world unreached, and by implication, deeming the rest of the world either reached or at least, reached enough. Maps were produced showing large parts of Latin America, Africa, and parts of Asia color-coded green (reached) using the 2 percent evangelical benchmark as its basis.[26]

"Minority Rules" is another sociological study supporting the idea that a minority percentage can impact a large majority. This research reveals that a very committed 10 percent population segment may influence the remaining 90 percent to adopt their views. Interestingly, the article maintains that when the subgroup falls below 10 percent, the minority opinion fails to affect the majority at all.[27]

---

[25] Patrick Johnstone, quoted in Sills, *Reaching and Teaching*, 109. Emphasis added.

[26] "Closing the Gap: Critical Issues and the Unfinished Task," PowerPoint slides (Richmond, VA: International Mission Board, SBC, 2010).

[27] "Scientists at Rensselaer Polytechnic Institute have found that when just 10 percent of the population holds an unshakable belief, their belief will always be adopted by the majority of the society. The scientists, who are members of the Social Cognitive Networks Academic Research Center (SCNARC) at Rensselaer, used computational and analytical methods to discover the tipping point where a minority belief becomes the majority opinion. The finding has implications for the study and influence of societal interactions ranging from the spread of innovations to the movement of political ideals.

"'*When the number of committed opinion holders is below 10 percent, there is no visible progress in the spread of ideas.* It would literally take the amount of time comparable to the age of the universe for this size group to reach the majority,' said SCNARC Director Boleslaw Szymanski, the Claire and Roland Schmitt Distinguished Professor at Rensselaer. 'Once that number grows above 10 percent, the idea spreads like flame'" [italics added]. Rensselaer Polytechic Institute, "Minority Rules: Scientists Discover Tipping Point for the Spread of Ideas," ScienceDaily,

Although a minor case can be made for a 10 to 20 percent threshold based on these two secular studies, no research supports a single digit benchmark. Nevertheless, the 2 percent evangelical threshold continues to serve as the standard for most modern mission strategy decisions.

UPG proponent Greg Parsons notes that some prioritization in missions is necessary.[28] Some groups must be targeted at the expense of others. When an unreached-people group (UPG) exceeds the threshold of 2 percent evangelicals in the total population, many believe the nationals can internally complete the mission task. Additionally, when a UPG exhibits no church planting activity, that people becomes unengaged and unreached (UUPG). Another category recently emerged, called UUUPGs or unengaged, unreached and *uncontacted* people groups. These are groups that have not yet been contacted by any Christians.[29] Ted Esler writes about these categories of missions "engagement":

> **The unengaged paradigm is reductionist**. Past definitions of un-reached people groups had some sort of a quantitative indicator for being reached. Most often used and quoted is two percent.... *Is two percent enough to be confident that the gospel message has been adequately absorbed in a culture? Is two percent enough for a people to be considered reached?*.... Perhaps that is why it is tempting to make the goal the deployment of workers to the unengaged. The larger goal (which is already rather reductionist) seems unattainable. Setting a lower goal makes our task easier.[30]

The current division of people groups to the smallest common denominator, however, results in an overanalysis of the situation and in one group being arbitrarily called reached and another unreached, based on questionable

---

"Science News," July 26, 2011, www.sciencedaily.com/releases/2011/07/110725190044.htm. See also J. Xie et al., "Social Consensus through the Influence of Committed Minorities," *Physical Review* E 84, no. 1 (July 2011): 1–9, DOI: 10.1103/PhysRevE.84.011130.

[28] Greg Parsons, "Will the Earth Hear His Voice?" (unpublished paper presented at the annual meeting of the International Society of Frontier Missiology, Atlanta, Georgia, September 24, 2014).

[29] According to Pratt, Sills, and Walters, UUUPGs "refers to the unreached, unengaged, and uncontacted people groups. Uncontacted peoples are those hidden, hostile or isolated people groups with whom no contact has ever been made for Gospel advance." Zane Pratt, M. David Sills, and Jeff K. Walters, *Introduction to Global Missions* (Nashville: B&H, 2014), 30.

[30] Ted Esler, "The Unengaged: An Engaging Strategy ... or Not?," *Evangelical Missions Quarterly* 51, no. 2 (April 2015): 136.

criteria.[31] Managerial missiology,[32] as some call it, carefully engages minute people groups numbering in the hundreds or thousands while overlooking larger, majority populations because the latter exceed the imaginary and contrived 2 percent evangelical threshold.

One researcher with a large missions agency received an overseas telephone call from a short-term volunteer pastor and his associate, who were searching for a specific UPG on the field. They had selected an unreached tribe and traveled to Africa to find "their people." After spending a few days in the country, the pastor told the researcher back at headquarters, "The people group was on the unreached list but we can't find them. Where are they?" They had traveled without establishing contact with anyone either overseas or in the home office. On the other side of the world, a missionary in South America was assigned to find unreached Native Americans from the Amazon Basin residing in the concrete jungles of one of the continent's largest cities. Despite the presence of multitudes of reachable people, the missionary had to focus on very difficult to find "hidden peoples" in one of South America's great cities.

When I worked in North Africa with the Beja people there were many other Muslim ethnicities numbering less than 2 percent evangelical (most under 0.2 percent evangelical). Although the homogeneous-unit principle helped determine the Beja needed priority in evangelism, I discovered as Muslims came to faith, their commonality was not in their ethnicity but because of their common experience as Muslim background believers (MBBs). Although I focused on the Beja, a number of other Muslim peoples joined the churches that emerged.

---

[31] Parsons, "Will the Earth Hear."

[32] Engel and Dyrness cite Samuel Escobar, who "coined the phrase 'managerial missiology' to refer to an unduly pragmatic endeavor 'to reduce reality to an understandable picture, and then to project missionary action in response to a problem that has been described in quantitative form.'"

They continue, "Once evangelism has been conceptualized into presentation of propositional truth, it is a logical deduction to declare a person (or even a people group) as 'reached' or 'evangelized' once they have 'heard.'" James F. Engel and William A. Dyrness, *Changing the Mind of Missions: Where Have We Gone Wrong?* (Downers Grove, IL: InterVarsity Press, 2000), 69.

The Mission of Missions and Multiple Mandates

Of course, there must be some basis for both the proportional deployment of mission personnel and for determining when a country or people group has attained self-sufficiency. Ralph Winter, in his book *The Twenty-Five Unbelievable Years: 1945–1969*, poses the question, "What is the mission of missions?"[33] Timothy Tennent warns against defining missions as, "'everything the church should be doing,' thus robbing the word of any distinctive emphasis or character."[34] Winter views the missions task as mainly a pioneering enterprise, where McGavran sees the evangelistic priority as reaping the harvest among the receptive. Although Crawley said in 2001 most mission agencies were pursuing a "both-and" strategy in regard to pioneer and harvest missions,[35] currently the former far exceeds the latter. Most mission entities have reassigned personnel through redeployment or attrition from traditional harvest fields to concentrate on unreached peoples.

The scriptures seem to present a dual mandate of missions to the last frontier as well as the harvest. All evangelicals agree that missions should prioritize evangelizing unbelievers. The missions philosophy question concerning the "mission of missions" revolves around whether missionaries should primarily proclaim the gospel to unreached peoples or also evangelize unbelievers in traditional mission fields? Engel and Norton argue for the broader view, writing:

> The Great Commission is not fulfilled, however, merely by proclaiming the message and exposing an offer to its claims. The convert is to be baptized and taught to observe all that Christ has commanded the church. . . . It appears then that the Great Commission contains three related but distinctly different communication mandates: (1) to *proclaim* the message; (2) to *persuade* the unbeliever; and (3) to *cultivate* the believer.[36]

---

[33] Winter, *Twenty-Five Unbelievable Years*, 99 (see chap. 4, n. 144).
[34] Timothy C. Tennent, *Invitation to World Missions: A Trinitarian Missiology for the Twenty-First Century*, Invitation to Theological Studies Series (Grand Rapids: Kregel, 2010), 54.
[35] Crawley, *World Christianity*, 75.
[36] Engel and Norton, *What's Gone Wrong*, 44 (see chap. 7, n. 26).

Lately, pioneer missions, last frontier missions,[37] or unreached peoples missions have been the primary kind of outreach deemed appropriate for expatriates in cross-cultural missions. Of course, the biblical mandate to reach the last frontier certainly exists. Jesus says in Acts 1:8, "But you will receive power when the Holy Spirit has come on you, and you will be my witnesses in Jerusalem, in all Judea and Samaria, and to the end the earth." Ralph Winter demonstrated that mission agencies had neglected the one-third of the world with little access to the gospel.[38]

Jesus's teachings, however, also emphasize reaping the harvest. Matthew 9:37–38 records these words of the Lord; "Then he said to his disciples, 'The harvest is abundant, but the workers are few. Therefore, pray to the Lord of the harvest to send out workers into his harvest.'" Lottie Moon, a Baptist missionary to China, wrote about the responsiveness of the Shantung Province and the need for more workers.[39] Donald McGavran, who popularized receptivity missions, writes:

> Since the gospel is to be preached to all creatures, no Christian will doubt that both the receptive and the resistant should hear it. *And since gospel acceptors have an inherently higher priority than gospel rejectors, no one should doubt that, **whenever it comes to a choice between reaping the ripe fields or seeding others, the former is commanded by God***. . . . If in any given sector the masses turn indifferent or hostile, then efforts to win them should be transferred to other sectors where unbelievers will hear and obey.[40]

Receptivity missions recognizes the variation in response to the gospel. McGavran says that where "the population is warmly responsive, it is sinful merely to hang on."[41] Current missions thinking often removes missionaries

---

[37] Pratt, Sills, and Walters write, "*The Last Frontier* is another term often heard in missions strategy. The IMB [International Mission Board] defines it as an 'unreached people for which the majority of its members have little or no access to the gospel of Jesus Christ. This represents 1.65 billion people in the world.'" Pratt, Sills, and Walters, *Introduction to Global Missions*, 30–31.

[38] John D. Robb, *Focus!: The Power of People Group Thinking: A Practical Manual for Planning Effective Strategies to Reach the Unreached* (Monrovia, CA: MARC, 1994), 2.

[39] Lottie Moon, May 17, 1887, letter published in September 1887 *Foreign Mission Journal*, in Harper, *Send the Light*, 216–18 (see chap. 4, n. 125).

[40] McGavran, *Understanding Church Growth*, 3rd ed., 207. Emphasis added.

[41] McGavran, 131.

from the field when believers reach the 2 percent evangelical threshold, placing these workers in new locales to start the sowing process from the beginning. Speaking of the church growth harvest mandate, McGavran says:

> That receptivity should determine effective evangelism methods is obvious. Unless Christian leaders in all six continents are on the lookout for changes in receptivity of homogeneous units within the general population and are prepared to seek and bring persons and groups belonging to these units into the fold, they will not even discern what needs to be done. An essential task is to discern receptivity and when this is seen, adjust methods, institutions, and personnel until the receptive are becoming Christians.[42]

Mike Morris contends, "McGavran believed that missionaries should be sent to unreached groups, but he believed that the responsive groups should be prioritized over the resistant groups."[43] Although the Beja people of North Africa proved more responsive than most Muslim tribes, they could not be called particularly receptive. What about the unreached populations in countries that show little response? McGavran answers these misgivings:

> Recognition of variations in receptivity is offensive to some missiologists because they fear that, if they accept it, they will be forced to abandon resistant fields. Abandonment is not called for. Fields must be sown. Stony fields must be plowed before they are sown. No one should conclude that if receptivity is low, the church should withdraw evangelistic efforts.

> Correct policy is to occupy fields of low receptivity lightly. The harvest will ripen someday. Their populations are made up of men and women for whom Christ died. While they continue in their rebellious and resistant state, they should be given the opportunity to hear the gospel in as courteous a way as possible. But they should not be heavily occupied lest, fearing they will be swamped by Christians, they become even more resistant.

> They should not be bothered and badgered. . . . Resistant lands should be held lightly.

---

[42] McGavran, 192.

[43] John Michael Morris, "McGavran on McGavran: What Did He Really Teach?," *Southern Baptist Journal of Missions and Evangelism*, no. 2 (Fall 2016): 13.

While holding them lightly, Christian leaders should perfect organizational arrangements so that when these lands turn responsive, missionary resources can be sent in quickly. . . . Reinforcing receptive areas is the only mode of mission by which resistant populations that become receptive may be led to responsible membership in ongoing churches.[44]

Winston Crawley states that a mission organization can hold to more than one mission philosophy. Speaking for the Southern Baptist Foreign Mission Board (now IMB), he says:

The Board is committed to both responsive and unresponsive fields. . . . Furthermore, our foreign missions philosophy and strategy have always been eclectic. That is, we have adopted insights, concepts, and approaches derived from many sources, if we feel they can be useful and are harmonious with our basic understanding of our mission and with the main thrust of our work.[45]

Despite Crawley's advocacy of dual mandates in the twentieth century, in the twenty-first century UPG missions reigns supreme among competing mission philosophies. Whatever mission theory one adopts—last frontier, receptivity, spiritual warfare, kingdom, eschatological, or doxological—the missiologist should balance their perspective to include multiple views.

CONCLUSION

This chapter demonstrates that normally one's mission philosophy will determine the direction of an agency's strategy and methods. Those adhering to a last frontier orientation will utilize discreet access strategies and one-on-one evangelism approaches. Church growth-harvest oriented missionaries will be interested in mass evangelism, and the training apparatus necessary to disciple the vast number of converts coming into the kingdom of God. The next chapter examines the myriads of mission methods being used in the strategies in the world.

---

[44] McGavran, *Understanding Church Growth*, 3rd ed., 190–91.
[45] Crawley, *A Story to Tell*, 275.

READING FOR FURTHER STUDY

Tennent, Timothy C. *Invitation to World Missions*. Grand Rapids: Kregel, 2010.
Terry, John Mark, and J. D. Payne. *Developing a Strategy for Missions: A Biblical, Historical, and Cultural Introduction*. Grand Rapids: Baker Academic, 2013.

9

Missions Strategy and Methods

W hile working at the home office of a large mission agency, I received a
visitor who presented a new method for starting churches along the
Amazon River in Brazil. Noting the lack of airstrips in the smaller villages,
and expense and slowness of ships, the guest proposed a novel idea. He favored
equipping missionaries with motorized hang gliders to swoop into villages by
air and preach the gospel. Stunned, I probed the guest about the seriousness of
his intentions. Indeed, he was sincere.

INTRODUCTION

As David Hesselgrave says, "A mind-boggling variety of approaches to 'discipling the nations' has been advocated during the era of modern missions."[1]
Although some techniques proved admirable, others did not. Philosophies,
strategies, and methods often overlap. First, a mission philosophy describes the
perspective by which one sees the missionary task. Second, a missions strategy portrays an overarching plan for effectively marshalling resources with a
mission organization's church or person's philosophy. The third term, methods,
describes the detailed tactics that accomplish the strategic plan.

---

[1] Hesselgrave, *Paradigms in Conflict*, 184 (see chap. 3, n. 31).

STRATEGY

Winston Crawley states, "The [Southern Baptist] Foreign Mission Board did not make formal reference to mission strategy until 1965 but both the process and many principles of strategic planning were followed by staff and missionaries in earlier generations. The concept of an overall plan for missions was not new."[2] Before examining particular strategies, Gailyn Van Rheenen presents a helpful list of broad strategy categories. These include (1) standard-solution strategies, (2) being-in-the-way strategies, (3) plan-so-far strategies, and (4) unique-solutions strategies.[3]

Strategy Categories

Standard-Solution Strategies. Standard-solution strategies come from a belief that one approach will solve the world's missions problem. Often a particular ministry, successful in America, will seek to export their strategy overseas. Working in the home office of a large mission agency, I received a visitor eager to present his idea. The earnest Christian said, "I believe the best way to reach the world is to put all of the International Mission Board's 5,000 missionaries[4] on two ships and sail them around the world. These boats would travel from port to port, evangelizing and discipling every country on the globe." He theorized that using ships would eliminate the need for missionary housing and transportation.

Being-in-the-Way Strategies. Being-in-the-way strategies in some manner resemble noncontextualized contextualization. No-strategy strategies hold that long-range planning infringes on God's sovereignty and interferes with the Holy Spirit's direction. Eschewing the strategic planning process, missionaries of this stripe attempt to follow God's leading rather than set goals and objectives. Van Rheenen cautions, "This strategy eliminates the possibility of failure and negates personal responsibility. If things go wrong it is because God has other plans."[5] When I supervised 400 missionaries in eastern South

---

[2] Crawley, *A Story to Tell*, 262 (see chap. 1, n. 45).
[3] Gailyn Van Rheenen, *Missions: Biblical Foundations and Contemporary Strategies*, 1st ed. (Grand Rapids: Zondervan, 1996), 142–45.
[4] As of February 8, 2019, the IMB counted 3,665 missionaries serving on the field.
[5] Van Rheenen, *Missions*, 144.

America, some personnel resisted setting ministry goals and objectives. One missionary said his strategy consisted of riding around a large Brazilian city and evangelizing those God brought his way. Although Christians should always be alert for opportunities, having no plan is no plan at all.

Plan-so-Far Strategies. Plan-so-far strategies frequently make an initial impact but often demonstrate weaknesses in follow-up. Planning occurs at the outset, but plan-so-far strategies often assume the Holy Spirit will bring the ministry effort to a successful conclusion. Sometimes, but not always, volunteer mission teams exhibit this weakness. When short-term teams minister with local churches either at home or overseas, sometimes little follow-up occurs because future plans for it have not been made. Despite a successful beginning, the end game suffers.

Unique-Solutions Strategies. Obviously preferring this category because he mentions it last, Van Rheenen says that unique-solutions strategies view each country, culture, and situation differently. Of course, the wording begs the question because every situation presents unique challenges. One could argue that a church-planting strategy should be developed for every circumstance. The strategy would not change, only the culture. Some strategies, however, only succeed under certain circumstances. When I served in North Africa, war and famine ravaged one of the three countries where the Beja people resided. Since the people group lived on both sides of an international border, a human-needs strategy suited the situation. Through agricultural, water, sanitation, and vocational training projects, the mission engaged the people group on both sides of the border for evangelism and church planting. If, however, the tribe had lived in a rich country like Saudi Arabia, such a strategy would not have been appropriate.

STRATEGY AND METHODS

Church Planting

Church-Planting Strategy. Church planting constitutes the dominant strategy for most mission agencies overseas, and increasingly in North America. This means that the focus of their ministry methods is the founding of new churches. Denominations and organizations of this persuasion view the establishing of new churches as the primary way of retaining their evangelism efforts and fulfilling the Great Commission. They agree with Donald McGavran's statement: "Today's supreme task is the effective multiplication of churches in the receptive societies of earth."[6] Although there is no command to plant churches in the Bible,[7] there is the command to make disciples. J. D. Payne, commenting on this reality, says, "Throughout the Bible, we read of the birth of churches—*after* disciples are made. Biblical church planting is evangelism that results in new churches."[8]

Most church-planting strategies follow a certain sequence. David Hesselgrave identifies a nine-step process: (1) the missionaries commissioned, (2) the audience contacted, (3) the gospel communicated, (4) the hearers converted, (5) the believers congregated, (6) the faith confirmed, (7) the leaders consecrated, (8) the believers commended, and (9) the relationships continued.[9] J. D. Payne, however, lists six sequential elements in the church-planting progression. He calls these the (1) pre-entry stage, (2) entry stage, (3) gospel stage, (4) discipleship stage, (5) church formation stage, and (6) leadership stage.[10] Rodney Harrison delineates seven church planting steps. These include: (1) cast a vision for multiplying, (2) identify the ministry focus group, (3) enlist planners and partners while clarifying roles, (4) discover and commit resources, (5) mobilize sponsoring congregations, (6) support birthing process and ongoing evaluation, and (7) celebrate and communicate church multiplication.[11] Gus Suarez sees the church planting process as six stages. These are: (1) creating a healthy environment, (2) identifying the called out, (3) equipping the church planter,

---

[6] McGavran, *Understanding Church Growth*, 3rd ed., 31 (see chap. 1, n. 27).

[7] E. Elbert Smith, *Church Planting by the Book* (Ft. Washington, PA: CLC Publications, 2015), 157.

[8] J. D. Payne, *Apostolic Church Planting: Birthing New Churches from New Believers* (Downers Grove, IL: IVP Books, 2015), 17.

[9] David J. Hesselgrave, *Planting Churches Cross-Culturally: North America and Beyond*, 2nd ed. (Grand Rapids: Baker, 2000), 93–293.

[10] Payne, *Apostolic Church Planting*, 53–54.

[11] Rodney A. Harrison, *Seven Steps for Planting Churches* (Alpharetta, GA: North American Mission Board, 2004), 5–59.

(4) mobilizing, (5) planting, and (6) multiplication.[12] Church planting represents the major strategy in missions in the twenty-first century.

Donald McGavran says "the multiplication of churches ... is a *sine qua non* in carrying out the purposes of God."[13] David Hesselgrave claims, "The primary mission of the church and, therefore, of the churches is to proclaim the gospel of Christ and gather believers into local churches where they can be built up in the faith and made effective in service; thus new congregations are to be planted throughout the world."[14] C. Peter Wagner agrees, writing, "*The single most effective evangelistic methodology under heaven is planting new churches.*"[15] Most mission agencies overseas and in North America adhere to this philosophy.[16] Church planting, also known as church founding, church starting, or church extension, has attained primacy in missions because local churches are able to conserve the results of evangelism, nurture new and existing believers, and pass the faith on from one generation to the next.

Although existing churches should be strengthened, new congregations must be planted because older churches often stagnate, while others die. Furthermore, new churches evangelize more effectively than older congregations because their members more easily embrace new ideas and methods.[17] Aubrey Malphurs says, "Church planting is an exhausting but exciting venture of faith that involves the planned process of beginning and growing local churches."[18] As might be expected, church planting methods vary greatly. Some of these methods can be combined with other approaches to missions.

---

[12] Gustavo V. Suarez, *Connections: Linking People and Principles for Dynamic Church Multiplication* (Friendwood, TX: Baxter Press, 2004), 203.

[13] McGavran, *Understanding Church Growth*, 2nd ed., 6–7 (see chap. 6, n. 23).

[14] Hesselgrave, *Planting Churches Cross-Culturally*, 17.

[15] C. Peter Wagner, *Church Planting for a Greater Harvest* (Ventura, CA: Regal, 1990), 11.

[16] Winston Crawley says the dominant personnel need in Southern Baptist missions is for those focused on church planting. Speaking of the church planter, he says, "The assignment is essentially that of seeking to evangelize a region through church planting, multiplying, and strengthening churches." Crawley, *A Story to Tell*, 161.

[17] Aubrey Malphurs, *Planting Growing Churches for the 21st Century: A Comprehensive Guide for New Churches and Those Desiring Renewal*, 3rd ed. (Grand Rapids: Baker, 2004), 44.

[18] Malphurs, 27.

Church Planting Methods

Historic Church Planting. Mike and Kay Minter started Reston Bible Church in 1974 with a Bible study in a golf course clubhouse in the Washington, DC, area. As a bivocational church planter, Mike worked at the golf course and won the manager, who became his first member, to the Lord. The first Sunday service began with twenty-five persons a year later. The church has grown in attendance to about 2,200 persons in 2018.[19]

Historic church plants begin in different ways. In this method of church planting, the church planter begins a group in a home, community center, school, or under a tree. In North America, the church planter usually becomes the senior pastor and the new church normally plans to either rent, build, or purchase a permanent facility.

Often an existing church will sponsor the church plant by temporarily lending or permanently commissioning some of their members to form the nucleus of a launch team. Church planting nomenclature calls this being "hived off" from the mother congregation, while Stuart Murray calls this phenomenon the "colonization" or "helicopter" model.[20] As the nascent group grows, the church may search for larger accommodations. Although the historic church plant often begins in a home, usually the new congregation desires to find a permanent location.

Alternatively, the historic church plant may use a team approach and recruit launch team members from several churches. Another model involves a denominational association of churches, a state convention, or a national missions entity sponsoring the church start.

House Church Planting. In the mid-1970s, while in seminary in the Dallas area, my wife and I joined a house church start in a community center. The fellowship was wonderful, the music inspiring, and the Bible teaching edifying. For spiritual growth, house churches offer unparalleled opportunities. From the beginning, however, the teaching of the children presented a problem. Since the participants came from a variety of church traditions, doctrinal

---

[19] Mike Minter, text message to Robin Hadaway, July 11, 2018. Minter is my former roommate.

[20] Stuart Murray, *Church Planting: Laying Foundations* (Scottsdale, PA: Herald Press, 2001), 237.

disputes also developed. Although a delightful experience for a few years, the church disbanded as families grew in size, and the members joined more established churches.

Many historic church plants start in homes, but the house church model advocates intend to always meet in homes or as a small group in a community center or other facility. When an individual house church reaches about twenty-five adults, home church proponents favor starting a new congregation so the close-knit fellowship offered by this model can continue. House church advocates see the home church as the biblical model.[21]

In a persecuted environment overseas, the low public profile of house churches keep them largely invisible to hostile governments. For this reason, house-church planting persists as the preferred method in places such as China, the Middle East, and Cuba. Cell-church groups meeting in homes differ from their house-church counterparts in both structure and content. Cell groups that meet in homes are linked organizationally with other cell groups, while house churches remain independent.[22] Ralph Neighbour says, "House churches tend to collect a community of 15–25 people who meet together on a weekly basis. Usually, each house church stands alone. While they may be in touch with nearby house churches, they usually do not recognize any further structure beyond themselves."[23]

The *Simple Church* concept represents a corollary to the house church paradigm. Coined by Tony and Felicity Dale, simple church consists of a movement of house churches in a geographical area. Using interactive Bible studies, believers are encouraged to find "persons of peace" who will agree to host a nascent church in their home. The churches are simple because they require no buildings, paid pastors, or worship instruments.[24] Simple church represents the Western version of the *Church Planting Movement*[25] church planting concept overseas.

---

[21] Wolfgang Simson, *Houses that Change the World: The Return of the House Churches* (Emmelsbüll, Germany: C&P Publishing; repr.,Tyrone, GA: OM Publishing, 2001), 140–41.

[22] Simson, 130–31.

[23] Ralph Neighbour Jr., *Where Do We Go from Here? A Guidebook for the Cell Group Church* (Houston: Touch Publications, 1990), 223.

[24] Martin Robinson, *Planting Mission-Shaped Churches Today* (Oxford: Monarch Books, 2006), 157, 160–61.

[25] The *Church Planting Movement* (CPM) concept will be explained later in this chapter.

The home church movement has operated largely unnoticed underground for several generations in the United States. Ed Stetzer references a Frank Viola article that lists eleven separate house church streams in North America. These include those influenced by diverse teachers such as Gene Edwards,[26] Watchman Nee, Witness Lee,[27] Kenneth Copeland, Kenneth Hagin, Sam Fife, George Warwick, and Bill Gothard.[28] Some house churches, of course, have emerged with no outside influences at all.

Whatever the culture, and despite their advantages, house churches have some significant drawbacks. Donald McGavran points out that meeting in homes for long periods of time becomes wearisome. Children and farm animals walking through the house church meeting are distracting.[29] Additionally, in countries with high crime rates, meeting in homes invites visitors with bad intentions to "case" the house for future crimes. House church proponents sometimes succumb to an elitist attitude, as most believe their model dates to the book of Acts and most closely resembles the early church.

Cell Church Planting. At a meeting of missionaries in South America in the late 1990s, cell church proponent and teacher, Ralph Neighbour Jr. said, "In church planting there is the cell church method and then there are all the other unbiblical models."[30] Cell church advocates believe their model most closely follows the Bible. They believe the cell church method combines the

---

[26] Gene Edwards represents the "radical wing" of the house church movement, advocating churches with no leadership, no structure, and no organization. See "Gene Edwards Controversy," Pentecostal Pioneers, "Heaven Sent Revival," accessed June 28, 2018, www.pentecostalpioneers.org/geneedwards1.html. Gene Edward's disciples began other smaller tributaries of the house church movement, including the New Covenant Apostolic Order (NCOO). The NCOO began with a group of former Campus Crusade for Christ leaders who left to establish the true New Testament church. Their "apostles" included Jon Braun, Peter Gillquist, Ray Netherly, Jack Sparks, and Gordon Walker. Eventually their house churches merged with the Antiochian Syrian Orthodox Church, headquartered in Damascus. My wife and I were involved in this house church movement while in seminary in the mid-1970s.

[27] Watchman Nee of China, and his disciple, Witness Lee, pioneered and popularized the view that house churches are the biblical model and there should be only one church in a geographic area.

[28] See Ed Stetzer, *Planting New Churches in a Postmodern Age* (Nashville: B&H, 2003), 168–71. Stetzer says Gothard's house churches adhere to the three "*h*'s,"—home church, home school, and home birth.

[29] McGavran, *Understanding Church Growth*, 2nd ed., 323.

[30] Ralph Neighbour Jr. remarks at a cell church training conference, Atibaia, Brazil, summer 1999.

advantages of the close fellowship of a weekly small group with the benefits of participation in corporate worship and teaching in a large venue. Cell church proponents see this model as the ideal wineskin for a new spiritual revolution to impact secular culture in the twenty-first century.[31]

In this model, cells meet (usually) in homes[32] and their small groups compose elements of a larger church. All the cells gather in a weekly, biweekly, or monthly mass meeting where everyone worships together. In this larger meeting, the lead pastor delivers a sermon for the entire church. The smaller weekly cell meetings gather for prayer, fellowship, and to study the weekly lesson prepared by the pastor of the large group. The cell church leadership controls the potentially large organization by permitting only authorized speakers and lessons to be delivered in the small groups. If an individual cell church leader teaches their own material, often they are reprimanded and sometimes dismissed.

There is no limit to the growth of a cell church, but individual cells are required to split or multiply when they reach a certain size, usually twenty-five persons (excluding children). Joel Comiskey says a cell church is "a church that has placed evangelistic small groups at the core of its ministry."[33] Cells multiply either when they reach a certain ceiling or every six months. There are two major variations of cell churches.

G12 Churches. Cesar Castellano developed this model in Bogotá, Colombia. Castellano began his cell church by discipling eight persons. Today more than 100,000 members gather in the capital city soccer stadium for the weekly mass cell church meeting.[34] This G12 concept might also be called the entrepreneurial model because the disciple chooses their own potential disciples. In this method, the leader disciples twelve persons in a cell. Each of these "disciples" mentors twelve other persons, starting cells themselves. In the G12

---

[31] William A. Beckham, *The Second Reformation: Reshaping the Church for the 21st Century* (Houston: Touch Publications, 1997), 235.

[32] Sometimes home cell groups meet in businesses. When I directed mission work for the IMB in eastern South America, my hairdresser and her husband led a cell church in their salon with their employees.

[33] Joel Comiskey, *Home Cell Church Explosion: How Your Small Group Can Grow and Multiply* (Houston: Touch Publications, 1998), 17.

[34] G12 Church, accessed June 28, 2018, https://g12church.com/.

model, anyone can be a cell group leader if they take the initiative to evangelize and disciple new cell group members.[35]

5 X 5 (Korea model). Paul Yonggi Cho[36] instituted the 5 X 5 model in Seoul, Korea. In this paradigm, the leadership of the cell church chooses leaders from existing cells. These leaders commission the new cell group leaders to start new cells. Cell church leaders closely supervise the individual leaders. Each cell contains five members (or ten persons in the case of couples) and a cell leader. Five cells make up a zone. The zone is supervised by a zone leader. A zone pastor then oversees twenty-five cells, and so on.[37]

Of course, the growth potential of either kind of cell church is limitless. Although cell congregations exist in North America, they tend to flourish best overseas. Independent-minded North Americans tend to bristle at the regimentation and hierarchical nature of cell church methodology.

Indigenous Church Planting. The concept of indigenous missions probably began with Henry Venn (1796–1873) in the nineteenth century. Wilbert Shenk writes:

> Venn and his American contemporary Rufus Anderson (1797–1880) sought to clarify the main goal of mission and the most effective means of realizing it. The concept of the indigenous church emerged as the central construct of mission theory. A church was judged to be indigenous when it was self-propagating, self-financing, and self-governing. Venn developed his theory of mission in a series of pamphlets and policy statements written in the years 1846 to 1865.[38]

Roland Allen (1868–1947) rediscovered Venn's theory and championed the "Nevius Plan" of self-support, self-government, and self-propagation for national Christian movements.[39] Allen published two important books as a

---

[35] Joel Comiskey, *Groups of 12: A New Way to Mobilize Leaders and Multiply Groups in Your Church* (Houston: Touch Publications, 1999), 22–25.

[36] Yoido Full Gospel Church near Seoul, Korea, claims to have 830,000 registered members, making it the largest church in the world.

[37] Neighbour, *Where Do We Go*, 45–46.

[38] Wilbert R. Shenk, in *Biographical Dictionary of Christian Missions*, ed. Gerald H. Anderson (New York: Macmillan Reference USA, 1998), s.v. "Venn, Henry," 698.

[39] Charles Henry Long, in *Biographical Dictionary of Christian Missions*, s.v. "Allen, Roland," 12–13.

result of his mission experiences in China. *Missionary Methods: St. Paul's or Ours?* (1912) and *The Spontaneous Expansion of the Church* (1927) argue for Allen's indigenous principles.[40] Concerning self-support, Roland Allen says it is wrong to think in terms only of money. Self-supporting congregations also support their pastors and supply their own meeting places.[41] Although largely ignored by his contemporaries, Allen's ideas are considered normative today. Charles Brock's *Indigenous Church Planting* advocates the concept.[42] Many of the succeeding methods, including Pioneer[43] and Four Fields[44] church planting, acknowledge the influence of Roland Allen and Charles Brock, who are in turn indebted to John Nevius.

The universal elements included in every church planting movement include two of the three "selfs" of John Nevius (local leadership and reproduction).[45] Ed Stetzer calls this the Apostolic Harvest Church Planter approach. In this model, the church planter or church planting catalyst preaches, plants a church, and then moves on.[46]

Often mission principles, philosophies, strategies, and methods seem to overlap, creating a certain ambiguity. Writing about Roland Allen's book *Missionary Methods: St. Paul's or Ours?*, David Hesselgrave points out that Allen fails to include any such methods; rather, the tome presents Allen's indigenous missions theory as the proper scriptural paradigm.[47] In the same way, church planting movements (CPM) contain elements that have been observed

---

[40] Lesslie Newbigin, foreword to *The Spontaneous Expansion of the Church* by Roland Allen (Grand Rapids: Eerdmans, 1962), iii.

[41] Roland Allen, *The Spontaneous Expansion of the Church*, 26–27.

[42] Charles Brock, *Indigenous Church Planting: A Practical Journey* (Neosho, MO: Church Growth International, 1994), 89–95.

[43] Thomas Wade Akins, *Pioneer Evangelism* (Rio de Janeiro: *Junta de Missoes Nacionais*, 1999), 9–10.

[44] Nathan Shank and Kari Shank, *Four Fields of Kingdom Growth: Starting & Releasing Healthy Churches*, rev. ed. (2014), Accessed September 13, 2018, https://static1.squarespace.com/static/588ada483a0411af1ab3e7ca/t/58a40ef11b631bcbd49c88c0/1487146760589/4-Fields-Nathan-Shank-2014.pdf.

[45] See David Garrison, *Church Planting Movements: How God is Redeeming a Lost World* (Midlothian, VA: WIGTake Resources, 2004), 172.

[46] Stetzer, *Planting New Churches*, 49–50.

[47] David J. Hesselgrave, "Paul's Missions Strategy," in *Paul's Missionary Methods: In His Time and Ours*, ed. Robert L. Plummer and John Mark Terry (Downers Grove, IL: IVP Academic, 2012), 127–29.

as being present when a large number of churches have been started. There are no methods or strategies presented in David Garrison's *Church Planting Movements*, only observations about what transpires when a CPM occurs. Garrison writes:

> A Church Planting Movement is *a rapid multiplication of indigenous churches planting churches that sweeps through a people group or population segment.* . . . You'll note that this definition describes what *is* happening in Church Planting Movements rather than describing what *could* or *should* happen.[48]

The distinctive feature of the CPM concept is the idea that churches can and should be planted rapidly. Whereas CPM is the philosophy of this kind of church planting, Training for Trainers (T4T) and Four Fields methods implement the theory. In other words, CPM missions has subsumed the indigenous church planting concept and added the idea of rapidity to it. The next chapter further addresses the complex topic of indigenous missions.

Pioneer Evangelism Church Planting. In 1989 Thomas Wade Akins developed the pioneer evangelism method to plant churches using mature laymen rather than ordained ministers.[49] This method trains laymen to lead inductive Bible studies in the homes of lost people to evangelize them and begin a church among them. Rather than starting the new church in the home of a Christian, this method seeks unchurched individuals willing to host a weekly group.

The cycle begins with introductory Bible lessons taught by the pioneer evangelist during weeks one through six. During the sixth lesson, most who have attended each session will come to faith in Christ. The succeeding six weeks constitute the discipleship process. On the twelfth week, the pioneer evangelist turns over the new congregation to a leader within the church. Although developed in Brazil, this method has been successfully replicated all over the world. The distinctive feature of this method is that the evangelist does not start the church in either his own house or the house of another

---

[48] Garrison, *Church Planting Movements*, 21.
[49] Akins, *Pioneer Evangelism*, 17.

believer. These churches are planted on the lost person's own turf so that other unbelievers feel comfortable attending.

Training for Trainers (T4T) Church Planting. Although originally trained as Clinical Pastoral Education (CPE) hospital chaplain missionaries, Ying and Grace Kai accepted the challenge of their mission to evangelize the lost and plant churches. After beginning in the year 2000, by the end of two years the Kais reported 906 small groups with more than 10,000 believers. By the ninth year the "new churches" reportedly numbered 158,993 with 1,718,143 baptisms.[50] The Training for Trainers (T4T) method requires the new member (trainer) to make a list of five non-Christian friends with whom he desires to share Christ. The trainer invites them into his home, shares his testimony and leads them to Christ. The disciple and his group of five become a new group. The trainer teaches his five disciples to share their testimonies with five others and so on.

Theoretically, the next week the trainer's first five disciples have led five non-Christians to the Lord, beginning their own groups. The original trainer leads his disciples through a six-week discipleship plan, while his disciples and their disciples lead new converts through the discipleship material and win others. As the movement multiplies, the new converts are only one week behind their leaders.[51] Often these new groups with week-old Christians are called churches. In 2004, I asked Ying Kai, during a T4T training meeting in Hong Kong, how many people actually follow instructions and witness to their friends. Kai replied, "about one in five." Of course, if even 20 percent of those who are led to Christ lead five more people to the Lord, the results are amazing.

Steve Smith argues that forming churches rapidly is appropriate and claims that in situations where all believers are new, it allows for young believers to become church leaders.[52] The T4T approach emphasizes the importance of each house-church member sharing their faith and discipling others to

---

[50] Steve Smith with Ying Kai, *T4T, A Discipleship ReRevolution: The Story behind the World's Fastest Growing Church Planting Movement and How It Can Happen in Your Community* (Monument, CO: WIGTake Resources, 2011), 21.

[51] Ying Kai, *Trainers: Establishing Successful Trainers,* 2nd ed. (Hong Kong: Ocean Printing, 2005), 5–6.

[52] Smith with Kai, *T4T,* 257, 266.

imitate them. Placing very new Christians in positions of leadership is an obvious weakness. Furthermore, most of the new groups amount to Bible studies
initially but sometimes proponents call them churches before they exhibit all
the biblical manifestations and requirements of church.

Four Fields Church Planting. Based on Mark 4:26–29,[53] this method
describes a church planting overview from the agrarian aspect of one of Jesus's
parables. The idea extrapolated from the parable presents as (1) *Sowers*—men
and women willing to cast the seed; (2) *Seed*—the word of God from the hand
of the sower; (3) *Soil*—the hearts of the lost in which the seed is cast; (4)
Season—commitment to the harvest; (5) *Sickle*—mobilized labor in the harvest force. Nathan and Kari Shank, authors of the Four Fields approach, train
church planters to follow this sequence in their work.[54]

The first phase of the Four Fields plan sees sowers arriving at an empty
field. In the second phase the sowers begin to seed the field with their gospel plan. The next step represents a "growing plan" in which the new believers disciple other new Christians. The fourth phase consists of the harvest, or
the sickle phase, of the Four Fields sequence. During this step, the harvesters
form new churches. Although Jesus's parables do not mention the starting of
churches, proponents see this implied as Jesus speaks about the kingdom of
God. This model has been used extensively in South Asia.

Seeker Sensitive Church Planting. The Seeker Sensitive church-
planting method focuses on the felt needs of the target demographic. The
method was started to reach baby boomers, who became the church "drop
out' generation,"[55] and their successors, Generation Xers, or "the Busters."[56]
Those born before 1945, "the Builders" until recently have controlled most

---

[53] "'The kingdom of God is like this,' he said. 'A man scatters seed on the ground. He sleeps
and rises night and day; the seed sprouts and grows, although he doesn't know how. The soil
produces a crop by itself—first the blade, then the head, and then the full grain on the head. As
soon as the crop is ready, he sends for the sickle, because the harvest has come.'"

[54] Shank and Shank, *Four Fields*, 12–15.

[55] Robert Wuthnow, *After the Baby Boomers: How Twenty- and Thirty-Somethings Are Shaping
the Future of American Religion* (Princeton: Princeton University Press, 2007), 1. "Baby boomers"
consist of those who were born between 1946 and 1964, corresponding to the higher birth rate
after the end of World War II and the Korean War.

[56] Ralph Moore, *Friends: The Key to Reaching Generation X*, rev. ed. (Ventura, CA: Regal
Books, 2001), 14. "Baby Busters" are the successors of the baby boomers, and are called so due to
the dip in the birth rate after 1964. See Wuthnow, *After the Baby Boomers*, 5.

congregations in the United States.[57] Bill Hybels, credited with popularizing the seeker-sensitive method, began Willow Creek Community Church in a rented movie theater in the Chicago area in 1975.[58] Seeker-sensitive churches and their variations feature contemporary music and relevant biblical messages in a relaxed atmosphere. When Harold Ockenga, the cofounder of Fuller Theological Seminary, rejected Christian separatism and advocated embracing some aspects of modernism, he laid the foundation for the seeker-sensitive approach.[59] Seeker-sensitive churches are basically receptor oriented. Sometimes those opposed to the worship styles, architectural innovations, and relaxed atmosphere of more contemporary-oriented churches are reacting to the wineskins and ignoring the quality of the wine inside.

Purpose-Driven Church Planting. Rick and Kay Warren founded Saddleback Community Church in Southern California in 1980. A unique feature of the Purpose-Driven (PDC) church plant is the concept of beginning large. In this method, a core group rehearses services in preparation for the launch service. Various types of media messages communicate the start date of the new church to the community. Daniel Sanchez says, "This means if they call twenty thousand people, two thousand will be willing to receive information. It is calculated that of these two thousand people, in general, about 10 percent or about two hundred, will attend the first meeting."[60] The polar opposite of a house-church plant, with its emphasis on smallness, Purpose-Driven churches begin large and then disciple from "crowd to core." A Purpose Driven church plant starts with as many people as possible and then disciples them through midweek small groups as well as Sunday night discipleship classes.[61]

---

[57] Stetzer, *Planting New Churches*, 106.

[58] Bill Hybels, *Just Walk Across the Room: Simple Steps Pointing People to Faith* (Grand Rapids: Zondervan, 2006), 226.

[59] Paul Chappell and John Goetsch, *The Savior Sensitive Church: Understanding and Avoiding Postmodernism and the Seeker-Sensitive Church Movement* (Lancaster, CA: Striving Together Publications, 2006), 47.

[60] Daniel R. Sanchez, Ebbie C. Smith, and Curtis Watke, *Starting Reproducing Congregations: A Guidebook for Contextual New Church Development* (Cumming, GA: Church Starting Network, 2001), 218.

[61] When the regional directors spent a week at Saddleback Church in 2001, Rick Warren told us the key to his church lay in the small groups. The large, seeker-friendly services only attract the crowds. The small groups and Saddleback's training classes—101, 201, 301, and 401—serve as their engine for discipleship.

Members are encouraged to grow in their faith by increasing personal commitment through taking training classes, joining a small group, and becoming involved in an outreach ministry.

Since 2003, Saddleback Church has been involved in missions through its PEACE Plan. With many thousands of members participating both on international mission trips and in local outreach, their website says, "This new model of mission [is] centered around providing tools and training in local churches, making the local church the engine for growth in a community."[62]

While there are many Purpose Driven churches in the United States, the Purpose Driven model is primarily implemented internationally, particularly in Africa and Latin America.[63]

Special-Purpose (Ethnic, Multiethnic, Language, and Affinity) Church Planting. This type of church plant focuses on a particular demographic as opposed to targeting a certain age group or serving a particular geographical area. In the United States, special-purpose congregations are often started to serve a specific language group or ethnicity. Stuart Murray calls these types of churches, "network churches," as they are composed of network relationships and common cultural components.[64] Chinese language church plants or African American church starts serve as examples. In previous decades, mission agencies called the former language-missions church planting.[65] Ed Stetzer says, "Monoethnic churches are safe environments because everyone shares a common narrative. Everyone fits, everyone belongs, and you don't need to explain or justify yourself. This safe environment creates a prime opportunity for evangelism that targets that particular ethnic community."[66]

---

[62] Saddleback Church, "The Peace Plan," accessed November 13, 2019, https://thepeaceplan .com/history/.

[63] When I supervised 400-plus missionaries in South America, I partnered with Saddleback Church to teach Purpose Driven church planting in Brazil. Rick Warren and his team trained over 1,500 pastors in Rio de Janeiro. As a result, a number of seeker-sensitive and Purpose Driven churches were begun.

[64] Murray, *Church Planting*, 133.

[65] The Home Mission Board (HMB) of the Southern Baptist Convention—now the North American Mission Board (NAMB)—had a Language Missions Department prior to the year 2000.

[66] Stetzer and Im, *Planting Missional Churches*, 104 (see chap. 1, n. 11).

Overseas, missionaries concentrating on a particular ethnicity exemplify special-purpose church planting. The missionary focuses on a specific people group rather than trying to reach the general population. This is also known as homogeneous unit principle (HUP).

The affinity[67] approach represents another variation of the special-purpose church planting concept. In this alternative, the church planter focuses on affinity groups such as cowboys, farmers, surfers, truckers, taxi drivers, sports-team fans, bikers, vacationers, and many others. In this paradigm, seekers are drawn because the church is composed of "their kind" of people. These churches are not built on excluding others but rather on attracting a certain demographic. Although conceding the advantage the affinity approach possesses as it focuses on a specific population segment, Stuart Murray objects to this concept:

> Even if the HUP is accepted as a component in a diversified mission strategy, the emergence of homogeneous churches is another matter. . . . The argument is that the development of more and more churches that simply mirror the divisions in society is not only questionable as a sustainable mission strategy, but is objectionable as a perversion of the gospel. The planting instead of multi-cultural churches would be an ecclesiological development with tremendous significance for mission.[68]

The type of church Murray favors—churches that are intentionally multi-ethnic (also known as "mosaic churches")—identify by their inclusive natures. These kinds of special-purpose congregations attempt to reflect all the ethnicities represented in their communities in order to demonstrate how Christ has broken down society's barriers[69] and provides a preview of heaven.

Taking the opposite view, McGavran champions realism. He contends that lost persons before conversion cannot be expected to act like regenerate individuals. The UPG method favors reaching people where they are, so they

---

[67] Not to be confused with international affinity groups. The International Mission Board (IMB) calls the ethnolinguistic people groups within certain geographical areas "affinities." For instance, all ethnolinguistic people groups originating in North Africa and the Middle East are part of the North Africa and Middle East Affinity.

[68] Murray, *Church Planting*, 136.

[69] Stetzer and Im, *Planting Missional Churches*, 106–7.

can be redeemed and subsequently begin to act like saved persons. McGavran
says:

> Men like to become Christians without crossing racial, linguistic, or
> class barriers. . . . Like the United States, most nations are composed
> of many unmeltable ethnics. India, for example, has more than 3,000
> units (castes and tribes) each of which practices endogamy.[70] . . . The
> biblical teaching is plain that in Christ two peoples become one.
> Christian Jews and Gentiles become one new people of God, parts
> of the One Body of Christ. But the One Body is complex. Since
> both peoples continue to speak separate languages, does not oneness
> cover a vast and continuous diversity? . . . It takes no great acumen
> to see that when marked differences of color, stature, income, clean-
> liness, and education are present, men understand the Gospel better
> when expounded by their own kind of people.[71]

Planting according to the HUP principle does not endorse racism but
rather recognizes the reality that people are best reached where they are most
comfortable. Once these lost persons become born again and are acculturated
into Christianity, many of them and most of their children will feel comfortable in the mosaic-like churches Murray prefers.

Emerging Churches. Emerging churches seem to attract some baby busters, but mainly Millennials to their congregations.[72] Emerging churches desire
new church forms for a postmodern society and engage in three core practices:
(1) identifying with the life of Jesus, (2) transforming secular space, and (3)
living as community. These churches focus, not on seekers, but on the believer.
Emerging church is a catch-all name for many diverse types of congregations.
Eddie Gibbs writes:

> Popularly, the term *emerging church* has been applied to high-profile,
> youth-oriented congregations that have gained attention on account
> of their rapid numerical growth, their ability to attract (or retain)

---

[70] The custom of marrying only within the limits of a particular tribe, caste, or community.

[71] McGavran, *Understanding Church Growth*, 2nd ed., 223–24, 227.

[72] Millennials compose that portion of the population born between 1980 and 2000. Thom S.
Rainer and Jess W. Rainer, *The Millennials: Connecting to America's Largest Generation* (Nashville:
B&H, 2011), 2. Baby busters, also known as Generation X, Generation Y, or both, fit between
the baby boomers and the Millennials within the years 1965 and 2000. Wuthnow, *After the Baby
Boomers*, 2.

twentysomethings; their contemporary worship, which draws from popular music styles; and their ability to promote themselves to the Christian subculture through websites and by word of mouth.[73]

Emerging church proponents do not desire to jettison Christianity, only its Western trappings. Simon Hall says, "My main aim for the community is not to be 'post' anything but to be 'and' everything. We are evangelical *and* charismatic *and* liberal *and* orthodox *and* contemplative *and* into social justice *and* into alternative worship."[74] Emerging churches desire to worship God differently and better than their parents and grandparents. Denver's (Colorado) Scum of the Earth Church exemplifies this paradigm's unorthodox attitude. Founded to reach persons other churches might reject, Scum of the Earth has been described as a punk-rock-goth-artist church. Their newsletter, titled "Rubbish," favors losing members as opposed to gaining them.[75] The founder, Michael Sares, includes a video tour of the church's bathrooms on its website. Although not everyone's cup of tea, emerging churches serve an untapped ecclesiological demographic. Some see this as the best alternative to reach the generation born between 2000 and 2020, tentatively being called Generation Z or the "Linksters." These young people have come of age during the electronic, internet era.[76]

Saturation Church Planting (DAWN). The saturation church planting concept interprets the "nations" in Matt 28:19 as literal countries as well as in its "ethnos" (ethnic-people group) sense. Therefore, the DAWN (Discipling A Whole Nation) strategy and resulting methods advocate planting at least one church in every community in every nation (political entity) on earth. Jim Montgomery says:

---

[73] Eddie Gibbs and Ryan K. Bolger, *Emerging Churches: Creating Christian Community in Postmodern Cultures* (Grand Rapids: Baker Academic, 2005), 41.

[74] Simon Hall in *Emerging Churches: Creating Christian Community in Postmodern Cultures* by Eddie Gibbs and Ryan K. Bolger (Grand Rapids: Baker Academic, 2005), 38–39.

[75] Jonathan Merritt, "Misfit Minister Says Pastors Should 'Pray Their Church Loses Numbers,'" Religion News Service, December 1, 2014, accessed June 28, 2018, https://religionnews.com/.../misfit-pastor-says-ministers-pray-church-loses-numbers/.

[76] Olivia Blair, "What Comes After Millennials? Meet the Generation Known as the 'Linksters,'" *Independent*, April 11, 2017, accessed June 24, 2018, https://www.independent.co.uk/life-style/millennials-generation-z-linksters-what-next-generation-x-baby-boomers-internet-social-media-a7677001.html.

DAWN aims at mobilizing the whole body of Christ in whole countries in a determined effort to complete the Great Commission in that country by working toward the goal of providing an evangelical congregation for every village and neighborhood of every class, kind, and condition of people in the whole country. . . .

When this is accomplished, it is not assumed the Great Commission for a country has been completed, but that the last practical and measurable goal has been reached toward making a disciple of that country and all the "nations" within it. . . . When this happens in every country in the world, we can almost hear the trumpet sound.[77]

The DAWN method does not prescribe the kind of evangelical churches that should be planted in a country but only stresses the necessity of saturating all countries with them. Although open to reaching people groups, the DAWN method views conquering and occupying geographic territory (countries) with the gospel as its primary objective. By reaching every city and town, DAWN proponents believe, as a by-product, no people group will be overlooked.[78]

Virtual Church Planting. In limited-access countries such as Saudi Arabia, where the persecution of Christians is fierce and the possibility of betrayal high, some church planters have resorted to virtual church planting. This model limits the contact within the church's membership to just a few trusted people. Generally speaking, only the church planter knows the membership of a virtual church. The church planter meets one-on-one with each church member in order to provide safety and security for the local body of Christ. Although rare, this type of church planting allows believers in high-persecution contexts to experience at least some level of church life.

Online church planting is a variation of the virtual church concept. Robert Wuthnow says, "Narrowly defined, the virtual church is a website or chat room to which people come to worship."[79] Originally, those interested in joining an event over the internet would stream the worship service live. With the advent of live video-conferencing tools and virtual-reality software, however, members

---

[77] James H. Montgomery, *DAWN 2000: 7 Million Churches to Go—The Personal Story of the DAWN Strategy* (Pasadena: William Carey Library, 1989), 12–13.

[78] Montgomery, 104.

[79] Wuthnow, *After the Baby Boomers*, 212.

in diverse locations will be increasingly able to join church services more interactively, even participating from remote locations. Although this concept is used currently by those on the margins of Christianity,[80] as technology improves evangelicals may join in as well. Micheal Pocock expresses some concerns as to the leadership of a virtual church. He writes, "Does the webmaster, by virtue of his or her role, assume the leadership? What about the scriptural teaching on the role of elders, deacons, or other leaders?"[81] Questions such as these must be addressed as this model is embraced.

Replanting and Revitalization Church Planting. Sometimes when an older, formerly large church dwindles to just a few members, the congregation or sponsoring denomination opts to restart a church by implementing an entirely new concept. For instance, a historic church might adopt a seeker-sensitive, emerging church, multiethnic, or mono-ethnic paradigm to attract a different sort of parishioner. This may be necessary because 94 percent of all churches are in decline.[82] Lyle Schaller says, "Periodically, every congregation either redefines its role and identity or it tends to drift into a passive state. . . . The research that has been done on this new generation of adults and on their outlook on religion suggests that the passive church will not be able to reach and serve many of these people, who view all institutions as suspect."[83]

The Mosaic Church in Los Angeles exemplifies a successful church revitalization and replant project. By 1964, the First Southern Baptist Church of East Los Angeles had declined to less than twenty persons. Called as pastor to basically bury the church, Tom Wolfe instituted a more contemporary worship style and changed the name of the congregation to "the Church on Brady." The Church on Brady attracted twentysomethings and thirtysomethings from

---

[80] A former Mormon missionary published a book advocating virtual witnessing and baptism. See Greg Timble, *The Virtual Missionary: The Power of Your Personal Testimony* (Springfield, UT: Cedar Fort, 2017). Another book espouses starting online congregations for those marginalized by traditional Christianity. See Jerold A. Garber, *Ministry to the Avatars: Building a Real Church in a Virtual World* (Bloomington, IN: Archway, 2017).

[81] Pocock, Van Rheenen, and McConnell, *Changing Face of World Missions*, 309 (see chap. 5, n. 2).

[82] Thom Rainer, quoted in Dottie Escobedo-Frank, *Restart Your Church* (Nashville: Abingdon, 2012), 5.

[83] Lyle B. Schaller, *Activating the Passive Church: Diagnosis and Treatment* (Nashville: Abingdon, 1981), 12–14.

across Southern California and began to grow. In 1994, Erwin McManus became the senior pastor and subsequently changed the name of the congregation again, to the Mosaic Church. Today, the Mosaic Church has grown to more than 2,000 members meeting weekly in multiple locations.

Capitol Hill Baptist Church in Washington, DC, achieved renewal in a different manner. Instead of changing the worship style and format, Pastor Mark Dever recommends the declining church "preach good sermons, move toward a plurality of elders, and be careful with the church's membership."[84] As a result of Dever's leadership, the church grew from 130 to about 1,000 people.[85]

Many stagnant or dying churches could benefit from a church revitalization or replant strategy. Tom Cheyney says a stagnant or declining church may need a transformational leader-change agent to help in refocusing a church.[86] A number of seminaries list church revitalization courses in their catalogs. The North American Mission Board, state conventions, local church associations, and other mission agencies assist churches in restarting their congregations.

Venue and Multicongregational Church Planting. From time to time, a large successful church elects to reproduce themselves by initiating church plants in the surrounding communities. Sometimes these churches anticipate becoming stand-alone congregations, while others intend to remain a part of the mother church. Sometimes venues are added because a small church with a large building needs rescuing.[87] More frequently, however, a large church with a regional presence desires to expand its footprint to other parts of an urban area. This can be achieved by starting medium- to large-sized churches or using small groups.[88]

Those using the multisite method often broadcast the weekly sermon from the mother church to the satellite churches in their orbit. In other situations, however, the local-site pastor may deliver his own Sunday sermon.

---

[84] Mark Dever, quoted in *A Guide to Church Revitalization: Guide Book No. 005*, ed. R. Albert Mohler (Louisville: SBTS Press, 2015), 69.

[85] Mohler, 65.

[86] Tom Cheyney, *The 7 Pillars of Church Revitalization and Renewal: Biblical Foundations for Church Revitalization* (Orlando: Renovate Publishing Group, 2016), 27–28.

[87] Ed Stetzer calls this the Adoption Method. Stetzer, *Planting New Churches*, 161–62.

[88] Wagner, *Church Planting for a Greater Harvest*, 66.

The internal venue model represents a variation on this paradigm. Here, a congregation primarily composed of one ethnic group plants a church or churches from other ethnic groups within its own building. For instance, the First Southern Baptist Church of Monterey Park (California), primarily composed of English-speaking Caucasians, started two Chinese-language churches (Mandarin and Cantonese) and a Spanish-speaking Argentinian congregation.[89] All four congregations successfully met at different times during the week, sharing the building and time slots on Sundays and weekdays. This represents an attractive option in urban areas where land, property, and building costs prohibit most new congregations from owning and operating their own facilities.

Urban Church Planting. Whether in North America or overseas, cities present the greatest challenge to church planting. Donald McGavran, writing about the urban puzzle, says, "In urban areas, where some conditions favor church growth and others inhibit it, sometimes churches multiply but mostly they do not. One cannot help asking why."[90] He points to the problems of mobile populations, long working hours, sophistication, and the indifference to religion caused by secularism.[91]

C. Kirk Hadaway, a sociologist and my brother, defines the word *urban* in his book *The Urban Challenge*:

> The terms *metropolitan* and *urban* are typically used interchangeably to refer to large cities, but each has a very distinct meaning as defined by the United States Census Bureau. Metropolitan areas, for instance, refer to Standard Metropolitan Statistical Areas. SMSAs, as they are called, are composed of one or more counties and must include at least 50,000 persons in a central city or urbanized areas. . . . The meaning of *urban*, as defined by the Census Bureau is quite distinct from that of *metropolitan*, even though the percent of Americans living in urban areas is nearly identical to the percent living in metropolitan areas. To be called urban an area must be within a city or town (place) with a minimum population of 2,500 or be an area surrounding an urban center which meets some minimum

---

[89] As a young man, I served as the pastor of this church from 1979–1983 before leaving for Tanzania to become an international missionary.

[90] McGavran, *Understanding Church Growth*, 2nd ed., 319.

[91] McGavran, 319.

population density requirements. Because of this definition, some towns which would seem hardly urban are included and some suburban and exurban territories surrounding very large cities would be excluded.[92]

Kirk Hadaway prefers "metropolitan" when speaking of urban areas.[93]

Increasingly, during the twenty-first century, more and more of the world's population will live in cities.[94] Today about 54 percent of the world's population is urban.[95] The United Nations projects that two-thirds of the world will live in cities by 2030.[96] Although acknowledging the paradigm shift from geographical missions to UPG missions in the twentieth century, Robert Garrett believes burgeoning cities constitute the next frontier in missions during this century.[97]

In the Western context, suburban church plants grow the fastest. For transitional neighborhoods in urban areas, Kirk Hadaway recommends ethnic churches, multiethnic congregations, regional churches, and satellite congregations of larger churches.[98] To this list McGavran adds house churches as being especially effective in city situations.[99]

---

[92] C. Kirk Hadaway, in *The Urban Challenge: Reaching America's Cities with the Gospel*, ed. C. Kirk Hadaway and Larry L. Rose (Nashville: Broadman, 1982), 10.

[93] Hadaway, 11.

[94] Roger M. Greenway and Timothy M. Monsma, *Cities: Missions' New Frontier*, 2nd ed. (Grand Rapids: Baker, 2000), 20.

[95] Chandan Deuskar, "What Does Urban Mean?" World Bank Blogs, June 2, 2015, https://blogs.worldbank.org/sustainablecities/what-does-urban-mean. Writing about the criteria for urban, Deuskar says, "The OECD [Economic Co-Operation and Development] methodology consists of three main steps: identifying contiguous or highly interconnected densely inhabited urban cores; grouping these into functional areas; and defining the commuting shed or 'hinterland' of the functional urban area. The OECD uses population size cutoffs (50,000 or 100,000 people, depending on the country) as well as population density cutoffs (1,000 or 1,500 people per sq. km.) to define the urban cores, and then selects those areas from which more than 15% of workers commute to the core as hinterlands."

[96] Edith M. Lederer, "UN Report: By 2030 Two-Thirds of the World Will Live in Cities," Associated Press, May 18, 2016, https://www.apnews.com/40b530ac84ab4931874e1f7efb4f1a22.

[97] Bob Garrett, "The Next Frontier: The Implications for Missions of Global Urbanization in the Twenty-First Century," in *Reaching the City: Reflections on Urban Missions in the Twenty-First Century*, ed. Gary Fujino, Timothy R. Sisk, and Tereso C. Casino (Pasadena: William Carey, 2012), 24.

[98] C. Kirk Hadaway, "Learning from Urban Church Research," in *Planting and Growing Urban Churches: From Dream to Reality*, ed. Harvie M. Conn (Grand Rapids: Baker, 1997), 42–43.

[99] McGavran, *Understanding Church Growth*, 2nd ed., 322.

Internationally, house churches make the best sense for metropolitan areas. Young men and women in large Muslim cities such as Cairo, Khartoum, and Istanbul embrace the anonymity of the city. An impossible option in rural areas where everyone knows everyone else's business, urbanites, whether male or female, can blaze their own trails economically, socially, and spiritually.

Concluding Remarks about Church Planting

The church planting methods presented in this chapter may be employed for either good or evil. Depending on the biblical doctrines embraced by the church planter or the church, the congregation may be orthodox, heretical, or somewhere in between. An emerging church start could be quite conservative theologically, while a historic church plant might deviate into liberalism. The music, worship, or size of a particular church model may seem to favor aberrant theology, but not necessarily. Although many might disagree, innovative methods need not preclude sound theology. Atlee Community Church in Richmond (Virginia),[100] a Southern Baptist church start with denominational assistance, adopted the seeker-sensitive format with a twist—a secular song would begin every service and congregational singing was not encouraged. Instead, a worship team performed all the songs in order for the target demographic, lost boomers and busters, to feel comfortable. At one service I attended, the worship team performed "Hotel California" by the Eagles rock band, followed by the pastor preaching a quite orthodox sermon on the reality of hell.

Church planting overseas by international missionaries differs significantly from their North American and European counterparts. In the West, the church starter usually becomes the founding pastor, at least in the beginning. Most of the time the church planter belongs to the same ethnic group and speaks the language of his new congregation as a native. Internationally, missionaries act more as catalysts, starting multiple churches simultaneously with a cadre of church planters they have trained from within the host culture. Generally speaking, international missionaries labor cross culturally, planting churches in a society and language not their own. In past generations, when

---

[100] Our family attended this church for several years while I worked at the home office of the International Mission Board (Southern Baptist Convention) in Richmond, VA. Our youngest daughter was baptized there.

international missionaries started a church, they pastored the congregation for a few years and then turned it over to a national believer. With over six billion persons on the planet, mission boards can ill afford to continue a strategy with a one-to-one church planter to church ratio.

Veteran missionary church planter Don Dolifka, my mentor during my first church planting assignment in Tanzania, says church planting internationally is very simple. The missionary needs to find a "couple of guys," disciple them, cast a church planting vision, and then mentor them as they begin multiple churches and train others.

EVANGELISM

Introduction

John Wesley famously said, "I set myself on fire and they come to see me burn."[101] Evangelism constitutes the fuel that ignites the fire of missions. Although different in scope, evangelism and missions go hand in hand. David Bosch sees missions as wider than evangelism and not synonymous with it.[102] Missions, however, cannot occur without evangelism. Evangelism produces the converts who become the new members of multiplying churches whose adherents evangelize others. Thomas Johnston declares:

> Evangelizing is the verbal proclamation of the Gospel of Jesus Christ to the unsaved in the power of the Holy Spirit to the end of persuading them to repent of their sin, to believe in the work of Jesus Christ on their behalf, and to accept Him as their Savior and Lord, with the intent to baptize them and teach them to observe all that Christ commanded, as committed members of a local NT church.[103]

Evangelism is the first step in the mission process. Over the centuries, Christians have employed many mission methods. Some methods of evangelism produce fruit in the foreign context, while other techniques are less

---

[101] John Wesley, quoted in Escobedo-Frank, *ReStart Your Church*, 2.

[102] Bosch, *Transforming Mission*, 409 (see chap. 1, n. 4).

[103] Thomas P. Johnston, *Evangelizology: A Biblical, Historical, Theological Study of Evangelizing*, vol. 1, *Motivation and Definition*, 2nd ed. (Liberty, MO: Evangelism Unlimited, 2011), 385.

effective. Although not exhaustive, this chapter outlines the broad categories of evangelism. John Havlik claims, "The task of the evangelistic church actually involves two things—evangelizing every person in the community and equipping (discipling) every person converted to Christ."[104]

Evangelism Strategies

Evangelism strategies, like church planting approaches, contain many methods. In some senses, evangelism and church planting strategies overlap and in other ways they do not. For instance, church planting cannot occur without evangelism to populate the new churches. When I arrived in North Africa there were no believers or churches in my area. The first priority was to implement an evangelism strategy to win new believers who would become members of the new church plants.

On the other hand, sometimes evangelism activities yield converts but no churches. Some evangelism strategies feature stand-alone methods that may result in churches or may not, depending on the intent of the tactician. Such methods might include personal evangelism, orality, church evangelism, mass event evangelism, or age-graded evangelism, to name just a few.

Discipleship Evangelism. Discipleship evangelism claims to capture the method of Jesus and his twelve disciples. Discipleship evangelism concentrates on a few disciples who in turn disciple others. The evangelist seeks "a person of peace"[105] and then disciples them. In areas that restrict conversion to Christianity this method often succeeds because the evangelist selects the disciples and can proceed as quickly or slowly as necessary. The G12 cell-church model uses the discipleship method of evangelism. In Colombia, an open (but sometimes violent) society, Cesar Castellanos began his cell church with twelve men. As these men discipled others, the multiplication movement now requires Castellano's church to hold their weekly meetings in a soccer stadium. Robert Coleman writes:

---

[104] John F. Havlik, *The Evangelistic Church* (Nashville: Convention Press, 1976), 17.

[105] The concept of seeking out those who are open to spiritual things is based on Luke 10:5–6: "Whatever house you enter, first say, 'Peace to this household.' If a person of peace is there, your peace will rest on him; but if not, it will return to you."

Men were his method. It all started by Jesus calling a few men to follow him. This revealed immediately the direction his evangelistic strategy would take. His concern was not with programs to reach the multitudes, but with men whom the multitudes would follow. Remarkable as it may seem, Jesus started to gather these men before he ever organized an evangelistic campaign or even preached a sermon in public. Men were to be his method of winning the world to God.[106]

Of course, every evangelistic approach favors discipling new converts, but the discipleship method believes this approach should be the primary methodology for reaching the lost. Billie Hanks points out that if one person discipled two people a year, and those disciples discipled others, in thirty-three years, 8.5 billion people would be reached for Christ.[107]

Evangelism through the Arts (Drama, Painting, and Music). In closed countries, Christian arts ministries can effectively present the gospel. In North Africa, Christian drama troupes perform "wordless plays" to Muslim audiences to great effect. Spellbound Muslims view the crucifixion and resurrection in such a dramatic way, no words are needed. Following the performance, silent evangelists visit one-on-one with the seekers who desire further information or to join a discipleship group.

Another innovative approach involves erecting an artist's easel in a city square in order to draw pictures, diagrams, or gospel narratives. In countries where the government prohibits open-air preaching the evangelist may relate stories without speaking. In this way, open-air campaigners' illustrated "paint talk" method shares the gospel with a large easel and a black light in about ten minutes. Crowds gather because of the interesting nature of the presentation.

Similarly, even in closed countries, Christian singers and musicians can attractively present the gospel with minimal offense to other religions. After believers perform their music on the street, in a park, or other public venue, some of those listening remain behind to converse with the musicians.

Direct Evangelism. When discussing the topic of evangelism, the idea of direct evangelism comes to mind first. Direct evangelism (also known as

---

[106] Robert Coleman, *The Master Plan of Evangelism* (Westwood, NJ: Fleming H. Revell, 1963), 21.

[107] Billie Hanks Jr. and Randy Craig, *Operation Multiplication 12 Session Guide: Multiplication by Mentorship* (Salado, TX: International Evangelism Association, 1999), 4.

confrontational evangelism), includes the tried-and-true methods of street preaching and door-to-door witnessing. Direct evangelism intimidates many because the evangelist usually has not formed a relationship previously with the unevangelized. Selecting a neutral site such as a coffee shop is one way of alleviating some of this anxiety. This kind of witnessing has been used throughout church history and should not be discarded because it is not socially acceptable. One of my North African colleagues would often buy a bus ticket from the capital city to the primary coastal city and preach to his fellow passengers during the 1,100 km journey.

Friendship Evangelism. Friendship evangelism, also known as web evangelism[108] or concentric circles evangelism,[109] starts with those the believer knows best. Friendship evangelism focuses on friends, family members, acquaintances, coworkers, and those who are in what Richard Jackson calls one's "daily traffic pattern of life."[110] Overseas, and especially in closed countries, web concentric-circle relationships represent the safest and most productive method of outreach. McGavran says:

> In Africasia,[111] the web counts tremendously. Every man has, knows, and is intimate with not merely brothers, sisters, parents, and grandparents, but also with cousins, uncles, aunts, great-uncles, sisters-in-law, mothers-in-law, godfathers and godmothers, grand-nieces and grandnephews, and many others. In his world, these are people who count. He can expect a night's hospitality in any of these houses. He belongs. Relatives will shield him from the law, try to get him a job, or help him select a wife or an ox in case he should need either.[112]

By using this kind of evangelism, any church model the church planter prefers can be employed to reach out to one's family, friends, and acquaintances.

---

[108] Not to be confused with the World Wide Web. Thinking of Donald A. McGavran, web relationships are extremely important to the "bridges of God." See the discussion in McGavran, *Understanding Church Growth*, 2nd ed., 359–63.

[109] See W. Oscar Thompson, *Concentric Circles of Concern: Seven Stages for Making Disciples*, rev. Claude V. King (Nashville: B&H, 1999).

[110] Richard Jackson, *How To's on the Highway to Heaven* (Phoenix: Exposition Press, 1985), 104.

[111] McGavran's term for peoples in Africa, Asia, and the Americas.

[112] McGavran, *Understanding Church Growth*, 2nd ed., 359.

Paul Little says, "Obedience in evangelism is one of the keys to spiritual health. It is vital to all Christians, individually and collectively."[113] Little suggests seven principles for witnessing to others based on Jesus's encounter with the woman at the well in John 4: (1) contact others socially, (2) establish a common interest, (3) arouse interest, (4) don't go too far [do not exceed the person's capacity to understand], (5) don't condemn [the sinner], (6) stick with the main issue, (7) confront him directly [present the gospel].[114] By using these principles, Paul Little says, the part-time evangelist can reach their friends and acquaintances.

Lifestyle and Servant Evangelism. Somewhat similar to friendship evangelism, lifestyle evangelism and servant evangelism seek to make outreach a part of one's everyday lifestyle, as opposed to a daily task to complete. Jim Petersen says there are two primary modes of evangelism in the New Testament: proclamation and affirmation. Proclamation is well known. Affirmation is "a process of incarnating the gospel message."[115] Lifestyle evangelism proponents desire to broadcast Christ in both word and deed. Lifestyle evangelism believes the outside world will understand the gospel through the works and witness of Christ followers.

Similarly, servant evangelism organizes concrete action plans to minister to the real needs of people. For example, some churches demonstrate Christ's love by painting a local elementary school or dispensing water in shopping center parking lots on hot days. Although servant evangelism of this sort may secure some community good will, sometimes no written or verbal witness explains why this ministry is taking place. Although lifestyle and servant evangelism portray Christians in a favorable light, the actual gospel of Christ has not been presented without some kind of verbal or written witness.

---

[113] Paul E. Little, *How to Give Away Your Faith* (Downers Grove, IL: InterVarsity Press, 1966), 25.

[114] Little, 26–45.

[115] Jim Petersen, *Evangelism as a Lifestyle: Reaching Your World with the Gospel* (Colorado Springs: NavPress, 1981), 42–43.

SPECIALIZED EVANGELISM

Student Evangelism. Bill Bright says, "Win the campus for Christ today, win the world for Christ tomorrow."[116] Consequently, the objective of Campus Crusade for Christ (now Cru) is to reach all academic communities in the United States by discipling the students, faculty, and staff of the institutions.[117] Student evangelism includes ministry among young children, youth, and college students. Although churches often have staff that minister to children, middle, and high school students, student evangelism represents very specialized and important work. Students are at an age when they are making major decisions in their lives and can best be evangelized while they are young.

Mass Evangelism. Leighton Ford believes the term "mass evangelism" misleads hearers to believe it is through mass hysteria people come to Christ en masse. He points out that the Bible gives many instances of the apostles preaching to large crowds. Ford says, "'Mass Evangelism' is a platform for personal evangelism. It differs from the regular preaching of the Word of God in the church only in degree, not in kind."[118]

I partnered with Operation Mobilization (OM) to rent a soccer stadium in the capitol city of a North African Muslim-majority country to present the gospel. Surprisingly, the OM director, a national believer, received a permit and 25,000 heard the claims of Christ in a country that persecutes believers and by law prohibits Muslims from becoming Christians.

Event evangelism (Mardi Gras, sports events, VBS, and holidays). Event evangelism takes advantage of occurrences in the calendar year. Christmas, Easter, New Year's, Halloween, Valentine's Day, and the Fourth of July exemplify prominent seasonal events that may be exploited by evangelists. Christians can participate in county fairs, sporting events, and neighborhood gatherings to present a witness. Such gatherings are nonconfrontational and focus the energy of the evangelists on one major emphasis. Thom Johnston says

---

[116] Bill Bright, *Come Help Change the World* (Old Tappan, NJ: Fleming H. Revell, 1970), 81.

[117] Campus Crusade for Christ International, *Sharing the Abundant Life on Campus* (San Bernardino: Campus Crusade for Christ International, 1972), iv.

[118] Leighton Ford, *The Christian Persuader: A New Look at Evangelism Today* (New York: Harper & Row, 1966), 71.

the disadvantage of event evangelism is that people may confuse entertainment with evangelism and "may create a talent-based ecclesiology."[119]

Sports Evangelism. Sports evangelism differs from evangelism at sporting events. A sports evangelist concentrates on evangelism to sports teams or by utilizing sports as an avenue for witness. For instance, a sports missionary in Uruguay decided to evangelize Uruguayans and plant churches among them by starting baseball teams across the country. Although baseball is almost unknown in Uruguay, the Uruguayans were attracted to it because of the novelty factor. Evangelists from sports as diverse as soccer, football, basketball, baseball, hockey, swimming, diving, surfing, wrestling, boating, and racing, including their coaches, players, and trainers, can have a remarkable impact on society.

On the other hand, missionaries witnessing at the quadrennial World Cup event seeking to reach the crowds would be an example of evangelism at a sporting event. Those witnessing at sporting events, obviously, do not need to have an expertise in any of the sporting contests.

Evangelism Presentations

The Scripture Method. Over the years Christians have developed a myriad different gospel presentations. The Scripture method, also known as the Romans Road, has the benefit of sticking to relevant Bible verses only. The Romans Road includes Rom 3:10; 3:23; and 6:23, which demonstrate to a lost person their need for salvation. This presentation contains the advantage of being strictly biblical. Some of the other methods feature many diagrams, charts, and ideas that may be true but are not exactly from the Bible.

Booklet Method. Often evangelists will share a small booklet that contains the main points they desire to explain. Cru's *Four Spiritual Laws*,[120] the Navigators' *Bridge to Life*,[121] and Billy Graham's *Peace with God*[122] represent prominent examples. Some evangelists prepare demographic survey questions as gospel presentation openers.

---

[119] Johnston, *Evangelizology*, vol. 2, *Commission, Practice, and Follow-Up*, 865.

[120] Bill Bright, *Have You Heard of the Four Spiritual Laws?* (Bright Media Foundation, 2003).

[121] The Navigators, *Bridge to Life* (Colorado Springs: NavPress, 1969).

[122] Tim Kenny, "Steps to Peace with God," Billy Graham Evangelistic Association, *Decision*, September 23, 2004, https://billygraham.org/decision-magazine/october-2004/steps-to-peace-with-god/.

Socratic Method. LifeWay Christian Resources' *Share Jesus without Fear* poses life questions (also called the Socratic method) to begin the conversation. Mike Shipman employs a question-and-answer approach for witnessing to South Asians on the subcontinent. The method begins with a series of probing questions and then moves to a gospel presentation depending on the level of interest. The *Any 3* method asks, "Are you Hindu, Muslim, Buddhist, or Christian?" or "What religion do you follow?"[123] The *Camel Method*, a strategy for witnessing to Muslims by using the Qur'an, has already been discussed in chapter 7.

The Testimony Method. The most popular method of witnessing currently is the testimony method. The evangelist gives a one- to five-minute testimony recounting, "(1) What my life was before I became a Christian, (2) What caused me to want Christ as my Savior, (3) How I became a Christian, (4) What being a Christian means to me."[124] This technique has the advantage of being credible, interesting, and irrefutable.[125] When using the testimony method, it is important to include the propositional truths of the gospel as well.[126]

The Diagram Method. *Three Circles: Life Conversation Guide*[127] represents another method of drawing biblical truth through the media method. This eighteen-page booklet is designed for the evangelist to share with a lost person how to fix his or her broken life. According to the presentation, every person has been created to reflect God's design. Sin, however, has resulted in each person on earth being broken. When a person repents and believes the gospel, his or her brokenness is repaired and that individual is restored to a right relationship with God.

---

[123] Mike Shipman, *Any-3: Anyone, Anywhere, Anytime: Lead Muslims to Christ Now* (Monument, CO: WIGTake Resources, 2013), 111–15.

[124] George E. Worrell, *How to Take the Worry out of Witnessing* (Nashville: Broadman Press, 1976), 46.

[125] Johnston, *Evangelizology*, vol. 2, 628.

[126] Mark Dever, *The Gospel and Personal Evangelism* (Wheaton, IL: Crossway, 2007), 73.

[127] *3 Circles: Life Conversation Guide* (Alpharetta, GA: North American Mission Board, 2014).

Church Evangelism and Visitation Evangelism

Roy Fish says, "The central activity of the church is to witness or to share. Sharing is the main work of the whole church throughout the whole world. Taking the message to 'every creature' suggests that the individual work of every Christian is to share with every unsaved person."[128] Charles Kelley points out that in past generations, church discipleship and evangelism occurred during the morning Sunday school hour and in the Sunday evening training hour.[129] He says Southern Baptist church evangelism prospered through decisional preaching using invitations, revival meetings, and the Sunday school. He says, "Integrating decisional preaching, personal evangelism, Sunday school and revival meetings, had a great farm that produced much fruit, creating growth throughout the SBC."[130] Sunday school pioneer Andy Anderson's Church Growth Spiral stressed the importance of enrolling non-Christians in Sunday school for the purpose of evangelism and ultimately starting new churches.[131]

For many reasons, the majority of church attenders in all denominations attend worship only, meaning that discipleship only occurs during the pulpit teaching ministry hour. Although many churches continue to operate Sunday schools or small groups, participation has declined. Most churches have shifted from a priority on discipleship to a focus on worship[132] and ceased to meet on Sunday and Wednesday nights. Although everyone values quality worship, it should not come at the expense of discipleship.

Much church evangelism rests on the related topic of visitation evangelism. Arthur Flake, famous for "Flake's Formula" for Sunday school growth, speaks of the absolute necessity of visitation evangelism.[133] Many churches do not recognize visitors during the worship service lest the newcomers become

---

[128] Roy J. Fish and J. E. Conant, *Every Member Evangelism for Today* (New York: Harper & Row, 1976), 6.

[129] Charles S. Kelley Jr., *Fuel the Fire: Lessons from the History of Southern Baptist Evangelism* (Nashville: B&H Academic, 2018), 187.

[130] Kelley, 180.

[131] Andy Anderson, *Where Action Is: How God Is Using a Simple Plan to Reach People for Christ* (Nashville: Broadman Press, 1976), 129.

[132] Kelley, *Fuel the Fire*, 189–90.

[133] Larry L. Lewis, *Organize to Evangelize: A Manual for Church Growth* (Nashville: Broadman Press, 1988), 26.

embarrassed.[134] Often churches encourage guests to complete a visitor's card if they would like to receive a personal call, or information from the church. These visitor cards have become the basis for prospects for a number of excellent visitation evangelism programs.

Evangelism Explosion. D. James Kennedy created Evangelism Explosion (EE) while serving as pastor of Coral Ridge (Florida) Presbyterian Church. The program visits those who have recently attended the church, either in their worship services or in Sunday school.[135] The EE approach asks two critical evangelistic questions: "(1) Have you come to a place in your spiritual life where you know for certain that if you were to die today you would go to heaven . . . ? (2) Suppose that you were to die today and stand before God and He were to say to you, 'Why should I let you into my heaven?' What would you say?"[136] Depending on the response, a gospel message is shared with the inquirer. Although not commonly used today as an evangelistic program, EE's two probing questions (Socratic method) remain popular with soul winners.

FAITH. The FAITH evangelism program represents another prominent visitation evangelism method. Founder Bobby Welch says, "FAITH is the commitment to combine Sunday School and evangelism with pastor, staff, and leadership, leading and equipping the laypeople of their local church to fulfill their Great Commission command in a way that produces powerful New Testament results."[137] FAITH[138] visitation teams contain three members each and visit prospects of the same age group as their Sunday school class. Whether they have visited the church or Sunday school, the goal is to enroll visitors in a Sunday school class, a Bible study, or a small group.

FAITH is an acrostic that uses the five digits of the human hand. Although FAITH is not as prominent today as it was, it represents well the propositional gospel presentation method. A summary of the FAITH technique follows:

---

[134] In Brazilian Baptist churches, often the pastor asks all non-Christians present to raise their hands—and they do.

[135] D. James Kennedy, *Evangelism Explosion* (Wheaton: Tyndale House, 1970), 13.

[136] Kennedy, 31.

[137] Bobby H. Welch, *Evangelism through the Sunday School: A Journey of FAITH* (Nashville: LifeWay Press, 1997), 37.

[138] I partnered with LifeWay and Bobby Welch to translate the FAITH method into Portuguese and bring the method to Brazil. A number of Brazilian Baptist churches implemented a contextualized version of FAITH called "Ponte" (Bridge).

(1) *F* is for forgiveness. Everyone has sinned and needs forgiveness, (2) *A* is for Available. God's forgiveness is available for all. (3) *I* is for Impossible. According to the Bible, it is impossible to get to heaven on our own, (4) *T* is for Turn. Turn means Repent, (5) *H* is for Heaven. Heaven is a place where we will live with God forever, (6) Invitation. Inquire, invite, insure.[139]

For churches without Sunday schools or small groups, visitation evangelism can be led by deacons or outreach team members. No matter the type or size of a church, some sort of visitation evangelism should be practiced.

EDUCATIONAL AND DISCIPLE-SHIP STRATEGY AND METHODS

Educational and discipleship strategies stress informal leadership training (discipleship), as well as more formalized educational endeavors such as secondary schools, lay institutes, colleges, and seminaries. These discipleship ministries see their role as training the future leaders in the national church. Education strategies generally operate within existing churches and proponents see the "teaching all things" portion of the Great Commission as their niche in missions. Some wonder whether this cultivating ministry should be part of the missionary task or should be left to the national church. Many agencies believe expatriate missionaries should concentrate solely on the pioneer missions undertaking. Although some missiologists agree with this position, the majority feel there is a role for missionaries to participate in educational ministries to nationals. This subject will also be covered in the next chapter.

Some mission groups see their roles as principally to educate and disciple new believers. Mission societies operate primary schools, secondary schools, colleges, seminaries, Theological Education by Extension (TEE), leadership training, vocational training institutes, and Bible study programs. For example, Kay Arthur's Precept Ministries, Bible Study Fellowship, Walk Thru the Bible, and Bruce Wilkinson's Teach Every Nation all have overseas components. These ministries and others like them often see discipleship as more important

---

[139] Bobby Welch and Doug Williams, *Faith Evangelism: Facilitators Guide* (Nashville: LifeWay Press, 2007), 10–11.

than church planting. Bruce Wilkinson told a group of mission administrators that the most important mission task is not church planting but Bible teaching. Wilkinson says:

> In 1998, I launched an organization with a 15-year goal: get a [Bible] teacher for every 50,000 people, in every country of the world, in 15 years' time. And after five years we were in 82 countries. That's a new country every 3 weeks. We had 33,000 trained Bible teachers.[140]

Those possessing a vision for educational training and discipleship see this ministry as the most important part of the Great Commission. They believe if all believers were sufficiently trained, church planting and church growth would take care of itself.

Tent Making

Tent Making as a Strategy. Of course, tent making, or marketplace ministry, harkens to New Testament days, and is one of the ministry methods employed by the apostle Paul. When Paul arrived in Corinth after his famous visit to Athens recorded in Acts 17, he found Aquila and his wife, Priscilla. Acts 18:3–4 says, "and since they were of the same occupation, tentmakers by trade, he stayed with them and worked. He reasoned in the synagogue every Sabbath and tried to persuade both Jews and Greeks." This verse well describes the role of tentmaker—someone who supports themselves with a secular occupation for the purpose of participating in Christian ministry. Although Paul received funds from some churches,[141] for the most part he supported himself during his missionary journeys.[142]

During the Great Depression in the United States in the 1930s, the Southern Baptist Foreign Mission Board could not support its missionaries. Many in Brazil found jobs in the private sector rather than return home. Most tentmakers today engage in this strategy, not primarily for economic reasons, but in

---

[140] Bruce Wilkinson, "Where Jabez Doesn't Cut It," Beliefnet, "Inspiration," accessed July 1, 2018, www.beliefnet.com/inspiration/2003/11/where-jabez-doesnt-cut-it.aspx.

[141] Speaking to the Corinthians in 2 Cor 11:8, Paul says, "I robbed other churches by taking pay from them to minister to you."

[142] When addressing the elders at Miletus in Acts 20:34, Paul said, "You yourselves know that I worked with my own hands to support myself and those who are with me."

order to enter a limited access country closed to normal missionary work. Some tentmakers secure employment in the fields of business, education, medicine, government, agriculture, or relief and development. Other missionaries of this stripe reside as long-term tourists or as retirees living from personal funds.

Tent-Making Methods. *Pure Tent Making.* The bi-vocational pastor model in North America constitutes a type of tent making. Often, smaller congregations cannot pay a full-time pastor, whether in North America or overseas. In this situation, the pastor uses his secular employment to supplement his ministry income. Tent-making circuit riders spread Christianity all over frontier America using this method. From time to time, a missionary cannot raise sufficient support at home, so he must secure a secular job overseas to meet the family needs. Occasionally, a missionary loses the support of their home agency and has to find work in the host country.

Strategic Tent Making. This type of missionary works as a tentmaker, not because of an economic necessity, but due to the restrictions of the host country. Many nations in the Muslim, Hindu, Buddhist, and Communist worlds do not issue missionary visas. Therefore, missionaries must enter another way. Paid by their mission boards, these missionaries work legitimate jobs, which provide them with a platform from which to perform ministry. Common missionary platforms include teaching, vocational training, sports, medicine, nursing, engineering, and relief ministry.

I placed teachers, engineers, a relief worker, and the writer of a novel in three countries in North Africa. A Korean mission agency posted a tae kwon do instructor in Sudan to teach the military this skill. When all else fails, missionaries may apply as tourists in order to gain residency. When a Western couple and their three children, however, ask for tourist visas over a multiyear period, host countries normally suspect the family are serving as missionaries.

Strategic tent making begs the question concerning ministry ethics. Is it proper to claim to be a doctor, a nurse, or an engineer in a country when being paid by a mission board? What ethical issues emerge when missionaries represent themselves as people with secular jobs, when their purpose in the country is spiritual in nature? Brother Andrew of Open Doors answers this dilemma by noting that Jesus "warned the disciples that they should tell no one that He was the Christ" (Matt 16:20 NASB). When forbidden to preach in the name of Jesus in Acts 4:18–20, the apostles replied, "Whether it's right in the sight of God for us to listen to you rather than to God, you decide; for we are unable to stop speaking about what we have seen and heard" (vv. 19–20). According to Brother Andrew, missionaries do not have to tell secular authorities everything about themselves. Additionally, Christian missionaries answer to an authority higher than secular governments, but must be ready to accept the consequences for their actions. Bruce Carlton writes, "Brother Andrew's ministry demonstrated that government restrictions forbidding missionary presence were not barriers to evangelization, and mission agencies."[143]

Business as Missions, or Marketplace Ministries. Business as Missions (BAM) represents a relatively new concept. BAM involves setting up a business for the purpose of elevating the economy of the host nation, making a profit, and providing a Christian witness. Neal Johnson quotes Tom Sudyk's definition of BAM as "the strategic use of authentic business activities to create cross-cultural opportunities to minister and evangelize within the business's spheres of influence with the aim of holistic transformation."[144] Mike Barnett says the BAM missionary has one foot planted in the ministry and another in the marketplace.[145] The BAM model attempts to avoid the ethical conundrum of tent making by energetically building a legitimate business while participating in as much ministry as possible.

Concluding Remarks Concerning Tent Making. I lived in a North African country for two years supervising three agricultural schemes, two water developments, a sanitation project, and a vocational training venture. I found overseeing secular relief work by day, while evangelizing, discipling, and starting churches in my spare time exhausting. After seven years supervising overseas tentmakers, I discovered the teachers, medical personnel, and relief workers under my supervision did not have much left in the tank by evening for the spiritual work. Tent making may be necessary in some church-planting

---

[143] R. Bruce Carlton, *Strategy Coordinator: Changing the Course of Southern Baptist Missions* (Eugene, OR: Wipf and Stock, 2010), 26.

[144] Tom Sudyk, quoted in C. Neal Johnson, *Business as Mission: A Comprehensive Guide to Theory and Practice* (Downers Grove, IL: InterVarsity Press, 2009), 29.

[145] Mike Barnett in *Business as Mission: From Impoverished to Empowered*, ed. Tom Steffen & Mike Barnett, Evangelical Missiological Society Series 14 (Pasadena: William Carey Library, 2006), 323.

situations, but the amount of work a marketplace minister can produce is limited.

HUMAN NEEDS

Strategy

Missionaries with compassionate predispositions often favor human-needs strategies. Relief and development schemes facilitate entry into countless communities otherwise closed to Christian ministry. Alleviating the deprivations of humankind allows the missionary to segue naturally from the physical realm into the spiritual sphere. Human needs include ministries such as medical (and wellness) programs, agricultural projects (including hunger relief, experimental farms, and agricultural assistance), institutions (orphanages, unwed mothers' homes, schools, and hospitals), vocational training projects, and infrastructure development (reservoirs, wells, latrines, and sanitation). I operated human-needs projects worth over $3 million dollars in North Africa in order to engage an unreached group.

Christians have always embraced the urgency of meeting human needs, whether at home or abroad. Jesus speaks of Christian compassion in Matt 25:35–36: "For I was hungry and you gave me something to eat; I was thirsty and you gave me something to drink; I was a stranger and you took me in; I was naked and you clothed me; I was sick and you took care of me; I was in prison and you visited me." The early church adopted the Lord's attitude toward the needy. Every missionary, no matter his or her assignment, will find themselves confronting human-needs situations calling for action on their part. Due to the close connection between spiritual needs and human needs, the latter must be addressed in order to meet the former.

Although some object to this approach, human-needs ministries may be used as an avenue to enter and maintain missionary residence in foreign countries. Whether an open or closed nation, governments have little incentive to grant missionaries visas if the missionary does not bring any value-added benefit to the country. Some view relief and development as one and the same, but in reality they differ. Relief usually means short-term emergency aid, while development seeks long-term transformation.

Methods

Medical Ministries. Missionary doctors, veterinarians, pharmacists, dentists, nurses, and public health workers have long been in the vanguard of missions. William Carey's associate served as a missionary doctor. These brave men and women founded and served in hospitals, clinics, and dispensaries all over the world. Southern Baptists entered India,[146] Paraguay,[147] Korea,[148] and a number of other fields through medical ministries. Although missionary health personnel must first perform their medical duties, they often excel at presenting a gospel witness and are instrumental in starting churches in the vicinity of their facilities. Their work often provides legitimacy for other kinds of mission work, allowing church-planting missionaries and others to reside in the country.

Agricultural Ministries. Since many third-world countries depend on agriculture, numerous nations welcome agricultural projects that assist communities in becoming self-sufficient in agronomy. Potential agricultural schemes may include farming, animal husbandry, soil conservation, well excavation, water retention, and reservoir construction. I conducted three agricultural projects and oversaw the construction of a reservoir in North Africa. While managing these projects during the day, I evangelized and planted churches weekends and evenings.

Disaster Relief. Relief ministries normally occur immediately after a major disaster. Such calamities include hurricanes, typhoons, tsunamis, floods, tornados, earthquakes, famines, pestilence, and volcanic eruptions. Immediately after a disaster, the most common kind of relief assistance consists of providing

---

[146] The International Mission Board entered India in 1973 by founding the Bangalore Baptist Hospital. See Bangalore Baptist Hospital, "About Bangalore Hospital," accessed June 29, 2018, www.bbh.org.in/about-bangalore-baptist-hospital/.

[147] The Baptist Hospital was founded in 1952, but land was purchased in 1948 as Baptists entered the country. See http://pbmcfoundation.org/yeah/wp-content/uploads/2017/12/Paraguay-NL-Vol-18-Issue-2_for-web.pdf, accessed June 29, 2018.

[148] Wallace Memorial Baptist Hospital was founded in 1951, shortly after Baptists entered the country. See https://hellobacsi.com, accessed June 29, 2018.

food, distributing potable water, and dispensing medicine. Relief ministries provide a temporary fix for immediate needs.

Sometimes, however, the calamity stems from a larger problem. Famines often occur because rainfall patterns have been altered due to deforestation that causes droughts. Population displacement due to political situations or poor farming techniques has triggered circumstances where people are starving. Although there are nonprofit entities (NGOs—Non-Governmental Organizations) and government organizations, including the United Nations, who specialize in this sort of work, missionaries are often cast into this role, willingly or unwillingly. Their participation in disaster relief marks them as caring people.

These events, by their very nature, are unpredictable, but a successful response by Christians can lead to a presence in limited-access countries and the beginning of new churches. The North American Mission Board of the Southern Baptist Convention wins high marks for its disaster relief response across the fifty states and Canada. Missions agencies have entered limited-access countries by responding to disasters. From a hotel in Ankara, Turkey, I learned of an earthquake in Iran. Using my relief and development contacts with other NGOs from my work in North Africa, I gained access to the country for my mission board.

Development and Persons-at-Risk Ministries. Whereas relief work primarily meets emergency needs, development projects strive for long-term solutions to systemic problems. This kind of ministry includes work with refugees, orphans, unwed mothers, the poor, widows, street children, the homeless, the blind, the deaf, the mentally handicapped, and the disabled. Often foreign countries do not value these marginalized persons and are only too happy to allow Christian charities and others to serve them. Unfortunately, institutions for the disadvantaged are expensive and many mission boards deemphasize them.

These kinds of ministries, however, dovetail well with the purpose of Christian missions, and missionaries can gain entry into many countries by working with marginalized persons. Recognizing this opportunity, the International

Mission Board has created a special emphasis to target deaf persons all over the world.[149]

Assisting refugees and displaced persons presents many challenges. First, the local country's government and the UNHCR (United Nations High Commission for Refugees) severely restrict access to refugees within host countries.[150] Secondly, this kind of work can be tedious and seem endless. Some refugees have lived in their camps for generations. I recommended to the UNHCR local commissioner a plan to disband several camps situated on the border between two countries in North Africa. I proposed that each nuclear family unit receive two camels, four goats, ten sheep, and then be sent home, disbanding the camp. The UNHCR looked at me, shook her head, and rejected my suggestion.

The issue of dependency presents a vexing problem for relief and development missions. Steve Corbett and Brian Fikkert argue in their popular book, *When Helping Hurts*, that some Western human-needs ministries cause more harm than good.[151] Taking the opposite position, Michael Badriaki chastises Corbett and Fikkert in his book, *When Helping Works*, for espousing a heartless and indifferent attitude toward desperately poor people needing assistance in the third world.[152] These complex issues will be explored in the next chapter concerning the role of the missionary.

Transformational Ministries. This relatively new aspect of human-needs ministry seeks to do more than just alleviate immediate and systemic human needs. Transformational development desires to improve the host society by investing time, resources, and personnel in challenging environments to improve peoples' lives spiritually, physically, and economically. Writing about

---

[149] "Fast Facts: Deaf," IMB, accessed August 5, 2019, https://www.imb.org/2016/09/04/fast-facts-deaf/.

[150] Refugees are those who have fled across an international border. Displaced persons have moved internally within their own country. The UNHCR is allowed to assist the former but not the latter.

[151] Steve Corbett and Brian Fikkert, *When Helping Hurts: How to Alleviate Poverty without Hurting the Poor . . . and Yourself*, 2nd ed. (Chicago: Moody, 2012), 27.

[152] Michael Bamwesigye Badriaki, *When Helping Works: Alleviating Fear and Pain in Global Missions* (Eugene, OR: Wipf and Stock, 2017), 5–7.

holistic missions, Roland Hoksbergen says transformational ministries seek to bring about the change God desires in a society.[153] He writes:

> In 2003 well-known evangelical pastor Rick Warren traveled to Rwanda at his wife's urging and witnessed poverty and suffering unlike any he had ever seen before. At about the same time he was led to read the Bible with fresh eyes, noticing now the over two thousand verses that address poverty and justice for the poor.... He responded by helping to set up a new organization, the PEACE Plan, that would address multiple needs of the poor the world over.[154]

Increasingly, this kind of mission approach appeals to Generation Xers and Millennials. Transformational development looks beyond human needs with a view toward improving lives for everyone in the third-world society. Additionally, implementing innovative ideas serves as a way to legitimize a missionary presence in a closed country. For instance, I explored the use of solar ovens.[155] In many poor countries, especially in Africa, women prepare the family meals using either firewood or charcoal. Deforestation due to drought and firewood foraging has caused cooking to become expensive and time-consuming. A solar oven, on the other hand, costs less than ten dollars and can prepare the family meal using mirrors that reflect and concentrate the sun's rays. Some mission societies employ this technology to form relationships with local residents and gain entry into limited-access areas.

A missionary in North Africa reports entering rural areas by holding village-wide public-health seminars. The missionary persuades villagers to place latrines in their communities. By using this transformational strategy, the missionary family has been able to please the government and the villagers, and share the gospel of Christ. Missionaries in Paraguay report evangelizing unreached areas without evangelical churches by dispensing eyeglasses and holding prenatal clinics for rural women.[156]

---

[153] Roland Hoksbergen, *Serving God Globally: Finding Your Place in International Development* (Grand Rapids: Baker Academic, 2012), 56.

[154] Hoksbergen, 1–2.

[155] Also known as solar cookers.

[156] Barbara Akins, *Ministry Based Evangelism* (Brasilia: IMB—Eastern South America, 2000), 68–69.

MEDIA

Strategy

Media strategies often constitute the first wave in an evangelism approach to start churches. Often media serves to plow the ground in a resistant mission field. A media strategy might first begin with a Bible-translation project that includes literacy training, and then the distribution of the finished product. A media strategy may also include book and tract translation and publishing, as well as producing films, television programs, and radio broadcasts.

Methods

Media ministries span the spectrum from print to electronics and from live action to film. Traditional media outlets include literature production, such as tracts, pamphlets, magazines, and books. For example, Chick tracts use a cartoon magazine format to convey a gospel story. Written by the late Christian artist Jack Chick, some tracts present a narrative from the Bible, while others address life and theological issues. United States based publishing houses sometimes have satellite operations overseas.

Bible translation, production, and distribution ministries also fall under this heading. The overseas vice president of the Wycliffe Bible Translators told a group of International Mission Board regional directors that the most important aspect of missions was not church planting but Bible translation. He noted the impossibility of planting a church without a Bible. Good point.

The production of Christian movies, film clips, television programming, and audio recordings presents the gospel to large audiences. All over the third world, the Jesus Film Project stages a film about the life of Christ taken from the Gospel of Luke. The *Jesus* film has been shown in every country in the world and translated into multiple languages.[157] Gospel Recordings began in the age of the phonograph but now provides recordings of scriptures, sermons, and narratives electronically. Internet and smartphone content production has emerged as an important ministry in the electronic media age, with the

---

[157] "Jesus Film Project," Cru, "Communities," accessed July 14, 2018, https://www.cru.org/us/en/communities/ministries/the-jesus-film-project.html.

production of computer resources, including websites, blogs, Twitter feeds, Facebook posts, Snapchat, as well as online witnessing and live video streaming. Of course, many formerly print-only publications produce online editions or have transitioned into an electronic-only format.

Christian radio and television stations work in North America and overseas. Some Christian stations in North America operate on a for-profit basis while others, like their overseas counterparts, are nonprofit or operate at a deficit. Prominent among the missionary broadcasters are companies like Far East Broadcasting Company (FEBC) and Trans World Radio (TWR). In closed countries, Bible correspondence schools represent an excellent method of follow-up for broadcast evangelism. "Precision harvesting," according to former missionary Chris Crossan, identifies prospects for evangelism and church planting by contacting those who have expressed interest in Christ by responding to a Christian radio program by electronic or print mail.

Chronological Bible Storying (CBS), Scripture memory, Scriptures In Use (SIU), and doctrinal recitation all fall under the category of orality ministries. The International Orality Network (IRN) defines orality as "a methodology for those who prefer or learn best through oral communication."[158] James B. Slack "describes five levels of literacy to be considered in presenting the gospel: (1) 'Illiterates' cannot read or write. . . . (2) 'Functional Illiterates' have been to school but do not continue to read and write regularly after dropping out of school. Within two years, even those who have gone to school for eight years often can read only simple sentences. . . . (3) 'Semi-literates' function in a gray transitional area between oral communication and literacy. . . . They learn primarily by means of narrative presentations. (4) 'Literate' learners understand and handle information such as ideas, precepts, concepts, and principles by literate means. They tend to rely on printed material as an aid to recall. (5) 'Highly literate' learners usually have attended college and are often professionals in the liberal arts fields. They are thoroughly print-culture individuals."[159] An orality method best serves the first three categories. Another group

---

[158] K. Carla Bowman and James Bowman, *Building Bridges to Oral Cultures: Journeys among the Least-Reached* (Pasadena: William Carey Library, 2017), xx.

[159] Issue Group on Making Disciples of Oral Learners, "Making Disciples of Oral Learners," Lausanne Occasional Paper 54, ed. David Claydon (a paper produced at the 2004 Forum for

to consider is those who can read and write but don't, known as secondary oral learners. James Slack defines these as "people who have become literate because of their job or schooling, but prefer to be entertained, learn and communicate by oral means."[160]

Carla Bowman claims traditional oral societies outnumber literate societies and must be reached through orality ministries.[161] Bible storying methodology summarizes scriptural narratives for presentation to non-literates. These condensations are extracted from Scripture but are not the exact words from the Bible. For this reason, Daniel Sheard advocates Bible verse memorization to accompany the stories, or memorizing and reciting the biblical stories word for word.[162] Carla Bowman's "Scripture In Use" (SIU) method urges memorizing short Bible stories directly from Scripture.[163] Bible memorization becomes of utmost importance when oral learners tackle nonnarrative literature genres, such as the Pauline Epistles. The memorization and recitation of doctrinal passages not usually associated with the storying method is called biblical oral pedagogy (BOP).[164] This technique allows the orality evangelist to deal with important doctrinal portions of the Bible often omitted in traditional oral presentations. Orality approaches and print methods should complement rather oppose one another. Missionaries should choose an approach tailored to their audiences.[165]

ANCILLARY MISSIONS

Support strategists see themselves as assisting the ministries of others. Aircraft, helicopters, and ships ferry missionaries and supplies to the mission field in order to assist front-line personnel. Short-term volunteers are another part in the broad scheme of support strategies. When trained and used properly,

World Evangelization, Pattaya, Thailand, September 29–October 5, 2004), accessed August 5, 2019, https://www.lausanne.org/docs/2004forum/LOP54_IG25.pdf.

[160] James Slack in *Making Disciples of Oral Learners*, 56.

[161] Bowman and Bowman, *Bridges to Oral Cultures*, xxii.

[162] David Sheard, *An Orality Primer for Missionaries* (self-pub., 2007), 38.

[163] Bowman and Bowman, *Bridges to Oral Cultures*, 239.

[164] Sheard, *Orality Primer for Missionaries*, 73.

[165] Bowman and Bowman, *Bridges to Oral Cultures*, 241.

volunteers may successfully augment the ministries of long-term missionaries by assisting them in carrying out their plans. Short-term missions will be addressed in the next chapter.

Combining Strategies

Missionaries may combine different strategies in order to achieve maximum effectiveness. The use of multiple methods better serves the missionary than simply holding to one tactic. Although all church-planting strategies should include evangelism, other approaches should also be embraced. Church planters in receptive societies often rely on media elements because they minister in an open climate. On the other hand, UPG missionaries often become tentmakers and prioritize human-needs strategies in order to access and minister to their people groups because these closed societies do not permit more open media methods.

CONCLUSION

This chapter presents current and past mission methods. By no means exhaustive, the list exemplifies the variety and complexity of the missionary enterprise. Church planting seems to be the most popular strategy, though church-planting methods vary widely both in North America and overseas. Evangelism methods have always been varied but are even more so today. With the advent of advanced technologies and communications, media ministries are advancing exponentially. Although innovation in missionary methods has surged, nothing can replace the missionary verbally telling others about Christ.

READING FOR FURTHER STUDY

3 Circles Life Conversation Guide. Alpharetta, GA: North American Mission Board, 2014.

Badriaki, Michael Bamwesigye. *When Helping Works: Alleviating Fear and Pain in Global Missions*. Eugene, OR: Wipf and Stock, 2017.

Corbett, Steve, and Brian Fikkert. *When Helping Hurts: How to Alleviate Poverty without Hurting the Poor . . . and Yourself*, 2nd ed. Chicago: Moody, 2012.

Hoksbergen, Roland. *Serving God Globally: Finding Your Place in International Development*. Grand Rapids: Baker Academic, 2012.

Johnston, Thomas P. *Evangelizology: A Biblical, Historical, Theological Study of Evangelizing*. Vols.1 and 2. Liberty, MO: Evangelism Unlimited, 2011.

Payne, J. D. *Apostolic Church Planting: Birthing New Churches from New Believers*. Downers Grove, IL: InterVarsity Press, 2015.

Pocock, Micheal, GailynVan Rheenen, and Douglas McConnell. *The Changing Face of World Missions: Engaging Contemporary Issues and Trends*. Grand Rapids: Baker Academic, 2005.

Rainer, Thom S., and Jess W. Rainer. *The Millennials: Connecting to America's Largest Generation*. Nashville: B&H, 2011.

Shipman, Mike. *Any-3: Anyone, Anywhere, Anytime: Lead Muslims to Christ Now*. Monument, CO: WIGTake Resources, 2013.

10

The Missionary

"Are you sure you can do this?" When the missionary candidate consultant met with me and my wife concerning our deployment to Tanzania, he wondered if a Los Angeles pastor and his family could survive in such a rural and economically depressed country. In 1983 Tanzania ranked as one of the poorest nations in the world, replete with potholed roads, fuel shortages, and empty store shelves.[1] Chickens sold for twenty dollars each and eggs cost twelve dollars a dozen. Missionaries were required to hunt game meat and ship supplies purchased from America in sea containers. This included everything from peanut butter to cooking oil to toilet paper. We were not sure we could survive in this economically depressed locale, but our call led us to accept the challenge.

INTRODUCTION

Often, when one thinks of a foreign missionary, an experience like our family had may come to mind. Missionaries labor, however, in every country in the world and their experiences differ significantly. Additionally, opinions vary about what constitutes the missionary role in the twenty-first-century world of rapid travel, instant communications, and global markets. Until the last generation, the heralds of Christ journeyed to the field by sea, relied on letters,

---

[1] Charles T. Powers, "Tanzania: A Vision Worn Thin," *Los Angeles Times*, May 31, 1981.

telegrams, and cables, and ministered in relative isolation.[2] How then should missionaries operate today and what kind of representatives should be sent out by churches and mission agencies?

The term "missionary" possesses a similar genesis to the concept of "missions" discussed in chapter 1. Christian missionaries, the "sent ones," communicate the gospel on behalf of their Lord, sending organizations, and themselves.

INCARNATIONAL AND REPRESENTATIONAL MISSIONARIES

David Hesselgrave addresses the subject of incarnationalism and representationalism in his book *Paradigms in Conflict:15 Key Questions in Missions Today*. Drawing on the insights of Andreas Köstenberger, Hesselgrave compares and contrasts these different models of missionary engagement. Resting on different interpretations of John 17:18[3] and John 20:21,[4] incarnationalists see Jesus as the model missionary, whereas representationalists view the apostle Paul as the ideal example.

Hesselgrave says incarnationalists include holistic-incarnationalists who desire to extend the kingdom of God to all of society, as well as conversion-incarnationalists who include the aggressive proclamation of the gospel.[5] Conversion-incarnationalists reject the liberation theology and social-gospel premises of many holistic-incarnationalists, but believe Jesus should be "our Model in the way he understood and carried out his mission."[6] Conversion-incarnationalists favor emulating Jesus's manner, means, and methods while simultaneously preaching Christ's salvation. Hesselgrave sees conversion-incarnationalists as very close to representationalists, coexisting with them

---

[2] Our family did not have a telephone in the house in either Tanzania or North Africa. Cell phones and email did not yet exist. In Tanzania, the mission communicated by shortwave radio or by the mission aircraft flying overhead, signaling that someone should meet them at the airport. In North Africa, few possessed telephone landlines. Expatriates relied upon telex messages that were sent and received at a local hotel.

[3] "As you sent me into the world, I also have sent them into the world."

[4] "Jesus said to them again, 'Peace be with you. As the Father has sent me, I also send you.'"

[5] Hesselgrave, *Paradigms in Conflict*, 133 (see chap. 3, n. 31).

[6] Hesselgrave, 134.

symbiotically.[7] In fact, most evangelicals who call themselves incarnationalists are really representationalists.[8]

Hesselgrave supports Köstenberger's contention that John Stott's incarnationalism "seems to be at odds with the Fourth Gospel's presentation of Jesus's incarnation as thoroughly unique, unprecedented, and unrepeatable (cf. especially the designation *monogenes* in 1:14, 18; 3:16, 18). The incarnation is linked with Jesus's eternal preexistence (1:1, 14) and his unique relationship with the Father (1:14, 18)."[9] Drawing on Köstenberger's work, Hesselgrave asks and answers three questions about the nature of the missionary, while arguing for representationalism:

> (1) First, what are missionaries to be in the world? . . . (2) Second, what are missionaries to say in the world? . . . (3) What is the missionary to do? . . . Literally and biblically, missionaries are representatives of an authoritative Sender, sent to certain places and peoples to fulfill a prescribed task. The sender-sendee relationship changes with new generations, cultures, peoples, and prescribed tasks in the missionary endeavor . . . . If one takes Jesus' mission as a model, what is the contemporary missionary to do about those aspects of mission and ministry that are not repeatable? We do know, for instance, that we should at least emulate Christ's obedience to the Father, his willingness to lay aside heaven's glory, his wisdom in speaking to the Samaritan woman about water and to Nicodemus about a second birth, and his practice of prayer. But should we emulate his cleansing of the temple with a tongue-lashing and the sting of a whip? Can we repeat the casting out legions of demons at the cost of a herd of swine or the raising of Lazarus to life when his body had already begun to decompose?[10]

---

[7] Hesselgrave, 137.

[8] Winston Crawley quotes from the philosophy statement of the Foreign Mission Board (SBC): "The board regards as basic the concept of the career missionary. The board is committed to the use of short-term and volunteer personnel, but the overwhelming, long-term need is for career missionaries who are committed to the truth of the incarnational principle—'the Word became flesh and dwelt among us'—dwelling among the people of some other land on a long-term basis." Crawley, *A Story to Tell*, 147 (see chap. 1, n. 45).

[9] Andreas Köstenberger, in Hesselgrave, *Paradigms in Conflict*, 138.

[10] Hesselgrave, *Paradigms in Conflict*, 137–39.

Most incarnationalists see Jesus as the "prototype" missionary—an example to replicate—an impossibility. Hesselgrave well declares that all Christians are incarnationalists in the sense of looking to Christ as the supreme example and trying to emulate him. Hermeneutical problems arise when evangelists confuse the descriptive portions of the Bible with the prescriptive. For example, missionaries cannot always adopt a lifestyle of poverty in the developing world because Jesus was poor, nor can they perform his miracles whenever they wish.[11]

Representationalists see the apostle Paul as the model for missionaries. Although some view Paul as more of a theologian, a writer, an ecclesiastical organizer, or strategist; most missiologists, until recently, have seen him primarily as a missionary evangelist and church planter. Roland Allen views Paul as the model for missionaries in the typical pattern sense.[12] Although the twenty-first-century missionary can obviously learn much from Jesus, their model for carrying out the Great Commission should be the apostle Paul.

PARTICIPATIONAL AND FACILITATIONAL MISSIONARIES

Each Nimitz Class aircraft carrier assigned to the United States Navy carries a contingent of about 6,000 sailors and airmen while at sea.[13] The International Mission Board at one time employed approximately 5,500 persons. Since America's largest denomination can only support about the same number of missionaries as can fill one aircraft carrier, mission agencies like it have reconsidered the role of their personnel overseas. As mentioned previously, formerly missionaries started churches and then served as their pastors. With 7.7 billion persons now in the world,[14] mission agencies are searching for ways to multiply the effectiveness of their people.

One issue is whether a missionary should do the work personally, or see that the mission is accomplished by someone. Many mission societies assign

---

[11] Hesselgrave, 144–45.

[12] Roland Allen, *Missionary Methods, St. Paul's or Ours? A Study of the Church in the Four Provinces,* 2nd ed. (London: Robert Scott, 1912; repr., n.p.: Crossreach Publications, 2017).

[13] "Nimitz Class Aircraft Carrier," Naval Technology, accessed July 18, 2018, https://www.naval-technology.com/projects/nimitz/.

[14] "Current World Population: 7.7 Billion," Worldometers, accessed August 5, 2019, www.worldometers.info/world-population/.

their personnel to a role where the missionary coordinates and facilitates the ministry of nationals, volunteers, and other mission agencies. Some missionaries contend their role should be limited to direct missions—preaching, teaching, and discipling. Often the mission organization urges their personnel to perform both roles simultaneously. This desire for "force multiplication" has birthed some new mission paradigms as well as the expansion and redefinition of the missionary role.

The Strategy Coordinator (SC), Non-Residential (NRM), and New Envoy Missionaries

While working for the International Mission Board (IMB) in 1987, Anglican researcher David Barrett (and others) proposed to former president Keith Parks the creation of a new kind of missionary to engage resistant blocks of people in countries not open to missionary residency. Initially started to enter China, the IMB created a new administrative and non-geographic area to engage unreached people groups.[15] Cooperative Services International (CSI) expanded from Asia into the Communist world, the Middle East and Islamic Africa. Non-Residential Missionaries (NRMs) were assigned, not to geographic nations, but to specific people groups that might span several countries. When NRMs found they could gain access to formerly impenetrable nations, the name was changed to Strategy Coordinator (SC) or Strategy Leader (SL).[16]

The SC, or New Envoy, gains residency by working in relief, development, medicine, or other secular occupations. Whether living inside or outside the country (or countries) of their people group, the strategy coordinator engages them by networking with national believers, other mission groups, and secular sources. For example, SCs often encourage Bible translator agencies to render the Scriptures into the language of their people group. Many SCs labor in third-world countries and provide services for refugees or the internally displaced members of their people group.[17] As missionaries, SCs often preach in

---

[15] Keith E. Eitel, *Paradigm Wars: The Southern Baptist International Mission Board Faces the Third Millennium* (Oxford, UK: Regnum Books, 2000), 96–97.

[16] Carlton, *Strategy Coordinator*, 79 (see chap. 9, n. 145).

[17] Tetsunao Yamamori, *God's New Envoys: A Bold Strategy for Penetrating "Closed Countries"* (Portland: Multnomah, 1987), 107–8.

churches or Bible conferences, and disciple new believers, while at the same time working a secular job.

As an NRM,[18] I lived inside a country in North Africa for two years, proclaiming the gospel in the evenings while supervising United Nations relief and development projects during the day. Part of the ministry with one of the people groups in North Africa included beginning two Bible translation projects.[19] I supervised twenty SCs in ten other countries who were performing the same kind of work. Although the strategy-coordinator paradigm effectively engages UPGs lacking a Christian witness, SCs essentially perform two full-time jobs. Their secular occupation allows the missionary family to maintain residency in a closed country, while their "real occupation" permits the evangelist to minister to an isolated people group. This dual role constitutes one of the first waves of a new kind of missions. Rather than the evangelist performing direct ministry, this new kind of missionary[20] initiates and coordinates the multiple ministries of others.

The Short-Term Missionary (Partnership Missions, Volunteer Missions, Mobilization Missions)

Many overseas workers multiply their ministries by mobilizing volunteers from Western churches. Often, the field missionary coordinates the partnership mission teams. The concept and possibility of short-term missionaries (STMs) emerged when international air travel became relatively affordable during the 1960s.[21] Frustrated by the sluggishness of traditional missions, George Verwer founded Operation Mobilization (OM) fifty years ago to send college students to proclaim the gospel.[22] OM, a very effective mission agency, also uses its short-term volunteer program to recruit, screen, and evaluate candidates for long-term service. In the fifty years since its founding, the number of

---

[18] My wife and I were among the first ten units assigned to the NRM (SC) program with the International Mission Board (SBC).

[19] One Bible translation used Arabic script, while the other used Roman script.

[20] Predictably, many who favor direct missions discount the value and effectiveness of the SC approach. Back in the day, some said NRM stood for "Not Really a Missionary."

[21] Eitel, Paradigm Wars, 94–95.

[22] David A. Livermore, Serving with Eyes Wide Open: Doing Short-Term Missions with Cultural Intelligence, 2nd ed. (Grand Rapids: Baker, 2013), 62.

North American STMs has grown from about five hundred to over a million annually.[23] Two out of every three short-term mission trips last two weeks or less,[24] and the majority of the participants are teenagers.[25] Youth with a Mission (YWAM) trains their teams for four months and sends them out for two months. The Short-Term Evangelical Mission (STEM) instructs their summer teams for two weeks and launches them for six weeks.[26]

Gordon Aeschliman believes short-term mission teams assist underprivileged national believers while growing the faith and commitment of the volunteers. He says short-term mission trips call upon Westerners to minister like Jesus.[27] On the other hand, David Livermore believes that STM proponents overstate the influence of short-term missions on both the participants and the recipients,[28] pointing to research that shows the impact is negligible.[29] Most likely, the truth lies somewhere in between. Many career missionaries receive their missionary call on a volunteer trip from their local church, college, or seminary. Although some Westerners practice non-indigenous methods overseas, many nationals are blessed by their contact with the North Americans. As churches and mission groups send out ever-increasing numbers of STMs, the church will need to devise ways to use them more effectively.

In order for short-term missions to become more successful, David Livermore urges believers to improve their cultural intelligence (CQ), "a way of measuring and improving the way we interact in different cultures."[30] According to him, most training materials for STMs includes only the first and the last of the four CQ capabilities:

---

[23] Roger Peterson, Gordon Aeschliman, and R. Wayne Sneed, *Maximum Impact Short-Term Mission: The God-Commanded Repetitive Deployment of Swift, Temporary Non-Professional Missionaries* (Minneapolis: STEMPress, 2003), 255.

[24] Robert J. Priest, Terry Dischinger, Steve Rasmussen, and C.M. Brown, "Researching the Short-Term Mission Movement," *Missiology* 34, no. 4 (October 2006): 433.

[25] Livermore, *Serving with Eyes Wide Open*, 53.

[26] Livermore, 67.

[27] Livermore, 261.

[28] Livermore, 56–57.

[29] Kurt Alan Ver Beek, "Lessons from the Sapling: Review of Quantitative Research on Short-Term Missions," in *Effective Engagement in Short-Term Missions: Doing it Right!*, ed. Robert J. Priest (Pasadena: William Carey Library, 2008), 475–76.

[30] Livermore, *Serving with Eyes Wide Open*, 110.

Cultural Intelligence includes four capabilities (Drive, Knowledge, Strategy, and Action), all of which are linked together. . . . The four capabilities of CQ are:

CQ Drive: Your level of interest, drive, and motivation to adapt cross-culturally.

CQ Knowledge: Your understanding of how cultures are similar and different.

CQ Strategy: Your ability to interpret cues and plan in light of your cultural understanding.

CQ Action: Your ability to behave appropriately when relating and serving cross-culturally.[31]

When churches and mission agencies select, train, and lead short-term missionaries to embrace all four facets of cultural intelligence, both the participants and recipients benefit. As STMs perform mission work more in line with indigenous principals they will help, rather than hurt the national churches.

THE MISSIONARY CALL (THE PROFESSIONAL MISSIONARY AND THE AMATEUR)

As the STM movement gathered momentum in the 1990s, Ralph Winter lamented what he called the "amateurization" of Christian missions. Winter believed short-term missionaries often fail to heed the lessons learned by previous generations of missionaries.[32] Hesselgrave argues that the difference between professionalism[33] and amateurism is that true mission work is a calling from God, not the choice of the individual.[34]

Is there a specific missionary call or is everyone a missionary, as many say today? Acts 13:2 records the sending of Paul and Barnabas by the church at

---

[31] Livermore, 111.

[32] Ralph Winter, in Hesselgrave, *Paradigms in Conflict*, 186.

[33] John Piper believes ministers should see themselves as prophets of God and not as professionals. Hesselgrave says, "So, in the context of Piper's book [*We are not Professionals*] professionalism has to do with attitude. Professionals tend toward pride and self-promotion, instead of humility and self-abnegation." Hesselgrave, *Paradigms in Conflict*, 188.

[34] Hesselgrave, *Paradigms in Conflict*, 189.

Antioch: "As they were worshiping the Lord and fasting, the Holy Spirit said, 'Set apart for me Barnabas and Saul for the work to which I have called them.'" When a local church sends out a short-term mission team, what is their status? Are they missionaries or should the title be reserved for long-term personnel who learn the language and the culture? Is the difference one of degree or substance?

Truly, every Christian should be a witness and willing to serve as a missionary. Mission trips help believers fulfill their responsibilities as Christian witnesses. They expose students, church members, and potential career missionaries to the opportunities and challenges of mission service. Just as not everyone receives a call to be a pastor or deacon, neither is everyone called to be a missionary. Missionaries, commissioned by a group of believers, proclaim the gospel, usually in a different location and often cross-culturally.

Short-term missionaries seldom receive cultural and linguistic training equal to their professional counterparts. Amateurism has some redeeming features. Each believer enters Christianity as a novice and begins the journey of discipleship. A new believer's passion for taking the gospel to the nations truly inspires. Enthusiasm, however, does not constitute a mission strategy. 2 Timothy 2:15 says, "Be diligent to present yourself to God as one approved, a worker who doesn't need to be ashamed, correctly teaching the word of truth." In order to make a lasting impact, long-term, called-of-God missionaries are needed.

Mark Twain observed, "The difference between the almost right word & the right word is really a large matter—it's the difference between the lightning bug and the lightning."[35] In a similar way, the professional missionary makes a lasting impact in comparison to his amateur equivalent.

THE SUPPORT MISSIONARY AND THE HOME OFFICE STAFF

Support missionaries and the home office staff comprise the unsung heroes in missions. These dedicated missionaries and professionals buy, service, and sell the cars; acquire and maintain the houses; process the financial receipts; conduct the audits; obtain the visas; provide the insurance; retain the lawyers;

---

[35] Mark Twain, quoted in Tom Warhover, "The Right Word," *MizzouAdvancedReporting* (blog), "Tips," accessed September 3, 2018, https://mizzouadvancedreporting.wordpress.com/.

translate the documents; clear the shipping containers; purchase the air tickets and supplies; obtain the MK school books; educate the children; raise the funds; communicate with the constituents; fly the aircraft; distribute the payroll; withhold and prepare the income taxes; raise the prayer support; coordinate the deputation; provide the retirement; select, train, and debrief the candidates; arrange the counseling; respond to accidents and disasters; support the organization's Internet and telephone communications; measure job performance; and generally administrate a complex organization across multiple time zones in every continent except Antarctica.

No mission organization can operate effectively without its logistics and home office personnel. In small mission fields, church planting missionaries perform double duty and execute some of the support services. In larger arenas, specialist missionaries carry out these essential administrative functions. Of course, the question arises, are these logisticians really missionaries? Yes. Besides laboring in their fields of expertise, these dedicated men and women engage in local evangelism and discipleship ministries and usually comprise an integral part of a local church-planting team. Many specialist missionaries rival their church-planting counterparts in spirituality, zeal, and commitment to evangelism.

THE MISSIONARY SPOUSE AND THE MISSIONARY FAMILY

Since the days of Lottie Moon, a single female missionary to China, thousands of women have performed effectively as career single missionaries. Although the apostle Paul served commendably as a single man almost 2,000 years ago, today almost all long-term male missionaries are married.[36] While single females perform jobs on the field designed for "head of household" missionaries, their married counterparts often receive the designation "church and home"

---

[36] Brazilian Baptist leaders told me that while single female career missionaries pose no problem the reverse is true concerning men. Their culture contends that an unmarried man is either "fooling around" or is "gay." Neither alternative mixes well with the missionary role.

missionaries. This means a couple has children and the care of the family requires the primary attention of one of the parents—usually the mother.[37]

It is impossible to overstate the importance of the missionary spouse. In primitive conditions with poor medical care, these women endure pregnancy, miscarry, give birth, raise children, lose children to death, home school, send children away to boarding schools and colleges, clean their homes without running water, prepare meals from scratch without reliable electricity or cooking gas, navigate horrendous traffic, and reside in isolation from family and friends. The missionary spouse tethers her TCKs (Third Culture Kids) to reality by preparing them to live as adults in their home nation. She does all of this while living a "fishbowl" existence where the nationals watch foreigners like her constantly.[38] Simultaneously, she masters a foreign language, adjusts to a complex culture, and welcomes visitors into her home.

Although the missionary spouse assists her husband in his ministry, most missionary women excel in evangelism and discipleship ministries. Since females compose over half of the world's population, a viable women's witness remains critical for reaching the nations for Christ. Countries that practice strict gender separation require female missionaries. Also, the missionary family serves as an important model for the national church. If only singles and couples without children serve as missionaries,[39] countries without a Christian tradition would have no example of a Christian marriage or family to observe and imitate.

Joyce Jackson describes the role of a North American church planter's wife as similar to the leeboard on a sailboat that keeps the craft from drifting.[40] The missionary spouse is the stabilizing force in the family. Despite her remarkable

---

[37] This is not always the case. Sometimes, particularly with female doctors, the husband is allowed into the country based on his wife's training and expertise. On other occasions, the husband and wife split their ministry and home duties fifty-fifty.

[38] Marjorie Foyle, *Overcoming Missionary Stress* (Wheaton: Evangelical Missions Information Service, 1987), 41.

[39] After a number of medical issues with the family, including the loss of a child at birth, the birth of a handicapped child, schistosomiasis, and amoebic dysentery, my mother told me, "I don't think people with children should be missionaries."

[40] Joyce Jackson, "The Role of a Church Planter's Wife," in *My Husband Wants to Be a Church Planter . . . So What Will That Make Me?*, ed. John M. Bailey and Sherri Jachelski (Alpharetta, GA: North American Mission Board, 2007), 49.

gifting, the church planter's wife in North America or overseas often experiences loneliness. While her husband receives fulfillment ministering in the culture, she remains at home with the children in an unfamiliar place with few friends. Niki Roberts urges the church planter's spouse to develop some close friendships among the local women.[41] I have observed, after supervising many families, that more missionaries return home due to family issues than for any other reason. Children's educational problems, health concerns, adjustment to a new culture, teenage rebellion, aging parents, and settling of estates conspire to bring missionaries home, either for a season[42] or permanently.

Building a Christian family in the ministry presents many difficulties. John Walvoord, the former president of Dallas Theological Seminary, told me when I was a student there in the mid-1970s, "You always have a wonderful idea of what a Christian family should be until you actually have a Christian family." Many missionary agencies provide various levels of member care for their personnel. Since missionaries often live in places without counseling services, Kelly O'Donnell recommends a member-care model composed of multiple layers:

> **Sphere 1: Master Care**. *Care from and care for the Master—the "heart of member care.... **Sphere 2: Self and Mutual Care**. *Care from oneself and from relationships within the expatriate, home, and national communities—the "backbone" of member care.... **Sphere 3: Sender Care**. *Care from sending groups (church and agency) for all mission personnel from recruitment through retirement*[43]—"sustainers" of member care.... **Sphere 4: Specialist Care**. *Care from specialists which is professional, personal, and practical—"equippers" of member care.... **Sphere 5: Network Care**. *Care from international member care networks to help provide and develop strategic, supportive resources—"facilitators" of member care.*[44]

---

[41] Niki Roberts and Nancy Sullivan, "The Loneliness of a Planter Wife," in Bailey and Jachelski, *My Husband Wants to Be*, 119, 121.

[42] The IMB permits missionaries to take an unpaid leave of absence for up to two years in order to resolve family or health issues.

[43] SIM (Sudan Interior Mission) operates a retirement village for its career missionaries in Sebring, Florida.

[44] Kelly O'Donnell, "Going Global: A Member Care Model for Best Practice," in *Doing Member Care Well: Perspectives and Practices from Around the World*, ed. Kelly O'Donnell (Pasadena: William Carey Library, 2002), 17–19.

By following such a strategy, missionaries, agencies, and churches can provide care for themselves and their personnel. Missionary life in a large society somewhat resembles being in the military. Mission agencies choose the housing, determine the transportation, decide the children's education, allot vacation, supervise travel, allocate communications, and regulate the time commitments[45] of their personnel. Some missionaries chafe under such regimentation.

THE HOME MISSIONARY

When I worked as a US Air Force radar officer in King Salmon, Alaska, in the early 1970s, Don and Marianne Rollins served in the civilian town as missionaries with the Home Mission Board (SBC).[46] Don flew aircraft equipped with skis in the winter that converted to pontoons for water landings during the summer months. The missionary hunted moose and caribou for meat for the table and traveled by dogsled in winter. Rollins competed in local dogsled races with the Native Americans, winning several contests. The missionary quickly learned to lose some of the races because the Aleuts did not appreciate a missionary from Florida beating them at their own games.

David Hesselgrave says the New Testament does not make a distinction between foreign and home missions.[47] North American home missionaries labored among Native Americans in the nineteenth century in conditions similar to those encountered in the third world during the twentieth century. Except for a few exceptions like the Rollins family, North American missionaries do not suffer the cultural dissonance, physical deprivations, or the isolation of their overseas counterparts. Sent on a mission to evangelize a particular group or geographical area, home missionaries coexist, however, with their overseas counterparts as missionaries in every sense of the word. North American church planters often minister in parts of their country indifferent or hostile to Christianity. Although the cultural differences may not be as pronounced

---

[45] Missionaries are prohibited from earning or receiving additional funds in their countries of residence, nor can they solicit funds in the USA except by permission.

[46] Now called the North American Mission Board. I served as the part-time youth director for the Rollinses at King Salmon Baptist Mission in 1973, my first position in the ministry.

[47] Hesselgrave and Rommen, *Contextualization*, 13 (see chap. 7, n. 5).

as overseas, the North American missionary is often viewed as an outsider with strange customs. Furthermore, the North American missionary foregoes pastoring an existing church with a nice salary or serving with a mission board that pays the family a stipend indefinitely.[48]

The North American Mission Board (SBC) fully supports some specialist home missionaries. They serve in social centers, plant ethnic churches, and work as catalytic missionaries. The latter oversee and coordinate a number of church planters. Additionally, some home missionaries serve as directors of missions for local associations of churches. Here, churches band together to support a missionary who assists existing congregations and plants new churches in a geographic area. Also, some home missionaries serve at the state denominational level where they assist churches by planting new congregations and revitalizing older ones.

THE MISSIONARY SOCIETY AND ORGANIZING FOR MISSIONS

Only Acts 13:2[49] records the sending out of missionaries and in this instance from a local congregation. For this reason, some denominations require missionaries to be sent by a specific local church,[50] even if the missionaries receive support from many other congregations. George Peters says that although Scripture does not make mention of mission organizations, biblical principles support the mission society concept—cooperative efforts among churches, selective appointment, and delegated authority.[51] A mission agency can more easily supervise and administer missionaries overseas thousands of miles away than is possible by a US church. Mission societies, if doctrinally sound and

---

[48] The North American church planter usually receives support for three or four years—each year receiving less money. After the third or four year the church planter is expected to be self-supporting.

[49] "As they were worshiping the Lord and fasting, the Holy Spirit said, 'Set apart for me Barnabas and Saul for the work to which I have called them.' Then after they had fasted, prayed, and laid hands on them, they sent them off."

[50] The American Baptist Association (ABA), not to be confused with the American Baptist Churches (ABC), requires missionaries to be sent from a local church. See www.religioustolerance.org/hom_aba.htm. Accessed July 25, 2018.

[51] Peters, *Biblical Theology of Missions*, 224–29 (see chap. 1, n. 7).

biblically based, can effectively assist local churches in fulfilling their Great Commission responsibilities. Most independent mission societies require a local church endorsement, while denominational mission boards insist on membership in their denomination.

All but a few mission agencies require their personnel to raise support. Normally, the mission agency's home office retains a small percentage of these funds for administrative costs. A few denominational mission societies, such as the International Mission Board (SBC), provide full support for their career missionaries and most of their short-termers (less than two years). In 1925 Southern Baptists established the Cooperative Program (CP), originally called the Unified Program or New Program, to meet the needs of the denomination,[52] including its home and foreign mission boards. The SBC asked each church to voluntarily contribute a certain percentage of its weekly offerings in order to relieve the churches from countless fundraising solicitations. Current CP distribution allots the two SBC missions agencies about 25 percent of the total denominational offerings that are sent from local churches.[53] Additionally, the mission boards collect two annual missions offerings: the Lottie Moon Christmas Offering for International Missions and the Annie Armstrong Easter Offering for North America Missions.

There was a day when missions organized themselves democratically overseas. They voted for budgets and personnel and issued internal operating regulations. With the advent of sophisticated communication and rapid transportation in the twentieth century, missions centralized their budgeting, personnel, and administration. Rather than each mission administering itself locally, agencies appointed area directors (or regional leaders) to more effectively manage them. Furthermore, each missionary was assigned to a supervisor

---

[52] Chad Owen Brand and David E. Hankins, *One Sacred Effort: The Cooperative Program of Southern Baptists* (Nashville: B&H, 2005), 96–98.

[53] In the rather complicated Baptist system, CP funds first pass from local churches to the local state Baptist convention. Each state convention retains a certain percentage for "state missions" and ministries. The remainder, about 50 percent of the monies received at the state level, is sent to the SBC Executive Committee (denominational offices in Nashville, TN) where the funds are divided among the entities of the SBC. A little over 50 percent of these monies go to the IMB and a little less than 25 percent to NAMB. The remaining about 25 percent is divided among the six SBC seminaries and a few other agencies. For more information, see Crawley, *A Story to Tell*, 123.

instead of operating independently. This centralization of administration only promises to continue. With the advent of increased communications, many mission teams have become "virtual," with members scattered around a country or continent. Despite the communication advances, virtual teams are challenged by misunderstandings that come from being isolated.[54]

Once controversial, most mission agencies now require their missionaries to set goals and objectives in their ministries. Peter Wagner says, "Strategy cannot be accurately planned or effectively evaluated without measurable goals."[55] Some missionaries disagree, saying evangelism is God's work. They see goals and objectives as presumptive and not following the Holy Spirit. Donald McGavran counters:

> Nothing focuses effort like setting a goal. As Christians seek to do effective evangelism, they need to set membership goals. This focuses their efforts on the main task. Goal setting requires securing needed facts. It reminds pastors and missionaries of their basic responsibilities and available resources. It forces them to arrange their priorities aright. It locks them onto their polestar. . . . Goal setting helps it to do so. Missiology is not a mishmash of many different ingredients. Rather it is that science whose steady aim is world evangelization in all six continents.[56]

I can testify to the value of goal setting. My assignment included working among a people group with no known believers in three adjacent countries in North Africa. I set a goal to start a church in each of the countries within five years. Although no churches were planted in two of the nations, in one of them over a hundred churches among a Muslim people group resulted. Goal setting, in this instance, certainly focused my attention.

---

[54] Pocock, Van Rheenen, and McConnell, *Changing Face of World Missions*, 312–14 (see chap. 5, n. 2).

[55] Peter Wagner, in McGavran, *Understanding Church Growth*, 2nd ed., 421 (see chap. 6, n. 23).

[56] McGavran, 412–13. McGavran's discussion on "How to Set Goals," 426–33 is worth reading.

THE MISSIONARY AND INDIGENOUS PRINCIPLES

A tenderhearted missionary in Tanzania loved to help people and had difficulty saying no to nationals. Locals would often ask for rides in the mission vehicle. One day the missionary hit upon an idea where he would not disappoint anyone, or so he thought. On a fifty-one-mile trip from Kyela to Mbeya, he decided to oblige every hitchhiker who asked for a lift. In order to accommodate everyone though, the first person who entered his car at the start of the journey had to exit when the van was full and so on. The missionary's short-term trip solution helped everyone a little but satisfied no one's long-term need. This story illustrates one of the problems in missions: the needs are many but are impossible to fulfill. King Solomon, in Eccl 1:15, well observes, "what is crooked cannot be straightened; what is lacking cannot be counted."

The question of indigenousness persists as one of the most vexing issues in missions. The previous chapter discusses some of the elements of the indigenous mission philosophy. Henry Venn, credited with originating indigenous principles, states national churches should be self-propagating, self-governing, and self-supporting.[57] Few disagree with the first two principles. The meaning and extent of self-support, however, generates quite an enormous amount of conflict. This section, therefore, will cover the issue of financial subsidy and assistance in missions today. As Melvin Hodges says, "Self-support is not necessarily the most important aspect of the indigenous church, but it is undoubtedly the most discussed."[58]

Interestingly, most missionaries favor "indigenous mission principles" in theory, but in practice they often make exceptions when pressed by their "special situations," or interpret the "self-supporting" concept in creative ways. In the early twentieth century, Roland Allen lamented the extensive financial subsidies he claimed were holding back the development of churches in India.[59] Many believe financial assistance to individuals and churches compounds rather than alleviates the root problem. Steve Corbett and Brian Fikkert write:

---

[57] See the discussion on indigenous church planting in the previous chapter.

[58] Melvin L. Hodges, *The Indigenous Church: A Complete Handbook on How to Grow Young Churches* (Springfield, MO: Gospel Publishing House, 1976), 74.

[59] Allen, *Missionary Methods*, 90.

Needs-based development focuses on what is lacking in the life of a community or a person. The assumption in this approach is that solutions to poverty are dependent upon outside human and financial resources. Churches and ministries using a needs-based approach are often quick to provide clothes, food, shelter, and money to meet the perceived, immediate needs of low-income people, who are often viewed as "clients" or "beneficiaries" of the program. Pouring in outside resources is not sustainable and only exacerbates the feelings of helplessness and inferiority that limits low-income people from being better stewards of their God-given talents and resources. When the church or ministry stops the flow of resources, it can leave behind individuals and communities that are more disempowered than ever before.[60]

This is a complex issue. Many in the developing world view the situation quite differently. Sometimes people question why it is appropriate for Westerners to support Western missionaries but not national missionaries and pastors? This question overlooks the fact that when American churches pay American missionaries they practice the indigenous principle of self-support by sustaining their own missionaries. When American churches, however, subsidize overseas national pastors and missionaries, the reverse is true.

Michael Badriaki, however, takes Fikkert and Corbett to task for negatively stereotyping both majority world persons and ministries to them. Badriaki says:

> He [Fikkert] wishfully concocts a bystander's missionary strategy for the Western church to practice in the majority world. An approach that restricts generosity, heightens anxiety and promotes the release of the stress chemical in the body called cortisol, which also inhibits empathy, that's how and when not helping hurts. As a Ugandan, I find Fikkert's conclusion off, because the mind-set he is promoting is based on negative and wrong assumptions. . . . It is as though Fikkert and anyone who embraces such advances, remain convinced that giving to people who are not Westerners while on missions violates Western-generated development principles that supersede biblical mandates about helping. What have missions come to? [61]

---

[60] Corbett and Fikkert, *When Helping Hurts*, 120 (see chap. 9, n. 153).
[61] Badriaki, *When Helping Works*, 8 (see chap. 9, n. 154).

Tension always exists between donors and recipients. When benefactors desire to address systemic problems with a strategic and broad response—usually development schemes that train the recipients rather than dispense food and funds—nationals sometimes perceive the contributors as heartless if the aid is not given immediately and indiscriminately. Speaking for many in the third world, K. P. Yohannan asks Westerners to sponsor poor children and financially support national pastors and missionaries. He says:

> Born into affluence, freedom and divine blessings, Americans should be the most thankful people on earth.
>
> But along with privilege comes a responsibility. . . .
>
> Throughout Scripture, we see only one correct response to abundance: sharing.
>
> God gives some people more than they need so that they can be channels of blessing to others. God desires equity between His people on a worldwide basis. . . .
>
> The Bible advocates and demands that we show love for the needy brethren. Right now, because of historical and economic factors that none of us can control, the needy brethren are in Asia. The wealthy brethren are in the United States, Canada and a few other nations. The conclusion is obvious: These affluent believers must share with the poorer churches.[62]

Short-term volunteers and long-term missionaries participate in missions and send resources overseas to help their less-fortunate brethren. National pastors, leaders, and individuals are only too willing to solicit and receive the assistance. Agents for third-world orphanages, hospitals, schools, denominations, pastors, and churches, span the globe competing for financial assistance from Western donors. Some recruit multiple benefactors to support their endeavors. Unfortunately, (relatively) inexpensive air travel, an increase in disposable time and income of Westerners, and the North American penchant for wanting to fix everything acerbates the situation. North Americans desire to help but they struggle with whether the sort of subsidy Yohannan proposes creates

---

[62] K. P. Yohannan, *Revolution in World Missions* (Carrolton, TX: GFA books, 1998), 83–84.

dependency, causing nationals to neglect their own stewardship and development. John Nevius cautioned against paying nationals in 1886.[63]

Addressing this conundrum in missions, Donald McGavran advocates a middle position. As a proponent of indigenous missions, McGavran favors indigenous principles in new work areas most of the time. He advises caution, however, writing:

> It is not true that "indigenous church principles make churches grow anywhere".... There is a grave danger that indigenous principles will become a new idol, and God's servants will say, "whether the church grows or not, whether churches multiply or not, we will adhere strictly to indigenous principles."... Indigenous principles are good, but it is a serious oversimplification to imagine that they are the only factor or even the chief factor in growth or non-growth.... The cause of world evangelization will not be advanced by dividing into camps for and against indigenous church principles, but rather by understanding when and how these exceedingly useful tools can be used in discipling the nations.[64]

McGavran advocates indigenous principles in responsive areas but says in highly resistant fields the mission agency may need to depend initially on missionaries and paid nationals at the supervisory level.[65] Some mission agencies pay the travel and lodging expenses for nationals to attend training conferences and for special evangelistic outreach trips. I hold that indigenous principles normally should be practiced. In the early stages of work in closed countries, some assistance may be given to a few nationals to begin the work. There are those who say, however, that once financial assistance starts, it is difficult, if not

---

[63] Nevius wrote, "The Employment System tends to excite a mercenary spirit, and to increase the number of mercenary Christians. Of course, we fully admit that many paid agents are sincere, earnest men and that they bring into the church sincere and earnest believers, some perhaps would not otherwise be reached. We are here simply pointing out an evil influence and tendency which are connected with one system and avoided by the other [not paying pastors].... When this mercenary spirit enters a church, it has a wonderful self-propagating power and follows the universal law of propagating after its kind. The mercenary preacher, whether paid or hoping to be paid, as naturally draws to himself others of like affinities as a magnet attracts iron filings." John L. Nevius, *The Planting and Development of Missionary Churches* (Shanghai: Presbyterian Press, 1886; Hancock, NH: Monadnock Press, 2003), 25.

[64] McGavran, *Understanding Church Growth*, 2nd ed., 383–84.

[65] McGavran, 387.

impossible to stop. The words of Melvin Hodges ring true more than ever even though written almost seventy years ago:

> Here is the key to the problem: As missionaries, we have too often trained the converts in dependence upon us rather than in *responsibility*. It may be because we have an overprotectiveness for our converts; it may be that unconsciously we desire that we be the head and have people look to us as the indispensable man; it may stem from our lack of faith in the Holy Spirit to do His work in maturing converts. But for whatever reason, the fact remains weak churches are often the product of the missionaries' wrong approach to their task.... There is one "pearl of great price" in building the church, and that is *a sense of responsibility* among the converts.[66]

Unfortunately, each generation of missions practitioners has to learn the indigenous lesson for themselves. Usually it is learned the hard way—by doing it wrong. There is probably more subsidy by outsiders of national believers, churches, and entities today than ever before. The proliferation of mission entities and short-term volunteers, coupled with Western affluence and ease of travel, has placed more people in overseas situations. Hopefully, the next generation can more effectively instill the responsibility in new church plants that has been advocated, but rarely applied over the last 175 years.

CONCLUSION

Some contend the necessity of sending foreign missionaries has ceased and the responsibility of the Western church should be limited to financial aid and prayer support.[67] Others argue for the continuing relevancy of the career missionary.[68] Most likely the role of the residential expatriate evangelist will endure for a number of reasons: (1) Mission agencies and churches desire accountability for the funds that they send. Just sending the money does not appeal to many. (2) The Great Commission extends to each Christian and some perceive God is calling them overseas. That some disagree does not negate one's

---

[66] Hodges, *Indigenous Church*, 17.
[67] Yohannan, *Revolution in World Missions*, 147.
[68] Crawley, *A Story to Tell*, 147, 151.

missionary call. (3) There are places on earth with few Christians and these countries require missionaries. Often, churches in persecuted environments or neighboring countries do not possess the resources or inclination to reach out to their "near culture" comrades. Western missionaries often fill this void. (4) In some places, long-simmering ethnic conflicts or racial prejudice effectively restrict the natural flow of the gospel from one people group to another within the same country. Often, a foreigner receives a better hearing than a fellow citizen because of these internal issues, rivalries, and conflicts. (5) Although the national church in many nations can evangelize and provide some training for themselves, many local believers desire missionaries to fill positions in theological education and other discipleship ministries. Increasingly, secular governments require qualified professors to teach in accredited Christian schools at all levels.[69]

If the third part of the Great Commission consists of "teaching all things," how long should this activity continue? Should the cultivating ministry be part of the missionary task or should it be left to the national church? Some mission agencies hold that expatriate missionaries should concentrate solely on the pioneer missions undertaking. I contend the teaching aspect of the Great Commission is still in force, is a portion of the missionary task, and remains part and parcel with the true mission of missions.

READING FOR FURTHER STUDY

Hesselgrave, David J., and Edward Rommen. *Contextualization: Meanings, Methods, and Models.* Pasadena: William Carey Library, 2003.

Hesselgrave, David J., and Ed Stetzer. *MissionShift: Global Mission Issues in the Third Millennium.* Nashville: B&H, 2010.

Livermore, David. *Serving with Eyes Wide Open: Doing Short-Term Missions with Cultural Intelligence*, 2nd ed. Grand Rapids: Baker, 2013.

---

[69] Usually the nationals desire a continuing missionary presence, while the mission boards generally oppose deploying large numbers of missionaries for this kind of ministry. In most cases a PhD (or its equivalent) is required.

11

Conclusion: The Future of Twenty-First-Century Missions

The Evangelical Missiological Society (EMS) gathered expectantly to listen to renowned missiologist Ralph Winter address a breakout session at its 2008 annual meeting. I positioned myself on the front row in order to hear the speaker clearly. Winter delivered a paper on a surprising topic. He urged mission agencies to prepare to engage extraterrestrial aliens from outer space when they arrive.[1] Needless to say, the members of EMS were surprised to hear about the emergence of people groups from other planets. Although missions may not be this forward thinking, what does the future hold for the twenty-first century?

Scott Sunquist describes the difficulty with projecting the future:

> No scholar—or as far as that goes, not even a madman—predicted that at the end of the twentieth century Christianity would not be recognized even as a cultural factor in Europe by the nations that compose the European Union. No prognosticator predicted that more Christians would be worshipping each Sunday in China than in Europe or North America. And, what might be surprising to us today, even the greatest mission leaders at the Edinburgh Missionary Conference in 1910 had pretty much given up on Christianity in Africa. Most of the missionary leaders, even in their most optimistic

---

[1] I sat on the front row of this presentation. Winter was not joking.

277

moments, thought Islam had the upper hand and believed Africa would become a Muslim continent. Fast-forward and we find that the opposite is true, for there are more Christians than Muslims in Africa today.

Yes, the twentieth century surprised the religionists, the historians, and the politicians. . . .

Close to 9 percent of France is Muslim, which means that there are more active Muslims in France than active Christians.[2]

In the same way, what will transpire in the twenty-first century is impossible to predict. Secular events often spawn unintended consequences both positively and negatively. David Hesselgrave says, "The church is a storm center of contemporary society."[3] Of course, storms break both ways. Wet weather brings needed rain to parched terrain. On the other hand, gales can cause significant damage. Both kinds of storms occurred in missions and society at large during the twentieth century. Missions and evangelism reached new zeniths while societal evils soared simultaneously. Church history shows that sometimes after a moral ebb, revival and spiritual renewal follow.

Patrick Johnstone lists nine global demographic challenges the world will face during this century. These include (1) population, (2) migration, (3) urbanization, (4) health and disease, (5) climate change, (6) economy, (7) energy resources, (8) politics and freedom, and (9) water resources.[4] Some of these challenges have already been covered previously. This chapter addresses some of the issues that might influence missions.

The population explosion and urbanization of Asia and Africa, and to a lesser extent, South America, has caused many refugees to seek residency in Europe and North America. This significant migration has caused social upheaval in multiple Western countries as these nations struggle to absorb the new religions and cultures of the émigrés. Although some native inhabitants lament the loss of their homeland's homogeneity, many new residents arrive

---

[2] Scott W. Sunquist, *The Unexpected Christian Century: The Reversal and Transformation of Global Christianity, 1900–2000* (Grand Rapids: Baker Academic, 2015), xvi–xvii.

[3] Hesselgrave, *Planting Churches Cross-Culturally*, 17.

[4] Patrick Johnstone, *The Future of the Global Church: History, Trends, and Possibilities* (Downers Grove, IL: InterVarsity Press, 2011), 1–19.

sympathetic to the gospel. This openness constitutes one of the positive receptive factors listed by the church-growth school. Donald McGavran says, "Today's inflooding immigrant populations also are notably responsive."[5]

McGavran says the situations that positively impact receptivity include (1) new settlements, (2) returned travelers, (3) conquest, (4) nationalism, (5) freedom from control, and (6) acculturation.[6] Any church planter can attest to the fact that it is easier to start a church in a new suburb than the inner city. The same is true overseas. Even new squatter settlements are more responsive than the comfortable enclaves of the wealthy in the world's major metropolitan areas.

Veterans of both World War I and World War II exemplify receptive returned travelers in the US. Many former servicemen moved to the western United States after these global conflicts and either joined or started churches with their new families. Their foreign travel while in the war made them more willing to chance bettering their lives in a new part of the country. Similarly, frequently the victims of conquest prove responsive to the gospel. Often those in subjugated nations reach such a low point in their lives that the good news brings hope to them.

Nationalism also influences responsiveness. Sometimes the church provides an outlet for political protest of authoritarian regimes. Similarly, the freedom of control that occurs when a dictatorship declines can spark an openness to the gospel. This happened when the Berlin Wall fell and the Soviet Bloc crumbled in 1989. One can only imagine what will happen when North Korea and Cuba break free from their repressive regimes.

The final receptivity factor, acculturation, comes into play when nations cut off from outside influence suddenly are exposed to other lifestyles and ways of thinking. Globalization and the Internet have increased this phenomenon. As the Muslim world, particularly Saudi Arabia, is confronted with the secularism of the West through popular culture, perhaps the truth of the gospel will prove attractive to many.

Politically, pragmatism and economic self-interest have replaced the strident dogmatism of doctrinaire socialism, communism, and Marxism. Communist

---

[5] McGavran, *Understanding Church Growth*, 2nd ed., 246 (see chap. 6, n. 23).
[6] McGavran, 248–52.

countries such as China and Vietnam have adopted the capitalist theories of Adam Smith[7] while paying lip service to Karl Marx.[8] Many believe China will replace the United States as the predominate country in the world by 2050.[9] One analyst projects the US to be in third place economically by the midpoint of this century, behind both China and India.[10] Production, branding, and marketing have replaced collective farms, communes, and planned economies. The steady hum of the production line based on supply and demand drowns out socialist slogans and jingoism. The truly communist nations such as North Korea and Cuba remain isolated and are searching for ways out of their economic quagmires. A prerequisite for political leadership in the new century seems to rest more on one's economic abilities than an individual's diplomatic, political, or military expertise. As in previous centuries, a leader's personal magnetism remains important.

In a similar vein, countries seem more interested in economic advancement than adhering to a particular political ideology. China and other Asian countries have adopted a "whatever works" development theory as long as the overarching political structure is not challenged. Muslim countries follow this path as well. Despite the rise of Islamic fundamentalism, most governments are more committed to creating new jobs than promoting Muslim orthodoxy—so long as development occurs within an Islamic framework.

The seldom considered crisis in water resources looms as a potential conflict generator between nations this century. Ethiopia, Egypt, and Sudan have sparred diplomatically over the issue. Ethiopia's construction of a super dam

---

[7] Adam Smith, considered the father of modern Capitalist thought, believed people are guided in their economic behavior, whether owners or laborers, by self-interest, according to the laws of supply and demand. See Alan B. Krueger's introduction to Adam Smith, *The Wealth of Nations* (New York: Bantam Classics, 2003).

[8] Karl Marx, the founder of communism, decries economic self-interest as freedom to exploit one's fellow man. The Marxist solution abolishes the ownership of private property and the accumulation of wealth. Karl Marx and Friedrich Engels, *Manifesto of the Communist Party* (Chicago: Encyclopedia Britannica, Inc., 1952), 420, 425.

[9] Jim VandeHie, "China is the Greatest, Growing Threat to America," Axios, May 21, 2018, accessed August 22, 2018, https://www.axios.com/china-united-states-future-2025-2050-infrastructure-trade-d7091849-235f-4aa1-b63c-e86477e9cfe6.html.

[10] "The World in 2050: The Long View: How will the Global Economic Order Change by 2050?" PwC Global, accessed August 23, 2018, https://www.pwc.com/gx/en/issues/economy/the-world-in-2050.html.

near its border with Sudan may spark a war with Egypt.[11] The Grand Ethiopia Renaissance Dam (GERD) will divert water from Ethiopia's Blue Nile from which Egypt receives 85 percent of its water. Ethiopia objects to the colonial era treaties that allocated Egypt 62 percent of Nile water, 22 percent to Sudan, and 0 percent to Ethiopia. Although a reallocation treaty was signed in 2015, tensions remain. The Nile River[12] impacts the water resources of Tanzania, Uganda, Rwanda, Burundi, the Democratic Republic of Congo (DCR), Kenya, Ethiopia, Eritrea, South Sudan, Sudan, and Egypt.[13] As world population grows, regional conflicts such as this one will only increase.

Scott Moreau points out that the ultimate conflict lies in "the ability of humanity to wipe ourselves out of existence."[14] Although nuclear bombs were last detonated in wartime in 1945, there is no assurance this could not happen again. Furthermore, globalization has increased the possibility of another great plague[15] sweeping the earth. The earth's interdependency could spawn a global economic crisis to rival the Great Depression of the 1930s. The rise of cryptocurrencies might spell disaster for financial markets. The Bitcoin phenomenon was seen as a response to the artificiality of government manipulation of

---

[11] Samantha Raphalson, "In Africa, War over Water Looms as Ethiopia Nears Completion of Nile River Dam," NPR, *Here & Now*, February 27, 2018, https://www.npr.org/2018/02/27/589240174/in-africa-war-over-water-looms-as-ethiopia-nears-completion-of-nile-river-dam.

[12] The White Nile originates in Lake Victoria (touching the countries of Kenya, DCR, Rwanda, and Burundi) and emerges from Tanzania and Uganda and streams into southern Sudan and then into Sudan. The Blue Nile emanates from Ethiopia near the Eritrean border into Sudan. The Blue Nile and White Nile join in Khartoum to form the Nile River, which subsequently empties north into Egypt.

[13] "Hydro-Economics: Egypt, Ethiopia and the Nile," Al Jazeera, "Counting the Cost," October 22, 2017, accessed August 21, 2018, https://www.aljazeera.com/programmes/countingthecost/2017/10/hydro-economics-egypt-ethiopia-nile-171022074240615.html.

[14] Scott Moreau, "Looking Backward While Going Forward, A Response to Winter's Vision," in *MissionShift*, ed. Hesselgrave and Stetzer, 199 (see chap. 4, n. 97).

[15] Kenneth Scott Latourette writes, "Beginning a few years before 1350, successive epidemics of Bubonic Plague, the 'Black Death,' swept over the region and are said to have reduced the population of Northern Europe by as much as a third and that of England by a half." Latourette, *History of Christianity*, vol. 1, 602–3 (see chap. 4, n. 13).

national currencies.[16] Despite its unlikeliness, a direct hit on the planet by a large meteor[17] also might occur.

With the advent of relatively cheap air travel and global business opportunities, governments, even within closed countries, are willing to allow a Western presence even if perceived to be religious in nature. These countries often overlook Christian pursuits in order to gain the hard currency and the economic impact they generate. Governments do not mind Christian activity as long as the church does not challenge the existing order nor has much success in winning converts.

Despite these technological innovations, many people have been left behind economically. Migrants tend to cluster in the large cities, which contributes to urban sprawl. These émigrés join other marginalized populations and compete with them for jobs and social services. This situation plunges both groups further into poverty. This reality often spirals into a dependence on drugs, alcohol, and other controlled substances in order to cope with boredom, futility, and hopelessness. The poor overall economies in most of these countries exacerbates the situation for the most needy persons.

How do these new realities impact missions? Negative crises can yield positive results. Donald McGavran writes, "Dissatisfactions, wars, oppression, deprivation, shock, hostility, erosion of belief in the old gods, and a thousand others—bring a given population into a condition where it can 'hear' the Good News."[18]

All these trends bode well for the short-term missions (STM) movement. Doubtless, as simultaneous translation software improves, fairly seamless conversations can occur between individuals who do not speak the same language. Additionally, video conferencing capabilities will allow for a mission experience overseas without the participant leaving home. Affordable global Wi-Fi will further facilitate uninterrupted worldwide communication. Although these

---

[16] Benjamin Wallace, "The Rise and Fall of Bitcoin," *Wired*, "Business," November 23, 2011, accessed September 28, 2018, https://www.wired.com/2011/11/mf-bitcoin/.

[17] Asteroid strikes are unnerving but common. An asteroid the size of a warehouse passed just by the earth on April 14, 2018. See Eric Mack, "Asteroid as Big as a Warehouse Is Freakiest Near Miss in Years," CNET, April 16, 2018, accessed September 7, 2018, https://www.cnet.com/news/asteroid-2018-ge3-is-freakiest-near-miss-earth-in-15-years/.

[18] McGavran, *Understanding Church Growth*, 2nd ed., 196.

innovations will allow for greater interaction at a surface level, it is not a given the participants will understand one another's cultures. Despite these hurdles, the involvement of short-term missionaries can be expected to increase during this century. Career missionaries will still be needed, however, to learn the culture and heart language of the people groups of the world and facilitate the flood of volunteers.

Into this bleak narrative, Christ offers hope. Missions and missionaries both overseas and in North America will always be needed. Hostilities exist within nations composed of different ethnicities to such an extent that only cross-cultural missionaries can influence them. Donald McGavran says, "near neighbor" people groups within a country cannot reach their own citizens because of this.[19]

What will missions resemble in the future? What will be the challenges? For one, Westerners will always struggle with the desire to fix everything. Many North Americans subconsciously believe problems overseas can be solved by throwing money at them. Kosuke Koyama wrote an interesting book titled, *Three Mile an Hour God*.[20] Koyama, a Japanese Christian, suggests that if the Son of God walked at a pace of three miles an hour to accomplish his Father's work, perhaps the people of God should slow down. Since Jesus and the apostles traveled without significant logistical support, how much in the way of finance and infrastructure is really necessary to preach the gospel and make an impact?

Missionaries will also grapple with how to live on the mission field. Unreached people groups almost by definition reside in hard-to-access places. Living like the nationals places stress on families, as many locales are dangerous, isolated, or both. It can seem romantic to live without running water and electricity until one actually tries it. Third Culture Kids (TCK) struggle with their identity. Just before our family's first missionary furlough, my son, Seth, and his friend Ritchie discussed their families' impending visits to their respective countries. Ritchie, the son of Canadian Pentecostal missionaries, said to Seth, "Seth, you are an American. I am a Canadian." Seth replied, "Yeah."

---

[19] McGavran, *Understanding Church Growth*, 2nd ed., 62–63.
[20] Kosuke Koyama, *Three Mile an Hour God* (London: SCM-Canterbury Press, 1979), 7.

Neither five-year-old could remember their home countries but were convinced of their nationalities and the accompanying sentiments.

Missionaries will still struggle with how to begin their work. Missionaries must be self-starters and are asked to produce something out of nothing in a foreign culture, while learning a complex language. When our family arrived in a closed country in North Africa for the first time, the challenge was daunting. I began by asking the few other missionaries in the country if they knew any Christians from among my target people group. Two believers were identified and I began with them. One of the believers was blind, however, and the other a depressed former communist. The thought crossed my mind, "Are there not any nationals better than these?" In mission work, one must begin with whom the Lord brings one's way. Although the original two believers never prospered, working with them led me to discover two more reliable nationals who began a movement that still continues.

Missionaries also will battle with the notion of "What am I trying to produce?" Previous missionaries desired to plant churches of their denominational stripe in their host nations. Today's missionaries, however, often aspire to start New Testament churches without any denominational affiliation. How should the global church look? Are denominations outdated? It has been my experience that every group eventually becomes affiliated with some belief system. It is natural for like-minded churches to cooperate with other congregations for ministry. How churches accomplish this task in either North America or overseas is a big question mark.

Missionaries will still grapple with their relationships. Although most missionaries agree with the three-self[21] mission philosophy, a fourth self has been added to the equation. Originally postulated by Paul Hiebert, the fourth-self idea favors allowing nationals to conceptualize their own indigenous theologies.[22] Danger lurks when any one nation or continent invents new religious dogmas. John Mbiti, an African theologian, says there are certain aspects of

---

[21] Henry Venn's Self-Propagating, Self-Supporting, and Self-Governing concept was implemented by John Nevius in Korea. See Bruce F. Hunt, preface to *The Planting and Development of Missionary Churches*, by John L. Nevius, 4th ed. (Hancock, NH: Monadnock Press, 1985), 14.

[22] Richard E. Trull Jr., *The Fourth Self: Theological Education to Facilitate Self-Theologizing for Local Church Leaders in Kenya* (New York: Peter Lang, 2013), 26.

the faith that are nonnegotiable.[23] Although often disparaged as a Western religion, Christianity was born in the Middle East and its creeds forged in church councils held in Central Asia (the Anatolia region of Turkey) during the middle of the first millennium. It is true that the West currently dominates the practice of Christianity but its doctrines are not Western. Christians of all stripes must not insist that their understandings are necessarily the correct ones. William Dyrness says, "I underline the importance of my conviction that only Scripture, not some particular interpretive schema, is transcultural."[24] When the global church rallies around the Bible for their interpretation and practice, only then can unity prevail. The Majority World church can assist the Western church by the richness of its experiences. For instance, when Westerners share Christ with non-Christians they often reference Blaise Pascal who said there is a "God-shaped vacuum" in everyone's heart that can only be filled by God.[25] The Buddhist, however, describes the urgency of mankind's life condition as one's turban is ablaze and for "the extinguishing thereof one must put forth extra desire, effort, endeavor, exertion, impulse, mindfulness and attention."[26] The Western analogy stresses what man does not have—peace. The Asian metaphor speaks of a real emergency—a turban on fire.

Ralph Winter postulates that First-Inheritance Evangelicalism (FIE) during the First (eighteenth century) and Second (1815–1840) Great Awakenings in America produced a Christianity that sought to save souls and transform society.[27] Winter contends that the Second-Inheritance Evangelicalism of the late nineteenth century and early twentieth century moved away from social action to concentrate principally on evangelism. He advocates and predicts a return to what he calls the "full-spectrum gospel" of FIE.[28] Early

---

[23] John Mbiti in Trull, *The Fourth Self*, 36.

[24] William A. Dyrness, *Learning about Theology from the Third World* (Grand Rapids: Zondervan, 1990), 31.

[25] The exact quote of Blaise Pascal is, "There is a God-shaped vacuum in the heart of every man which cannot be filled by any created thing, but only by God the Creator, made known through Jesus Christ." See Chris Lutes, "The Secret That Will Change Your Life," *Christianity Today*, accessed September 7, 2018, https://www.christianitytoday.com/iyf/hottopics/faithvalues/8c6030.html.

[26] Koyama, *Three Mile an Hour God*, 38–39.

[27] Winter, "Evangelicals in Missions," in Hesselgrave and Stetzer, *MissionShift*, 175.

[28] Winter, 178, 190.

in his ministry Winter held that biblical mission primarily had to do with evangelizing the world. Later in life, he changed his mind and according to Hesselgrave, seemed "to have made social action at least necessary to evangelism and church growth."[29] This trend seems likely to continue.

More importantly, however, the missionary task projects as a spiritual undertaking. Many of the normal rules of success do not apply. Bible study and prayer must remain at the forefront. A dependence on sociology and modern technology can potentially prevent the missionary from taking a leap of faith with God's Spirit. Although technology and the social sciences can assist in discerning demographic trends, they are no substitute for the leading of God. The inability to predict the future is exemplified by an instance Donald McGavran describes in the 1980 second edition of *Understanding Church Growth*:

> An extraordinary happening has gone almost unmarked in the world of missions. One of the four great non-Christian religions has died in the last fifty years. In 1920 Confucianism, the religion of four hundred million Chinese, was a powerful faith. The communist conquest of China has radically altered the situation. The whole family system, so basic to Confucianism, has been liquidated. Inside mainland China, Confucianism has lost its power. True, it is still practiced by some Chinese of the dispersion and may continue in vestigial form for decades or centuries, but as a great faith, Confucianism is finished.[30]

McGavran was wrong here. As with Christianity, Confucianism in China went underground but did not die. One wonders if the opposite might occur with the Muslim faith. Could Islam, so strong in the early twenty-first century, be fading in eighty years? It is difficult to predict.

Above all, modern missions must rediscover the power of God in prayer. George Peters says, "The Bible is a record of supernatural manifestations, interventions and activities. Many of these happenings are direct answer to prayers. 'It is a noteworthy fact that there are 657 definite requests for prayer in the Bible, not including the Psalms, and 454 definitely recorded answers.' Prayer is a prominent subject in the Bible and a most significant exercise of

---

[29] Hesselgrave, "Conclusion," in Hesselgrave and Stetzer, *MissionShift*, 274, 292.
[30] McGavran, *Understanding Church Growth*, 253.

faith by the saints and the church."[31] When I attempted to enter a closed North African country in 1990, I was stymied at every turn. For six months, I visited numerous mission agencies and Christian aid organizations across the United States to locate someone who could obtain a residence visa for the Hadaway family. One day, at my home in Phoenix, Arizona, I fell on my knees and prayed, "Lord, if you'll get me into this country, I will live there with my family." Twenty minutes later the telephone rang. A woman with a Christian aid organization from the Horn of Africa called to say that someone from North Africa was coming to the US. She thought he could help me enter the country. I flew to Fort Wayne, Indiana, and met with the director of a refugee relief agency who agreed to sponsor the family's visa. For over ten years this agency sponsored all the residence permits for my mission society. Many churches were planted as a result.

Although prayer is important for any Christian, it is an absolute necessity on the mission field. The missionary resides in enemy territory and only prayer can thwart the powers of darkness. Once, in a North African country, one of the nationals threatened to tell the Muslim government of the evangelistic purpose for my relief and development projects. The Christian national leaders committed the matter to prayer. After a few days, the man became sick and was taken to a hospital in a nearby port city. Within a week the man died. Although sobered and sad, the leaders saw the hand of God in this event.

Six months later, a leader in a large port city of this Muslim country also threatened to expose the existence of my nascent church to the fundamentalist government. Again, the nationals and I committed the matter to prayer. A few weeks later this man drove through the desert with two women. After becoming trapped in the sand, they hailed a passing bus for a lift. The bus lost its way in the trackless desert. Forty-eight passengers, including the man who had threatened the church's work, were found on the side of the road, having died of thirst. The nationals proclaimed, "God did this." Indeed, in both instances God had protected his work.

The apostle Paul writes in 1 Cor 13:12, "For now we see only a reflection as in a mirror, but then face to face. Now I know in part, but then I will know

---

[31] Peters, *Biblical Theology of Missions*, 339 (see chap. 1, n. 7).

fully, as I am fully known." Unfortunately, this is all mankind can know of both the present and the future—our vantage point is indirect and our view indistinct. Although Christian missions may seem to the observer as haphazardly planned, unevenly distributed, and haltingly executed, God takes the long view and sees a greater purpose for the ages. Each generation rightly desires to "finish the task" of world missions and history is replete with examples of this kind of thinking. If each century produces approximately four generations of mankind, then about eighty generations have come and gone since Jesus's day. We are tempted, as were his apostles, to ask God when the task will be complete and when Jesus will return. Acts 1:6–8 says, "So when they had come together, they asked him, 'Lord, are you restoring the kingdom to Israel at this time?' He said to them, 'It is not for you to know times or periods that the Father has set by his own authority. But you will receive power when the Holy Spirit has come on you, and you will be my witnesses in Jerusalem, in all Judea and Samaria, and to the ends of the earth.'"

Westerners, particularly pragmatic Americans, desire to forecast, predict, plan, set goals, budget, coordinate, control, systematize, analyze statistics, and evaluate the progress of their mission work. Spiritual endeavor, however, is not so easily domesticated. Sometimes there is no explanation for the events that transpire. McGavran says, "Sudden ripenings, far from being unusual, are common. No one knows or has counted the ripenings of the last decade, but it is safe to say that they total hundreds.[32]

The opposite tendency is also dangerous. Sometimes people blame God for their poor planning or lack of effort. When I served in the United States Air Force a common joke consisted of the phrase, "My work is so secret, even I don't know what I'm doing."

Who could have predicted during the Fundamentalist-Modernist controversy[33] of the 1920s that sixty-five years later seeker-sensitive, but theologically

---

[32] McGavran, *Understanding Church Growth*, 2nd ed., 247.

[33] The Fundamentalists came into existence about 1914 to support the fundamentals of the faith, *vis-à-vis* the higher criticism of the Bible and evolutionary teaching prevalent in the last years of the nineteenth century. Fundamentalists, who preferred to be called evangelicals or conservatives, supported the inerrancy of the Bible, the deity of Christ, his virgin birth, and bodily resurrection. See Latourette, *History of Christianity*, 2:1264, 1421. The Fundamentalist-Modernist controversy climaxed in the Scopes Monkey Trial in Dayton, Tennessee, in 1925. This court case pitted three-time Democratic presidential candidate William Jennings Bryan

conservative, churches would develop? The only guarantee in the future of missions is that the world of twenty-first-century missions will surprise the church as much as the preceding centuries amazed our forebears. Hessselgrave wrote, "If, as is universally acknowledged, 'every man is his own historian,' it follows that every person is his or her own missiologist."[34] This book was written to assist Christians in developing competency in this area. Søren Kierkegaard postulated that there would come a time when everything was so easy the only thing left was to make things more difficult.[35] This could be said of missions today. Ralph Winter says, "The future of the world hinges on what we make of this word 'mission.'"[36] Some try to make the concept difficult, but it is simple. In his Word, Jesus repeats to the church what he said to his twelve apostles eighty generations ago—it is not for you to know. But we are to be his witnesses throughout the world, in the power of the Holy Spirit proclaiming the gospel of Jesus's death, burial, and resurrection and making those who believe into his disciples. This is missions.

READING FOR FURTHER STUDY

Johnstone, Patrick. *The Future of the Global Church: History, Trends, and Possibilities.* Downers Grove, IL: InterVarsity Press, 2011.

Koyama, Kosuke. *Three Mile an Hour God.* London: SCM-Canterbury Press, 1979.

Noll, Mark A. *The New Shape of World Christianity: How American Experience Reflects Global Faith.* Downers Grove, IL: IVP Academic, 2009.

Sunquist, Scott W. *The Unexpected Christian Century: The Reversal and Transformation of Global Christianity 1900–2000.* Grand Rapids: Baker Academic, 2015.

---

against Clarence Darrow, attorney for the plaintiff, John Thomas Scopes. Scopes, a part-time substitute teacher, was recruited to challenge Tennessee's law prohibiting the teaching of evolution in the public schools. Scopes and evolution lost the battle but eventually evolutionary teaching became standard scientific belief in America. See Ray Ginger, *Six Days or Forever: Tennessee vs. John Thomas Scopes* (Chicago: Quadrangle Books, 1969), 29.

[34] Hesselgrave, "Conclusion," in Hesselgrave and Stetzer, *MissionShift*, 267.

[35] Hesselgrave, 256–57.

[36] Ralph D. Winter, "The Meaning of Mission: Understanding This Term Is Crucial to the Completion of the Missionary Task," *Missions Frontiers*, March-April 1998, quoted in Hesselgrave and Stetzer, *MissionShift*, 274.

Appendix A: Baptism

Since baptizing is mentioned as a key component of the Great Commission, the practice merits discussion in a book about missions. One enters the Christian community, the church, through baptism, beginning the lifelong discipleship process. The baptizing (βαπτίζοντες) of new Christians forms an important part of evangelizing and discipling the nations in the Great Commission. Often baptism is just assumed. There is, however, disagreement about some aspects of baptism.

In the papyri the verbal form was used to speak of a "submerged" boat and in another instance, more figuratively of someone "'flooded,' or overwhelmed by calamities."[1] Albrecht Oepke, writing on *baptizo* (βαπτίζω)[2] in the *Theological Dictionary of the New Testament (TDNT)* says the term means "to dip in or under." He writes, "The intensive βαπτίζω occurs in the sense of 'to immerse' from the time of Hippocrates, in Plato, and especially in later writers." Furthermore, it meant "to sink," "to suffer shipwreck," and "to drown."[3]

For these reasons, Baptists and many other evangelicals have held that the mode of baptism, immersion, is important.[4] Louis Berkhof disagrees:

> Is immersion the only proper mode of baptism? The generally prevailing opinion outside of Baptist circles is that, as long as the

---

[1] Moulton and Milligan, *Vocabulary of the Greek Testament*, 102 (see chap. 2, n. 13).
[2] Albrecht Oepke, *Theological Dictionary of the New Testament*, s.v. "βαπτίζω, baptize," 529.
[3] Oepke, 530.
[4] Interestingly, although the Catholic and Orthodox communities baptize infants by pouring or sprinkling water, when an adult converts to their faith, the new convert is baptized by immersion.

fundamental idea, that of purification, finds expression in the rite, the mode of baptism is quite immaterial. It may be administered by immersion, by pouring or affusion or by sprinkling. . . . The Baptists assert, however, that the Lord did command baptism by immersion, and that all those who administer it in a different way are acting in open disobedience to His authority.[5]

George R. Beasley-Murray argues that immersion is implicit in the symbolism of Christ's death, burial, and resurrection. He says, "Despite the frequent denials of exegetes, it is surely reasonable to believe that the reason for Paul's stating that the baptized is *buried* as dead, rather than he *died* (as in Rom 6:6), is the nature of baptism as immersion."[6]

The question of infant baptism also generates controversy. Although Berkhof concedes that adults should be believers in Christ prior to baptism, he argues that infant baptism is allowable because Scripture does not prohibit it.[7] Some proponents of infant baptism hold that baptism based upon their parents' faith seals children into the covenant of God, while others see it as a promise of presumptive regeneration.[8] Beasley-Murray counters that infant baptism was not practiced by the early church and baptism was intended for believers only.[9] A Presbyterian minister said, "If it is proper to administer baptism to infants, then the import of baptism must be the same for infants as for adults. It cannot have one meaning for infants and another for adults."[10]

Baptism remains important. Overseas, especially with Muslims, Hindus, and Buddhists, it means the convert has crossed the line. Often seekers from other religions will try out Christianity. When challenged with baptism, however, they frequently demur. When someone is willing to be baptized, they burn their bridges with their former religion and embrace Christ. Baptism by immersion symbolizes a whole-hearted commitment to Christianity, and as such, is part and parcel with the Great Commission and the Christian faith.

---

[5] Berkhof, *Systematic Theology*, 629 (see chap. 3, n. 35).

[6] George Raymond Beasley-Murray, *Baptism in the New Testament* (Grand Rapids: Eerdmans, 1962), 133.

[7] Berkhof, *Systematic Theology*, 637.

[8] Berkhof, 639.

[9] Beasley-Murray, *Baptism in the New Testament*, 359.

[10] John Murray, quoted in Beasley-Murray, *Baptism in the New Testament*, 360.

Appendix B: Ecclesiology

The question arises what kind of church[1] should be planted? This is important because, especially in pioneer situations, missionaries are called on to begin churches by choosing not only the leadership, but the polity of the nascent church. This is a sobering and humbling task, shaking the missiologist to his core. In North America, the founding pastor, church planting team, or sponsoring church usually decide the question.

As with most biblical controversies, there are sound arguments and evidence for each view. Since Anglicans, Lutherans, Bible churches, and Baptists all plant churches, either through their denomination or as members of a mission agency, these issues must be addressed in the church-planting process. Church polity is not a fundamental of the faith like the virgin birth or resurrection of Christ, but remains important.

In Acts, the three words representing the three major forms of church government appear in the same chapter and seem to be used interchangeably, leading many to believe the three words refer to the same person. Due to the complexity and controversialism of the issue, each term and form of government will be addressed. The pertinent Bible verses are as follows:

> Acts 20:17: "Now from Miletus, he sent to Ephesus and called for
> the **elders** [*presbuteros*, πρεσβυτέρους] of the church." Acts 20:29: "Be
> on guard for yourselves and for all the flock that the Holy Spirit has

---

[1] A discussion and definition of church appears in chapter 3. This appendix deals only with the question of church polity.

appointed you to as **overseers** [*episcopas,* ἐπισκόπους] to **shepherd** [*poimainein,* ποιμαίνειν] the church of God, which He purchased with His own blood." [emphasis added]

The church offices and polity theories derived from these words present as follows:

1. Elders, Presbyters (*presbuteros,* πρεσβυτέρους).

Although this word originated from the concept of someone of an older age, this is not always the case. Gunther Bornkamm says:

> The peculiar problem of the use of πρεσβυτέρους [*presbuteros*] in Judaism and Christianity arises out of the twofold meaning of the word, which can be employed both as a designation of age and also a title of office. The two meanings cannot always be distinguished with clarity. . . . A surprising point in the Pastorals is that the bishop plays an important part here as well as the presbyters and that his functions are the same (cf. 1 Tim 5:17 προστῆναι [*prostainai,* managing or ruling] in 3:5; διδακτικόν [*didaktikov,* able to teach] in 3:2; cf. also Tt. 1:9). It is thus natural to suppose the offices are one and the same in the Pastorals. Only thus can one explain the fact that just after Titus is told to appoint elders (1:5) the portrait of a bishop is given (vv. 7 ff.). Yet one can hardly make a complete equation. This is proved by the simple fact that in the Pastorals [ἐπισκόπους] *episcopos* is always in the singular while the πρεσβυτέρους [*presbuteros*] form a college. [2]

Since there are a number of elders from Ephesus who are called to Miletus by Paul, this is seen as an argument for a plurality of elders in a local church. What is not clear is if the Ephesian elders were all from one large church in Ephesus or if there were a number of smaller Ephesian house churches affiliated with the larger one.

2. Overseer, Bishop (*episcopos,* ἐπίσκοπος).

This term speaks of the leader of a congregation but developed into a concept of a supervisor of churches in an area. Concerning the origin of the term, Herman Beyer says:

---

[2] Gunther Bornkamm, "πρεσβυτέρους, (*presbuteros*)," in *TDNT,* vol. 6.

The word ἐπίσκόπος is best rendered "overseer" or "watch." From this there develops a twofold use which only reunites in a stronger focus on Christian soil. In Greek ἐπίσκόπος is first used a. with a free understanding of the "onlooker," "watcher," "protector," "patron." . . . Therewith the word ἐπίσκόπος comes to be used b. as a title to denote various offices.[3]

This included state officials such as in Athens in the 4th and 5th centuries BC and the officers of secular societies. Furthermore, Beyer says that the higher-ranked apostles, prophets, and teachers are never called elders or overseers. This designation is reserved for responsible men in congregations who are called to the shepherding task. The more formalized title would come later.[4]

In the early church during the early and middle part of the first millennium, authority became more and more centralized in the hands of bishops. This phenomenon has come to be called the rise of the monarchical bishop. Although the Roman Catholic and Eastern Orthodox communions adopted this polity, generally speaking, many Protestant Reformation theologians moved away from it.

3. Pastor, Shepherd (*poimainein*, ποιμαίνειν)

Here the verb "to shepherd" appears, not the noun "shepherd" or "pastor." Although shepherds, like tax collectors and publicans, were so despised in everyday Jewish life they could not be witnesses in a court of law, both the Old Testament and New Testament speak of them figuratively in a positive way. King David calls God "my shepherd" [רֹעִי] in Ps 23:1 and Jesus proclaims himself the "good shepherd [ὁ ποιμὴν ὁ καλὸς, *poimai kalos*]" in John 10:11. Additionally, 1 Pet 5:4 describes Jesus as the great [or chief] shepherd [Ἀρχιποίμενος. *apex-poimenos*]. Only once is the office of pastor ποιμένας [*poimenas* or shepherd] mentioned in the New Testament (Eph 4:11) and there it is linked with teachers [*didaskalos*, διδασκάλους] leading many to believe the pastor-teacher role refers to one office.

Most congregational churches see the pastor-teacher as the church's sole elder and only overseer. Other ministers on a church staff or pastors of other

---

[3] Hermann W. Beyer, "(*episcopos*), ἐπίσκόπος," in *TDNT*, vol. 2.

[4] Beyer, "(*episcopos*), ἐπίσκόπος."

churches are considered elders and overseers as well. Generally speaking, however, the free-church tradition usually does not have plural elders.

The ambiguity and interchangeability of these three words in Acts 20:17, 28 should cause the theologian pause and allow the missiologist some flexibility when applying church polity on the mission field. A "biblical" case can be made for each of the major church polity persuasions—Episcopalian, Presbyterian, and Congregational. The Roman Catholic, Orthodox, Anglican, Episcopal, Lutheran, and Methodist communions organize themselves according to the episcopal model. Presbyterian, Reformed, and most Bible churches follow the plural elder (Presbyterian) format. Congregationalist churches, most Baptist denominations, Assemblies of God, and other independent groups are largely congregational in nature. Strict Congregationalists see the pastor as the sole elder and overseer in the church.

Mark Dever sees plurality of elders as the New Testament model. He writes:

> The Bible clearly models a plurality of elders in each local church. Though it never suggests a specific number of elders for a particular congregation, the New Testament refers to "elders" in the plural in local churches (e.g., Acts 14:23; 16:4; 20:17; 21:18; Titus 1:5; James 5:14). When you read through Acts and the Epistles there is always more than one elder being talked about.[5]

On the other hand, Bill Blanchard, in his book *Church Structure That Works*, sees the pastor as filling the overseer/elder/shepherding office. Any plurality would be, according to him, composed of other full-time vocational ministers serving on the church staff.[6] Over 80 percent of Southern Baptist churches follow this second model.

Of course, there are combinations of church government within the above three categories. Although Roman Catholic and Orthodox churches are strictly episcopal in structure, Methodists (also episcopal in structure) have pastors at the church level who are supervised by bishops in their regions. Further, some Baptist churches have plural elders but the congregation selects the elders,

---

[5] Mark Dever, *Nine Marks of a Healthy Church*, rev. ed. (Wheaton: Crossway, 2000), 215–16.
[6] Bill Blanchard, *Church Structure That Works: Turning Dysfunction into Health* (Sisters, OR: VMI, 2008), 29–30.

including the teaching elder. Stephen and Kirk Wellum define proper congregationalism as a plurality of elders with the congregation as the final court of appeal. They write:

> The purpose of this chapter, then, is to argue in favor of a congregational form of church government. The congregationalism we defend is *not* what sometimes is caricatured as congregationalism. It's not some form of radical individualism in which everyone does what is right in his own eyes. It's not some "direct democracy" in which every decision concerning every issue must be put to a congregational vote, thus displacing any role for God-ordained leaders/elders. Instead, we defend the view that, under the lordship of Christ and under the authority of divinely given elders who lead, the last and final court of appeal in matters related to the local church is the congregation itself.[7]

Of course, this is more a redefinition of congregationalism than an example of it. Most free churches operate by committees and/or ministry teams and avoid the abuses the Wellums abhor. Similarly, even pastors in episcopal governed churches are better served by listening to their lay leadership rather than acting unilaterally.

The issue is important in missions as the church planter must determine the kind of church that will be started. Recently the International Mission Board of the Southern Baptist Convention issued a "Foundations" document supporting a plurality of elders. The document states, "The consistent pattern in the New Testament is for churches to have a plurality of pastors/elders/overseers."[8]

What is not clear is where these elders were serving. Were they serving in one church or was there one elder serving a number of smaller churches? The early church met in homes for security reasons and because there were no church buildings. I have visited the ruins of Ephesus twice. It is quite possible that there were a number of house churches throughout this sprawling city,

---

[7] Stephen J. Wellum and Kirk Wellum, "The Biblical and Theological Case for Congregationalism," in *Baptist Foundations: Church Government for an Anti-Institutional Age*, ed. Mark Dever and Jonathan Leeman (Nashville: B&H, 2015), 49.

[8] "Foundations," The International Mission Board (Richmond, VA: International Mission Board, 2018), 62.

each led by an elder. Those of the free-church persuasion have traditionally interpreted the three terms to mean that the pastor is the single elder (*presbyter*, πρεσβυτέρους) and overseer (*episcopos*, ἐπισκόπους) of a particular church. When an ordination council is convened, all the local pastors (elders and overseers) constitute the ordination council (or the presbytery).

As missionaries operate in pioneer areas, usually there is a small pool of potential local leaders. This is probably why Paul left some of his lieutenants as pastors of mission churches along the way—there were few, if any, scripturally[9] qualified candidates.

For instance, I planted a church in a suburb of Mwanza, Tanzania, the second-largest city in the country. I took a young apprentice with me as I walked through the village composed of grass huts. After I preached under a tree, a number of African Traditional Religion adherents believed, including the village chief and medicine man. When I organized the church a year later, I was in a quandary about who to choose as a church leader. I chose and installed a married, twenty-two-year-old young man over the older men in the congregation. The reason was that the other candidates were witch doctors, polygamists, or both.

Like in the New Testament, most of the other churches in China, especially those started by the T4T method, are small. In a house church of fifteen it seems it would best reflect the biblical model to have a single elder/pastor/overseer form of church government.

I have served as all three in my ministerial career. As a young man, I served as the elder of an independent Bible-church plant. Before departing for the mission field, I worked as the sole pastor of two traditionally organized Southern Baptist churches in California and Arizona. On the mission field in Tanzania, I functioned in apostolic roles that could be called, at times, filling the office of overseer. This is because in Tanzania and North Africa I basically supervised churches.

Although in the Scripture there are strong hints of direction in church government, perhaps exactness in church polity has been left by the Holy Spirit intentionally vague. Although the character and qualifications for church leaders is quite clear, the actual structure for new churches is not.

---

[9] The New Testament was in the process of being written.

Bibliography

3 Circles Life Conversation Guide. Alpharetta, GA: North American Mission Board, 2014.

Abdalati, Hammudah. *Islam in Focus.* 2nd ed. Indianapolis: American Trust Publications, 1993.

Abrahams, R. G. *The Nyamwezi Today: A Tanzanian People in the 1970s.* Cambridge: Cambridge University Press, 1981.

Ahmed, Akbar S. *Islam Today: A Short Introduction to the Muslim World.* London: I. B. Tauris, 1999.

Akins, Barbara. *Ministry Based Evangelism.* Brasilia: IMB—Eastern South America, 2000.

Akins, Thomas Wade. *Pioneer Evangelism.* Rio de Janeiro: *Junta de Missoes Nacionais,* 1999.

Allen, David L., Eric Hankins, and Adam Harwood, eds. *Anyone Can Be Saved: A Defense of "Traditional" Southern Baptist Soteriology.* Eugene, OR: Wipf and Stock, 2016.

Allen, Roland. *Missionary Methods, St. Paul's or Ours?: A Study of the Church in the Four Provinces.* 2nd ed. N.p.: Crossreach Publications, 2017. First published 1912 by Robert Scott (London).

———. *The Spontaneous Expansion of the Church.* Grand Rapids: Eerdmans, 1962.

Allison, B. Gray. *Winsome Words for the Willing Witness.* Memphis: Allison Evangelistic Association, undated.

Anderson, Andy. *Where Action is: How God is Using a Simple Plan to Reach People for Christ.* Nashville: Broadman Press, 1976.

Anderson, Courtney. *To the Golden Shore: The Life of Adoniram Judson.* Valley Forge, PA: Judson Press, 1987.

Anderson, Justice A. "An Overview of Missiology." In Terry, *Missiology,* 3–18.

———. "Medieval and Renaissance Missions (500–1792)." In Terry, *Missiology*, 157–71.

Ausenda, Gregory. "Leisurely Nomads: The Hadendowa (Beja) of the Gash Delta and their Transition to Sedentary Village Life (Sudan)." PhD diss., Columbia University, 1986.

Badriaki, Michael Bamwesigye. *When Helping Works: Alleviating Fear and Pain in Global Missions*. Eugene, OR: Wipf and Stock, 2017.

Bailey, John M., and Sherri Jachelski, eds. *My Husband Wants to Be a Church Planter . . . So What Will That Make Me?* Alpharetta, GA: North American Mission Board, 2007.

Baker, Charles F. *A Dispensational Theology*. 2nd ed. Grand Rapids: Grace Bible College Publications, 1972.

Bakhtiar, Laleh. *Sufi: Expressions of the Mystic Quest*. New York: Avon, 1976.

Barnwell, Katharine. *Introduction to Semantics and Translation: With Special Reference to Bible Translation*. 2nd ed. Horsleys Green, UK: Summer Institute of Linguistics, 1980.

Barrett, C. K. *A Commentary on the First Epistle to the Corinthians*. 2nd ed. London: Black, 1971.

Barrett, David B. *World Christian Encyclopedia: A Comparative Study of Churches and Religions in the Modern World, AD 1900–2000*. Nairobi: Oxford University Press, 1982.

Beasley-Murray, George Raymond. *Baptism in the New Testament*. Grand Rapids: Eerdmans, 1962.

Beekman, John, and John Callow. In *A Manual for Problem Solving in Bible Translation* by Mildred Larson. Dallas: The Summer Institute of Linguistics, 1975.

Beilby, James K., and Paul R. Eddy, eds. *Divine Foreknowledge: Four Views*. Downers Grove, IL: InterVarsity Press, 2001.

Bergreen, Lawrence. *Marco Polo: From Venice to Exandu*. New York: Random House, 2007.

Berkhof, Louis. *Systematic Theology: With a Complete Textual Index*. 4th ed. Grand Rapids: Eerdmans, 1949.

Blackaby, Henry T., and Claude V. King. *Experiencing God: Knowing and Doing the Will of God*. Nashville: LifeWay Press, 1990.

Blair, Olivia. "What Comes After Millennials? Meet the Generation Known as the 'Linksters'." *Independent*, April 11, 2017. https://www.independent.co.uk/life-style/millennials-generation-z-linksters-what-next-generation-x-baby-boomers-internet-social-media-a7677001.html.

Blanchard, Bill. *Church Structure that Works: Turning Dysfunction into Health*. Sisters, OR: VMI Publications, 2008.

Blight, Richard. *Translation Problems from A to Z*. Dallas: Summer Institute of Linguistics, 1992.

Bosch, David J. *Transforming Mission: Paradigm Shifts in Theology of Mission.* Mary-knoll, New York: Orbis, 1991.

Boulos, Samir. *European Evangelicals in Egypt (1900–1956): Cultural Entanglements and Missionary Spaces.* Leiden, The Netherlands: Koinklijke Brill, 2016.

Bowman, K. Carla, and James Bowman. *Building Bridges to Oral Cultures: Journeys among the Least Reached.* Pasadena: Wm. Carey Library, 2017.

Boyd, Gregory. "The Open-Theism View." In Beilby and Eddy, *Divine Foreknowledge,* 13–47.

Brand, Chad Owen, and David E. Hankins. *One Sacred Effort: The Cooperative Program of Southern Baptists.* Nashville: B&H, 2005.

Braswell, George W., Jr. *Islam: Its Prophet, Peoples, Politics and Power.* Nashville: Broadman and Holman, 1996.

Bratcher, L. M. *The Apostle of the Amazon.* Nashville: Broadman Press, 1951.

Bright, Bill. *Come Help Change the World.* Old Tappan, NJ: Fleming Revell, 1970.

———. *Have You Heard of the Four Spiritual Laws?* Bright Media Foundation, 2003.

Brock, Charles. *Indigenous Church Planting: A Practical Journey.* Neosho, MO: Church Growth International, 1994.

Brown, Richard. "Response to Point 2." *International Journal of Frontier Missions* 24, no. 1 (2007): 8–9.

Bruce, F. F. *The Acts of the Apostles.* Grand Rapids: Eerdmans, 1949.

Bryan, Lynn. *Understanding Bible Prophecy.* Bloomington, IN: WestBow Press, 2012.

Budge, Ernest Alfred Wallis. *The Egyptian Sudan: Its History and Monuments.* London: Kegan Paul, Trench, Trubner, 1907.

Caballeros, Harold. "Defeating the Enemy with the Help of Spiritual Mapping." In Wagner, *Breaking Strongholds,* 119–40.

Cairns, Earle E. *Christianity through the Centuries: A History of the Christian Church.* Rev. ed. Grand Rapids: Zondervan, 1954.

Cameron, Geoffrey, and Benjamin Schewel. *Religion and Public Discourse in an Age of Transition: Reflections on Baha'i Practice and Thought.* Baha'i Studies. Ontario: Wilfrid Laurier University Press, 2018.

Campus Ministry. *Sharing the Abundant Life on Campus.* San Bernardino, CA: Campus Crusade for Christ International, 1972.

Carey, William. "An Enquiry into the Obligation of Christians to Use Means for the Conversion of the Heathens." In Winter and Hawthorne, *Perspectives,* 312–18.

Carlton, R. Bruce. *Strategy Coordinator: Changing the Course of Southern Baptist Missions.* Eugene, OR: Wipf and Stock, 2010.

Carter, Charles W., and Ralph Earle. *The Acts of the Apostles.* Grand Rapids: Zondervan, 1973.

Caughey, Ellen. *Eric Liddell: Olympian and Missionary.* Ulrichville, OH: Barbour, 2000.

Chang, Po-tuan. *Understanding Reality: A Taoist Alchemical Classic.* Translated by Thomas Cleary. Honolulu: University of Hawaii Press, 1987.

Chappell, Paul, and John Goetsch. *The Savior Sensitive Church: Understanding and Avoiding Postmodernism and the Seeker-Sensitive Church Movement.* Lancaster, CA: Striving Together Publications, 2006.

Cheyney, Tom. *The 7 Pillars of Church Revitalization and Renewal: Biblical Foundations for Church Revitalization.* Orlando: Renovate Publishing Group, 2016.

Chittick, William C. *Sufism: A Short Introduction.* Oxford: Oneworld, 2005.

Clark, W. T. "Manners, Customs and Beliefs of the Northern Beja." *Sudan Notes and Records (SNR)* 21, no. 1 (1938): 26–27.

Coleman, Robert. *The Master Plan of Evangelism.* Westwood, NJ: Fleming H. Revell, 1963.

Comiskey, Joel. *Groups of 12: A New Way to Mobilize Leaders and Multiply Groups in Your Church.* Houston: Touch Publications, 1999.

———. *Home Cell Church Explosion: How Your Small Group Can Grow and Multiply.* Houston: Touch Publications, 1998.

Corbett, Steve, and Brian Fikkert. *When Helping Hurts: How to Alleviate Poverty without Hurting the Poor . . . and Yourself.* 2nd ed. Chicago: Moody, 2012.

Corduan, Winfried. *Neighboring Faiths: A Christian Introduction to World Religions.* 2nd ed. Downers Grove, IL: InterVarsity Press, 2012.

Craig, William Lane. "The Middle Knowledge View." In Beilby and Eddy, *Divine Foreknowledge*, 119–43.

Crawley, Winston. *Global Mission: A Story to Tell: An Interpretation of Southern Baptist Foreign Missions.* Nashville: Broadman Press, 1985.

———. *World Christianity, 1970-2000: Toward A New Millennium.* Pasadena: William Carey Library, 2001.

Cummings, Joseph. "Muslim Followers of Jesus?" In *Understanding Insider Movements: Disciples of Jesus within Diverse Religious Communities*, edited by Harley Talman and John Jay Travis, 11–23. Pasadena: William Carey Library, 2015.

de Léry, Jean. *History of a Voyage to the Land of Brazil, Otherwise Called America.* Translated by Janet Whatley. Berkeley: University of California Press, 1992.

Dent, Don. *The Ongoing Role of Apostles in Mission: The Forgotten Foundation.* Bloomington, IL: Crossbooks, 2011.

Deuskar, Chandan. "What Does Urban Mean?" *World Bank Blogs,* June 2, 2015. https://blogs.worldbank.org/sustainablecities/what-does-urban-mean.

Dever, Mark. *The Gospel and Personal Evangelism.* Wheaton: Crossway, 2007.

———. *Nine Marks of a Healthy Church.* Rev. ed. Wheaton: Crossway, 2000.

Diem-Lane, Andria. *Ahimsa: A Brief Guide to Jainism.* Walnut, CA: Mt. San Antonio College Philosophy Group, 2016.

Donohue, John J., and John Esposito, eds. *Islam in Transition.* New York: Oxford University Press, 2007.

Duesing, Jason G. "Ambition Overthrown." In *Adoniram Judson: A Bicentennial Appreciation of the Pioneer American Missionary*, edited by Jason G. Duesing, 55–76. Nashville: B&H Academic, 2012.

———. *Seven Summits in Church History*. Nashville: Rainer Publishing, 2016.

Durie, Mark. "Messianic Judaism and Deliverance from the Two Covenants of Islam." In Ibrahim and Greenham, *Muslim Conversions*, 265–82.

Dyrness, William A. *Learning about Theology from the Third World*. Grand Rapids: Zondervan, 1990.

Eitel, Keith E. *Paradigm Wars: The Southern Baptist International Mission Board Faces the Third Millennium*. Cumbria, CA: Regnum Books, 2000.

Elliot, Elisabeth. *A Chance to Die: The Life and Legacy of Amy Carmichael*. Grand Rapids: Revell, 1987.

Elton, Lord. *General Gordon*. London: Collins Press, 1954.

Emhardt, William Chauncey, and George M. Lamsa. *The Oldest Christian People: A Brief Account of the History and Traditions of the Assyrian People and the Fateful History of the Nestorian Church*. Eugene, OR: Wipf and Stock, 2012.

Engel, James F., and William A. Dyrness. *Changing the Mind of Missions*. Downers Grove, IL: InterVarsity Press, 2000.

Engel, James F., and Wilbert Norton. *What's Gone Wrong with the Harvest?* Grand Rapids: Zondervan, 1982.

Ensminger, Sven. *Karl Barth's Theology as a Resource for a Christian Theology of Religions*. London: Bloomsbury T&T Clark, 2014.

Ernst. Carl W. *The Shambhala Guide to Sufism*. Boston: Shambhala Publications, 1997.

Escobar, Angel F. Sanchez. *A Brief History of the Byzantine Church*. Winston-Salem, NC: St. Stephen Harding College Publishing House, 2009.

Escobedo-Frank, Dottie. *Restart Your Church*. Nashville: Abingdon, 2012.

Esler, Ted. "The Unengaged: An Engaging Strategy . . . Or Not?" *Evangelical Missions Quarterly* 51, no. 2 (April 2015): 136.

Esposito, John, and Dalia Mogahed. *Who Speaks for Islam? What a Billion Muslims Really Think*. New York: Oxford University Press, 2007.

Esposito, John, Daniel Fasching, and Todd Lewis, eds. *World Religions Today*. 3rd ed. New York: Oxford University Press, 2009.

Estep, William R. *Whole Gospel Whole World: The Foreign Mission Board of the Southern Baptist Convention, 1845–1995*. Nashville: Broadman and Holman, 1994.

Eusebius. *Eccles III*. New York: Mason and Lane, 1839.

Fenton, John Y., Norvin Hein, Frank E. Reynolds, Alan L. Miller, Niels C. Nielsen Jr., and Grace G. Burford. *Religions of Asia*. Edited by Robert K. C. Forman. 2nd ed. New York: St. Martin's, 1988.

Finney, John. *Recovering the Past: Celtic and Roman Missions*. London: Darton, Longman and Todd, 1996.

Fish, Roy J., and J. E. Conant. *Every Member Evangelism for Today*. New York: Harper & Row, 1976.

Fletcher, Jesse C. *Wimpy Harper of Africa*. Nashville: Broadman Press, 1967.

Ford, Leighton. *The Christian Persuader: A New Look at Evangelism Today*. New York: Harper & Row, 1966.

Fort, Wana Ann G., and Kim Davis. *A Thousand Times Yes: Two Doctors Who Answered God's Call*. Birmingham, AL: New Hope, 2013.

Foxe's Book of Martyrs. Edited by Marie Gentert King. Old Tappan, NJ: Fleming H. Revell, 1968.

Foyle, Marjorie. *Overcoming Missionary Stress*. Wheaton: Evangelical Missions Information Service, 1987.

Gallimore, Howard. *Erik (Eurico) Alfred Nelson Papers: 1891–1975, AR 363*. Nashville: Southern Baptist Historical Library and Archives, 2012.

Gamst, F. C. "Beja." In *Muslim Peoples*. Vol. 1. Westport, CN: Greenwood Press, 1984.

Garber, Jerold A. *Ministry to the Avatars: Building a Real Church in a Virtual World*. Bloomington, IN: Archway, 2017.

Garland, David E. *1 Corinthians*. Grand Rapids, MI: Baker, 2003.

Garrett, Bob. "The Next Frontier: The Implications for Missions of Global Urbanization in the Twenty-First Century." In *Reaching the City: Reflections on Urban Missions in the Twenty-first Century*, edited by Gary Fujino, Timothy R. Sisk, and Tereso C. Casino, 19–33. Pasadena: William Carey Library, 2012.

Garrison, V. David. *Church Planting Movements: How God Is Redeeming a Lost World*. Midlothian, VA: WIGTake Resources, 2004.

"Gene Edwards Controversy." In *Heaven Sent Revival*. Pentecostal Pioneers. www.pentecostalpioneers.org/geneedwards1.html, June 28, 2018.

Gerla, M. R. *Jainism: In 13 Chapters*. Self-published, Create Space, 2017.

Gibbs, Eddie, and Ryan K. Bolger. *Emerging Churches: Creating Christian Community in Postmodern Cultures*. Grand Rapids: Baker Academic, 2005.

Ginger, Ray. *Six Days or Forever: Tennessee vs. John Thomas Scopes*. Chicago: Quadrangle Books, 1969.

Goerner, H. Cornell. *All Nations in God's Purpose: What the Bible Teaches about Missions*. Nashville: Broadman Press, 1979.

Goheen, Michael W. *A Light to the Nations: The Missional Church and the Biblical Story*. Grand Rapids: Baker Academic, 2011.

Gordon, April A., and Donald L. Gordon. *Understanding Contemporary Africa*. 3rd ed. Boulder, CO: Lynn Reiner, 2001.

Greear, J. D. *Breaking the Islam Code: Understanding the Soul Questions of Every Muslim*. Eugene, OR: Harvest House, 2010.

Greenway, Roger M., and Timothy M. Monsma. *Cities: Missions' New Frontier*. 2nd ed. Grand Rapids: Baker, 2000.

Greeson, Kevin. *The Camel*. Arkadelphia, AR: Wigtake Resources, 2007.

Grudem, Wayne. *Systematic Theology: An Introduction to Biblical Doctrine*. Grand Rapids: Zondervan, 1994.

Hadaway, C. Kirk. "Learning from Urban Church Research." In *Planting and Growing Urban Churches: From Dream to Reality*, edited by Harvie M. Conn, 35–45. Grand Rapids: Baker, 1997.

Hadaway, C. Kirk, and Larry L. Rose, eds. *The Urban Challenge: Reaching America's Cities with the Gospel*. Nashville: Broadman Press, 1982.

Hadaway, Robin Dale. "Balancing the Biblical Perspective: A Missiological Analysis." *Journal of Evangelism and Missions* 2 (Spring 2003): 103–14.

———. "Tropical Preaching: Proclaiming Biblical Truth Cross-Culturally." *Midwestern Journal of Theology* 14, no. 1 (2015).

Hanh, Thich Nhat. *The Heart of the Buddha's Teaching*. New York: Broadway Books, 1999).

Hankins, Eric. "Commentary on Article 6: Election to Salvation." In Allen, Hankins, and Harwood, *Anyone Can Be Saved*, 90–102.

Hanks, Billie, Jr., and Randy Craig. *Operation Multiplication 12 Session Guide: Multiplication by Mentorship*. Salado, TX: International Evangelism Association, 1999.

Harper, Keith, ed. *Send the Light: Lottie Moon Letters and Other Writings*. Macon, GA: Mercer University Press, 2002.

Harris, Laird R., Gleason J. Archer Jr., and Bruce K. Waltke, eds. *Theological Wordbook of the Old Testament*. Vol. 1. Chicago: Moody, 1980.

Harrison, Rodney A. *Seven Steps for Planting Churches*. Alpharetta, GA: North American Mission Board, 2004.

Hatcher, William S., and J. Douglas Martin. *The Baha'i Faith: The Emerging Global Religion*. Wilmette, IL: Baha'i Publishing, 2002.

Havlik, John F. *The Evangelistic Church*. Nashville: Convention Press, 1976.

Hefley, James, and Marti Hefley. *Uncle Cam: The Story of William Cameron Townsend Founder of the Wycliffe Bible Translators and the Summer Institute of Linguistics*. Huntington Beach, CA: Wycliffe Bible Translators, 1995.

Hesselgrave, David J. *Communicating Christ Cross-Culturally*. 2nd ed. Grand Rapids: Zondervan, 1991.

———. "Conclusion: A Scientific Postscript—Grist for the Missiological Mills of the Future." In Hesselgrave and Stetzer, *MissionShift*, 256–95.

———. *Paradigms in Conflict: 15 Key Questions in Christian Missions Today*. Edited by Keith Eitel. 2nd ed. Grand Rapids: Kregel, 2018.

———. *Planting Churches Cross-Culturally: North America and Beyond*. 2nd ed. Grand Rapids: Baker, 2000.

Hesselgrave, David J., and Edward Rommen. *Contextualization: Meanings, Methods, and Models*. Pasadena: William Carey Library, 2000.

Hesselgrave, David J., and Ed Stetzer, eds. *MissionShift: Global Mission Issues in the Third Millennium*. Nashville: B&H, 2010.

Hexham, Irving. *Understanding World Religions*. Grand Rapids: Zondervan, 2011.

Hiebert, Paul G. *Anthropological Insights for Missionaries*. Grand Rapids: Baker, 1985.

———. *The Gospel in Human Contexts: Anthropological Explorations for Contemporary Missions*. Grand Rapids: Baker Academic, 2000.

———. *Transforming Worldviews: An Anthropological Understanding of How People Change*. Grand Rapids: Baker Academic, 2009.

Hiebert, Paul G., and Eloise Hiebert Meneses. *Incarnational Ministry: Planting Churches in Band, Tribal, Peasant, and Urban Societies*. Grand Rapids: Baker, 1995.

Hiebert, Paul G., Daniel R. Shaw, and Tiete Tiénou. *Understanding Folk Religion: A Christian Response to Popular Beliefs and Practices*. Grand Rapids: Baker, 1999.

Hodges, Melvin L. *The Indigenous Church: A Complete Handbook on How to Grow Young Churches*. Springfield, MO: Gospel Publishing House, 1976.

Hoksbergen, Roland. *Serving God Globally: Finding Your Place in International Development*. Grand Rapids: Baker Academic, 2012.

Houssney, Georges. *Engaging Islam*. Boulder, CO: Treeline Publications, 2010.

Howell, Brian M., and Jenell William Paris. *Introducing Cultural Anthropology: A Christian Perspective*. Grand Rapids: Baker, 2011.

Hubbard, Ethel Daniels. *The Moffats*. New York: Friendship Press, 1944.

Hunt, Dave, and James White. *Debating Calvinism*. Sisters, OR: Multnomah, 2004.

Hunter, J. H., *A Flame of Fire: The Life and Work of Rowland V. Bingham*. Toronto: Sudan Interior Mission, 1961.

Hybels, Bill. *Just Walk across the Room: Simple Steps Pointing People to Faith*. Grand Rapids: Zondervan, 2006.

Ibrahim, Ayman S., and Ant Greenham, eds. *Muslim Conversions to Christ: A Critique of Insider Movements in Islamic Contexts*. New York: Peter Lang, 2018.

Islamic Affairs Department. *Understanding Islam and the Muslims*. Washington, DC: Embassy of Saudi Arabia, 1989.

Issue Group on Making Disciples of Oral Learners. *Making Disciples of Oral Learners: To Proclaim His Story Where It Has Not Been Known Before*. Lausanne Occasional Paper 54, edited by David Claydon. Paper produced at the 2004 Forum for World Evangelization, Pattaya, Thailand, September 29–October 5, 2004. https://www.lausanne.org/docs/2004forum/LOP54_IG25.pdf.

Jackson, Joyce. "The Role of a Church Planter's Wife." In Bailey and Jachelski, *My Husband Wants to Be a Church Planter*, 47–57.

Jackson, Richard. *How To's on the Highway to Heaven*. Phoenix: Exposition Press, 1985.

Jacobsen, Frode F. *Theories of Sickness and Misfortune among the Hadendowa Beja of the Sudan: Narratives as Points of Entry into Beja Cultural Knowledge*. London: Kegan Paul, 1998.

Johnson, C. Neal. *Business as Mission: A Comprehensive Guide to Theory and Practice*. Downers Grove, IL: InterVarsity Press, 2009.

Johnston, Sammie. *Dream Builders: The Story of the Forts of Africa*. Birmingham, AL: New Hope, 1989.

Johnston, Thomas Paul. *Evangelizology*. 2nd ed. 2 vols. Liberty, MO: Evangelism Unlimited, 2011.

———. *Examining Billy Graham's Theology of Evangelism*. Eugene, OR: Wipf and Stock, 2003.

Johnstone, Patrick. *The Future of the Global Church: History, Trends, and Possibilities*. Downers Grove, IL: InterVarsity Press, 2011.

Josephus, Flavius. *Antiquities of the Jews*, chap. 3. In *Josephus Complete Works*. Translated by William Whiston. Grand Rapids: Kregel Publications, 1960.

Kai, Ying. *Trainers: Establishing Successful Trainers*. 2nd ed. Hong Kong: Ocean Printing, 2005.

Kane, J. Herbert. *A Global View of Christian Missions: From Pentecost to the Present*. Rev. ed. Grand Rapids: Baker, 1975.

Kapteijns, Lidwein. "The Historiography of the Northern Sudan from 1500 to the Establishment of British Colonial Rule: A Critical Overview." *International Journal of African Historical Studies* 22, no. 2 (1989): 251–66.

Karrar, Ali Salih. *The Sufi Brotherhoods in the Sudan*. Evanston, IL: Northwestern University Press, 1992.

Kato, Byang. *Theological Pitfalls in Africa*. Kisumu, Kenya: Evangel, 1975.

Kelley, Charles S., Jr. *Fuel the Fire: Lessons from the History of Southern Baptist Evangelism*. Nashville: B&H Academic, 2018.

Kennedy, D. James. *Evangelism Explosion*. Wheaton: Tyndale House, 1970.

Kenny, Tim. "Steps to Peace with God." Billy Graham Evangelistic Association. *Decision*, September 23, 2004. https://billygraham.org/decision-magazine /october-2004/steps-to-peace-with-god/.

Khan, Gabriel Mandel. *Buddha: The Enlightened One*. San Diego: Thunder Bay Press, 2005.

Kirimura, Yasuji. *Outline of Buddhism*. Tokyo: Nichiren Shoshu International Center, 1981.

Koyama, Kosuke. *Three Mile an Hour God*. London: SCM Press, 1979.

Kraft, Charles. "Dynamic Equivalent Churches in Muslim Society." In *The Gospel and Islam: A 1978 Compendium*, edited by Don McCurry, 114–28. Monrovia: Missions Advanced Research and Communication Center, 1978.

Kreider, Alan. *The Patient Ferment of the Early Church: The Improbable Rise of Christianity in the Roman Empire*. Grand Rapids: Baker Academic, 2016.

Ladd, George Eldon, *A Theology of the New Testament*. Grand Rapids: Eerdmans, 1974.

Lancaster, Daniel B. *The Bagbys of Brazil: The Life and Work of William Buck Bagby and Anne Luther Bagby, Southern Baptist Missionaries*. Austin, TX: Eakin Press, 1999.

Latourette, Kenneth Scott. *A History of Christianity*. Vol. 1, *Beginnings to 1500*. Rev. ed. New York: Harper & Row, 1975.

Lederer, Edith M. "UN Report: By Year 2030 Two-Thirds of the World Will Live in Cities." Associated Press, May 18, 2016. https://www.apnews .com/40b530ac84ab4931874e1f7efb4f1a22.

Lemke, Steve W. "Five Theological Models Relating Determinism, Divine Sovereignty, and Human Freedom." In Allen, Hankins, and Harwood, *Anyone Can Be Saved*, 169–78.

Lingenfelter, Sherwood G., and Marvin K. Mayers. *Ministering Cross-Culturally: An Incarnational Model for Personal Relationships*. 2nd ed. Grand Rapids: Baker Academic, 2003.

Little, Paul E. *How to Give Away Your Faith*. Downers Grove, IL: InterVarsity Press, 1966.

Livermore, David A. *Serving with Eyes Wide Open: Doing Short-Term Missions with Cultural Intelligence*. 2nd ed. Grand Rapids: Baker, 2013.

Leupold, H.C. *Exposition of Genesis*. Vol. 1. Grand Rapids: Baker, 1942.

Lewis, B. A. "Deim el Arab and the Beja Stevedores of Port Sudan." *Sudan Notes and Records (SNR)* 43 (1962): 60.

Lewis, I. M., ed. *Islam in Tropical Africa*. 2nd ed. London: Hutchinson University Library for Africa, 1980.

Lewis, Larry L. *Organize to Evangelize: A Manual for Church Growth*. Nashville: Broadman Press, 1988.

Lewis, C. S. *The Great Divorce: A Fantastic Bus Ride from Hell to Heaven—A Round Trip for Some but not for Others*. New York: Macmillan, 1946.

Lewis, Rebecca. "Insider Movements: Retaining Identity and Preserving Community." In Winter and Hawthorne, *Perspectives*, 673–76.

Liddon, H. P. *Explanatory Analysis of St. Paul's Epistle to the Romans*. Minneapolis: James and Klock, 1977.

Lindsay, Thomas M. *The Church and Ministry in the Early Centuries*. Minneapolis: James Family Publishing, 1977.

Levi-Strauss, Claude. "The Sorcerer and His Magic." In *Magic, Witchcraft and Religion*, edited by Arthur C. Lehmann and James E. Myers, 182–91. Mountain View, CA: Mayfield, 1985.

Logan, David. "Known Knowns, Known Unknowns, Unknown Unknowns and the Propagation of Scientific Enquiry." *Journal of Experimental Botany* 60, no. 3 (March 1, 2009): 712. https://doi.org/10.1093/jxb/erp043.

Luther, Martin. *Commentary on Romans*, translated by Theodore Mueller. Grand Rapids: Kregel, 1954.

———. "Treatise on Christian Liberty (1520)." https://history.hanover.edu/courses /excerpts/165luther.html

MacArthur, John. *1 Corinthians*. Chicago: Moody, 1984.

———. *Romans 9-16*. Chicago: Moody, 1994.

Mack, Eric. "Asteroid as Big as a Warehouse is Freakiest Near Miss in Years." CNET, April 16, 2018. https://www.cnet.com/news/asteroid-2018-ge3-is-freakiest-near -miss-earth-in-15 years/.

Magnusson, Sally. *The Flying Scotsman: A Biography*. New York: Quartet Books, 1981.

Mair, Victor H. Preface to *Tao Te Ching* by Lao Tzu. Translated by Victor H. Mair. New York: Bantam Books, 1990.

Malphurs, Aubrey. *Planting Growing Churches for the 21st Century: A Comprehensive Guide for New Churches and Those Desiring Renewal*. 3rd ed. Grand Rapids: Baker, 2004.

Manchester, William. *A World Lit Only by Fire: The Medieval Mind and the Renaissance: Portrait of an Age*. New York: Little, Brown, 1991.

Marshall, Paul, Roberta Green, and Lela Gilbert. *Islam at the Crossroads: Understanding Its Beliefs, History, and Conflicts*. Grand Rapids: Baker, 2002.

Martin, Judith N., and Thomas K. Nakayama. *Experiencing Intercultural Communication*. 2nd ed. Boston: McGraw-Hill, 2005.

Martin, Walter R. *The Kingdom of the Cults: An Analysis of the Major Cult Systems in the Present Christian Era*. Minneapolis: Bethany Fellowship, 1965.

Marx, Karl, and Friedrich Engels. *Manifesto of the Communist Party*. Chicago: Encyclopedia Britannica, 1952.

Mbiti, John S. *African Religions and Philosophy*. 2nd ed. Oxford: Heinemann, 1989.

McBirnie, William Stuart. *The Search for the Twelve Apostles*. Wheaton: Tyndale House, 1973.

McGavran, Donald A. "The Bridges of God." In Winter and Hawthorne, *Perspectives*, 335–46.

———. *Understanding Church Growth*. 2nd ed. Grand Rapids: Eerdmans, 1980

———. *Understanding Church Growth*. 3rd ed. Grand Rapids: Eerdmans, 1990.

McIntosh, Gary L. *Donald A. McGavran: A Biography of the Twentieth Century's Premier Missiologist*. Boca Raton, FL: Church Leader Insights, 2015.

McNeile, Alan Hugh. *The Gospel According to St. Matthew: The Greek Text with Introduction, Notes, and Indices*. Grand Rapids: Baker, 1980.

Miley, George. *Loving the Church, Blessing the Nations: Pursuing the Role of Local Churches in Global Mission*. Waynesboro, GA: Authentic Media, 2003.

Miller, James. *Daoism: A Beginner's Guide*. Oxford: Oneworld, 2003.

Millroth, Berta. *Lyuba: Traditional Religion of the Sukuma*. Uppsala, Sweden: Studia Ethnographica Upsaliensia, 1965.

Moffat, J. *The First Epistle of Paul to the Corinthians*. MNTC 7. London: Hodder & Stoughton, 1938.

Montgomery, James H. *DAWN 2000: 7 Million Churches to Go—The Personal Story of the DAWN Strategy*. Pasadena: William Carey Library, 1989.

Montgomery, John Warwick. "Luther and Missions." *Evangelical Missions Quarterly* (July 1967): 2.

Moore, Ralph. *Friends: The Key to Reaching Generation X*. Ventura, CA: Regal Books, 2001.

Moreau, Scott. *Contextualization in Missions: Mapping and Assessing Evangelical Models*. Grand Rapids: Kregel, 2012.

———. "Looking Backward While Going Forward, A Response to Winter's Vision." In Hesselgrave and Stetzer, *MissionShift*, 192–202.

Morgan, Diane. *The Best Guide to Eastern Philosophy and Religion*. New York: Renaissance Books, 2001.

Morris, Edmond. *Theodore Rex*. New York: Random House, 2001.

Morris, John Michael. "McGavran on McGavran: What Did He Really Teach?" *Southern Baptist Journal of Missions and Evangelism* no. 2 (Fall 2016): 9–23.

Mosely, Donald C., Leon C. Megginson, and Paul H. Pietri. *Supervisory Management: The Art of Inspiring, Empowering, and Developing People*. Mason, OH: Thomson-SouthWestern, 2005.

Moulton, James Hope, and George Milligan. *The Vocabulary of the Greek Testament: Illustrated from the Papyri and Other Non-Literary Sources*. London: Hodder and Stoughton, 1914–1929; Grand Rapids: Eerdmans, 1976.

Muller, Roland. *Honor and Shame: Unlocking the Door*. Bloomington, IN: Xlibris, 2000.

Murray, Stuart. *Church Planting: Laying Foundations*. Scottsdale, PA: Herald Press, 2001.

Musk, Bill. *Kissing Cousins? Christians and Muslims Face to Face*. Oxford: Monarch Books, 2005.

Muthuraj, Joseph. *We Began at Tranquebar*. Vol. 1, *SPCK, the Danish-Halle Mission and Anglican Episcopacy in India (1706-1843)*. Delhi: Indian Society for Promoting Christian Knowledge, 2010.

Nadeau, Randall L. *Asian Religions: A Cultural Perspective*. Oxford: John Wiley & Sons, 2014.

Nadel, S. F. "Notes on Beni-Amer [Beja] Society." *SNR* 26 (1945): 53–94.

Nasr, Seyyed Hossein. *Islam: Religion, History, and Civilization*. New York: Harper Collins, 2003.

Nasr, Vali. *The Shia Revival: How Conflicts within Islam Will Shape the future*. London: W. W. Norton, 2006.

The Navigators. *Bridge to Life*. Colorado Springs: NavPress, 1969.

Navlakha, Suren, trans. *The Thirteen Principal Upanishads*. London: Wordsworth, 2000.

Neighbour, Ralph, Jr. *Where Do We Go from Here? A Guidebook for the Cell Group Church*. Houston: Touch Publications, 1990.

Nellis Air Force Base. "Mission." Nevada Test and Training Range: Units. https://www.nellis.af.mil/Units/NTTR/.

Nix, Preston. "Commentary on Article 10: The Great Commission." In Allen, Hankins, and Harwood, *Anyone Can Be Saved*, 143–56.

Neely, Lois. *Fire in His Bones: The Official Biography of Oswald J. Smith*. Wheaton, IL: Tyndale House, 1982.

Nesbitt, Eleanor. *Sikhism: A Very Short Introduction*. 2nd ed. Oxford: Oxford University Press, 2016.

Nevius, John L. *The Planting and Development of Missionary Churches*. Hancock, NH: Monadnock Press, 2003.

Newbigin, Lesslie. Foreword to *The Spontaneous Expansion of the Church*, by Roland Allen. Grand Rapids: Eerdmans, 1962.

Newell, Peggy E., ed. *North American Mission Handbook: US and Canadian Protestant Ministries Overseas, 2017-2019*. Pasadena: William Carey Library, 2017.

Newport, John P. *The New Age Movement and the Biblical Worldview: Conflict and Dialogue*. Grand Rapids: Eerdmans, 1998.

Nhat Hanh, Thich. *The Heart of the Buddha's Teaching: Transforming Suffering into Peace, Joy, and Liberation*. New York: Broadway Books, 1998.

Niebuhr, H. Richard. *Christ and Culture*. New York: Harper & Row, 1975.

Numani, Shibli. *'Umar: An Abridged edition of Shibli Numani's 'Umar al-Faruq*. London: I. B. Tauris, 2004.

O'Donnell, Kelly. "Going Global: A Member Care Model for Best Practice." In *Doing Member Care Well: Perspectives and Practices from Around the World*, edited by Kelly O'Donnell, 13–22. Pasadena: William Carey Library, 2002.

Olson, C. Gordon. *Beyond Calvinism and Arminianism: An Inductive Mediate Theology of Salvation*. 3rd ed. Lynchburg, VA: Global Gospel Publishers, 2012.

Otis, George, Jr. *Informed Intercession: Transforming Your Community through Spiritual Mapping and Strategic Prayer*. Ventura, CA: Renew Books, 1999.

"Our History." Norwegian Church Aid. https://www.kirkensnodhjelp.no/en /about-nca/our-history/.

Overmyer, Daniel L. *Religions of China: The World as a Living System*. Long Grove, IL: Waveland Press, 1998.

Page, Dave. *Church Planting Notebook: A Strategy for Birthing and Growing Churches*. Auburn, CA: Church Planting Resources, n.d.

Parshall, Phil. *Bridges to Islam: A Christian Perspective on Folk Islam*. Grand Rapids: Baker, 2007.

———. "Going Too Far?" In Winter and Hawthorne, *Perspectives*, 663–67.

Parsons, Greg. "Will the Earth Hear His Voice?" Paper presented at the annual meeting of the International Society of Frontier Missiology, Atlanta, Georgia, September 24, 2014.

Patai, Raphael. *The Arab Mind*. Rev. ed. New York: Hatherleigh, 2002.

Payne, J. D. *Apostolic Church Planting: Birthing New Churches from New Believers*. Downers Grove, IL: InterVarsity Press, 2015.

Pentecost, J. Dwight. *Things to Come: A Study in Biblical Eschatology*. Grand Rapids: Zondervan, 1958.

Peters, George W. *A Biblical Theology of Missions*. Chicago: Moody, 1972.

Petersen, Jim. *Evangelism as a Lifestyle: Reaching Your World with the Gospel*. Colorado Springs: NavPress, 1981.

Peterson, Robert A. "Undying Worm, Unquenchable Fire: What Is Hell—Eternal Torment or Annihilation? A Look at the Evangelical Alliance's *The Nature of Hell*." *Christianity Today*, October 23, 2000 https://www.christianitytoday.com /ct/2000/october23/undying-worm-unquenchable-fire.html.

Peterson, Robert A., and Michael W. Williams. *Why I Am Not An Arminian*. Downers Grove, IL: InterVarsity Press, 2004.

Peterson, Roger, Gordon Aeschliman, and R. Wayne Sneed. *Maximum Impact Short-Term Mission: The God-Commanded Repetitive Deployment of Swift, Temporary Non-Professional Missionaries*. Minneapolis: STEM Press, 2003.

Pikkert, Peter. *Protestant Missionaries to the Middle East: Ambassadors of Christ or Culture?* Hamilton, ON: WEC Canada, 2008.

Piper, John. *Let the Nations be Glad: The Supremacy of God in Missions*. Grand Rapids: Baker, 1993.

Plueddemann, James E. *Leading across Cultures: Effective Ministry and Mission in the Global Church*. Downers Grove, IL: IVP Academic, 2009.

Plummer, Robert L., and John Mark Terry, eds. *Paul's Missionary Methods: In His Time and Ours*. Downers Grove, IL: InterVarsity Press, 2012.

Powers, Charles T. "Tanzania: A Vision Worn Thin." *Los Angeles Times*, May 31, 1981.

Pratt, Zane, David M. Sills, and Jeff K. Walters. *Introduction to Global Missions*. Nashville: B&H Academic, 2014.

Priest, Robert J., Terry Dischinger, Steve Rasmussen, and C. M. Brown. "Researching the Short-Term Mission Movement." *Missiology* 34, no. 4 (October 2006): 433.

Race, Alan. *Thinking About Religious Pluralism*. Minneapolis: Fortress, 2015.

Rainer, Thom S., and Jess W. Rainer. *The Millennials: Connecting to America's Largest Generation*. Nashville: B&H, 2011.

Raphalson, Samantha. "In Africa, War over Water Looms as Ethiopia Nears Completion of Nile River Dam." NPR, *Here & Now*, February 27, 2018. https://www.npr .org/2018/02/27/589240174/in-africa-war-over-water-looms-as-ethiopia-nears -completion-of-nile-river-dam.

Ravindra, Ravi. *The Bhagavad Gita: A Guide to Navigating the Battle of Life*. Boulder, CO: Shambhala, 2017.

Rhae, Sarah J. *Life of Henry Martyn: Missionary to India and Persia, 1781–1912*. Self-published, Create Space Publishing Platform, 2016.

Richardson, Don. "Redemptive Analogies." In Winter and Hawthorne, *Perspectives*, 430–36.

Robb, John D. *Focus! The Power of People Group Thinking*. Monrovia, CA: MARC Press, 1994.

Roberts, Nicki, and Nancy Sullivan. "The Loneliness of a Planter Wife." In Bailey and Jachelski, *My Husband Wants to Be a Church Planter*, 119–29.

Robinson, Martin. *Planting Mission-Shaped Churches Today*. Oxford: Monarch Books, 2006.

Rose, Jenny. *Zoroastrianism: An Introduction*. London: I. B. Taurus, 2011.

Ruthven, Malaise. *Islam in the World*. 3rd ed. New York: Oxford University Press, 2006.

Sanchez, Daniel R., Ebbie C. Smith, and Curtis Watke. *Starting Reproducing Congregations: A Guidebook for Contextual New Church Development*. Cumming, GA: Church Starting Network, 2001.

Sarma, Deepak. *Hinduism: A Reader*. Oxford: Blackwell, 2008.

Schaff, Philip. *ANF03. Latin Christianity: Its Founder, Tertullian*. https://www.ccel.org/ccel/schaff/anf03.html.

———. *History of the Christian Church*. 8 vols. Grand Rapids: Eerdmans, 1971.

Shah, Idries. *The Way of the Sufi*. London: Penguin Books, 1968.

Shank, Nathan, and Kari Shank. *Four Fields of Kingdom Growth: Starting and Releasing Healthy Churches*. Rev. ed., 2014. https://static1.squarespace.com/static/588ada483a0411af1ab3e7ca/t/58a40ef11b631bcbd49c88c0/1487146760589/4-Fields-Nathan-Shank-2014.pdf.

Sheard, David. *An Orality Primer for Missionaries*. Self-published, 2007.

Shearer, Alistair. *The Hindu Vision: Form of the Formless*. London: Thames & Hudson, 1993.

Skinner, Craig. *The Teaching Ministry of the Pulpit*. Grand Rapids: Baker, 1981.

Simpkins, C. Alexander, and Annellen Simpkins. *Simple Confucianism: A Guide to Living Virtuously*. Boston: Tuttle, 2000.

Simson, Wolfgang. *Houses That Change the World: The Return of the House Churches*. Waynesboro, GA: OM Publishing, 2001.

Singh, Jasprit, and Teresa Singh. *Style of the Lion: The Sikhs*. Ann Arbor, MI: Akal Publications, 1998.

Singh, Patwant. *The Sikhs*. New York: Doubleday, 1999.

Shaller, Lyle B. *Activating the Passive Church: Diagnosis and Treatment*. Nashville: Abingdon, 1981.

Shipman, Mike. *Any-3: Anyone, Anywhere, Anytime: Lead Muslims to Christ Now*. Monument, CO: WIGTake Resources, 2013.

Steffen, Tom, and Mike Barnett, eds. *Business as Mission: From Impoverished to Empowered*. Pasadena: William Carey Library, 2006.

Stetzer, Ed. *Planting New Churches in a Postmodern Age*. Nashville: Broadman and Holman, 2003.

Stetzer, Ed, and Daniel Im. *Planting Missional Churches: Your Guide to Starting Churches that Multiply*. 2nd ed. Nashville: B&H Academic, 2016.

Smith, Adam. *The Wealth of Nations*. New York: Bantam Classics, 2003.

Smith, Ebbie. "Contemporary Theology of Religions." In *Missiology: An Introduction to the Foundations, History, and Strategies of World Missions*, edited by John Mark Terry, Ebbie Smith, and Justice Anderson. 1st ed. Nashville: Broadman and Holman, 1998.

Smith, E. Elbert, *Church Planting by the Book*. Ft. Washington, PA: CLC Publications, 2015.

Smith, Huston, and Philip Novak. *Buddhism: A Concise Introduction*. New York: HarperCollins, 2003.

Guthrie, Stan. "Deconstructing Islam: Apologist Jay Smith takes a Confrontational Approach." *Christianity Today*, September 9, 2002. https://www.christianitytoday.com/ct/2002/september9/32.37.html.

Smith, Michael A. *From Christ to Constantine*. Downers Grove, IL: InterVarsity Press, 1971.

———. *The Church under Siege*. Downers Grove, IL: InterVarsity Press, 1976.

Smith, Steve, and Ying Kai. *T4T, A Discipleship ReRevolution: The Story behind the World's Fastest Growing Church Planting Movement and How It Can Happen in Your Community*. Monument, CO: WIGTake Resources, 2011.

Sookhdeo, Patrick. *Global Jihad*. MacLean, VA: Isaac, 2007.

Spencer, Robert. *The Complete Infidel's Guide to Iran*. Washington, DC: Regnery, 2016.

Stanford, A. Ray, Richard A. Seymour, and Carol Ann Seymour, *Handbook of Personal Evangelism*. Hollywood, FL: Florida Bible College, n.d.

Stewart, Laura Lee. *Through Christ Who Strengthens: A History of the Baptist Mission of East Africa, 1956–1976*. Nairobi: Baptist Publications, 1976.

Suarez, Gustavo V. *Connections: Linking People and Principles for Dynamic Church Multiplication*. Friendswood, TX: Baxter Press, 2004.

Sullivan, Regina D. *Lottie Moon: A Southern Baptist Missionary to China in History and Legend*. Baton Rouge: Louisiana State University Press, 2012.

Sunquist, Scott W. *The Unexpected Christian Century: The Reversal and Transformation of Global Christianity, 1900–2000*. Grand Rapids: Baker Academic, 2015.

Talman, Harley, and John Jay Travis, eds. *Understanding Insider Movements: Disciples of Jesus within Diverse Religious Communities*. Pasadena: William Carey Library, 2015.

Tennent, Timothy C. "Followers of Jesus ('Isa) in Islamic Mosques: A Closer Examination of C-5 'High Spectrum' Contextualization." *International Journal of Frontier Missions* 23, no. 3 (2006): 101–17.

———. *Invitation to World Missions*. Grand Rapids: Kregel, 2010.

Terry, John Mark. "The History of Missions in the Early Church." In Terry, *Missiology*, 141–56.

———, ed. *Missiology: An Introduction to the Foundations, History, and Strategies of World Missions*. 2nd ed. Nashville: B&H, 2015.

Terry, John Mark, and Robert L. Gallagher. *Encountering the History of Missions: From the Early Church to Today*. Grand Rapids: Baker Academic, 2017.

Terry, John Mark, and J. D. Payne. *Developing a Strategy for Missions: A Biblical, Historical, and Cultural Introduction*. Grand Rapids: Baker Academic, 2013.

Thiselton, Anthony C. *The First Epistle to the Corinthians*. Grand Rapids: Eerdmans, 2000.

Thompson, W. Oscar. *Concentric Circles of Concern: Seven Stages for Making Disciples*, revised and updated by Claude V. King. Nashville: Broadman and Holman, 1999.

Timble, Greg. *The Virtual Missionary: The Power of Your Personal Testimony*. Springfield, UT: Cedar Fort, 2017.

Travis, John J. "The C-Spectrum: A Practical Tool for Defining Six Types of 'Christ Centered Communities' found in Muslim Contexts." In Winter and Hawthorne, *Perspectives*, 664–67.

———. "Response One in Followers of Jesus ('Isa) in Islamic Mosques: A Closer Examination of C-5 'high spectrum' contextualization." *International Journal of Frontier Missions* 23, no. 3 (2006): 124–25.

Trull, Richard E., Jr. *The Fourth Self: Theological Education to Facilitate Self-Theologizing for Local Church Leaders in Kenya*. New York: Peter Lang, 2013.

Twain, Mark. *The Quotable Mark Twain: His Essential Aphorisms, Witticisms and Concise Opinions*, edited by R. Kent Rasmussen. New York: McGraw-Hill, 1998.

———. "Youth, Aging." In *The Wit and Wisdom of Mark Twain: A Book of Quotations*, 31. Mineola, NY: Dover, 1999.

Van Gelder, Craig, and Dwight J. Zscheile. *The Missional Church in Perspective: Mapping Trends and Shaping the Conversation*. Grand Rapids: Baker Academic, 2011.

van Pelt, Piet. *Bantu Customs in Mainland Tanzania*. Rev. ed. Tabora, Tanzania: Tanganika Mission Press, 1982.

Van Rheenen, Gailyn. *Communicating Christ in Animistic Contexts*. Pasadena: William Carey Library, 1991.

———. *Missions: Biblical Foundations and Contemporary Strategies*. 1st ed. Grand Rapids: Zondervan, 1996.

———. "Syncretism and Contextualization: The Church on a Journey Defining Itself." In *Contextualization and Syncretism: Navigating Cultural Currents*, edited by Gailyn Van Rheenen, 1–30. Evangelical Missiological Society Series 13. Pasadena: William Carey Library, 2006.

VandeHie, Jim. "China is the Greatest, Growing Threat to America." Axios, May 21, 2018. https://www.axios.com/china-united-states-future-2025-2050-infrastructure-trade-d7091849-235f-4aa1-b63c-e86477e9cfe6.html.

Wagner, Peter C., ed. *Breaking Strongholds: How to Use Spiritual Mapping to Make Your Prayers More Strategic, Effective and Targeted*. Shippensburg, PA: Destiny Image, 2015.

———. *Church Planting for a Greater Harvest*. Ventura, CA: Regal, 1990.

————. *Territorial Spirits: Practical Strategies for How to Crush the Enemy through Spiritual Warfare*. Shippensburg, PA: Destiny Image, 2012.

Warren, Rick. *The Purpose Driven Church: Growth Without Compromising Your Message and Mission*. Grand Rapids: Zondervan, 1995.

Watt, W. Montgomery. *Muhammad: Prophet and Statesman*. London: Oxford University Press, 1961.

Wehr, Hans. *Arabic-English Dictionary: The Hans-Wehr Dictionary of Modern Arabic*. Edited by J. Milton Cowan. Urbana, IL: Spoken Language Services, 1994.

Weingarten, Gene. "Joshua Bell." *Washington Post*. Reprinted in *Kansas City Star*, April 22, 2007.

Welch, Adam E. "Life and Literature of the Sukuma in Tanzania," East Africa. PhD diss., Howard University, 1974.

Welch, Bobby H. *Evangelism through the Sunday School: A Journey of FAITH*. Nashville: LifeWay Press, 1997.

Welch, Bobby H., and Doug Williams. *Faith Evangelism: Facilitators Guide*. Nashville: LifeWay Press, 2007.

Westcott, B. F. *The Gospel According to St. John: The Authorized Version with Introduction and Notes*. Grand Rapids: Eerdmans, 1975.

Wheatcroft, Andrew. *Infidels: A History of the Conflict between Christendom and Islam*. New York: Random House, 2004.

White, James. "Unconditional Election." In Hunt and White, *Debating Calvinism*, 91–116.

Wiersbe, Warren W. *50 People Every Christian Should Know: Learning from Spiritual Giants of the Faith*. Grand Rapids: Baker, 2009.

Wijsen, Frans, and Ralph Tanner. *"I Am Just a Sukuma": Globalization and Identity Construction in Northwest Tanzania*. Amsterdam: Rodopi Press, 2002.

Wilkinson, Bruce. "Where Jabez Doesn't Cut It." Beliefnet. www.beliefnet.com /inspiration/2003/11/where-jabez-doesnt-cut-it.aspx.

Williams, Augustus Warner. *The Life and Work of Dwight L. Moody: The Great Evangelist of the 19th Century*. Philadelphia: P. W. Ziegler, 1900.

Willis, Avery T., Jr., and Henry Blackaby. *On Mission with God: Living God's Purpose for His Glory*. Nashville: LifeWay Press, 2001.

Wilson, J. Christy, Sr. *Apostle to Islam: A Biography of Samuel M. Zwemer*. Pioneer Library, 2017.

Wimber, John. *Power Evangelism*. Bloomington, MN: Chosen Books, 2009.

Winter, Ralph D. "The Future of Evangelicals in Mission." In Hesselgrave and Stetzer, *MissionShift*, 164–91.

————. *The Twenty-Five Unbelievable Years*. Pasadena: William Carey Press, 1971.

Winter, Ralph D., and Steven C. Hawthorne, eds. *Perspectives on the World Christian Movement: A Reader*. 4th ed. Pasadena, CA: William Carey Library, 2009.

Winter, Ralph D., and Bruce A. Koch. "Finishing the Task: The Unreached Peoples Challenge." In Winter and Hawthorne, *Perspectives*, 531–46.

Wong, Eva. *Being Taoist: Wisdom for Living a Balanced Life*. Boulder, CO: Shambhala, 2015.

World Council of Churches. "*The Church toward a Common Vision: Faith and Order Paper No. 214*." Geneva: WCC Publications, 2013.

Worrell, George E. *How to Take the Worry Out of Witnessing*. Nashville: Broadman Press, 1976.

Wuthnow, Robert. *After the Baby Boomers: How Twenty- and Thirty-Somethings are Shaping the Future of American Religion*. Princeton: Princeton University Press, 2007.

Xie, J., S. Sreenivasan, G. Korniss, W. Zhang, C. Lim, and B. Szymanski. "Social Consensus through the Influence of Committed Minorities," *Physical Review* E 80, no. 1 (2011): 1, 9.

Yamamori, Tetsunao. *God's New Envoys: A Bold Strategy for Penetrating "Closed Countries."* Portland: Multnomah, 1987.

Yohannan, K. P. *Revolution in World Missions*. Carrolton, TX: GFA, 1998.

Zwemer, Samuel M. *Influence of Animism on Islam: An Account of Popular Superstitions*. New York: Macmillan, 1920.

Name Index

Subject Index

Scripture Index